The Cognitive Control of Motivation

The Cognitive Control of Motivation

The Consequences of Choice and Dissonance

Philip G. Zimbardo
Stanford University

Scott, Foresman and Company

Library of Congress Catalog Card No. 69-14438

Regional offices of Scott, Foresman and Company are located in Atlanta, Dallas, Glenview, Palo Alto, and Oakland, N.J.

Preface

Some years ago when Bob Cohen and I, and our students at New York University, began outlining the problems that form the basis of the research presented here, our concern was limited to testing several interesting derivations of Leon Festinger's theory of cognitive dissonance, using the rigorous methodology impressed upon us at Yale, especially by Carl Hovland and Neal Miller. However, as this program of research unfolded and other students and fellow social psychologists joined in the common enterprise, the focus widened until, as the reader will see, we were involved not only with basic issues of learning, motivation, and cognition, and their interactions with physiological processes, but also with the broadest philosophical implications about existence and being.

We believe that some of the appeal of our work, which we feel is appropriate for various types of psychology courses, both relatively basic and advanced, lies in its empirical demonstration of the extent to which, and the specification of the conditions under which, man can control the demands imposed by his biological drives and social motives. That man may thereby gain greater autonomy from environmental control of his behavior is a clear implication of this research. Those with a more humanistic orientation may focus primarily on this level of abstraction. Other students of psychology may instead attend to the systematic use of an elegant theory to guide our research endeavor, or to the varied methodology involved in turning soft concepts like choice and justification into hard variables.

Sadly, Bob's death prevented him from sharing in this realization of our plan. However, reflected throughout this book is the example he provided for those who knew and loved him, that even the reality of imminent death need not diminish man's capacity to choose, nor his commitment to freedom and to life. This work is dedicated to his memory.

The difficulties of translating ideas into actions and then into words were shared and alleviated by many in addition to the authors represented by their research articles. To the score of graduate and undergraduate psychology students who assisted with the execution and analysis of this research goes our sincere appreciation. Provocative discussions with George Kaufer, and most especially with my friend, Claude Faucheux, helped clarify and extend the theoretical implications, while the critical evaluation of parts of this book by Jack and Lee Brehm tightened much that was loose in our thinking and presentation. Marguerite Clark of Scott, Foresman, through her constant encouragement, perceptive editorial advice, and faith in the eventual completion of this book, proved to be an author's most valuable asset. Anne Zeidberg, my magnificent secretary, not only gave the words shape, but improved upon them. To

Rose and Adam Zimbardo, who suffered through what is worst in the researcher's agony over the uncertainty of his work and the writer's anguish over his inarticulateness, and still maintained a sense of humor about it all, thanks.

Without funds, basic research and the opportunity to communicate its findings and pursue its consequences would be impossible. The financial aid of the National Science Foundation and the National Institute of Mental Health helped to materialize our hypotheses into this book.

P. G. ZIMBARDO

Brooklyn, February 1, 1968

Contents

II. Social Motives and Personality Variables

INTRODUCTION

> Man of nature endowed with reason placed, as it were, in the middle between these two extremities [of appetite and will] may through his *choice* incline to sense or reach to understanding.
>
> Castiglione, 1528[1]

In what way is man unique or distinctive among living creatures? It is the attempt to answer this question which forms the common basis for the empirical research presented in this book. This research stems from a belief in the importance of cognitive factors for understanding human behavior and in the operation of choice as the one most essentially human characteristic. Contrasted with this approach is the generally prevailing orientation in modern psychology toward behaviorism (used in its broadest sense), which minimizes differences between man and other animals in its search for basic laws governing the behavior of *organisms*.

Before describing these two positions, I would like to make a cursory examination of earlier views on the question of man's singularity. First, I will attempt to show how the instinct doctrine drastically changed the centuries' old philosophical and theological view and then how behaviorism, although it was instrumental in the downfall of the instinct doctrine, has nevertheless retained one of its major premises about man.

For over twenty-five hundred years of recorded history, philosophers and theologians have kneaded the issue of man's place in the universe. In large measure their intellectual efforts were directed not toward understanding what man is but toward postulating special privileges for him. These formulations (cf., Beach, 1955) removed man from the Great Chain of Being, established his affinity with the god(s), and, by so doing, justified his unique right both to an afterlife and to the exploitation of lower animals.

It was possession of the godlike gift of reason which enabled men, if they willed, to understand right from wrong and to act freely to direct their behavior for the ultimate glorification of their immortal souls. Without a rational soul, an animal, of course, could not act freely and could never achieve the heavenly state of grace and everlasting life. The apparently organized, patterned, complex behavior of lower animals could, however, be readily explained by attribution of god's gift of "instincts" to these brutes. Their behavior was completely determined by built-in patterns of instinctual responding which were not under voluntary control but which did enable the animal to satisfy its basic needs.

The Darwinian revolution swept such distinctions aside with its evidence for continuity of species and for environmental adaptation which was sometimes irrational and impulsive in man as well as rational in other animals. McDougall's

---

1. Baldassare Castiglione, *The Courtyer*, originally published 1528; adapted from Sir Thomas Hoby's 1561 translation, in *Sixteenth Century English Prose*, K. J. Holzknecht (Ed.). New York: Harper, 1954, p. 217.

added psychological support (in his 1908 text, *Social Psychology*) brought man and beasts together again under the common roof of shared instincts.

Although the instinct doctrine was a dominant intellectual force for almost two decades, it withered under the combined attack of the cultural anthropologists and the newly emerging behaviorist school. The former replaced the universals of instinct with cultural and environmental relativity. The latter, in attacking the logic, assumptions, and implications of the instinct approach, advanced a more rational (empirically testable) view which saw behavior as emerging from the association of overt responses with discriminable stimuli, established through practice and strengthened through reinforcement.

Having overthrown the rule of instinct for the rule of learned behavior, the behaviorist position became the central orientation in psychology (or at least in American psychology). Interestingly, however, it did not deny the commonality of men and beasts—but rather underscored and then extended it.

The most general theoretical position underlying the research in the present volume has evolved in part from a dissatisfaction with many of the basic behaviorist presuppositions about what man is, how he is motivated, and how he relates to his environment. Before outlining these usually implicit assumptions of behaviorism, which may have fostered a distorted conception of the human organism, let us clarify the limits of our opposing view. The emergence of psychology as an objective, empirical science can be credited to the behaviorists' inductive approach and operational emphasis. It is hoped, in fact, that these characteristics are adequately reflected in the research to be presented here. While acknowledging that debt, however, it is not necessary to accept unquestioningly all of the derivatives of that approach.

Let us now consider some of the behaviorist assumptions most destructive of a view of man as a special creature.

THE BEHAVIORIST VIEW OF MAN

While recognizing that man has a special verbal repertoire of responses and a complex and well-differentiated system of higher mental processes, the behaviorists nevertheless have minimized differences between species, maintaining that the proper study of mankind proceeds from the study of simpler organisms, like the rat or pigeon. The species differences that are recognized are given the form of quantitatively different parameters (or empirically determined constants) rather than seen as resulting from the operation of qualitatively different variables. Functional laws of behavior have developed from a research strategy which studies a simple response of a relatively simple organism to a narrowly defined physical stimulus within a controlled and very limited environment. Extension of this model to the study of human behavior has had the effect of minimizing the complexity of human responding.

This empirical approach is also based upon a physical input-output model of behavior which views overt measurable behavior as the direct product of some physical property of some stimulus. The most important human attributes for many experimenters thus are limited to man's sensory apparatus and response effectors. While more liberal behaviorists mention the possibility of "mediators" between the terminal dependent variable and the initiating independent variable, the process of reducing mediational phenomena to ever smaller S's and R's has limited the challenge of this approach to the basic input-output model.

A corollary to this economical system of behavior is the implicitly passive role it assigns to the individual organism being studied. An individual (rat or human being) is *subjected* to the stimulus; thus, he becomes a "subject" who was "run" under given conditions. The very semantics of the experiment betray the passive, purely instrumental view that the experimenter develops toward the organism under investigation. In fact, the subject is not only viewed as, but is treated like, an object. What is studied is never human action but *reaction*. Here we see a kind of self-fulfilling prophesy in which humans are given the rules of the experiment, which deprive them of any initiative, creative responding, or freedom of action. The subject is really asked to suspend his disbelief and pretend that the experimental task has meaning—to role-play at being an experimental human subject who asks no questions and behaves in the predetermined simple fashion desired by the experimenter. The personal history of the subject as a human being who thinks, decides, gets involved, becomes committed and obligated, feels responsible, can be irrational, etc., becomes either irrelevant or part of what is considered "error variance." When human beings are treated this way, they will react according to the same functional laws of behavior as do lower animals. Under these standardized conditions the experimenter is able to posit a behavioral continuity—which in large part he has artificially created.

Behavioristic approaches to learning have done still more injustice to the integrity and uniqueness of man by their focus on appetite and extrinsic reward. For an experimental subject to be impelled to action, he must be motivated; and with both human and animal subjects, this motivation has been accomplished almost entirely by the arousal of appetites—since it is in their appetites that these subject populations are most similar. Drives aroused by deprivation states or by stimuli noxious to the senses are then satisfied by reinforcement administered by the experimenter. Secondary and presumably even social drives and rewards are assumed to be derivative of these primary, more biologically based operations, and the instigation and maintenance of all behavior are regarded as dependent on a functional relation between drive and reward based on their effects on appetite.

Does the reinforcement for a given response usually bear any *intrinsic* relationship to the nature of the response or task activity of the subject? No, the reinforcement is related to the response not logically, but mechanically, temporally, or instrumentally. The task given to the subject merely provides a convenient opportunity to observe some aspect of behavior which can be reinforced, the response and the reinforcement both being arbitrarily defined by the experimenter.

The use of such a task enables behavioral engineers to display the myriad ways both human and animal behavior can be brought under the control of the environment. However, a task of this kind is not adequate to reveal man's capacity to work and learn from the self-generated motives of curiosity or mastery of the environment (see Prentice, 1961) nor his role in attempting to control his own environment.

This point is eloquently made in the behavior of a preschool child solving a puzzle "for its own sake": after successfully putting the puzzle together for the first time, the child may immediately break it up and begin again—without first making any attempt to solicit praise for his completed performance. Also, we can see how inadequate the explanations are of how a child learns his native language if they are restricted to the principles of extrinsic reward and motivation. In fact, learning in humans may be adversely affected by the substitution of incentive-directed motivation for personal task-satisfaction motivation.[2]

Finally, we come to the point which will be most crucial in the development of the thesis of this book: the nature of the choice and freedom accorded to experimental subjects. Just as the rat or chimpanzee who is put into an apparatus which will deliver painful shocks is given no choice in this arrangement, the human subject similarly is given no choice of alternatives. He will receive an air puff to his eyelid, a shock to his finger, or engage in a boring task of learning nonsense syllables for an hour because he is a subject, or part of a "subject pool" required to participate. Where participation is voluntary, his freedom is virtually negated by having sufficient extrinsic justifications provided for engaging in the given task—such as money, course credit, social approval, or pressures toward conformity. That subjects in psychological experiments either perceive that they have little or no choice but to do what the experimenter desires or have adequate extrinsic justification for doing so is evidenced by the fact that few, if any, refuse, decline, or drop out, regardless of the degree of aversiveness of the procedures. We will consider this issue in greater detail subsequently in this book because it is in the operation of choice that man's psychological uniqueness is revealed.

THE RENAISSANCE VIEW OF MAN

This analysis of the behaviorist view of man leads us not to a new conception of man but rather back to the Renaissance and Elizabethan conception of the tripartite "soul."

> [I]n our soul there be three kinds of ways to know, namely, by sense, reason, and understanding. From sense there arises appetite or longing, which is common with brute beasts; from reason arises

2. Although monkeys show an intrinsic interest in certain kinds of puzzles and will explore and work on them for long periods of time, their performance deteriorates when solving the puzzles becomes associated with receiving food—an extrinsic source of justification (Harlow, Harlow, & Meyer, 1950).

election or choice, which is proper to man; from understanding by which man may be partner with the angels, arises will.

Castiglione, 1528[3]

In one sense, the intention of the research presented in this book is to provide empirical support for the conception of man described in the above passage. When man is motivated by appetite and is given no choice of whether to endure a state of deprivation or noxious stimulation, then he reveals his oneness with the beasts. When he is provided with cognitions which specify alternative courses of action available to him, then by the act of choosing man transforms himself from the object of actuarial determinism to the creator of his own existence.

COGNITIVE PHENOMENA

Since the variables of choice and justification with which we will be concerned are clearly cognitive ones—in contrast with the physical or biological variables more typically employed by behaviorists—let us first consider the general issue of the degree to which cognitive variables can affect behavior. After a brief exploration of some seemingly unrelated, general "cognitive phenomena," we will reformulate the rather lofty objectives previously advanced in terms of manipulable variables and their measurable consequences, and we will try to elucidate the theoretical assumptions which have guided this research on the cognitive control of man's biological drives and social motives.

The Placebo Problem

The rate at which Americans purchase drugs and the extent of their faith in the efficacy of aspirin, tranquilizers, stimulants, and other drugs is amply demonstrated by the financial success of our drug companies. Unfortunately, however, there is little demand for the drug which has proven to be the most effective one to be developed by the pharmaceutical laboratories—the *placebo*.

A thorough survey of its usage (Haas, Fink, & Hartfelder, 1963) revealed that in nearly one hundred independent studies of twenty-nine different symptoms and sicknesses—including multiple sclerosis, cancer, psychosis, alcoholism, migraine, colds, rheumatism, and even constipation—pain reduction was achieved in an average of 27 per cent of over 4500 patients. In another survey, Beecher (1959) reported that in fifteen test series, approximately one third of all American patients responded positively to this drug. In some specific studies, the incidence of pain reduction was as high as 75 per cent; in others, placebos were as effective as morphine in relieving postoperative pain. Interestingly,

3. Baldassare Castiglione, *The Courtyer*, originally published 1528; adapted from Sir Thomas Hoby's 1561 translation, in *Sixteenth Century English Prose*, K. J. Holzknecht (Ed.). New York: Harper, 1954, pp. 216–217.

patients complain of a wide range of negative side effects following administration of a placebo: nausea, headaches, sleepiness, and reduced concentration. *Believing* that a placebo will lead to pain reduction is sufficient to bring about major psychological (and perhaps physiological) reorganization, which not only alters the experience of pain but can produce new symptoms.

The convictions of a patient can do even more than make potent an inert drug; they can *reverse* the usual pharmacological effect of a medicine. Ipecac, which is normally used to induce vomiting, especially in cases of poisoning, "had healing effects on patients with nausea of pregnancy when it was suggested to them that they were receiving a good preparation" (cf., Haas et al., 1963, p. 27).

Psychological Factors in Disease

Despite these studies, drug companies continue to view these dramatic findings merely as "a problem" to be overcome by some improved methodology for evaluating "real" drugs, and most psychologists have successfully ignored the implications of the placebo problem. In fact, many hard-headed scientists and men of medicine are distressed by research like that reported above with ipecac, since they prefer to place their faith in physical rather than psychological variables. (One is reminded in passing of Sherrington's admonition to Pavlov to avoid the fad and Charybdis of the "mystical" phenomena of classical conditioning.) The interesting paradox is that they, too, are betrayed by their everyday language, which is replete with statements about disease causation in terms of "low resistance," "feeling run down," "being fatigued," "under stress," "feeling blue," "not having a will to live," etc.

But can psychological influences contribute to the process of infection and production of disease in man? Friedman and Glasgow, in a provocative report (1966), respond to this question in the affirmative, concluding their survey of recent research in this area by noting that "relatively subtle psychological and environmental factors appear to influence susceptibility to a wide range of infectious and parasitic agents" (p. 23).

In one study (Meyer & Haggerty, 1962), both streptococcal and non-streptococcal respiratory illnesses were about four times as frequent following family episodes judged to be stressful (in sixteen families studied periodically for twelve months). Another study (Hinkle & Plummer, 1952) found that among one thousand telephone operators, one third of the group accounted for two thirds of the absences, mostly from respiratory problems. Those highest in absenteeism differed from those lowest primarily in their psychological outlook: they were more unhappy, resentful, and frustrated. In addition, they suffered from twelve times as many respiratory illnesses.

Bush (1962), in emphasizing the importance of psychological stress in activating ACTH, notes that psychological factors have a greater effect than extreme physical stimuli (such as cold, frost, exhaustion) on increasing the secretion rate of cortisol and its concentration in peripheral blood. "The most important natural stimulus to the activity of the [adrenal cortex] gland is psychological in character."

Perhaps the most convincing evidence for a multifactor approach to disease etiology comes from a study by Friedman, Ader, and Glasgow (1965), using mice as subjects. Mice were stressed for three days (given cues for shock anticipation plus electric shock), then inoculated with Coxsackie B virus and stressed for four additional days. Neither stress alone (for some control groups) nor virus alone (for others) was sufficient to cause manifest disease. Only a combination of environmental stress with the viral agent resulted in disease.

These authors also present evidence from studies which show that respiratory illnesses are significantly greater among displaced Chinese students who have not adapted psychologically to their new way of life than among other Chinese students comparable in every way except for their perception of and acceptance of this change. Similarly, the anthropologist Scotch has shown (1963) that members of the Zulu tribe whose lives have been disrupted by moving to cities have excessively high rates of hypertension, while those remaining in the villages have very low rates. Also relevant here is Stamler's (1964) study of psychological stress and hypertension among Negro blue-collar workers in Chicago.

It has been demonstrated recently that even physical growth of children can be stunted by living in an emotionally upsetting environment during the early years of childhood. A group of thirteen children whose growth was abnormally retarded "demonstrated remarkable growth acceleration" when they were in a convalescent hospital away from the family strife, but they stopped growing again when they returned home (Powell, Brasel, Blizzard, & Taiti, 1967).

Psychological Expectancy Versus Physical Pain

With regard to behavioral and physiological reactions to psychological stress, Brady has reported (1962, 1965) that during the course of conditioning in rhesus monkeys, lever pressing and the release of 17 hydroxycorticosteroids were more influenced by the presentation of the conditioned stimulus (the psychological signal) than by the presentation of the unconditioned shock (the physical event). In another study (Sidman, Mason, Brady, & Thach, 1962), a significant elevation of 17-OH-CS was elicited even when not a single shock was received (perfect avoidance) during a two-hour experimental session.

As can be seen in Figure 1, at the outset of conditioning the conditioned stimulus has no effect upon subsequent behavior, while the shock clearly depresses responding. However, during the course of conditioning, the neutral stimulus is invested with meaning and becomes a signal for emotional responses in preparation for the shock. In fact, when the conditioned emotional response is fully established, behavior is suppressed only by the CS and *no longer by the shock!* It may well be that the psychological stress of anticipating the shock is more aversive than the shock itself. The occurrence of the physical shock may even be a "relief," signaling as it does the end of emotional preparation. When subjects were given the choice of either postponing a shock or taking the shock and thereby terminating the warning signal which preceded it, "the animals behaved in such a way as to terminate the (warning) stimulus as quickly as

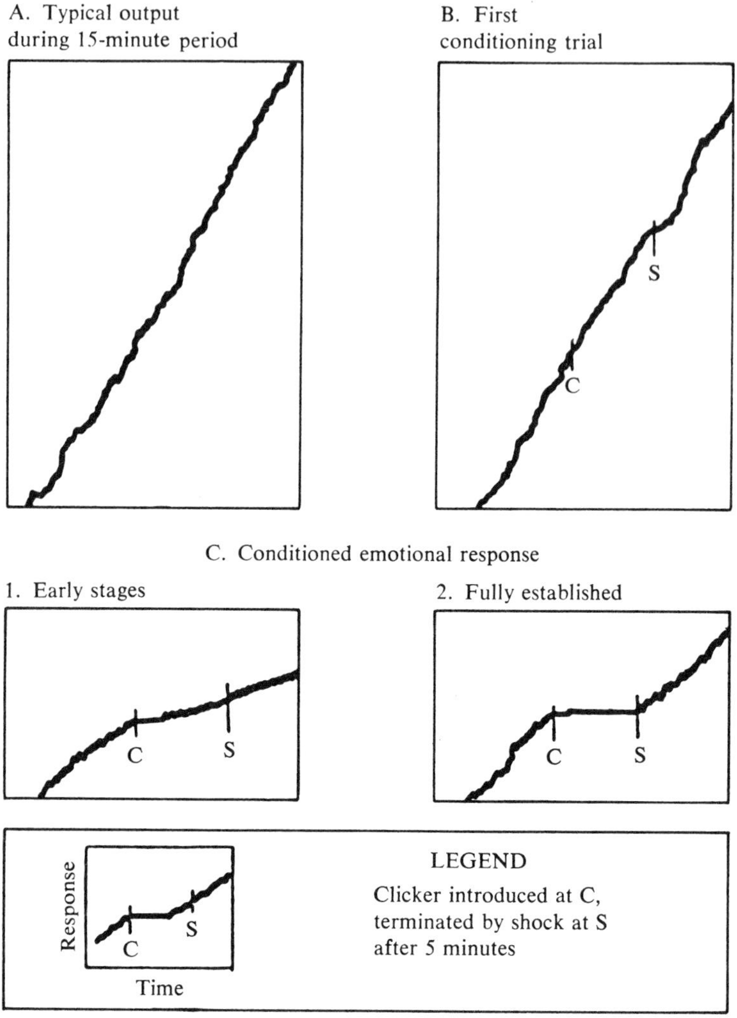

FIGURE 1
The conditioned emotional response as it appears typically in the cumulative response curve. Abscissae: time. Ordinates: cumulative number of responses. (From Hunt & Brady.)

possible, even though a shock accompanied each stimulus termination" (Sidman and Boren, 1957, p. 343).

Uncertainty and Control

It could be predicted that if the expectancy of an aversive event is more aversive than the event itself, an individual will elect to receive a stronger shock whose occurrence he can control rather than a weaker shock which either is delayed or is unpredictable in its temporal presentation. Such a prediction is in line with Mandler's (1965) conception of the importance of controlling uncertainty in the environment, and it finds support in a recent study by Gibbon (1967), who demonstrated that "when shock is inevitable on every trial, subjects terminate the threat of punishment at the cost of the punishing event itself. They, so to say, 'get it over with'" (p. 460).

Mason and Brady (1964) have demonstrated quite convincingly the sensitivity of psychoendocrine systems to social aspects of the environment. They describe a study in which steroid levels in one group were increased by uncertainty about a future event (the content of a movie) but remained at the normal level in another group which was provided with knowledge about this future event. In humans, when behavioral mechanisms habitually used to deal with distressing events or thoughts (such as denial of the imminent death of one's sick child) are undermined or are ineffective, mean levels of 17-OH-CS change in a highly reliable fashion (Wolff, Hofer, & Mason, 1964).

In a well-controlled study, Ikemi and Nakagawa (1962) tested thirteen subjects who had marked allergic sensitivity to the leaves of two common Japanese poisonous trees. When they were led to believe that they were being touched by the leaves of a harmless chestnut tree but were actually rubbed with the usually allergy-producing leaves, eleven of the thirteen failed to develop any skin reaction. On the other hand, when the procedure was reversed and they thought the control leaves were the allergy leaves, eleven subjects did develop dermatitis.

Janis' classic study (1958) of expectancies and anxiety about a future threatening event, surgery, revealed that postoperative physical recovery was greatest for surgical patients whose anxiety was moderate. High levels of preparatory anxiety made for ineffective coping, while low levels of anxiety failed to initiate realistic expectancies about the future pain, or to start the "work of worrying" prior to the event. Rate of recovery from serious surgery may therefore be related to the impact of cognitive inputs to the patient, such as communications which create realistic expectancies and which provide adequate information about those aspects of the novel environment which the patient perceives but is helpless to control overtly.

MOTIVATION IN THE LABORATORY AND IN THE REAL WORLD

The broader context in which I wish to place our research on cognitive processes and motives may be better appreciated if I sketch another contrast. Using any issue of the *Nebraska Symposium on Motivation* as testimony, we can assert that it is both common and relatively easy to obtain dramatic, immediate effects across a wide range of behaviors when motivation is induced in the laboratory. However, outside the lab, where people are no longer subjects, greater intensities of motivation (due to prolonged hunger, thirst, sleep deprivation, isolation, vigilance, or even celibacy) often yield few, if any, effects of comparable psychological significance. While it might be true that this difference is in part attributable to the greater sensitivity of measurement possible in the laboratory, I believe there are other, more important underlying factors.

Perhaps I can illustrate the point by comparing the fatigue, boredom, and impairment in performance typically found in laboratory studies after an hour or so on a pursuit-rotor task (or some comparable activity) with the failure of a recent study to find evidence of fatigue among *volunteer* drivers who drove 70 mph for 24 consecutive hours! "Each of these [seven] *S*s was verbally informed prior to volunteering about what would be expected of him in the experimentation" (Safford & Rockwell, 1966). They then drove a 160-mile route eight times in 24 hours at top speeds, with a 15-minute rest during refueling every two and one half hours—drove in silence, each with an experimenter sitting behind him.

Since only two drivers were unable to finish the 24-hour driving task (they drove only 21 hours each), the study was interpreted as a "failure." "The fact that the subjects did not 'break down' or 'fall asleep' during the experimental task does not enable the subjects' data to be scrutinized for a pattern in the performance measures which might be used to foretell a complete breakdown or cessation of performance" (Safford & Rockwell, 1966, p. 17).

For our purposes, this study is closer to what happens in real life than in the laboratory, because the individuals involved voluntarily committed themselves to the experience with some knowledge of what was expected of them and with a clearly specified task goal (24 hours of continuous driving), on a task which they fully understood. Under such conditions, these subjects (all college students) were able to exert a considerable degree of control over their behavioral and physiological reactions to a task which *ought* to have induced extreme fatigue.

As we saw in our earlier discussion, the behavioristic tradition in psychology, focusing as it does upon infrahuman species, has provided a model of motivated behavior which, naturally, is cognitionless. Consequently, most studies of human motivation based upon such a model have not taken seriously the role of the individual's cognitions in his entrance into and acceptance of deprivation states and aversive stimulation. In this sense, what is usually studied in the laboratory is not really comparable to human behavior in the real world where people may exercise volition in choosing their commitments and accept responsibility for the consequences of their performance.

THE COGNITIVE APPROACH

Most hard-headed psychologists prefer to avoid incorporating a term like "cognition" into the glossary of a scientific psychology, for the same reason that physical scientists and medical researchers prefer to ignore all psychological concepts which do not have immediate and direct empirical referents which can be isolated and studied *in vacuo*. For behaviorists, like Verplanck (1957), *cognition* is a term with scientific pretensions but with no more scientific prestige than literary, conversational, or intuitive remarks. There is little difference between such a modern view of cognition and the earlier dismissal by William James of "consciousness." In his *Essays in Radical Empiricism* (1912), James pronounced that consciousness "is the name of a nonentity, and has no right to a place among first principles. Those who still cling to it are clinging to a mere echo, the faint rumor left behind by the disappearing 'soul' up in the air of philosophy."

Verplanck's glossary does, however, provide a starting point by defining cognition as a hypothetical S → S association or perceptual organization postulated to account for expectancies. Wallach's analysis (1949) of perception and cognition makes perception a more primitive concept arising as a direct consequence of the physical effect of a stimulus upon the receptors; cognition is defined as perception integrated with associated memory traces.

Most congenial with the viewpoint underlying the use of cognition in this monograph is the position of Zajonc (1967): A functional definition of cognition and other major psychological constructs should indicate the specific source which accounts for most of the response variability. Thus, for motivation this source is deprivation or arousal, for learning it is practice and reinforcement, for perception it is stimulation, for the sensory psychologist it is energy transformations of the stimulus, while for the cognitive psychologist it is the informational or signal value of stimuli.

If cognitions represent "knowledge, opinion or belief about the environment, about oneself or one's behavior" (Festinger, 1957), then cognitive organization represents the psychological ordering and structuring of prior information processing and becomes a predictor of future motivational, attitudinal, or behavioral effects. Cognitive analysis is no longer concerned with how social phenomena are organized in descriptive categories (see Scheerer's earlier approach, 1954), but rather with how cognitions interact to modify and control behavior.

Cognition and Computer Simulation

The major impetus for legitimizing a cognitive approach to the study of human behavior has not come from social psychologists but from those interested in computer simulation and information processing. It is curious, therefore, to see hard-headed experimental psychologists continue to regard cognition with the same jaundiced eye as instinct, mind, or even soul because of its vague and indeterminate boundaries, while cognition has become a central concept in computer simulation of behavior, where it is necessary to operationalize explicitly every concept and process (see Simon & Newell, 1964).

Simon has recently (1967) proposed an information-processing theory of human thinking in which cognition and affect interact to influence both the process and the outcome. In this theory, the central nervous system is regarded as a serial processor of information with an interpreter system which systematically examines a hierarchy of subroutines until it arrives at the most elementary one. Completion of a particular subroutine allows processing of the next higher, more complex one. Built into such a model are "aspiration achievement" (attainment of subgoal), "satisficing" (adequate, though not complete subgoal achievement), "impatience" (selection of best alternative in a given period of time) and "discouragement" (cessation of processing after a given number of failures). Such a system can have multiple goals and multifaceted criteria of any single goal, as well as an operation for "noticing" when conditions have arisen that require ongoing programs to be set aside because real-time needs of high priority are encountered. Such real-time needs may arise from unexpected environmental events, physiological demands, or sudden awareness of cognitive associations.

Thus a cognitive approach is seen as having utility in understanding complex human information processing, and as such it will probably come to occupy a position of major importance in all psychological models dealing with meaningful human behavior.

The Cognitions of Choice and Justification

We have seen that although the Renaissance conception deemed choice as proper to man, it has been largely ignored as an independent variable in psychological research because of the traditional view of the experimental subject as a passive reactor to contrived environment. To give man, the subject, a choice is to complicate any interpretation of his responding and to make tenuous any comparisons with chimps, dogs, cats, pigeons, rats, cockroaches, and planaria.

In sharp contrast, existential philosophy has rectified the doctrine of choice. Sartre (1957) makes choosing the indispensable attribute of man: "Man makes himself"; and "Through his choice he involves all mankind, and he cannot avoid making a choice." It is precisely because man can exercise choice that he is free to control and is not simply controlled. In a sense, this optimistic view of human potentiality contradicts the behaviorists' basic assumption of determinism. For the existentialist, "man is free, man is freedom." As Sartre goes on to say, "I am creating a certain image of man of my own choosing. In choosing myself, I choose man."

It may well be that psychology has not been forced to consider this concept of choice seriously because the existential analysis is too idealistic. Choice may be man's liberation, but perhaps we have not created the conditions in which man *wants* freedom of choice. "He who has a choice has trouble," according to an old Dutch proverb. Man is born free, but at every opportunity he shackles himself with compulsion, ritual, obligation, and conformity in order to live thoughtlessly, to conceal his weaknesses, and to gain respectability.

Why should choice make trouble? The ability to choose first involves psychological freedom to specify what the alternatives are, or to perceive those that are available. The act of deciding upon one alternative and rejecting the others requires consideration of the attributes, implications, utility, and costs of each. The commitment to take action transforms what is originally a continuum of theoretical response alternatives into a concrete dichotomy with one degree of freedom, thereby changing abstract intellectual involvement into immediate ego-involvement. Since the consequences of any act cannot be fully known at the time of the choice, there is always some risk that the decision may be the wrong one. It is fear of this possibility that keeps people from choosing. If one chooses freely, then one bears personal responsibility for the consequences of the choice. If there are outcomes which can be evaluated as right or wrong, good or bad, wise or stupid, then the individual himself can be evaluated according to the consequences of his choice. Where the alternatives are mutually exclusive, the choice irrevocable, and the consequences involve important aspects of the individual's aspirations, values, and attitudes, then his very self-definition is at stake. As long as the individual knows he could have done otherwise, or that others he respects might have made a different choice, then, unlike Pontius Pilate, he cannot wash his hands of it.

In place of true choice, which allows the possibility of denigrating self-evaluation, one can give the appearance of choosing by putting himself in situations which force the choice or by arranging for others to act so he can merely react. It is only when the individual sees no exit, perceives that his freedom to choose is minimal, conceives of himself as helpless, victimized, and passive, that he can be free in the negative sense of not being responsible. However, in this process of choosing not to choose, man relinquishes a major part of his human integrity.

Choice and Chance: Gamblers, Neurotics, and Schizophrenics. For many people the ideal is to have an illusion of choice within a system where external forces actually determine the decision and thus must bear responsibility for any negative consequences, while positive outcomes can be attributed to the individual. This is like betting against the odds on a long shot: if you lose, no one could have reasonably expected any other outcome; but if you win, then you earn the right to be credited with having made a smart choice. To extend this analogy further, the impulsive gambler prefers to play only when the outcome is entirely determined by chance, for then he need not be concerned with the restraints upon action which reason or foreknowledge impose. Winning is not affected by ability, merit, desire, effort, or any skill, but by uncontrollable and capricious luck only.

This avoidance of the consequences of making important decisions is manifested in its extreme form among neurotics, who can see no alternatives to the ineffectual compulsions they have substituted for meaningful action. Or, they go to great lengths to preserve their self-esteem from further threats produced by "wrong" decisions by allowing themselves to feel controlled by other people, situations, or magical formulas. It may be that even among schizophrenics, choice avoidance becomes a major dynamic process. Perhaps the last choice they make is to reject the choosing of "real" self in favor of an apparent self who can experience no frustration either because choice is irrelevant to a supposedly motive- and goal-less person or because the outcomes of imaginary choices are guaranteed within their newly fabricated level of reality. Some support for such a view comes from an intensive observational analysis of back ward schizophrenics by Hershkowitz (1962) at West Haven, Connecticut, Veterans Hospital. These patients created a subculture, without the aid of any verbal communication, in which every action, however trivial, was guaranteed to have a predictable, desired outcome; no action was ever subjected to chance. Thus, for example, if one of these patients wanted a cigarette, he need not risk making a decision to ask someone who might not have one or would not share; rather, he would always get one if he asked certain cigarette-offering patients when they were sitting in specific chairs denoting accessibility to such requests.

Justification Undercuts Freedom of Choice. There are many occasions when it is impossible to deny that one had alternatives other than that chosen. Under such circumstances of obvious choice, individual responsibility may be abrogated by invoking sources of justification to adequately explain why anyone would have made the same choice. Statements like "I did it for the money," ". . . out of fear of God," ". . . to get a good grade," ". . . to avoid punishment or ridicule," ". . . to gain the approval or love of another person," etc., are all attempts to provide justification extrinsic to the task itself or to the nature of the alternative chosen—which will be respected by the individual's reference group and will also be convincing to himself.

No Choice—Adequate Justification. When the individual perceives that he has no choice but to behave according to the rules of a particular game or when he sees no other alternatives, but is provided with adequate justification for why he had to act as he did, then he divests himself of the possibility of genuinely interacting with his environment. Stimulus input can then be processed with minimal cognitive "interference," and the output behavior should be relatively well correlated with the intensity of that input. Under these circumstances, human behavior *is* reducible to basic principles derived from motivational theories based upon infrahuman species.

Choice—Minimal Justification. On the other hand, if the individual cannot explain away his behavior because he *did* have a clear and explicit choice to behave differently and, in addition, had justification which, though increasing the likelihood of his choice, did not completely determine it, then he must directly confront the environment his choice has created for him. Under these circumstances, man may alter his external environment by modifying and controlling his internal environment. There is no longer a one-to-one correspondence between stimulus intensity and reactivity because cognitive processes have intervened to increase response variability. Block and Bridger (1962), while they support this general position, place an upper boundary upon response variability:

> Man does gain the capacity to interpret the environment historically, to essentially modify the impact of stimuli upon himself. Since stimulus variability and response variability go hand-in-hand, we cannot expect to find rigid stimulus-response relationships such as LIV [Law of Initial Values] when man's higher activities can effectively intervene between stimulus and response. However, the stimulus-modifying capacity of man is limited. Novel threatening stimuli, strong psychological stimuli and physical stimuli such as drugs cannot be effectively modified, and thus will tend to produce responses conforming to rigid input-output laws (p. 12).

To rephrase the implication of this entire approach, if one's behavior is not perceived as being externally determined, then the locus of causality shifts from an external to an internal point of reference, and man actively engages in his environment rather than passively submits to the demands put upon him.

RELEVANCE OF DISSONANCE THEORY

Because Festinger's theory of cognitive dissonance (1957, 1964), and especially Brehm and Cohen's extension of it (1962), implicates these variables of commitment, choice, and justification as central in human decision making, it has been used as the conceptual basis underlying the present research in order to generate empirically testable predictions.

When a person has the cognition that he has voluntarily chosen to commit himself to a behavior which has negative consequences for the satisfaction of some relevant, salient motive, a state of cognitive dissonance is created. The knowledge that the tension associated with a given motive is uncomfortable is inconsistent with the knowledge that one has agreed to accept it, continue to endure more of it, or postpone behavior directed toward available goals which could reduce the drive.

This theory of cognitive dissonance assumes the existence of a basic tendency within each individual toward consistency of cognitions about oneself and one's environment. When two or more cognitive elements (or sets) are in a *psychologically* inconsistent relation, dissonance is aroused. Although dissonance is cognitive in origin, the theory essentially follows drive-reduction motivational principles: Dissonance is defined as a general tension state which motivates behavior, the terminal response of which results in a reduction in the level of tension.

The dynamic or motivating force of the theory can be ascribed to the (apparently) culturally learned need for internal consistency among behavior, attitudes, values, and beliefs, as well as to perceived pressures toward uniformity of these cognitions with social reality. Festinger's earlier theories of informal social communication (1950) and social comparison processes (1954) focused on this latter, extra-individual source of motivation, while dissonance theory is primarily centered upon the intra-individual source. Both of these processes, however, may be subservient to more basic phenomena which characterize this approach as a "face-saving theory," in which the individual is motivated to modify and distort both internal and external reality in order to make them appear consistent with having made the "correct" decision.

It is assumed that dissonance can give behavior both energy and direction, the necessary characteristics of a drive (cf., Cofer & Appley, 1964). Pressures to reduce dissonance vary as a function of the magnitude of this cognitive drive, which in turn is specified as a weighted proportion of cognitions which are inconsistent with the commitment to those which support it. This ratio increases and dissonance becomes intensified as the unchosen alternative is relatively more attractive (more will be lost) and as the unchosen alternative has more positive attributes not shared by the chosen alternative. Finally, dissonance also increases with the importance of the decision. However, since dissonance is defined in terms of a ratio, if importance contributes equally to all elements, its effect will be canceled out. Norah Rosenau's perceptive thesis (1964) clarifies this issue by demonstrating that the magnitude of dissonance produced by an act of choice varies directly with the importance of the consequences of the choice if the outcome is intimately linked to the act of choice (e.g., if the subject's personality will be evaluated directly from the kind of choice made). When the act of choice only establishes a path by which the outcome could eventually be achieved (e.g., choosing a particular medical school in order to become a doctor), then the effect of importance will vary inversely with the amount of time, the number of events, or the additional behavior after the act of choice necessary to fully determine the value of that outcome.

Dissonance Reduction

Efforts to reduce dissonance will be in the nature of attempts to redefine the situation by adding new cognitions or modifying existing ones which will decrease the ratio of inconsistent over consonant cognitions. Dissonance may be reduced by enhancing the attractiveness of the chosen alternative relative to the unchosen, by seeking social support or information in favor of the decision, by denial or misperception of discrepant cognitions, by decreasing the importance of the decision, by increasing the cognitive overlap between alternatives, and by minimizing the discrepancy between one's attitudes or values and those of another person. These are, of course, only some of the most general dissonance-reducing strategies, since the object and magnitude of the dissonance must be individually determined (extra-theoretically) in each application of the theory and since the ways in which the dissonance can be reduced depend upon the past reinforcement history of the individual, his current motivation, and the constraints of the given situation.

Since dissonance is an assumed intervening process inferred from the antecedent operations establishing inconsistency and from its measurable behavioral effects, obviously there can be no independent metric to measure it directly. Rather, it should be conceived as a heuristic device for generating a great many hypotheses about behavior from a small number of assumptions and postulates. (See Zajonc, 1967, and Abelson, Aronson, McGuire, Newcomb, Rosenberg, and Tannenbaum, 1968, for an excellent review of recent research stimulated by the theory and for a classification and analysis of the major issues.)

The Forced Public Compliance Paradigm

Our present concern is limited to one aspect of the cognitive dissonance theory—the arousal and reduction of dissonance as a consequence of publicly behaving in ways which are psychologically inconsistent with one's beliefs, opinions, and values. This forced public compliance occurs in everyday life whenever we engage in activities that we don't really want to engage in—such as going to a job we don't like, entertaining disliked friends or relatives, studying instead of going on a date, eating unpleasant but nutritious foods, or a host of similar public activities that are not congruent with our underlying private attitudes.

Recently, Jack Brehm (1962) has extended this application of dissonance theory to investigate what happens when an individual behaves in a way which is not predictable from a given state of motivation, that is, when an already motivated person voluntarily commits himself to a state of additional or prolonged deprivation. The relevant cognitions are one's awareness of the aversiveness of the stimulation or of the tension associated with the drive on the one hand and the knowledge that one has chosen to be exposed to such a state on the other hand. The dissonance occasioned by such a commitment, however, may be reduced by a third cognitive element which can be consistent with this public action. The greater the coercive force exerted to induce the choice, the more the commitment is externally determined and consequently "rationally" justified. Thus, the magnitude of dissonance decreases as the incentive for making the commitment to deprivation—or the punishment for not making it—increases. Dissonance therefore will be maximal when the individual perceives that there are alternative ways for him to act and that the external support for any one of these alternatives is not sufficient to justify completely its selection (see Aronson, 1966). Under these conditions, he is personally responsible for the consequences of his choice.

These theoretical variables of choice and justification are not in psychologically independent dimensions, since the perception of no choice is typically accompanied by maximum justification for one course of action, while completely free choice is possible only when the alternatives have equivalent utilities. However, within a considerable range they are free to vary independently. Moreover, choice may involve first perceiving that alternatives are available and then that, regardless of the utilities involved, the choice is still completely open (i.e., it is still possible to bet against the odds, make the unpopular or deviant choice, etc.). It also seems evident that people vary in the extent of the disproportionality in utilities they require before selecting one alternative and rejecting the others (along a risk-conservative continuum). Dissonance theory specifies that after the commitment is made, the values of each alternative will be modified, the chosen alternative increasing and the rejected one decreasing in value.

DISSONANCE PREDICTIONS

Since it is difficult to deny the reality of the behavioral commitment or to modify the external environment directly, a highly probable dissonance-reducing behavior should be the modification of the cognition least resistant to change—the subjective appraisal of the drive stimulus itself. If one perceives oneself to be less hungry, thirsty, sexually aroused, or in pain (whatever the drive), one's commitment to further deprivation or noxious stimulation becomes less dissonant. If resulting attempts to reduce this dissonance lead to an alteration of the noncognitive as well as this cognitive component of any motivational state, then the drive itself will be functionally lowered. If the drive is actually reduced in the service of dissonance reduction, then we should be able to demonstrate that the various associated consummatory and physiological behaviors—as well as the motive-related subjective and instrumental reactions—have been decreased.

Our conventional paradigms of motivation lead us to expect that three of the factors which cumulate to intensify motivational effects on performance are: (1) high level of drive, (2) reward for commitment to the drive, and (3) strong threat or more intensified stimulation or deprivation.

However, consideration of the role which cognitions play in directing motivation forces a re-evaluation of traditional hypotheses which relate strength of instrumental or consummatory behavior in a direct way to physical or temporal properties of the drive-arousing stimuli. This is seen to hold because dissonance will be greater as: (1) the perceived freedom of choice increases, (2) the initial drive level increases, (3) the severity of anticipated future deprivation or stimulation increases, and (4) the incentives or justification for commitment to deprivation or excessive stimulation decrease. Under these circumstances, there will be greater pressure to reduce dissonance, which, if channeled effectively, could actually lower the drive and lead to a lowered level of relevant instrumental or consummatory behavior.

Thus, what we hope to show in the empirical research that follows is that in the process of reducing cognitive dissonance, an individual may actually alter his own state of motivation, thereby controlling his internal environment and reducing the impact upon his behavior of any given biological drive or social motive.

GENERAL RESEARCH STRATEGY

In most of the research presented here, drive states are experimentally induced in the laboratory by standard, simple operations of deprivation, isolation, relevant stimulation, or blockage of goal attainment. In the more recently performed studies, control groups, treated identically to dissonance groups, but given no choice in commitment to the discrepant behavior, are employed to replicate previously established experimental results relating selected "motivated behaviors" to stimulus input intensity. These control groups, therefore, are used to demonstrate the effects of high versus low levels of arousal on a variety of responses, "unbiased" by interference from the additional variables of choice and justification. As such, they provide the limits within which the dissonance treatment groups can be expected to array themselves.

In all of these experiments, the forced public compliance paradigm was used to study changes in motivated behavior as a consequence of cognitive variables assumed to arouse dissonance. We will be examining, therefore, a series of studies which incorporate a common set of intervening variables, a similar set of cognitive-input variables, and a wide variety of response measures (reflecting several levels of analysis). Predictions will be made about changes in physiologically based drives (hunger, thirst, pain), socially learned motives (achievement, aggression, approval), and attitudes (toward specific things).

Criticism of Dissonance Research

Respecting the relevant arguments of the critics of earlier research on dissonance theory (e.g., Chapanis & Chapanis, 1964; Jordan, 1964; Rosenberg, 1966; and Zajonc, 1967), we have tried to be compulsive about our precision and rigor in executing and analyzing these experiments; to utilize standard procedures within uncomplicated situations; to develop reliable measures adequately pretested; to employ unconfounded research designs with proper control groups; to collect data bearing upon alternative explanations; to use independent, "blind" analysis of subjective data; and to minimize experimenter bias within the experimental procedure. Statistical evaluation of treatment means has typically proceeded from an overall analysis of variance or covariance (or related IBM analysis) to multiple comparisons of subgroups' means with a two-tailed alpha level of .05.[4] Subjects have been eliminated from data analyses for only the most generally accepted reasons, such as occasional apparatus failure, but never after examining their data, except for explicitly labeled internal analysis to uncover some suspected relationship.

During the five-year span represented by this research, we have attempted a systematic, cumulative development of a relatively circumscribed problem in which clusters of studies refine the methodology of previous work, clarify alternative interpretations, strengthen the basic theoretical model, and extend the implications of earlier results.

The Self-Selection Issue

If subjects have a choice in whether to expose themselves to a situation assumed to be unpleasant, the best test of the validity of both the choice and the aversiveness of the situation occurs when some members of the experimental group refuse to commit themselves to that situation. However, if there is a greater self-selection by subjects in the dissonance conditions than in the control groups—the greatest self-selection being, as would be expected, in the High Dissonance group—then we may be introducing a bias in the results (see Brehm & Cohen, 1962, and Chapanis & Chapanis, 1964). This can be true only if those who refused the commitment have lower thresholds for the relevant stimulation, thus ensuring that their self-selection would automatically inflate the mean of the distribution of the remaining subjects and make the High Dissonance group appear to be less reactive to the drive operations. This does not appear to be the case in the data we will present, since subjects who refused are not more sensitive or disturbed by the stimulation or anticipated deprivation. It is probable that they are simply more independent, autonomous, and self-assertive than those who remain. This evidence comes from several studies whose designs enabled us to collect comparable data on refusal and committed subjects, and from many

4. The professional convention of presenting various statistical values in addition to the probability level will not be followed here in order to increase readability; however, concerned readers may solicit them directly from the authors.

of the other studies which offer data on the initial reactions of all subjects prior to choice.

PLAN OF THE BOOK

The experiments are not presented in the chronological order in which they were originally performed; rather, they are arranged in two parts and subdivided into sections to provide a meaningful sequential development of the basic propositions being tested. In the first part, on the more biologically based drives, there are three studies related to hunger and food preferences, three on thirst, and three on pain and anxiety about pain. In the second part, dealing with social and personality variables, studies on need for achievement, failure avoidance, and need for social approval are followed by two reports on research on interpersonal aggression. Finally, several studies relating dissonance variables to premeasured individual-difference variables demonstrate the utility of this integration of social and personality phenomena. The editor's comments after each study sometimes include supplementary data from related studies, attempt to make salient some particular aspect of the study, or raise questions generated by the experiment but answerable only by subsequent research.

Although all the articles have been edited to increase their comparability in organization and style and to integrate them better into the overall design of this text, each is presented in sufficient detail to convey the original quality and "feel" of the work.

Let us now turn to this empirical evidence to answer our initial question of whether man can claim uniqueness by controlling his environment through the exercise of choice.

Part I

Biological Drives

Section A

Hunger

The Fox and the Grapes

The Fox had gone without breakfast as well as without dinner, so when he found himself in a vineyard his mouth began to water. There was one particularly juicy-looking bunch of grapes hanging on a trellis. The Fox leaped to pull it down, but it was just beyond his reach. He went back a few steps, took a running start, and jumped again. Again he missed. Once more he tried, and once more he failed to get the tempting prize. Finally, weary and worn out, he left the vineyard. "*I really wasn't very hungry*," he said, to console himself. "Besides, I'm sure those grapes are sour."

Aesop, Sixth century B.C.[1]

Did the Fox say he wasn't hungry in an attempt to rationalize away his heightened drive state? Or did he, in fact, effectively reduce his hunger drive by some cognitive process?

1. MODIFICATION OF HUNGER BY COGNITIVE DISSONANCE

Jack W. Brehm

Let us consider a hypothetical example in order to see how cognitive dissonance might affect hunger. Picture a professor busily engaged in writing a paper. His work is going well when lunch time arrives, and he is reluctant to take time out to eat. He considers going but finally decides to stay and work.

1. *Aesop's Fables*. New York: Golden Press, Inc., 1965, p. 23. (Italics mine.)

SOURCE: Brehm, Jack W., "Modification of Hunger by Cognitive Dissonance." Adapted from "Motivational Effects of Cognitive Dissonance" reprinted from *Nebraska Symposium on Motivation*, edited by M. R. Jones, by permission of University of Nebraska Press and the author. Copyright 1962 by the University of Nebraska Press. Supplementary material from *Explorations in Cognitive Dissonance* by J. W. Brehm and A. R. Cohen (New York: John Wiley & Sons, Inc., 1962), pp. 133–136.

Readers familiar with dissonance theory will recognize that the professor in our example is in a dissonance-creating situation. He is confronted with two attractive alternatives: going to lunch and continuing to work on the paper. Once he has decided to stay and work, then the known or imagined benefits of going to lunch are dissonant with his decision. What are these benefits? The particular benefit we are interested in is the consummatory behavior of eating, which will be as rewarding as the professor is hungry. We can see, therefore, that his decision to go without lunch is dissonant with his knowledge that he is hungry. Note that I refer to his *knowledge* of his own hunger rather than to his physiological condition.

The next logical question concerns how the professor might try to reduce his dissonance. From the introductory discussion of dissonance theory, we know that he might try to increase the number or importance of cognitions that are consonant with his decision. Thus, he might try to magnify the importance of working on the paper at this time while his thoughts on the subject are clear; or he might imagine that the value of the paper depends upon its early publication; and so on. Our main interest, however, is in the most probable alternative way of reducing dissonance, namely, to decrease the number or importance of dissonant cognitions. Specifically, we are concerned with the possibility that the professor might reduce his dissonance by *minimizing or eliminating the cognition that he is hungry*. For if only he can convince himself that he is not hungry, then surely the major reason for his going to lunch is eliminated, and hence, so is his dissonance. In summary, a possible way for dissonance to occur is through a decision to deprive oneself of food when one is hungry, and a possible way to reduce that dissonance is by convincing oneself that one is not hungry.

Although it seems relatively unequivocal that dissonance could be aroused in connection with a decision to deprive oneself of food, it is perhaps less clear that attempts at dissonance reduction could take the form of changing one's knowledge about how hungry one is. What is necessary, from the point of view of dissonance theory, is that the resistance to change of this cognitive component of hunger be relatively lower than that of the cognition about the behavioral commitment to deprivation. In other words, a person must be able to change either how hungry he is or, at a minimum, how hungry he thinks he is. Although we assumed that a person could change his cognition about how hungry he is, it was necessary to perform an experiment in order to see whether or not this assumption was in fact tenable.

One final theoretical point must be made before the first experiment in this series of interrelated studies is described, and to make that point I shall return to our professor, who has given up his lunch and is busily working on a paper. Having decided to deprive himself of lunch, he has presumably experienced dissonance. But how much dissonance? The amount of dissonance is a function of the ratio of weighted dissonant to consonant cognitions. Hence, the professor's dissonance will be greater the greater his hunger prior to the decision and the less important his working on the paper. If this ratio is large enough, the professor will decide to go to lunch. But let us confine ourselves to the range of cases in which the decision is to remain and work on the paper.

Let us suppose that just before deciding whether or not to go to lunch, the professor receives a telephone call from his wife, who happens to be worried about his weight. She tells him that if he skips today's lunch, she will give him a certain art book that he has long wanted. This additional benefit of giving up lunch is consonant with the decision to stay and work rather than go to lunch. Consequently, it will *reduce* the magnitude of dissonance that would result from a decision to miss lunch, even though it has nothing to do with the writing of the paper, which may remain the main motivation. In turn, the reduced magnitude of dissonance will produce relatively fewer attempts at dissonance reduction, and there will be *less reduction in hunger*. In our example, the professor whose wife promised an additional reward for going without lunch will remain relatively hungry even after deciding not to have lunch. In summary, and in conceptual terms, the greater the *extrinsic* reward for choosing to deprive oneself, the *less* the reduction in self-judged hunger from before to after the decision.

OVERVIEW OF EXPERIMENTAL DESIGN

To test this hypothesis, an experiment was designed and conducted by Jon Christopher Crocker and myself. In this experiment, we attempted to get hungry people to commit themselves to further food deprivation for either a high or a low extrinsic reward. To find what differential effects these two conditions would have on the cognitive component of hunger, we obtained self-ratings of hunger both before and after the commitment to further deprivation.

PROCEDURE

Male college students in an introductory psychology class were given the opportunity to participate in a study of "the effect of food deprivation on intellectual and motor functioning." They were told it would be necessary for them to go without breakfast and lunch on the day they were to report for a testing session in the afternoon, and they were also asked to keep the evening of the same day free. Participation was voluntary and worth a "credit point" toward the student's final grade in the introductory course (a minimal, uniform incentive for all subjects).

Twenty-two subjects were scheduled for individual sessions and were assigned alternately to one of the two experimental conditions. When each subject arrived at the experimental room, he was reminded that the study concerned the effect of food deprivation on certain kinds of intellectual and motor performances. His attention was then drawn to some sandwiches, candies, cookies, and milk lying at the side of the testing table, with the comment that he would be able to eat at the end of the testing session (obviously this should have increased the salience of hunger and eating).

Each subject was then told that it was necessary to determine just how hungry he was at the time of taking the tests and for that reason he should indicate his hunger on a rating scale. The subject was asked to be as accurate and honest as he could in making this rating. He was then given a 61-point scale, with each tenth point (starting with 0) labeled by the words *Not at all*, *Very Slightly*, *Slightly*, *Moderately*, *Quite*, *Very*, and *Extremely*, and was asked to mark the single point closest to how he felt.

Each student was then asked to perform the tests of intellectual and motor functioning, consisting of a pegboard task, naming objects made of wood, and problem solving. These tasks were included simply because they fit the rationale of the experiment. Since they are irrelevant to the experiment's true purpose, they will not be discussed further.

Deprivation Operation

After completion of these tasks (which took 15 minutes), the commitment to further deprivation was introduced by the experimenter in this way:

> You will recall that we asked you to keep your evening free since some people were to be asked to return for further testing in the evening. You are one of the people being asked to return for the later testing. This is, of course, up to you but let me explain what is involved. You will have to go without any food until about 8 or 9 o'clock this evening. Then we will give you some more tests of your intellectual and motor performances. There will be sandwiches, cookies, and milk for you to eat at the end of the testing session.

Dissonance Arousal

In order to create High Dissonance, the experimenter went on to say:

> Unfortunately, we cannot give any more experimental credit points for the evening session. You get your point for having taken part this afternoon so don't think you have to come this evening. But we would appreciate your help. If, however, you don't feel like doing it, that's okay because we can get someone else to do it.

If the subject hesitated, he was given further (standardized) encouragement.

To create Low Dissonance, the experimenter said:

> Unfortunately, we cannot give any more experimental credit points for the evening testing session. However, we can pay anyone willing to come back since we do need your help. The amount is $5.00.

We tested eleven subjects in the Low Dissonance condition, one of whom refused to commit himself to further deprivation; we also tested eleven subjects in the High Dissonance condition, two of whom refused to commit themselves to further deprivation. The data for these three subjects were deleted from our final analysis (and here, of course, there is no problem with differential subject self-selection).

Postcommitment Hunger Rating

After the subject had committed himself to going without dinner and was scheduled for an evening session, he was asked to fill out the hunger-rating scale again. It was explained that people had been found to change in their hunger from one moment to the next, some persons changing one way, some the other, and that he should again make as careful and accurate an estimate of his hunger as possible.

Another Measure of Hunger: Appetite

Finally, the subject was asked how many sandwiches, cookies, and (pint-sized) cartons of milk he would like to have brought to him for his eating at the end of the evening testing session. A simple count of these items would presumably offer another measure of hunger.

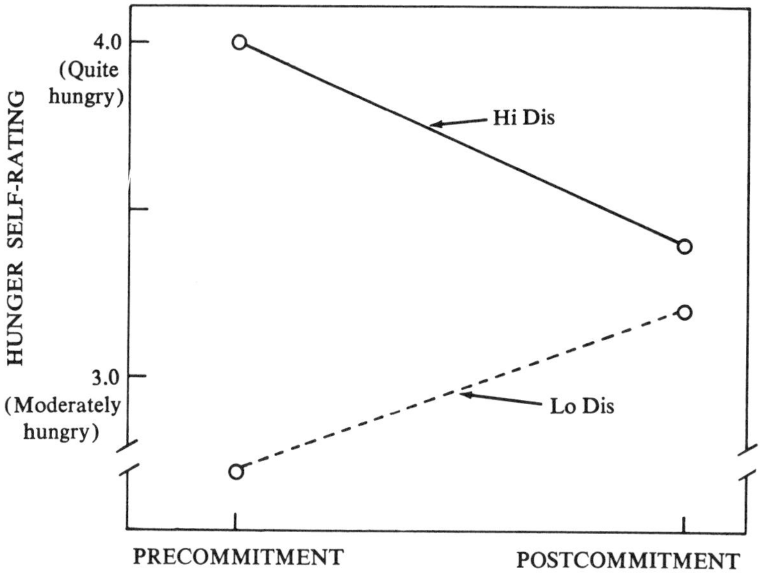

FIGURE 1

Mean self-ratings of hunger.

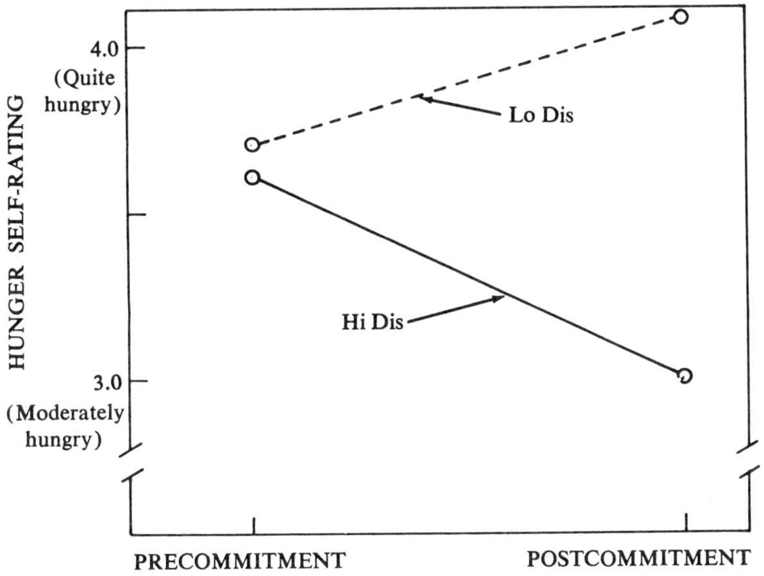

FIGURE 2

Mean self-ratings of hunger for selected subjects matched on precommitment scores of hunger.

RESULTS

You will recall that we expected those subjects who committed themselves to food deprivation for no incentive to experience relatively great dissonance and to try to reduce that dissonance by reducing how hungry they thought themselves to be. The obtained changes in the self-ratings of hunger are presented in Figure 1. They are clearly consistent with our expectation: with ratings on our 61-point scale scored from 0 to 6.0, the High Dissonance subjects *reduced* their rating by 0.57, and the Low Dissonance subjects *increased* their rating by 0.43. The difference between the rating changes, which go in opposite directions, in these two conditions is significant beyond the 1 per cent level using a *t*-test. These data are clearly consistent with our hypothesis that the cognitive aspect of this motivation is a function of dissonance and its reduction.

Initial-Difference Artifact

There are, however, some problems with these data. Perhaps the most serious problem is that there was a difference between the *initial* ratings in the two conditions. As can be seen in Figure 1, the High Dissonance subjects rated themselves as considerably more hungry to begin with than the Low Dissonance subjects. Whether this difference is due to sampling error or to some difference in the experimental conditions, it suggests that there may have been some reasons other than dissonance for the later changes in the hunger ratings. We can rule out some of these reasons by an internal analysis of the data in which only those subjects whose initial scores were similar are compared. When we do this, as shown in Figure 2, we find that the changes in hunger ratings are nearly identical to those of the unselected subjects. We can conclude, therefore, that the initial difference in hunger self-ratings (or its cause) does not account for the obtained differences in the change of hunger scores. Thus, the qualification of our conclusion that the data support the hypothesis is not serious, although the interpretation of the pre-experimental difference is still ambiguous.

Food Ordered

Additional evidence for our hypothesis is available from the count of the number of food items ordered by subjects for the evening testing session. If subjects in the High Dissonance condition had been trying harder than those in the Low to convince themselves that they were not hungry, then they should have ordered fewer items. This expectation is confirmed by the obtained averages: only 2.7 items of food in the High Dissonance condition compared with 4.2 in the Low (significant by *t*-test beyond the 1 per cent level).

CONCLUSIONS

The data thus support the theoretical notion that the cognitive aspects of motivation are affected by dissonance in much the same way as are other types of cognitions, like opinions. More specifically, they support the hypothesis that the dissonance aroused by the inconsistency between being motivated, on the one hand, and being committed to further deprivation of motive reduction, on the other, can be reduced by a decrease in the experienced intensity of the motivation. The resolution thus effected makes the knowledge that one has low motivation consonant with the knowledge that one has committed oneself to not experience motive reduction for a relatively long period of time.

Editor's Comments

Brehm's experiment demonstrates that self-ratings of hunger are reduced when hungry subjects commit themselves to a period of further food deprivation for minimal justification. In addition, these subjects order fewer items of food to eat at the conclusion of the experiment. While these measures are viewed as indicative of a reduction of hunger motivation in High as compared to Low Dissonance subjects, there are some questions as to alternative explanations.

The author himself has suggested one alternative, namely, that the perceived severity of the food deprivation for the Low Dissonance subjects is intensified by the offer of \$5.00 to undergo it. "If the deprivation is worth \$5.00, then I must be (or will be) quite hungry," might be a typical response to this inducement. Or, the money might make more salient the experience of hunger for these subjects. This methodological problem can be (and has been) handled in subsequent studies in two ways: (1) by using, instead of money, variations in the number of rational arguments to justify commitment; and (2) by telling subjects in all conditions that the deprivation experience has a constant value to the experimenter (e.g., "It is worth \$10.00.") and then introducing differential justification by telling those in the High Dissonance group that the experimenter can give them only \$1.00 for their participation, while telling those in the Low Dissonance condition he can give them only \$5.00.

In this first study, there were no control groups without the explicit choice of commitment to further deprivation, nor was there any attempt to induce different levels of hunger arousal. What was tested was only the basic comparison between experimental groups given differential justification under similar conditions of choice.

The unexplained difference in initial self-ratings of hunger, while apparently not affecting the pattern of the results (as demonstrated in the internal analysis of the data), nevertheless requires additional replication of this general procedure. The next experiment not only attempts such a replication but provides for a more demanding test of the cognitive control of hunger motivation. It is one thing for subjects to tell the experimenter they are not so hungry; it is quite another matter for them to alter their physiological reactions to food deprivation. To what extent, then, can a noncognitive component of hunger, such as release of free fatty acids into the blood, be affected by the operation of choice and justification in the process of commitment to food deprivation?

2. A PHYSIOLOGICAL EFFECT OF COGNITIVE DISSONANCE UNDER FOOD DEPRIVATION AND STRESS

Mary L. Brehm, Kurt W. Back, and Morton D. Bogdonoff

Brehm and Cohen (1962) suggest that changes in the cognitive components of motivation (e.g., self-reports) may have correlated consequences on the non-cognitive components. It is precisely this aspect of motivation that the present exploratory studies intend to examine: Are the cognitive changes produced by dissonance also reflected in changes in physiological variables?

A study was designed that allowed the examination of certain cognitive and physiological changes as functions of commitment to further deprivation and exposure to stress under High and Low Dissonance conditions. The deprivation period was 24 hours, which permitted examination of possible relatively enduring dissonance effects. Since the physiological measure of hunger required venipuncture and the taking of blood samples and since for many subjects this procedure is fear arousing, we were also able to examine physiological reactions to situational fear arousal as a function of dissonance.

The physiological measure employed was the change in concentration of plasma-free fatty acids (FFA) in the blood stream. The mobilization of FFA has been shown to be a reliable measure of autonomic-nervous-system activity in response to increased energy demands upon the individual. Such demands are made during fasting, the length of which has been found to correlate positively with FFA level (Dole, 1956; Klein, Bogdonoff, Estes, & Shaw, 1960). The FFA measure is also highly responsive to central-nervous-system activity. In arousal situations, such as the introduction of a needle to take a blood sample, sharp rises in FFA occur, followed by a return to the basal rate after a short recovery period (Bogdonoff, Estes, & Trout, 1959; Cardon & Gordon, 1959). In addition, this measure has been found to be sensitive to conditions of social interaction (Back, Bogdonoff, Shaw, & Klein, 1963).

DISSONANCE PREDICTIONS

Dissonance theory holds that dissonance and consequent minimization of hunger *increase* as justification for committing oneself to deprivation *decreases*.

SOURCE: Brehm, Mary L., Kurt W. Back, and Morton D. Bogdonoff, "A Physiological Effect of Cognitive Dissonance Under Food Deprivation and Stress." Adapted from "A Physiological Effect of Cognitive Dissonance Under Stress and Deprivation," *Journal of Abnormal and Social Psychology*, 1964, *69*, pp. 303–310.

Since FFA is directly related to length of deprivation, and thus presumably to actual hunger, subjects who commit themselves to deprivation for little justification, and who therefore convince themselves they are not hungry, would be expected to show less increase in FFA than those given high justification.

Similarly, since FFA during continuing deprivation increases from the stress of puncture alone, subjects who commit themselves to a second puncture under low justification (High Dissonance arousal), and presumably try to minimize the fearfulness of the puncture, would tend to show less increase in FFA in response to the second puncture than those under high justification (Low Dissonance).

EXPERIMENT I: OVERVIEW OF EXPERIMENTAL DESIGN

Hunger was induced by having subjects forego eating for 16 hours prior to the start of the experiment. The level of free fatty acid in the blood and self-ratings of hunger were the major response measures taken at three key times: after the original deprivation period, immediately after subjects committed themselves to an additional 8 hours of food deprivation under High or Low Dissonance conditions (varying justification), and again after the full-day fast.

PROCEDURE

The subjects (male college students) were told that the experiment would involve fasting and having blood samples taken and that three course-credit points were offered for participation. During the afternoon prior to the experiment, subjects in groups of three to six reported to the hospital clinic for a briefing session. Size of the groups was determined only by clinic scheduling problems. The subjects were told by the experimenter (a physician) that they must maintain a strict fast from that time (4:30 P.M.) until the following morning. In order to emphasize the importance of the fast, they were given wafers supposedly containing a traceable chemical element that would reveal any intake of caloric substances. The purpose of the experiment was minimally described as "an examination of blood chemistry in normal young males following a fast of 16 hours."

Initial Measures of Hunger Arousal

On their arrival at the clinic at 8:30 A.M. the following morning, the subjects were first asked by a research technician to rate themselves as to "how hungry they felt at the moment." Ratings were made on a 61-point scale, with each tenth point (starting with zero) successively labeled by *Not at all*, *Very Slightly*, *Slightly*, *Moderately*, *Quite*, *Very*, and *Extremely*. Then, an indwelling Cournand needle was inserted in an antecubital vein and the first blood sample drawn. This sample will be referred to as the *puncture level.*

A recovery period of 20 minutes elapsed, wherein the subjects sat quietly filling out questionnaires including semantic-differential items and measures of social desirability and anxiety. The information from these questionnaires (taken in conjunction with a separate study) was used here primarily to provide a standard time and activity prior to the taking of the second, or *resting level,* blood sample. Since analysis of the data from these questions is not germane to the present study, it will not be discussed further, beyond remarking that no differences were found between answers given under different experimental conditions. During this time, an assortment of sandwiches, candy, cookies, and milk were on obvious display in the experimental room (to increase the salience of food for all subjects). After the second blood sample was drawn, the subjects were seen individually by the physician-experimenter.

Subjects

The subjects, all males recruited from introductory sociology courses, were randomly assigned to the two dissonance conditions. Of the twenty subjects recruited, nine were assigned to the Low and eleven to the High Dissonance condition. Three subjects, two in High and one in Low Dissonance, declined further commitment because of prior arrangements. Two subjects in High Dissonance committed themselves and failed to return in the afternoon. Thus, there were eight Low and seven High Dissonance subjects.

High Dissonance

In the High Dissonance (low justification) condition, the experimenter introduced himself, briefly reiterated the ostensible reason for the experiment, and asked the subject whether he would be willing to continue the fast for another 8 hours. He reassured the subject that his commitment to the experiment was completed, that he already had earned his credit points, and that further continuance was up to him and was merely a convenience to the research team so they could "gather additional data on a full 24-hour fast." If the subject hesitated, he was told that it was entirely his choice and that scheduling problems would be alleviated if he could continue.

Low Dissonance

In the Low Dissonance (high justification) condition, each subject was likewise told that his commitment to the study was completed, but that it was highly important to medical research, to science, and to the success of the project to get additional data and that the study was therefore willing to pay a stipend of

$25 for a further 8-hour period of fasting. In both experimental conditions, the necessity of not discussing the experiment on campus was stressed.

Immediate Postcommitment Measures

For both conditions, a third blood sample* was drawn and the needle was removed. The technician again asked each subject to rate his degree of hunger on a separate, identical scale. The subject was told that people change in the amount of hunger they feel, even in the space of an hour—some changing one way, some the other, and some not at all—and that he should again be as accurate as possible. He was then asked to order items of food like those displayed to be available at his return for the afternoon session.

Delayed Measures—Full Fast Period

On their return to the clinic at 4:30 P.M., subjects were asked to rate themselves on the hunger scale (for the third time) and another puncture-level sample was drawn. A period of 20 minutes elapsed while the subjects filled out questionnaires similar to those administered in the morning. Then, the fifth and last sample was drawn, and the experiment was concluded.

While eating the food they had ordered, the subjects were fully apprised of the nature of the research, and all, regardless of expectation, were paid $25.00.

RESULTS

Self-ratings

Although the difference between the mean initial morning ratings of the High and Low Dissonance groups is not significant, there is a significant difference between their rating changes immediately following commitment (see Table 1). Five out of seven High Dissonance subjects decreased their self-ratings of hunger, whereas only one of the eight Low Dissonance subjects did so ($p < 0.10$). This one subject complained of nausea following the drawing of the second blood sample and subsequently decreased his hunger rating by 18 points. No other subjects complained of nausea. Without this subject, the difference between conditions in reported hunger change is significant at the 2 per cent level. This corresponds to the results obtained under similar conditions in the previous study by Jack Brehm (Article 1).

---

* Blood Sample 3 was taken directly following agreement to continue in order to determine whether there was any immediate response. However, this few minutes proved to be too short a period to produce any stable difference between that sample and the resting level. Other studies in lipid research have also shown that 15 to 20 minutes are required for the FFA reaction. Therefore, Sample 3 was not used in the analysis.

TABLE 1

MEAN SELF-RATINGS OF HUNGER*

Rating	Condition	
	High dissonance (Low justification)	Low dissonance (High justification)
Morning:		
Precommitment	35.1	29.5
Postcommitment	33.1	29.4
Difference	−2.0	−0.1 ($p < 0.10$)
Afternoon:		
Final	40.1	36.0
Difference (from precommitment)	+5.0	+6.5 (n.s.)

* Negative difference values indicate a decrease over time in the amount of hunger felt, while positive difference values reflect an increase. A score of 40 corresponds to the verbal label "Quite hungry."

It should be noticed that High Dissonance subjects tended to have higher ratings in the afternoon ($p = 0.10$, Mann-Whitney U test), but this was apparently a function of the initial (precommitment) differences, since changes in ratings from precommitment to afternoon were not significantly different.

As in the previous experiment, one plausible alternative to the dissonance explanation for the significant difference in rating changes immediately after commitment is that the monetary reward promised in the Low Dissonance condition might have convinced the subjects that their discomfort must be rather high. In the present experiment, however, we notice that the difference occurs not because the hunger increased with Low Dissonance but because it decreased with High Dissonance. This latter effect cannot be explained in terms of the magnitude of the incentive's altering the anticipated severity of the deprivation for the Low Dissonance subjects.

It appears, then, that the two variations in justification used to induce commitment did differentially affect the degree of felt hunger immediately following the commitment. However, none of the changes from morning to afternoon were significantly different between conditions.

Mean FFA Levels

Mean FFA levels of the five blood samples are shown in Table 2. Direct comparison of the samples between High and Low Dissonance conditions indicates no significant differences. The first index to be examined is the change in resting level from morning to afternoon (Samples 2 and 5). It can be seen from Table 2 that there is no difference between the two dissonance conditions on this index, since the mean levels rise equally as hours of deprivation increase (from FFA values in the 700's to the 1200's). This would appear to be evidence contrary to our predictions.

Internal Analysis Based on Hunger Ratings

However, Brehm and Cohen (1962, p. 139) suggest that subjects who report only slight hunger after a period of food deprivation should be deleted from the analysis since they do not meet the conditions necessary for testing the dissonance hypothesis. If initial deprivation has had little effect, commitment to further deprivation will not be a dissonant-producing experience. It follows, therefore, that the average values for the entire group may have little meaning.

In the present study, when subjects are divided on the basis of a median split on initial reported hunger (see Figure 1), those in the High Dissonance condition who are relatively hungry do clearly show less increase in FFA from morning to afternoon (Samples 2 and 5) than those who initially report not being hungry ($t = 1.84$, $p < 0.10$). That this is not an artifact or regression effect due to initial levels of FFA is shown by the fact that subjects in the Low Dissonance condition show a difference in the opposite direction—those initially not hungry showing less of an increase (interaction $F = 3.29$, $p < 0.10$). Of the four subgroups, it is those who presumably experience the most dissonance—namely, those in the low-justification condition who were hungry at the time they committed themselves to further deprivation—who show the least increase in FFA during the period of subsequent deprivation and end up with the lowest resting level.

Thus, under conditions of Low Dissonance, hungry subjects show a greater increase in FFA than those initially not hungry, which is to be expected from the "normal" relation between hunger and FFA levels. Under High Dissonance conditions, however, the opposite is true: those not hungry initially show a much greater increase than subjects who were hungry at the start. In fact, hungry High Dissonance subjects are more similar to not hungry Low Dissonance subjects than they are to any other subgroup. This is, of course, what would be expected if they were successful in convincing themselves that they were not hungry during the period of deprivation and if this self-persuasion had a corresponding effect on physiological variables.

TABLE 2

MEAN FFA LEVELS (μ Eq/L)*

Sample	Condition	
	High dissonance (Low justification)	Low dissonance (High justification)
Morning:		
(1) Puncture	1155	960
(2) Resting	729	776
Afternoon:		
(4) Puncture	1405	1586
(5) Resting	1224	1212

* Blood samples were analyzed for FFA by a modification of the method of Dole (Trout, Estes, & Friedberg, 1960). The unit of measurement is micro-equivalent per liter.

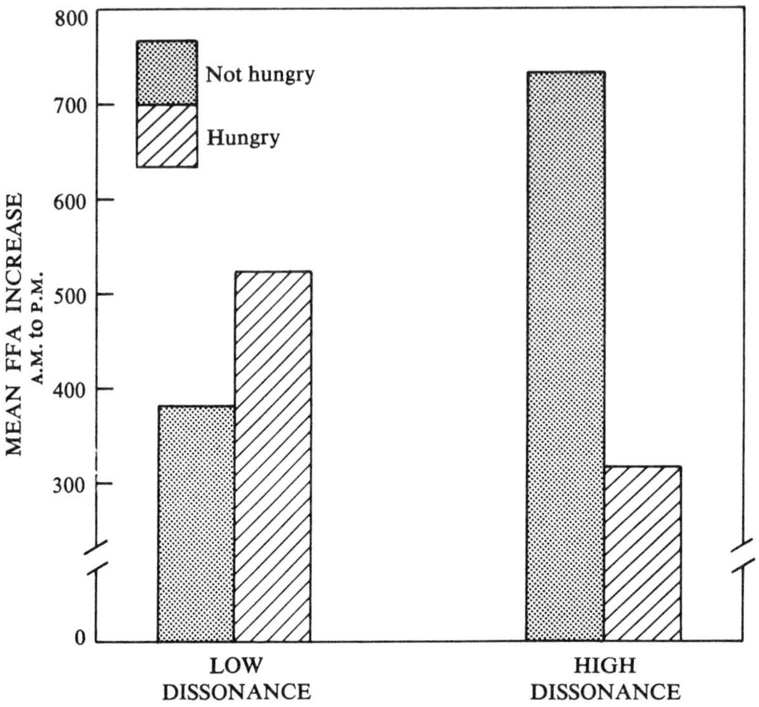

FIGURE 1
Internal analysis of changes in resting levels of FFA by justification condition for subjects reporting themselves to feel hungry or not hungry on their first rating.

It is possible that subjects who initially rated their hunger low after the 16-hour fast were strongly committed from the beginning of the fast to undergo whatever was required, for a variety of reasons. In this case, strong social motivation to comply with the requests of the experimenter would support the commitment to deprivation and would itself lead to the suppression of the deprivation effect. The stronger this reinforcement, the less the increased stress. We shall return to this point after we have dealt with a second experiment, in which initial commitment was an important factor.

Stress Reaction

The second index to be examined is the subject's reaction to the needle puncture —specifically, the ratio of puncture level to resting level, or Sample 1 divided by Sample 2 for the morning and Sample 4 by Sample 5 for the afternoon session. These data are presented as percentages in Table 3. It can be seen that High Dissonance subjects became less aroused in the afternoon than they had become in the morning prior to the commitment, which involved both further fasting and another needle puncture. By contrast, the Low Dissonance subjects became

TABLE 3

FAA RATIOS OF PUNCTURE LEVEL TO RESTING LEVEL
(in per cents)

Sample	Condition		Difference
	High dissonance	Low dissonance	
Morning	157	124	33
Afternoon	112	132	20
Difference	−45	+8	

slightly more aroused. An analysis of variance yields a significant interaction ($p < 0.05$), with nonsignificant main effects.

Again, if one divides the groups on the basis of the dimension relevant to dissonance, in this case initial arousal (Sample 1 divided by Sample 2), it is clear that the difference between dissonance conditions occurs only with those subjects who exhibited greater tension at the threat of needle puncture, as can be seen in Table 4. The figures represent the morning and afternoon ratios and the difference between the two, with a minus indicating decreased situational arousal. Thus, subjects who commit themselves to a fearful and hence physiologically arousing situation tend to show less physiological arousal later to the extent that justification for the commitment is minimal and dissonance is presumably high. Again, the extent of the difference among the highly aroused subjects may be partly due to the unusually high morning ratio of the High Dissonance subjects; but regression cannot account for the fact that they have a lower ratio in the afternoon than the Low Dissonance subjects.

EXPERIMENT II: A REPLICATION

To increase the size of the sample, the study was repeated. The procedure was essentially the same as in the previous study except that individual monetary

TABLE 4

AROUSAL RATIOS IN INITIALLY AROUSED AND NOT-AROUSED SUBJECTS
(in per cents)

Condition	Subjects initially aroused			Subjects initially not aroused		
	Arousal ratio		Difference	Arousal ratio		Difference
	Morning	Afternoon		Morning	Afternoon	
High Dissonance	193	123	−70	109	99	−10
Low Dissonance	136	149	13	112	116	4
Difference	57	26	—	3	17	—

reward was omitted from the high-justification condition in order to give the results more external generalizability. In addition, a full-day condition was run here as a control on the effects of fasting without a change in expectations. Control subjects were told on first contact (prior to any fasting) that they were expected to return twice and to fast for 24 hours. The rationale given at the morning session was the same as that given previously in the high-justification condition.

Subjects

There were 11 subjects in each of the justification groups and 7 full-day Control subjects. Commitment was obtained from all 22 experimental subjects, and all subjects returned for the afternoon session. This rather impressive degree of cooperation may have been partly due to the fact that these subjects were recruited from campus groups which were promised a lump-sum payment for procuring the services of a group of their members. One subject was deleted from the High Dissonance group owing to an inadequate fast prior to the morning session. One Low Dissonance subject suffered a syncopic reaction in the afternoon, and his blood measures were deemed unreliable.

RESULTS

Self-ratings of Hunger

Surprisingly, none of the predicted differences between groups in self-ratings of hunger were significant. Initial ratings in all three groups were considerably lower than in the first study (by an average of 5 score points). Nine subjects from the experimental groups and two from the Control group rated themselves as only "slightly hungry" or less, after foregoing two meals. It may be that the special recruiting conditions inadvertently increased the initial level of commitment motivation and thereby biased the hunger ratings.

Mean FFA Levels

It is difficult to make direct between-group comparisons on the measure of mean increase in FFA level because of an unusually low puncture level in the Low Dissonance group. Not only was this initial morning puncture level more than 200 M Eq/L units less than either the Control or the High Dissonance group, but it was even lower than its own subsequent resting level!

Internal Analysis by Initial Hunger Report

If the groups are divided again according to the first hunger rating, the same pattern emerges as in the previous study (see Figure 2). The difference between initially hungry and not-hungry subjects in the increase in FFA resting levels from morning to afternoon (Samples 2 and 5) was greatest in the Low Dissonance conditions: the hungry subjects increased their FFA levels by 1058 units, while those not hungry showed an increase of only 430 units. This effect is much weaker in the full-day Control group (a difference of 167 units) and is considerably attenuated in the High Dissonance group. There, the hungry subjects showed an increase of 857 FFA units, while not-hungry subjects revealed only a slightly lower increase of 779 units (a difference of 78 units).

Thus, among the initially hungry subjects there is less increase in the High Dissonance condition than in the Low Dissonance condition, whereas the reverse is true for the initially not-hungry subjects. (An analysis of variance yields a significant effect for hunger—$p < 0.005$—and a significant interaction—$p < 0.025$). However, the difference in increase between the hungry and not-hungry subjects in the High Dissonance condition is not significant, and the obtained interaction effect is a function of the significant difference in increase between the hungry and the not-hungry subjects only in the Low Dissonance condition. There was a similar effect, though not significant, in Experiment I.

FFA levels evidently are affected in a predictable fashion by manipulations

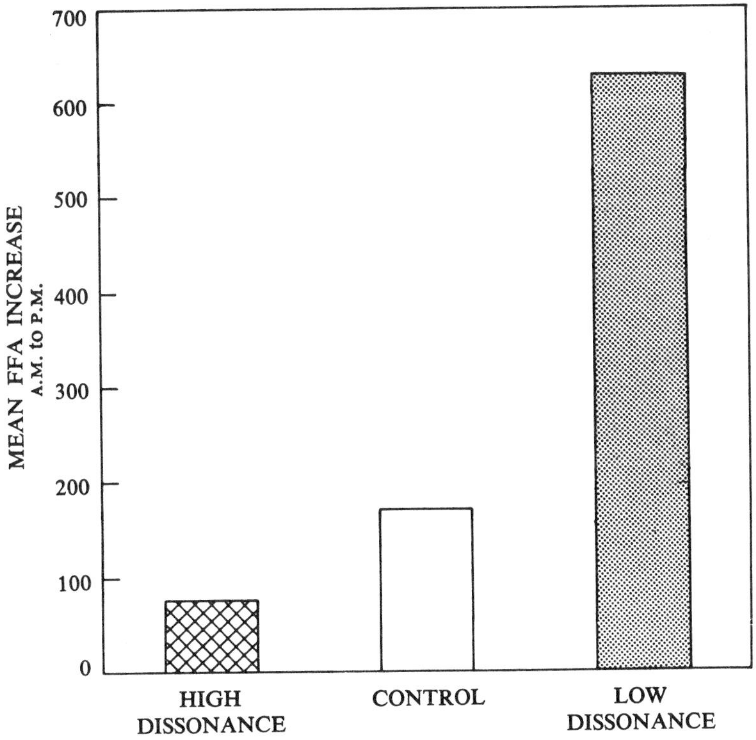

FIGURE 2
Mean difference in FFA increase (from morning to afternoon resting levels) between the initially hungry and not-hungry subjects in each condition.

that create cognitive dissonance if the subjects perceive themselves to be hungry at the time when they commit themselves to further deprivation. This physiological difference distinguishes those subjects who are hungry from those who are not in the Low Dissonance condition. However, the effects of high dissonance on reducing hunger minimize the physiological difference between reportedly hungry and not-hungry subjects.

Control of Stress Reaction

If we look at this study as one concerned not with commitment to fasting and hunger but rather with commitment to the stressful event of vein puncture, an indwelling needle, and the removal of blood, then dissonance aroused by voluntary commitment for minimal justification should lead to a reduction in experienced stress. This effect, clearly shown in our first study, was replicated in this study, where those subjects who were originally most aroused (stressed) by the needle puncture subsequently showed less stress to the puncture if they were given the High Dissonance treatment. There were no differences in treatments for those subjects who were not initially stressed by the needle puncture.

DISCUSSION

The first question posed in this research was whether the cognitive reorganization produced by dissonance following commitment to further deprivation is accompanied by physiological changes. In Experiment I, subjects who initially reported themselves to be hungry and committed themselves under conditions of minimal justification (High Dissonance) showed the least increase in fat mobilization over the extended period of food deprivation. A similar pattern was observed in Experiment II (although this must be qualified because of unexplained precommitment differences).

Using FFA responsiveness to stress as the dependent measure, the results in both studies indicate that the same stressful event of venipuncture was tolerated more by those subjects given low as compared to high justification for voluntarily committing themselves to more of this procedure. This increased tolerance to stress (ratio of puncture level to resting level) was most marked for the High Dissonance subjects who exhibited least tolerance to this stress prior to their discrepant commitment (i.e., who were initially most aroused).

There are several differences between Experiments I and II that deserve mention. The first FFA level taken in the second study was significantly lower than the comparable sample in the first study ($p = 0.02$), and a similar difference between studies occurred on blood Sample 2 (p about 0.10). In corresponding fashion, the initial hunger ratings in Experiment II were lower than those in the first experiment.

An interesting possible explanation for some of these contrasting results is that the main cognitive reorganization in support of one's commitment tends to occur at the time one originally becomes highly motivated to engage in whatever one has committed himself to, for whatever reason. Such motivation and reorganization would take effect, then, at the time of arousal—in this case, at the morning session. But apart from dissonance theory, and somewhat at variance with it, a person may also be highly motivated to engage in a given behavior by a strong "pitch" or selling job, as when personal, societal, and scientific benefits are stressed. This kind of motivation would be effective from the time of recruiting or, at the latest, in the first afternoon briefing session—that is, before measurements are taken. In short, then, a person may reorganize his cognitions in support of his behavior not only in response to dissonance but also, more generally, whenever he has any strong motivation to engage in that behavior. In the second study, the hungry subjects can be assumed to make their decision at the time of the morning session and subsequently to respond to dissonance, while the subjects who rated themselves as not hungry may have *already* reduced the cognitive and physiological symptoms of their hunger by the time of the morning session.

Katz (1960) has distinguished several functions of attitudes and motivation that correspond to the different kinds of motivation that may have been operating between the two studies. One such function is fulfilling "the need for consistent knowledge," a dominant motive in Experiment I, leading to dissonance reduction within the experimental session itself. However, in recruiting subjects for the second experiment, a second function of motives was utilized—"the value-expressive function." Volunteering for the study and the anticipated fast was in part an expression of loyalty to a campus group of which the subject was a member. This group, rather than the subject, received a sum of money for each member who participated in the research. Reorganization of cognitions related to this function could have resulted in a greater level of nonspecific motivation throughout the second experiment for all subjects.

The two studies, especially the first, suggest that an already-motivated person who commits himself to further deprivation experiences dissonance and subsequently attempts to minimize the magnitude of his motivation. Within a few minutes after commitment, such a person tends to report that he is less motivated than he had reported he was prior to commitment. This self-convincing process goes beyond changes in the cognitive components of motivation and results in modification of a physiological response known to be related to the type of motivation involved. After having convinced himself that he does not feel so deprived, the individual responds physiologically as if indeed he were not as deprived as he actually is. To the extent that this finding, here only marginal, is substantiated in other research, it has rather widespread implications for the understanding of human motivation.

Editor's Comments

In Experiment I we have a replication of Jack Brehm's finding that self-estimates of hunger are lower for subjects who commit themselves to food deprivation for minimal as compared to high justification (here $25.00 plus a scientific rationale). More important, however, is the effect of the dissonance manipulation on the physiological variable of the level of free fatty acids (FFA) in the blood. Although adequate testing of the theory demanded internal analyses that separated initially hungry subjects from those initially not hungry (and thus placed a limit on the generalizability of the results), both Experiments I and II demonstrated that the normally greater release of FFA for hungry than nonhungry subjects is inhibited under conditions of High Dissonance (as compared to Low Dissonance). In fact, in Experiment I, this dissonance-produced inhibition resulted in less than half as much of an increase in FFA over the period of deprivation for hungry as for nonhungry subjects.

The authors rightly introduce a note of caution in making inferences from the data since there are sizable initial differences between groups and between the two experiments in both FFA levels and hunger ratings prior to the dissonance manipulation. The problem may be traced to the methodology, which essentially creates two situations of dissonance: the first occurs under uncontrolled conditions outside the laboratory, after the subject agrees to participate in the study and miss several meals; the second occurs when he is asked to extend his fast for an additional period.

Dissonance following the initial commitment increases as the subject becomes hungry and voluntarily foregoes eating two meals. In the course of doing so, some subjects may be forced to justify this behavior to parents, roommates, etc. Doing so should increase their commitment and should force them to generate intrinsic justifications ("I'll feel better if I cut down on my food intake"), as well as extrinsic ones ("I'm doing it for an important scientific experiment," or "because a respected teacher asked me to"). Such responses, of course, weaken the differences in justification that are provided later by the experimenter when he assigns the subjects to the High and Low Dissonance groups. By sampling error alone, this uncontrolled process of commitment and justification will occur with differing frequency and intensity in different subjects. Thus, there may be sizable differences in commitment, prior effort expended, and level of hunger (already influenced by dissonance reduction) when the subjects arrive to take part in the formal, controlled laboratory part of the study. The second commitment may interact with this initial level of dissonance in a complex and unknown manner.

For our purposes, then, it would be better to create the initial commitment to deprivation or aversive conditions in the laboratory where extraneous influences on the subject can be minimized and the subject's options are more limited. This should reduce initial differences between conditions and allow a more direct and unambiguous test of the control of motivation following dissonance arousal. When such a procedure has been followed, as in a number of the experiments to be reported in the sections on thirst and pain, the results have been correspondingly less equivocal.

The theoretical status of the full-day fast group in Experiment II is somewhat questionable if it is to be considered as a Nondissonance Control group. These subjects voluntarily agreed in the beginning to undergo 24 hours of food deprivation, while the dissonance subjects initially volunteered for only 16 hours of deprivation. The only difference between the treatments is the *change* in the expectations of the experimental subjects after the 16-hour period, and it is not clear whether or not this created more dissonance than the original commitment or than was experienced by the full-day fast controls (who knew, after 16 hours, that they had already agreed to 8 additional hours of deprivation). In a sense, this Control group resembles the drivers in the Introduction, who, after volunteering for 24 hours of continuous driving, completed the task with no signs of fatigue (Safford & Rockwell, 1966). It is not surprising, therefore, that the data for these Controls look more like those for the High than for the Low Dissonance subjects.

The use of FFA level as a dependent variable indicative of the reduction of hunger motivation by cognitive dissonance is somewhat complicated since it is a measure that is sensitive also to stress. It is, then, a "two-for-one measure," and the experimenters take advantage of this fact to demonstrate both phenomena: that there is less of an increase in "stress" among High Dissonance subjects than among Lows (the strongest finding reported), as well as less of an increase in "hunger." Although the stress measure is reported as "an index of the subject's reaction to the needle puncture" and operationally consists of a ratio of puncture level to resting level, it might also reflect a different source of stress—the more chronic level of stress associated with hunger. Another study is obviously required in which commitment to the stressful event is independent of fasting and hunger, thus ruling out possibly confounding interactions.

One of the general conclusions that the reader may have drawn from this study is that physiological measures are not the Royal Road to Scientific Truth that one would like to believe they are. They are no more "direct" reflections of motivational processes than are behavioral measures, nor is their interpretation unequivocal. For example, in the second study reported here, the FFA response to the puncture is not even "reasonable," since the puncture level is lower than the resting level. In a sense, the FFA measure is both an autonomic- and a central-nervous-system thermometer, and it is susceptible to stimuli other than those studied in this research.

In passing, it should be mentioned that fatty acid mobilization is also affected by strenuous exercise and hypnotically induced imagery. In a recent study (Cobb, Ripley, & Jones, 1967), FFA levels were first measured while subjects were at rest and then while they underwent strenuous exercise on a bicycle ergometer. A day later, subjects were given a hypnotic suggestion to imagine they were again on the bicycle, pumping faster and faster. FFA levels were taken arterially every 3 minutes and showed an almost identical pattern of increase in the real and hypnotically imagined exercise periods (an average increase of 95 per cent of the resting level). A major difference between the two conditions occurred after the experimental period when FFA levels diminished gradually following the actual exercise but fell to normal immediately after the hypnotic state ended. In another part of this experiment, FFA levels were again significantly elevated when hypnotized subjects recalled traumatic emotional experiences.

These comments are not intended to detract from the valuable contribution of Brehm, Back, and Bogdonoff in demonstrating the inhibition of hunger at both a physiological and a cognitive level. They are made, rather, to suggest the susceptibility of their physiological measure to influence by other motivational states that may or may not be correlated with hunger and by other sources of response variability, thus accounting for some of the marked initial differences that limit the generalizability of their conclusions.

Because of complications like these in reliance upon physiological measures to assess the noncognitive components of motivation, another strategy has been employed by researchers in this area, involving the use of consummatory and instrumental behaviors that are assumed to vary as a function of drive level. In the studies presented so far in this section, it has been assumed that attempts at dissonance reduction have resulted in a general lowering of hunger motivation. But can it be shown that there is a causal relationship between dissonance conditions and changes in liking for a specific food? The next study considers the possibility of increasing the positive attraction to (i.e., appetite for) a highly disliked food by arousing high levels of dissonance. Moreover, this study tests the reasonable assumption that to the extent that the effect is specific to the food involved in the dissonant choice, then the effects of dissonance reduction ought not to generalize to other foods that are not part of the same class. Finally, this study raises the provocative question of the role of the coercive agent: Does it make a difference if the person who influences you to engage in forced compliant behavior is positive (nice, warm, considerate, likeable) or negative (aloof, cold, condescending, unfriendly)? Which one will be most effective in changing your attitude about the disliked food?

3. CHANGING APPETITES FOR EATING FRIED GRASSHOPPERS WITH COGNITIVE DISSONANCE

Philip G. Zimbardo, Matisyohu Weisenberg, Ira Firestone, and Burton Levy

One of the most widely held generalizations in social psychology is that the effectiveness of a persuasive communication is increased if its source is "credible." The early research by Hovland and Weiss (1951) and by Kelman and Hovland (1953) that gave substance to this conclusion has recently been extended to demonstrate the efficacy of credible communicators even when the amount of change advocated is extreme (Aronson, Turner, & Carlsmith, 1963).

SOURCE: Zimbardo, Philip G., Matisyohu Weisenberg, Ira Firestone, and Burton Levy, "Changing Appetites for Eating Fried Grasshoppers with Cognitive Dissonance." Adapted from "Communicator Effectiveness in Producing Public Conformity and Private Attitude Change," *Journal of Personality*, 1965, *33*, pp. 233–255. Reprinted by permission of the authors and the Duke University Press.

Credibility has been defined traditionally in terms of communicator attributes that are perceived by the audience as being relevant to the topic of the communication. However, positive and negative source traits that bear no objective relevance to the topic can also be effective in modifying attitudes toward its conclusions. The potent effect of such irrelevant communicator characteristics has long been utilized in practical influence situations outside the laboratory: by lawyers aware of the importance of dress and demeanor of their clients upon jury attitudes, by advertisers sensitive to the "topic-free" nature of a sexy communicator, and more recently by politicians interested in creating an image by appropriate "packaging" of irrelevant traits. That irrelevant aspects of communicator credibility are important determinants of attitude change has been shown empirically in a study in which the race of a communicator influenced the acceptance of a speech which extolled the virtues of arithmetic to sixth-grade students (Aronson & Golden, 1962).

Such objectively irrelevant characteristics are of great importance in interpersonal communication situations in which attitude change is often mediated by a host of physical, social, and psychological traits of the influencing agent. If pressure is put on a person to engage in behavior discrepant with his relevant attitudes and values, then obviously the degree of this pressure is a determining factor in what the person will do. If it is too weak, he will not comply and his attitudes will remain unchanged; if it is too strong, he will comply publicly but likewise his private attitudes should remain stable. If the overt compliance can be completely justified in terms of its being instrumental to rewards and punishments controlled by the communicator, then there is no further need to adjust one's attitude to this discrepant behavior. But as the probability of compliance approaches a value of 0.5 in any given population, it becomes increasingly likely that characteristics of the communicator which are essentially irrelevant to the content of the behavior will be used as justification—as, for example, in statements like, "I did it because he's a nice guy."

If, on the other hand, a person complies to the inducement of a negative communicator—i.e., someone disliked—clearly he cannot justify the discrepant behavior by invoking the personal characteristics of the communicator as justification. Zimbardo (1960) has suggested on the basis of dissonance theory that such a person should be likely instead to change his attitudes toward the discrepant behavior to bring them in line with his actions. Compliance with a negative communicator should produce greater dissonance than compliance with a positive communicator.

DISSONANCE PREDICTIONS

If attitude change is the major dissonance-reducing mechanism utilized, then the general hypothesis that can be experimentally tested is that public compliance with a negative communicator (compared to a positive one) will result in greater attitude change in the direction indicated by the overt behavior. If the overt discrepant behavior involves eating an extremely disliked food, then we should observe positive increases in liking for this specific item of food as a function of dissonance arousal and reduction, without correlated changes in attitude toward the communicator.

OVERVIEW OF EXPERIMENTAL DESIGN

Attitudes toward a highly disliked food—fried grasshoppers—were measured before and immediately after an inducement by a communicator to eat the food and after compliance or noncompliance with that inducement. For half the subjects, the communicator adopted a friendly, positive role; for the others, he adopted an unfriendly, negative role. A money incentive was used as a second possible source of justification for half the subjects in each communicator treatment; no monetary incentive was given to the other subjects. Control groups were also used, whose attitudes were measured twice, with no experimental manipulation between.

PROCEDURE

Subjects

All the subjects who participated in this study were required to do so; there were no volunteers. Two groups of subjects were used: 50 males from the introductory psychology class at University College of New York University participated as part of a course requirement, and 102 Army Reservists from an Army Reserve Center adjacent to the N.Y.U. campus were used. The Reservists, all privates and corporals, were only a few years older than the students and were roughly equivalent in educational background. Within these two groups, the subjects were randomly assigned to the two communicator treatments and the two treatment levels of incentive.

Control Groups

There were five groups of Control subjects (an additional 68 Reservists), who were not given an inducement or opportunity to eat grasshoppers but whose attitudes were measured before and after a time interval equivalent to that of the experimental groups. In different Control groups minor aspects of the procedure were varied; but since there were no differences among them, their data will be combined for comparison with the experimental treatments.

Communicator Characteristics

Because the communicator was an officer in the college's ROTC program, it was possible to determine how he was usually perceived by those ROTC members ($N = 53$) with whom he worked by means of their responses on an alleged officer-rating survey. From the personality-trait profile[1] that emerged from this analysis, a set of experimental role behaviors was developed that would operationally define this man as a positive or negative communicator by emphasizing certain of his traits and minimizing others.

For all conditions, the communicator had to be perceived as conscientious, capable, organized, industrious, and concerned about the subjects' reactions, in order to guarantee an appropriate level of attention and seriousness on the part of the subjects. In addition, the communicator's role could not evoke hostility in the subjects because of his direct interaction with any one of them.

Positive Role. Under both role treatments, the subjects' perception of the communicator was based primarily on his interaction with his "assistant," which was determined by a prearranged script. For the Positive condition, the communicator gave politely phrased requests to the assistant, called him by his first name, responded to a "mistake" by the assistant with equanimity, and in general was considerate and pleasant. Nevertheless, at all times it was clear that he was the experimenter and in control.

Negative Role. However, in the Negative condition, the communicator was to be perceived as someone personally unpleasant—a person one would not want to know, work with, or work for. This perception was guided by actions designed to make him appear snobbish, demanding, tactless, bossy, cold, and hostile to others. These actions were incorporated in his quite formal interaction with the assistant, whom he always referred to by last name and ordered about and with whom he was exacting, somewhat annoyed, and irritated. When the assistant "mistakenly" brought in the "wrong" experimental food (a tray of eels in aspic), the communicator, who was in the process of talking to the subjects in his most pleasant manner, suddenly blew up and said, "Oh, dammit, can't you remember the schedule? That food is for the next group . . . Let's get with it and hurry up about it!" As the assistant left, obviously embarrassed, the communicator shrugged his shoulders disgustedly, then caught himself short, *reversed his role behavior in front of the subjects*, apologized for the interruption, and proceeded in the same pleasant tone as before.

The effectiveness of these role variations in producing differential perceptions of the communicator and the validity of our measuring instruments were first tested in our laboratory with a college sample, before being slightly modified to make them appropriate for the Army Reservists. The procedure used with the Reservists will not be detailed here, since there was little difference between the methodology used with the two samples.

Initial Attitudes

The subjects were first brought to a lecture hall in large groups ($N = 100$ on each of three testing sessions, some of whom were used to test hypotheses not relevant to our present study). There, one of the authors was introduced as a

1. The adjective check list was taken from Gough's list as presented by Newcomb (1961, pp. 279–280).

civilian liaison from the Quartermaster Corps interested in some aspects of food preferences. All Reservists then completed a nine-point attitude scale of degree of liking of a wide range of food items,[2] among them fried Japanese grasshoppers. (The student subjects had completed this scale in class several weeks before.) The randomly assigned experimental subjects were then sent to an adjoining room, while the Controls were sent to a third room where they completed a second attitude scale, without any intervening manipulation. There was no contact between those who had completed the experiment and those waiting to begin. Although subjects were run in groups of about 10 men, interaction was minimized by instructions and by partitions between them.

Inducement to Eat Grasshoppers

The previously mentioned differences in the experimenter's role behavior commenced as soon as the subjects entered the experimental room. After the subjects completed a hunger and eating-habit questionnaire, heard a talk about the needs of the new mobile army, and witnessed the assistant's "mistake," a plate of five fried grasshoppers was placed in front of each man, as the experimenter was saying:

> Before asking you to eat the experimental food, I want to make it clear that this part of the experiment is *voluntary*, and *no one* has to eat these fried grasshoppers if they don't want to. However, for the purposes of the study, I would like you to try at least one and preferably to eat all on the plate. In order to get as many people as possible to try one, I will pay, right now, fifty cents to each person who eats one. [Pause] Take a moment to decide. I will place the money next to each plate. Those of you who are willing to try the grasshopper, please indicate it by pulling the plate and money toward you. Those of you who are unwilling to even give it a try, leave the plate and money where they are and raise your hand to indicate you don't want to eat any. All right now, go ahead and eat.

Obviously, money was not mentioned in the No Incentive condition. Note that every subject had to make some response, whether or not he chose to eat.

Postcompliance Attitudes

The final ratings, which were made in yet another room, were in the absence of the Communicator. The assistant of the alleged civilian liaison told the subjects that he wanted to evaluate various aspects of the experiment and get more information from them. At this time the experimental subjects completed: (1) a

2. This hedonic scale, which was anchored at every point with verbal labels from "like extremely" to "dislike extremely," has a reliability coefficient of 0.96 (Peryam, Polemis, Kamen, Eindhoven, & Pilgrim, 1960).

postexperimental measure of attitudes toward a number of foods, including grasshoppers; (2) a measure of willingness to endorse eating grasshoppers; (3) checks on the experimental conditions of choice, pressure, etc.; and (4) several indexes of evaluation of both the communicator and his assistant.

RESULTS

Unpopularity of Eating Grasshoppers

The unappealing nature of grasshoppers as a food was established prior to this experiment by comparative ratings of it and a number of other unusual foods like snake, octopus, eel, etc. In this comparative rating, grasshopper was evaluated most negatively among ten such foods by an additional sample of 217 college students; fewest of these students had tried it, and 57 per cent said they would not try it! They were asked to list all the things they thought about when they considered eating grasshoppers. Some of the negative cognitions they associated with this food were: ugly, greasy appearance, slimy, shiny, charred, repulsive, squirming, eyes, wings, dirty, rat feces, might hurt me, burned them as a child, biology laboratory, graveyard, and not kosher.

Public Compliance

Despite these generally aversive reactions toward eating fried grasshoppers, about 50 per cent of the men in each communicator condition accepted the inducement to eat at least one. There were no differences between the college and Army samples, Positive and Negative Communicator conditions, or monetary-incentive treatments in the *frequency* with which grasshoppers were eaten or in the *amount* eaten (a mean of about two grasshoppers per eater in each condition).

Thus, the public conformity of accepting the inducement to eat a novel, disliked food was not affected by our experimental conditions but was probably related to individual differences that were equally distributed across our groups.

Freedom of Choice to Eat Grasshoppers

It should also be noted that although the subjects accurately perceived that they had little choice in whether or not to come to the experiment (since they were not volunteers), nevertheless they reported having a high degree of choice in whether or not to eat the experimental food. The difference between the perception of the lack of choice to participate in the study and the free choice to eat was highly significant for all comparisons ($p < 0.001$). In addition, the subjects felt that the communicator did not exert much direct pressure upon them to eat.

We had, therefore, established the ideal conditions for testing our dissonance hypothesis: There was an equal percentage (about 50 per cent) of people who agreed or refused to engage in the discrepant behavior, they all perceived that they had a free choice to eat or not, and they made that choice following a request from an agent they clearly liked or disliked (as we shall show subsequently). Finally, there were no group differences in the subjects' initial attitudes toward the experimental food.

DISSONANCE EFFECTS

Attitude Change Toward Eating Grasshoppers

Figure 1 presents the attitude-change data in terms of net percentages of all subjects who changed in the direction of increased liking for grasshoppers and

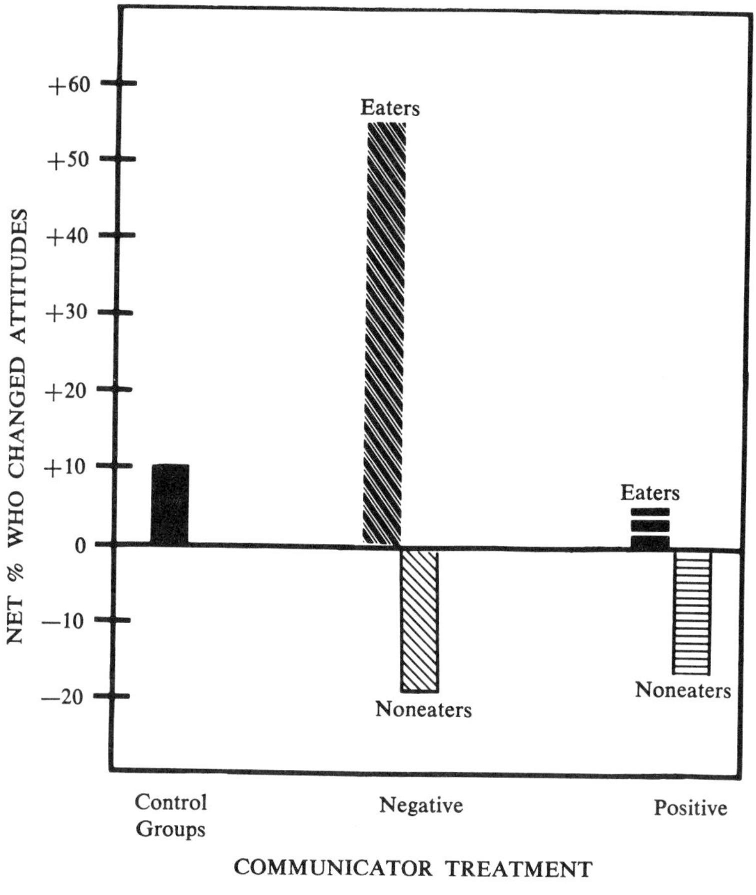

FIGURE 1
Net proportion of subjects within Communicator and Eating groups who changed their attitudes toward fried grasshoppers to be more favorable as against those who changed to less-favorable attitudes.

who changed in the opposite direction (a measure derived from Hovland, Lumsdaine, & Sheffield, 1949; positive changes minus negative changes, omitting those who showed no change).

The pattern of results was similar and dramatic for both college students and Army Reservists. While 60 per cent of all those who ate the unpleasant food changed their attitudes to like it more, 34 per cent of those who refused to eat showed a boomerang effect, liking it even less ($p < 0.01$). Among Eaters, the Negative Communicator was much more effective in changing attitudes in the predicted direction (55 per cent) than the Positive Communicator (only 5 per cent). Among Noneaters, approximately the same boomerang effect was produced by both communicators. The difference in the net proportion of change as a function of communicators is statistically significant (critical ratio $= 2.00$, $p < 0.05$).

If the data are analyzed according to magnitude of attitude change for all subjects in each condition (i.e., mean scale distance), the results are similar to those obtained with the above-mentioned frequency measure of change. Eaters changed by a greater amount than did Noneaters (combined over subsamples, $p < 0.001$). While the mean change for the Control groups was $+0.3$ units, it was $+0.6$ for the Positive Communicator Eaters and twice that, or $+1.2$, for the Negative Communicator Eaters. Although this Positive Communicator condition does not differ significantly from the Control groups (by a Duncan Multiple-Range Test), the amount of change in the Negative Communicator condition is significantly greater ($p = 0.02$) than that in the Control.

Extrinsic Justification: Monetary Incentive

The difference between Eaters and Noneaters was greatest when there was least justification for compliance—i.e., with a Negative Communicator and no monetary incentive (although the Negative Communicator produced more attitude change than the Positive Communicator even when monetary justification was provided). However, between-cell incentive comparisons are of marginal significance ($p < 0.10$) because of the variable meaning of the fifty-cents offer, which some men viewed as a bribe or even an insult rather than as a source of positive incentive.

Personal Endorsement of Grasshoppers

Another way the effects of the communicator variable on private acceptance were assessed was by means of a specially devised measure of the extent to which each Reservist was willing to endorse or recommend grasshoppers to other soldiers. It was felt that such a measure would be a more stringent, yet more valid, test of the hypotheses since it involved a public (behavioral) commitment to one's attitude, less anonymity, and greater possible consequences to the individual subject.

After completing the postexperimental attitude questionnaire, the Army

Reservists were told that it was the job of the present research team to prepare a manual to be used by men about to enter a survival course. They were informed, "We feel that one of the best understood, most honest and effective techniques is to prepare a report in which the actual information and statistics are supplemented by personal endorsements by men like yourselves who have had some direct experience with the food." They were then given an endorsement-release form presenting six quotations pertinent to eating grasshoppers. The quotations were arranged and labeled in order from "strongest endorsement" through "weak endorsement" to "no endorsement," and they were prefaced by an introduction stating that the respondent authorized the use of his name in association with the statement he had signed. The subject had to select one of the six statements, write in the name of the food he ate, and then sign and date his statement. The endorsements varied from "I've tried (the food) personally, found it to be very tasty, and would certainly recommend it" to "If you try eating (the food) as I did, you'll find that they're not so bad, in fact they had no taste at all."

Among those Army subjects who ate at least one grasshopper, there was a significant degree of association between postexperimental attitude and level of endorsement. Of those with negative attitudes, 94 per cent gave a weak endorsement, while 88 per cent of those with positive attitudes gave a strong endorsement. The majority (66 per cent) of those with moderate attitudes (neutral or barely positive) tended to give weak rather than strong endorsements (chi square value yields a $p < 0.001$ and contingency coefficient of 0.48). The results obtained with this measure are in agreement with those presented previously: 37 per cent of the subjects in the Negative Communicator condition gave strong endorsements, while only 11 per cent in the Positive condition did so.

Specificity of Cognitive Reorientation

It should be noted that attitude change toward grasshoppers was specific to food items in the same class. While changes in grasshopper attitudes were unrelated to attitude changes for ten nonsurvival foods, the generally positive change for those who ate grasshoppers generalized to the majority of ten other survival foods in both college and Army subjects. Similarly, the negative change shown by Noneaters was mirrored by negative changes only toward other survival foods. These effects were more consistent in the Negative than the Positive Communicator condition.

Communicator Traits

In both the college and Army samples, there was a vast difference in the perception of the communicator that was congruent with his manipulated role behavior. The Negative Communicator role resulted in an evaluation of him as possessing more negative and fewer positive traits than the Positive Communicator role ($p < 0.001$). Subjects preferred not to have to work with or hire as an experimenter the Negative Communicator in contrast with either the Positive Communicator or even the assistant ($p < 0.001$). An analysis of the 22 specific traits employed revealed that there were no differences on those (seven) traits that indicated competence (on which we tried to maintain a constancy across conditions). On each of those (eight) traits directly incorporated into the role behaviors, the differences between communicator treatments were beyond the 0.01 level of significance; on the other traits, only indirectly linked with the experimental induction, the differences were at the 0.05 level.

Attitudes Toward Grasshopper vs. Communicator

The final point to be made is that within the Negative condition the Eaters did not view the communicator more favorably than did the Noneaters on even a single trait; in fact, Noneaters felt he was more capable ($p < 0.05$) and more industrious ($p < 0.05$) than did Eaters. For the Positive Communicator, there were differences between Eaters and Noneaters on four traits, and on each of these, Eaters felt the communicator was more positive than did Noneaters. He was fairer ($p < 0.05$), less egotistical ($p < 0.05$), more genuinely interested in them ($p = 0.05$), and more mature ($p < 0.10$).

Thus, Eaters under the Negative Communicator condition changed their attitudes toward the object of their induced public behavior—fried grasshoppers—but did not develop more favorable attitudes toward the communicator (a postexperimental measure only). Positive Communicator Eaters, on the other hand, did not much change their attitudes toward the food but did tend to justify their eating in terms of personal characteristics of the communicator, which were irrelevant to the eating of grasshoppers.

CONCLUSIONS AND IMPLICATIONS

In this study, attitudes toward eating fried grasshoppers became more positive following dissonance arousal, and this effect was carried over to related (survival) foods but not to dissimilar foods. Greatest changes in attitude were noted for men who complied with the request of a Negative Communicator and ate a grasshopper with no monetary incentive.

The study indicates that a communicator who advocates public compliance to behavior discrepant from a person's attitudes and values can influence attitude change without specifically communicating persuasive arguments and conclusions. Those who behaviorally accept the inducement tend to change their attitudes to support their actions, while those who do not comply often show boomerang effects, adopting more extreme positions in the original attitude direction. This dissonance-induced attitude change following public compliance is greater when the behavior cannot be as readily justified in terms of communicator characteristics, i.e., when the person reacts negatively to the communicator. Thus, factors that are irrelevant to communicator credibility may operate in interesting and subtle ways.

These findings may have considerable generality, since there were no differences in the pattern of results for college and Army Reserve samples, and our Army Reservists appeared to be comparable to the regular Army subjects used in related research on food preferences by Peryam et al. (1960).

Editor's Comments

Resolution of dissonance-induced motivation takes the form of coordinating internal response systems with overt public compliance to a related discrepant behavior. If the commitment is to prolonged fasting, then a person under high dissonance arousal (created by maximum choice and minimal justification) perceives himself as less hungry, orders fewer items of food, and releases less free fatty acid into his blood. If commitment is to eat a disliked food under these same dissonant conditions, cognitions toward the food are significantly modified to make its eating acceptable. Thus, both general and specific cognitive components of motivation related to hunger and eating can be brought under some degree of cognitive control.

This last study shows that dissonance reduction involves more than a simple process of denial of relevant cognitions (one interpretation of the reduced hunger motivation considering the first two studies alone). Here, High Dissonance subjects did not deny the characteristics of the communicator; in fact, they were preceived quite veridically. Subjects did not justify their dissonant behavior by distorting their attitudes toward the agent of coercion but rather by changing the cognitive element that would result in the greatest reduction in the dissonance between eating grasshoppers and disliking them: they modified their dislike in a positive direction.

These findings replicate those of Smith (1961) on the efficacy of a low-justification source in producing attitude change, and the absolute size of the change produced in both his study and the present one is considerably greater than is typical in attitude-change studies not involving a behavioral commitment. Smith's study also used a noncollege sample of Army Reservists, which permits somewhat greater generalizability than is usual with college-sophomore-saturated research.

The results of this study lead us to conclude that the decreased ratings of hunger noted in the two previous studies do not reflect generalized decrements in motivation but are specific to the cognitions associated with the hunger drive. The present study, however, suffers from the same weakness as Brehm's: there was no systematic variation of choice and no control group that engaged in the discrepant behavior under conditions of low personal choice. Such a comparison is, of course, theoretically crucial and will be required in our future studies.

Despite some problems with interpretation of initial group differences, the necessity to resort to internal analysis, and the absence of some control conditions, this first body of data encourages us to examine the effects of these same cognitive variables as they operate on a different primary motive—thirst.

Section B

Thirst

4. COMMITMENT TO THIRST: THE COGNITIVE CAMEL COMPLEX

Jack W. Brehm

We assume that thirst has a cognitive component which can be affected by dissonance and that the demonstration of such an effect might have important implications for the understanding of the physiological aspects of thirst. This study utilized a second independent variable in addition to the same kind of manipulation of justification for deprivation as was used in the hunger studies. This second variable may be conceptualized as the *salience*, or immediate availability, of the goal object. Ordinarily, one would expect that making the goal object salient would increase the magnitude of the motivation, at least at the cognitive level. But if a person has committed himself to deprivation of the goal object, the presence of the goal object should magnify the consequent dissonance, partly by enhancing the initial motivational level and partly by making what becomes the dissonant cognition more salient. It should be noted that our experiment on hunger (Article 1) was performed under constant conditions of high salience of relevant stimulation; i.e., food was present on the testing table throughout the experimental session. In this present study, then, we expected to find that the absence of relevant stimulation for thirst would result in less thirst reduction after commitment to deprivation than its presence.

OVERVIEW OF EXPERIMENTAL DESIGN

The design consisted of exposing already thirsty subjects to low or high stimulus-relevant salience (absence or presence of pitcher of water) and then inducing

SOURCE: Brehm, Jack W., "Commitment to Thirst: The Cognitive Camel Complex." Adapted from "Motivational Effects of Cognitive Dissonance" reprinted from *Nebraska Symposium on Motivation*, edited by M. R. Jones, by permission of the University of Nebraska Press and the author. Copyright 1962 by the University of Nebraska Press. Supplementary material from *Explorations in Cognitive Dissonance* by J. W. Brehm and A. R. Cohen (New York: John Wiley & Sons, Inc., 1962), pp. 133–136.

them with either low- or high-value (monetary) rewards to agree to further abstention. Two additional, control conditions were run in order to reveal the effects of the high- or low-relevant stimulation and general experimental procedure on changes in self-ratings of thirst during the experimental session. Everything about these control conditions was the same as in the experimental conditions except that the inducement to further deprivation was omitted. The dependent measures were change in self-rating of thirst and amount of water drunk after commitment to further abstention.

DISSONANCE PREDICTIONS

Since the salience of water to subjects prior to the commitment should tend to increase thirst, subjects in the High Salience condition should tend to show more initial thirst than subjects in the Low Salience condition. When a thirsty person commits himself to deprivation of liquids, he should experience dissonance, and the magnitude of that dissonance should be greater in persons with high thirst than in persons with low thirst. At the same time, the amount of dissonance experienced should tend to be reduced by whatever rewards or incentives there are for making the commitment to deprivation. Hence, subjects in the High Salience condition (water present) should experience relatively high dissonance if they are given a minimal reward for commitment and less dissonance if they are given a sizable reward for commitment. Subjects in the Low Salience (water absent) condition should also experience dissonance, but to a lesser degree. To the extent that a person does experience dissonance, he will, we assume, try to reduce it by changing his cognition of how thirsty he is. The more dissonance he experiences, the more he will try to feel less thirsty. While a person can try to reduce dissonance in other ways as well, and may actually do so, we assume that most people will attempt at least some dissonance reduction through the reduction of how thirsty they feel.

PROCEDURE

Both male and female introductory psychology students at Duke University were given an opportunity to participate in what was called "a study of the effect of thirst on motor and intellectual functioning." They were told that if they volunteered to participate, they were to go without liquids from bedtime of the evening before the day of their experimental session until the session in the afternoon. They were promised one "experimental credit point" for their participation.

The procedure of this study was similar to that of my hunger study (see Article 1). The subjects, tested individually, were first reminded of the purpose of the study. They were then asked to indicate how thirsty they were, using the same multiple-response scale as in the hunger experiment. About 15 minutes were then spent in work on motor and intellectual tests.

Deprivation Inducement

The offer of further deprivation, which was introduced at this point, was changed in certain ways from that of the hunger study. The subjects in this study had not been warned ahead of time that they might be asked to come back again; so the experimenter introduced this possibility by saying that some subjects were being asked to go for another day without liquids and then to come back for additional testing.

Dissonance Manipulation

The experimenter continued with these words:

> Unfortunately, I can't offer you further credit for participating further, but since research has shown that going without water for this amount of time could become very uncomfortable, I would like to offer you something if you will participate further. I think it is worth $10.00, but because of a departmental regulation, I can only offer you $1.00 for participating. Of course, it's entirely up to you.

The $1.00 payment indicated in the above instructions was intended to create a High Dissonance commitment. Subjects in the Low Dissonance condition were offered $5.00 instead.

After the commitment to further deprivation, subjects worked for a few minutes on a problem-solving task (e.g., how to get a cannibal and a missionary across a canyon) and then were asked to indicate how thirsty they were, using the same scale as before. Again the experimenter explained that people change in how thirsty they feel from one moment to the next, and that some change one way, some change the other, and some do not change at all. [This is a standard procedure used in attitude-change studies to legitimize the changing of a subject's responses without biasing the direction.]

Salience

Salience was manipulated simply by having in the subject's view a pitcher of water and cups in one condition (High Salience) and not having these relevant cues present in the other condition (Low Salience).

Evaluation of Incentive Manipulation

Subjects were then asked to respond on a rating scale designed to measure the success of the incentive manipulation. The question asked was how appropriate they thought the payment was for the further deprivation and testing, and the answers on the scale ranged from "Extreme overpayment" through "Appropriate" to "Extreme underpayment." It was explained that this information was needed for the planning of future research.

Measure of Water Consumption

Finally, we attempted to measure the consummatory effects of our manipulations. In order to be able to let the subjects drink, it was, of course, necessary to release the subjects from the impression that the deprivation would be continuous. Although this release would have the effect of reducing the magnitude of dissonance due to the commitment, we hoped that enough differential thirst would remain to show up in the amounts of water consumed.

The offer of water was introduced by the following instructions:

> Now, although you will not be allowed to drink any liquids after you leave here, you may drink as much much water as you would like right now. I will be back in a moment and we will continue the tasks. You may drink all the water you want right now.

The subject was given a pitcher of water and some paper cups (in the High Salience condition they were already there), and the experimenter then left the room for a few minutes in order to make the subject feel free to drink however much he wanted. Unknown to the subject, the pitcher of water contained exactly 1000 cc. of water, which allowed us to measure precisely the amount he drank.

Upon returning to the room, the experimenter explained that the experiment was really over and disclosed its true purposes, reasons for deceptions, and so on.

Subject Loss

In running the experiment, we found we could not get all of the subjects to commit themselves to the further deprivation and retesting. We had not warned them in advance that they would be asked to return, and many had "legitimate business" that prevented their committing themselves. Previous plans for going out of town or for participating in some athletic event were typical of what was considered legitimate. Other subjects simply decided that they did not want to go another day without liquids. Some of the subjects who declined might have been induced to make the commitment to further deprivation if we had applied more pressure. However, increased pressure would also have tended to reduce the magnitude of dissonance in the subjects who did comply and might therefore have minimized the experimental effect for the bulk of our subjects. About one fourth of the subjects who were given the choice refused to commit themselves to further deprivation. The proportion of refusals was not different between the two dissonance conditions. However, it is noteworthy that about two thirds (19 of 29) of the refusals were in the High Salience condition. This suggests that the presence of the pitcher of water did indeed make subjects more thirsty prior to the commitment decision.

The strategy employed, therefore, was to recruit and test subjects until we had 10 males and 10 females in each condition who were committed to further deprivation. However, a few of these subjects indicated on the first self-rating of thirst that they had little or no thirst. Since a person who feels no thirst after a deprivation period would not necessarily experience dissonance from a commitment to further deprivation, these few subjects were deleted from our final analysis. Although this "purification" of our data did not involve many subjects, it does indicate a possible theoretical limitation of the generality of our results. This interpretation assumes that it is the cognitive component of thirst rather than the number of hours of deprivation of liquids that is crucial to the arousal of dissonance following commitment to further deprivation; thus, it was necessary to eliminate those subjects who did not think of themselves as thirsty even after the extended pre-experimental deprivation period. (This approach was also used by Brehm, Back, and Bogdonoff in Article 2.)

RESULTS

Success of Incentive Treatment

Information on the success of our incentive manipulation of dissonance is available from the postexperimental question on the appropriateness of the amount of payment offered. The averages for each experimental condition and for males and females separately are presented in Table 1, where the positive figures indicate judgments of overpayment and the negative, underpayment.

We had expected that the high incentive would be seen as either appropriate or overpayment and the low incentive as underpayment. This expectation seemed to be met fairly well by the males but not by the females. The females seemed to think themselves overpaid whether they received $1.00 or $5.00; in fact, in the

TABLE 1

MEAN RATINGS* OF APPROPRIATENESS OF PAY FOR EACH EXPERIMENTAL TREATMENT

Condition	Males			Females		
	n	Mean	Variance	*n*	Mean	Variance
High Dissonance ($1.00):						
High Salience	7	−0.1	4.8	9	0.3	1.4
Low Salience	7	−0.2	4.7	10	0.9	5.4
Low Dissonance ($5.00):						
High Salience	9	0.4	0.7	10	2.0	3.2
Low Salience	9	0.4	1.1	8	0.2	0.2

* A negative mean indicates pay was regarded as inappropriately low. The size of each positive mean indicates perceived extent of overpayment.

Low Salience condition, they thought themselves more overpaid with $1.00 than with $5.00! It is evident that the females did not conform to the experimental conditions necessary for an adequate test of the present hypothesis. Why they did not conform is unclear, although it may be related to the fact that the experimenter was also a female. Or they may perhaps have had a different attitude toward research or toward payment for participation. For the sake of simplicity, then, we will confine our report of further results to the male sample.

Self-Ratings

The self-ratings of thirst prior to the commitment to further deprivation enabled us to see whether or not the presence of the relevant stimulation, that is, the pitcher of water, had the expected effect of making subjects feel more thirsty. Let me summarize these data by saying that the subjects in the High Salience condition did rate themselves as somewhat more thirsty than did those in the Low Salience condition. Although this difference is not statistically reliable, it is in the direction expected and gives us some confidence that the relevant stimulation was noticeable and had some effect on thirst.

Figure 1 presents the thirst-rating changes from before to after the commitment to further deprivation. In the Low Dissonance (high incentive, or $5.00) condition there was a slight increase in thirst, while in the High Dissonance (low incentive, or $1.00) condition there was a decrease in thirst. Furthermore, as

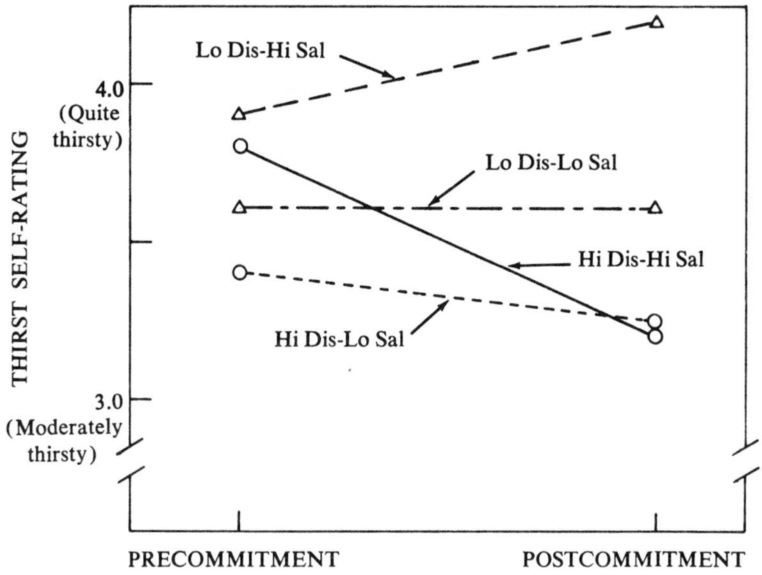

FIGURE 1
Mean self-ratings of thirst for groups differing in justification and salience of goal object.

predicted, the greatest decrement in thirst occurred in the High Dissonance condition in which the goal object was present. An analysis of variance of these data reveals that the dissonance-manipulation effect is significant at the 5 per cent level. Neither the salience manipulation nor the interaction of the manipulations is significant, although the interaction reveals a moderately strong trend ($p < 0.10$). The only statistically reliable difference between pairs or conditions is that between the High and Low Dissonance conditions within the High Salience condition ($p < 0.05$).

These results, then, are very much like those of the study on hunger (Article 1). When a relevant goal object is present, a person who thinks of himself as in need and who commits himself to further deprivation will tend subsequently to think of himself as less in need. This tendency is *inversely* proportional to the magnitude of the incentive that induces or helps to induce the commitment. Low salience of the goal object at the time of the commitment tends to reduce these effects.

Control-Group Change

The thirst change among subjects in the Control condition (thirsty, but no voluntary commitment to additional deprivation) raises questions about the interpretation of the experimental results. Subjects in both of these conditions showed some decrement in thirst, with those in the High Salience condition showing more (−0.47) than those in the Low Salience condition (−0.09). These thirst changes, it will be noted, are not clearly different from the corresponding changes in the High Dissonance condition. Should one conclude, therefore, that our obtained differences between the dissonance groups occurred not because the High Dissonance subjects became less thirsty but because the Low Dissonance subjects became significantly more thirsty? Unfortunately, we cannot tell from the present data, for the Control condition did not really control for all other factors but only for the magnitude of dissonance (i.e., choice in and justification for commitment to further deprivation). In particular, the Control condition differed from the experimental conditions in terms of the subjects' expectations about when they would be able to drink liquids after their initial deprivation period. It seems plausible to assume that this difference, along with other possible differences, accounts for the decreased thirst among control subjects. In effect, then, this Control condition was not really adequate as a baseline against which to compare the effects of dissonance.

NONCOGNITIVE ASPECTS OF MOTIVATION

Now that there is some evidence that a cognitive component can be changed by dissonance, let us reconsider the relationship between the cognitive and noncognitive components of hunger and thirst. It will be recalled that a change in cognition does not necessarily imply a change in the represented event. When the represented event is ambiguous, change in its corresponding cognition can easily occur. Suppose, for example, that a person is watching a moving object in a room that is slowly getting darker and darker. While the room is still quite illuminated, the person could hardly convince himself that the object is any place other than where it actually is. But as the room becomes so dark that he can no longer be sure he is seeing the object, it becomes increasingly easy for him to be convinced that the object is somewhere other than where it really is. In other words, the stimulus to which his cognition of location corresponds becomes increasingly ambiguous, and as it does so, its corresponding cognition becomes easier to change by other forces.

This same sort of thing may also happen with hunger and thirst, at least for the moderate periods of deprivation we have used. How hungry or thirsty a person is may simply be ambiguous within a certain range of deprivation. This analysis would imply that within the usual periods of deprivation, the degree of a person's motivation might well be controlled by many factors other than the deprivation itself. One such factor could be cognitive dissonance. Another might be the availability of the goal object, or expectations about its availability, as well as other situational determinants.

Are dissonance-induced changes in motivation limited to its cognitive component—that is, to the experienced perception of how hungry or thirsty one is, or of one's stomach contractions or hot, dry mouth? The free-fatty-acid findings would suggest not, but the interpretation of this measure is complex because of its sensitivity to stress or fear as well as to hunger. Could the consumption of the goal object directly linked to the drive state be influenced by cognitive pressures? If we assume that noncognitive components of motivation are relatively more resistant to change than are the cognitive components, dissonance reduction would generally be in the direction of reevaluation of the expectation of goal attainment or increased justification for the commitment. If, however, such cognitive changes are blocked by situational constraints, then there might be attempts at dissonance reduction on the noncognitive level. The movement from saying "I feel less thirsty" to acting less thirsty and then being less thirsty is the direction in which cognitive changes might eventually result in noncognitive change and thus in a change in the drive itself. Do thirsty subjects who commit themselves to further deprivation under dissonant conditions actually drink less water than those in Control or Low Dissonance groups?

Water Consumption

It will be recalled that subjects were told that they could drink as much of a pitcher of water as they wanted at the beginning of the period of additional deprivation. Unfortunately, this procedure would help subjects reduce whatever dissonance had been aroused by their agreement to forego liquids; thus it does not provide a very good test of implications for consummatory behavior. Nevertheless, the data which are presented in Figure 2 did yield the expected pattern among experimental conditions. Although none of the differences is statistically reliable, there was an apparent trend for the subjects in the con-

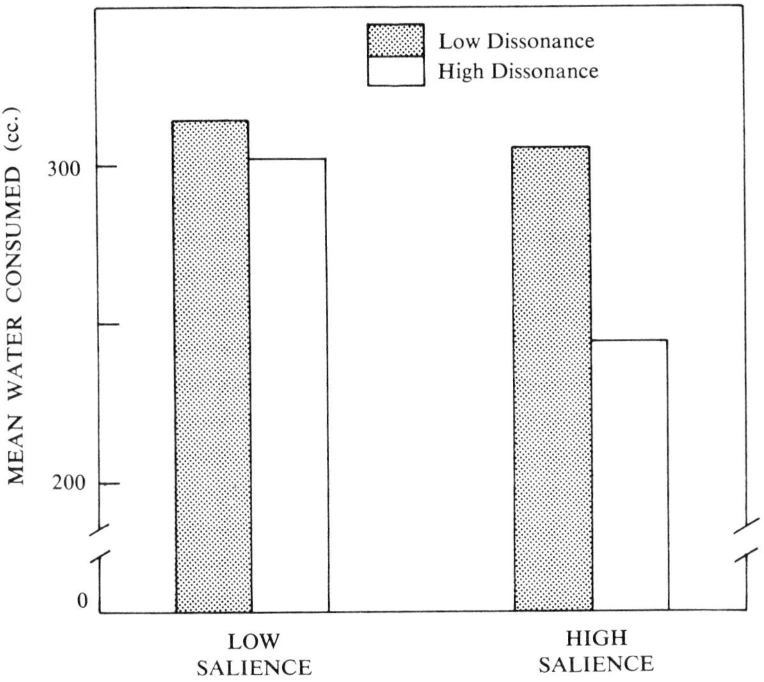

FIGURE 2
Mean cubic centimeters of water consumed by High and Low Dissonance groups varying in the prior salience of water.

dition of greatest dissonance, the High Dissonance-High Salience condition—who showed the greatest decrease in self-ratings of thirst—to drink the least water. These data, too, then, suggest that the effects of dissonance may well include consummatory behavior.

CONCLUSIONS

In summary, the understanding of motivational phenomena may be increased by some attention to the factors that influence cognition. It is now clear that the cognitive aspects of even physiologically based motivations, such as hunger and thirst, may be influenced by a person's attempt to reduce dissonance. Although it may sometimes be true that cognitive change has no corresponding effect on noncognitive motivational components, it seems likely that at least some noncognitive components can be affected, as indicated by the evidence on consummatory behavior in the present study and on the mobilization of fatty acids in the blood in the earlier study. Finally, it remains to be seen how induced changes in the cognitive aspects of motivation will fit into our general understanding of the role of motivation in other psychological processes such as perception, learning, and performance.

Editor's Comments

This study shows that self-ratings of thirst (like those of hunger) are reduced more in High Dissonance than in Low Dissonance conditions. In addition, this effect extends to drinking behavior (although this finding is not statistically significant). The average amount of water drunk was about 60 cubic centimeters less in the High Dissonance-High Salience group than in any other. Brehm concludes that the amount of decrease in thirst is an inverse function of incentive for deprivation and a direct function of water-relevant stimulation.

Unfortunately, these results cannot be generalized across sexes since the females responded in a rather bizarre way to the experimental induction; they did not respond appropriately to the differences in monetary incentive or to the manipulation of salience. Because of this, their data were not utilized in testing the hypotheses. However, it can be said that while the changes in rated thirst were extremely weak for females, the trend was in the same direction as for the males, with the only *decrease* in thirst (-0.07) exhibited by the High Dissonance-High Salience group, while the Low Dissonance-Low Salience group increased in thirst ($+0.31$). We will have to rely on the data from our subsequent studies, however, to increase our confidence that we are not concerned with only a masculine phenomenon.

In the present experiment, some subjects had to be deleted from the analyses because they were not thirsty after the deprivation period. It is not clear whether in fact 16 hours of water deprivation produced no experience of thirst in them, or whether (as was suggested in connection with the research by Brehm, Back, and Bogdonoff) their lack of felt thirst was a reflection of dissonance reduction (or some other competing motivational process) that took place during the uncontrolled interval between the initial agreement to go thirsty and the time of arrival at the laboratory for the subsequent controlled arousal of dissonance. In the next paper in this section, Brock and Grant present a technique for the experimental arousal of thirst in the laboratory that helps overcome this source of ambiguity in analyzing drive-arousing operations.

In interpreting the water-consumption data, Brehm attributes less drinking in the High Dissonance condition to lowered physiological demands as a result of dissonance reduction. However, it could also be argued that drinking is correlated with self-ratings of thirst partly in an attempt to maintain response consistency. Thus, if a subject had said he was not very thirsty, he would probably drink less than he would if he had said he was thirsty, simply to be outwardly consistent (by observing his own behavior—a position postulated by Bem, 1967). Brock and Grant's study also provides valuable data on changes in consummatory strength of thirst as a *direct* channel for dissonance reduction.

This next study also attempts to answer the provocative question of whether cognitive dissonance can be aroused below the level of the subject's verbalizable awareness. A positive resolution of this issue would permit the extension of our present analysis to the area of unconscious motivation where repression has placed one (or more) cognitions outside of the subject's awareness.

5. DISSONANCE, AWARENESS, AND THIRST MOTIVATION

Timothy C. Brock and Lester D. Grant

This experiment deals with two problems related to dissonance theory. Can dissonance be aroused between two inconsistent cognitions when the person has limited awareness of one of them? Can change in consummatory strength of motives and drives be an avenue of dissonance reduction? Affirmative answers to these questions would extend the domain of applicability of dissonance theory.

"Awareness" in dissonance arousal has not received experimental attention, but the problem has been explicitly stated. Rosenberg and Hovland wrote:

> Festinger makes no assumption about whether the organism consciously "experiences" dissonance, although at one point he does speak of a subject's "having learned, during the course of his existence, how unpleasant dissonance is." The whole problem of whether responsiveness to inconsistency requires awareness seems to be an open one (1960, p. 222).

The research presented in this book suggests that reduction in the strength of a motive or drive is a direct function of magnitude of dissonance. Of special concern to us is the research on hunger and thirst presented earlier by Brehm (Articles 1 and 4) and by Brehm, Back, and Bogdonoff (Article 2). In these studies, drive was induced by deprivation of food or water for about 16 hours. As has been noted, unexpected differences in initial drive level between groups as well as unclear sex effects may have been consequences of uncontrolled variables operating during the period of deprivation outside the laboratory. These two issues, then—awareness and motive change—were brought together in the present experiment by the laboratory manipulation of degree of thirst, the hypnotic induction of an inconsistent sensation (water bloatedness), and the measurement of amount of water consumed in the waking state when amnesia for the posthypnotic suggestion was established.

DISSONANCE PREDICTIONS

The primary experimental hypothesis was derived from four assumptions: (1) dissonance between two cognitions can be produced even if the person is unaware

SOURCE: Brock, Timothy C., and Lester D. Grant, "Dissonance, Awareness, and Thirst Motivation." Adapted from "Dissonance, Awareness, and Motivation," *Journal of Abnormal and Social Psychology*, 1963, *67*, pp. 53–60.

of one of them; (2) a feeling of extreme water satiation creates more dissonance in a person who knows he is very thirsty than in a person who knows he is only slightly thirsty; (3) such dissonance may be reduced by decreasing the magnitude of the thirst drive; and (4) water consumption is a valid index of magnitude of thirst.

The hypothesis concerned water consumption by experimental hypnotic subjects, who were given the "bloated" suggestion, and Control hypnotic subjects, who were given an irrelevant suggestion. It was predicted that the *difference* in water consumption between very thirsty and slightly thirsty Control subjects would be significantly greater than the corresponding difference for experimental subjects. In other words, drinking by very thirsty subjects would greatly exceed drinking by slightly thirsty subjects in the Control group but not in the experimental (Dissonance) group. In fact, high thirst plus dissonance might lead to *less* water consumption than low thirst for experimental subjects if the difference between initial thirst levels was not extreme.

OVERVIEW OF EXPERIMENTAL DESIGN

Subjects were randomly assigned to one of two thirst-arousal conditions within each of the following three treatments: (1) hypnotized and given a dissonant suggestion of feeling a water-bloated stomach; (2) hypnotized and given a suggestion irrelevant to thirst, i.e., that they would feel fatigued; (3) not hypnotized and asked to role play having the feeling of water bloatedness. First, thirst was experimentally aroused by having all the subjects eat a hot sauce on crackers. Then the subjects in the first two treatments, who had previously been trained in hypnosis, were hypnotized and given suggestions either discrepant with their feeling of thirst or irrelevant to it, as well as amnesia for the hypnotic suggestion itself. The subjects in the third group were not hypnotized and were asked merely to act out the dissonant feeling, i.e., water bloatedness. When the hypnotic trance was removed and while the role playing was still in effect, the subjects were offered water (the amount consumed being the major dependent variable) and then were asked to fill out a questionnaire relevant to their drive state and to their reactions to various parts of the experiment. The hypnotic trance was then reinduced, the amnesia suggestions were removed, and the subjects were awakened; for the subjects in the third treatment, the role playing was ended. All subjects were then offered water again and questioned about their reactions.

PROCEDURE

Subjects and Research Setting

There were 20 high-school students, 10 male and 10 female, in each of the three groups: Dissonance, Control, and Role-Play Control. The 60 subjects figuring in the present results were part of a larger sample of 92 who were initially approached about the experiment (see p. 70 for analysis of the subject attrition). The 60 subjects were eligible for or were members of a special evening seminar for high-school students seeking advanced exposure to topics in the humanities and sciences via lectures from experts and authorities from nearby communities. Since eligibility was based primarily on scholastic excellence, the present sample was from the top 5 per cent of high-school students in several school districts in Westmoreland County, Pennsylvania.[1] Initial contact was made by the authors, who appeared briefly at the beginning of an evening seminar and asked students interested in participating in research using hypnosis to obtain their parents' consent. In sum, then, the present subjects were superior in intelligence and motivated to explore new experiences beyond those provided in the regular school curricula.

At the beginning of the experimental session, the experimenter introduced the study to the individual Dissonance and Control subjects as a two-part research project, the first part involving hypnosis and the second, food preferences, as part of a market-research study. (The experimental procedure for the Role-Play Controls will be discussed later.)

Hypnotic Induction

An attempt to induce hypnosis was made and the following tests were passed before the experiment was continued:[2] complete relaxation, eye fluttering and catalepsy, kinesthetic delusion (head levitation and lowering), positive cutaneous hallucination (warmth), partial amnesias (counting backwards from 100, forgetting number after 90; inability to remember own name), arm catalepsy, finger rigidity and analgesia, positive hallucination of viewing funny movie, and compliance with posthypnotic suggestion of return to hypnosis upon specified signal. In terms of Weitzenhoffer's (1953) summary of scales by Hull (1933), Davis and Husband (1931), Barry, Mackinnon, and Murray (1931), Friedlander and Sarbin (1938), and Van Pelt (1949), the present subjects were placed in *at least* a "medium trance." For example, according to the Davis-Husband scale, subjects retained in the analysis of results reached the level of Score 20 and, in addition, showed systematized posthypnotic amnesia (Score 28 in "somnambulistic" phase). Finally, each hypnotized subject was repeatedly told:

> After you wake up, if I say the word "brown" you will want to go deep asleep, deeper asleep than you are now. You will not remember me telling you this but you will want to go deeper asleep than you are now when I say the word "brown."

---

1. The authors are indebted to the parents and educators whose cooperation was essential, especially T. W. Fullerton, Superintendent; P. R. Bingaman, R. M. Crawford, and W. E. Yates, principals; B. F. Browne, J. W. Minder, G. Rutter, and R. J. Simmons, teachers; and M. Kepple, counselor. At the county level, F. E. Kauffman, Superintendent, was extremely helpful in overall planning and coordination of facilities and subject recruitment.

2. The hypnotist, or "operator," had had extensive experience with hypnosis for several years, with initial training and supervision provided by a practicing hypnodontist.

Thirst Arousal

The random assignment of the subjects into High and Low Thirst conditions was made by one experimenter, with the assignment being concealed from the hypnotist-experimenter, or "operator." When the subject was awakened from the initial hypnotic induction, the experimenter handed him two ordinary saltine crackers with approximately two teaspoons of sauce on each and he was told to eat them as part of the product-testing research. In the Low Thirst condition, the recipe for the sauce was 1 teaspoon of water to 3 tablespoons of ordinary catsup. In the High Thirst condition, 4 teaspoons of hot sauce were added to 3 tablespoons of catsup. Louisiana hot pepper was the critical ingredient in the hot sauce, sold commercially as "Frank's Red Hot Sauce." Sauces in both conditions were identical in appearance and viscosity. When the subject had just finished swallowing the crackers and sauce, the experimenter turned the subject's attention again to the operator, who rapidly induced hypnosis by employing the previously suggested signal, "brown."

Dissonance Cognition

The Dissonance subjects were told under hypnosis:

> This time when you wake up you will feel that you have drunk a great deal of water. You will feel extremely bloated with water, but you will not remember my telling you this. You will simply feel extremely full of water, that you have drunk a tremendous amount of water and are now completely bloated with water. You will not know why you feel this way but you will feel extremely bloated with water.

Control Group

The procedure for the control hypnotic subjects was the same except that they were told:

> When you wake up you will feel extremely tired and fatigued, that you have exerted yourself a great deal. You will feel extremely tired but not sleepy. . . .

In addition, all subjects were told that they would be unable to remember any part of the hypnosis except that it had been a relaxing and pleasant experience. Subjects were reminded again of the "brown" signal, awakened, and asked to turn their attention to the experimenter.

Opportunity to Drink

The experimenter produced a paper cup and a quart pitcher of water and asked if the subject would like some water "to wash away the taste of the crackers and sauce." Water was continually supplied until the subject indicated he had had enough. If the subject declined water initially, he was asked "Are you sure you wouldn't like water? There's lots here." Then the subjects were asked to fill out a questionnaire, giving self-reports of perceived thirst, of enjoyableness of eating the crackers, and of success of the hypnosis or role-playing performance (each on a 60-point scale). Water was then offered again, and probes for failure of amnesia were made. The subject's attention was turned once again to the operator, who used the previously described signal to induce hypnosis.

Final Session

During this final session under hypnotic trance, the suggestion for feeling bloated or tired was removed and the subjects were told that they would be unable to remember any part of the experiment conducted under hypnosis "until the results are reported next month at the seminar." On being awakened, the experimental subjects were again offered water. Before the experimenter dismissed each subject, he placed him on his honor not to discuss the experiment until the lecture on the results was given to the seminar.

The entire session with each subject took about 35 minutes, 20 of which (on the average) were devoted to the initial induction of hypnosis. About a month later, the authors reported results to the subjects and their seminar and led a lively discussion on hypnosis and psychology. At this time, it was ascertained that no subject perceived a connection between the food testing and the hypnosis.

Role-Play Control Group

This condition was run after the two hypnotic conditions were completed. The introduction to the research was the same except that the first project was described as being concerned, not with hypnosis, but with developing tests aimed at discovering role-playing talent and dramatic ability. Emphasis was placed on the ability to portray and "really experience something without using words." In a warm-up session, subjects were asked to close their eyes and convey the following experiences: watching a hilarious movie, sucking a lemon, getting control of a car after it had been forced off the road at high speed, bidding good-by to best friend on train pulling slowly out of station, etc. Subjects were encouraged after each "scene," and "really experiencing it" was reemphasized. The remaining procedure was the same as for the experimental hypnotic subjects, except that the hypnosis and the hypnotic patter and phrasing were not employed. Instead, the experimenter said, "Now imagine that you have drunk a great deal of water, that you feel extremely bloated with water . . . ."

Dependent Measures

The major dependent variable was the number of cubic centimeters of water drunk during the time water was made available. In addition, questionnaire ratings attempted to measure reactions to the cracker-sauce combination and to the success of the hypnotic and role-playing procedures, as well as to measure extent of amnesia.

SUBJECT ATTRITION AND SELECTION

Of the 92 subjects initially approached, 16 were either unwilling to participate or were unable to obtain their parents' written consent. In addition, 3 subjects were lost because of illness and 2 because a convenient appointment could not be arranged. Of the subjects who reported for the research, 4 could not be hypnotized and 3 others, although hypnotizable to some extent, could not pass the depth-of-hypnosis tests specified above. These 7 subjects were excused with the usual request to reveal nothing. In addition, data from the following subjects were omitted in the analysis of the results: two subjects who had perfect recall of the entire procedure; one subject who reported remembering the signal word, "brown"; and another who had a sore throat. The results, therefore, are based on the 60 subjects who satisfied the a priori criteria of admissibility established for this study.

RESULTS

Factors Affecting Experimental Purity

A primary concern was the subjects' posthypnotic forgetting of the critical suggestion. Although the waking amnesia suggestion was for the hypnotic experience in general and not specifically for the bloated or tired feelings, the general ban on recalling any part of the hypnosis was apparently potent: none of the 40 hypnotic subjects verbalized the induced feeling either spontaneously or after the experimenter's probing. With the exception of occasional memory for the earliest suggestions of the initial induction period, the subjects retained in the analysis of results were able to write or say little more than that the hypnosis had been a pleasant, relaxing, and enjoyable experience; they recalled nothing else of the hypnotic instructions. In contrast, the subjects wrote accurate and detailed descriptions of the "product testing" in which they described their reactions, compared the sauce to other foods, commented on its marketable qualities, etc.

Some evidence on the effectiveness of the thirst manipulation is presented in Table 1, where it can be seen that subjects in the High Thirst condition found the cracker-sauce combination less enjoyable and more thirst arousing than did the Low Thirst subjects (two-tailed t-test, p's < 0.01); these differences were approximately the same in the three major treatment groups. There were no differences between treatments in the extent to which the hypnosis or role playing was subjectively experienced as successful.

TABLE 1

MEAN SELF-RATINGS OF THIRST, ENJOYABLENESS, AND FEELING OF SUCCESS*

Treatment	Thirst†	Enjoyableness‡	Success§
High Thirst:			
Male, bloated¶	34.0	19.0	46.0
Female, bloated	32.8	17.0	39.0
Male, tired	32.0	17.0	39.0
Female, tired	39.6	16.0	42.0
Male, role play	30.8	15.0	41.6
Female, role play	42.4	14.0	33.6
Low Thirst:			
Male, bloated	20.4	44.4	43.6
Female, bloated	11.6	42.0	48.0
Male, tired	27.4	34.2	46.0
Female, tired	24.2	32.6	40.0
Male, role play	20.8	44.0	38.0
Female, role play	21.6	32.4	32.2

* Each mean based on $N = 5$.

† The higher the mean, the greater the thirst attributed to eating the crackers with sauce.

‡ The higher the mean, the greater the enjoyableness attributed to eating the food.

§ The higher the mean, the greater the extent to which hypnotic subjects felt hypnosis "worked" on them; for role-play subjects, the greater they perceived the successfulness of their performance.

¶ Male subjects who were given the crackers and hot sauce combination (High Thirst) and the hypnotic suggestion of water bloatedness.

Test of the Dissonance Hypothesis

The mean water-consumption scores presented in Figure 1 clearly support the hypothesis. In the two Control groups, subjects who ate the hot sauce (High Thirst) drank two to four times as much water as subjects who received diluted catsup (Low Thirst). This effect was reversed in the experimental groups, where the High Thirst subjects drank *less* than the Low Thirst subjects. The effect cannot be attributed to hypnosis alone, since the Control groups were also hypnotized but given suggestions irrelevant to thirst; nor can it be attributed to the bloated instructions alone, since the role-playing group operated under this effect. The magnitude of the hypnotically induced dissonance arousal (having a hot, dry mouth and simultaneously feeling bloated) is evidenced by the fact that eight of the ten High Thirst subjects in this condition completely refused to drink any water, while there were only two refusals in the corresponding Low Thirst condition ($p < 0.05$).

An analysis of variance of water-consumption scores for hypnotic subjects yielded significant main effects for thirst and the bloated-tired classification. There were no sex differences. In general, the "bloated" subjects drank less than the "tired" subjects ($p < 0.001$). The interaction between the bloated-tired classification and magnitude of thirst was quite significant ($p < 0.001$).

Since the data did not approximate a normal distribution (there was marked heteroscedasticity), the Freeman-Tukey variance-stabilizing square-root transformation, as described by Mosteller and Bush (1954, p. 326), was employed in a re-analysis. The main effect of High-Low Thirst was no longer statistically significant, but the significance of the bloated-tired main effect and the interaction of this variable with magnitude of thirst were both increased.

Correlations between subjective ratings of thirst and amount of water consumed were significantly positive in the Control group ($r = +0.45$, $p < 0.05$), indicating that those who drank more water reported feeling more thirsty. However, for the experimental group, amount of water consumed was not correlated with subjective thirst ($r = -0.03$).

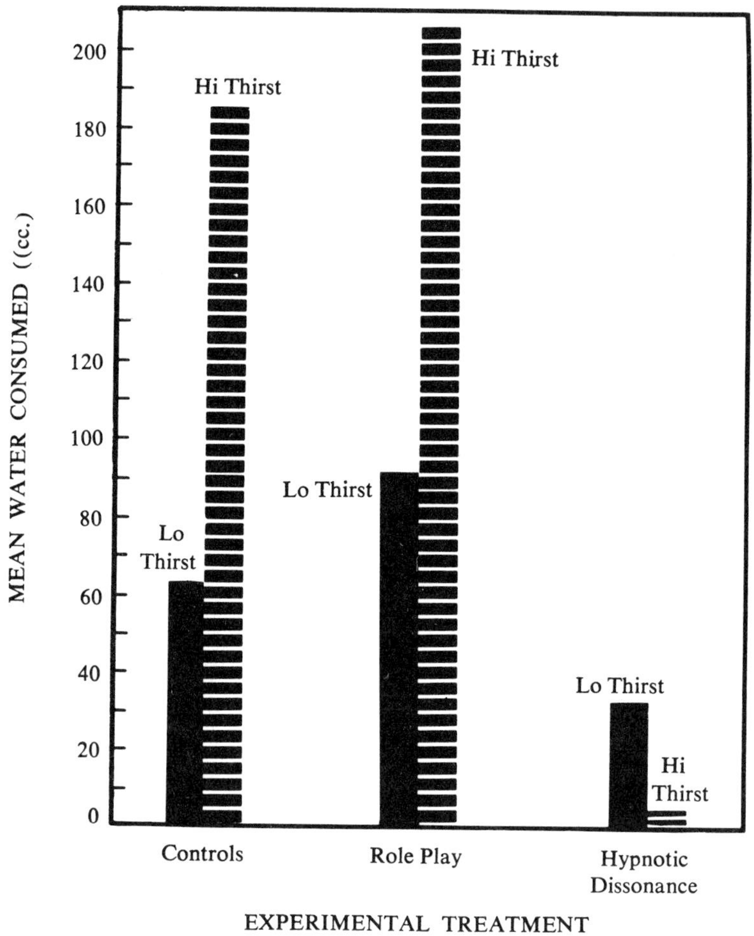

FIGURE 1

Mean water consumption for subjects varying in thirst arousal under Control, Role Play, and hypnotically induced Dissonance conditions.

TABLE 2

MEAN AMOUNT OF WATER (CC.) CONSUMED BY DISSONANCE SUBJECTS AFTER REMOVAL OF "BLOATED" SUGGESTION*

Sex	High Thirst	Low Thirst
Male	16.4	29.8
Female	15.8	40.4

* Cell $N = 5$.

Persistence of Dissonance Effect

The experimenter routinely offered water to experimental subjects after the bloated suggestion was removed. The data in Table 2 suggest that decrement in magnitude of thirst persisted even when the dissonant element, "bloatedness," was no longer hypnotically present. High Thirst subjects continued to require less water than Low Thirst subjects ($p < 0.05$). Apparently, there was an enduring reduction in the strength of the thirst drive by subjects in the experimental dissonance group.

DISCUSSION

The main finding, that very thirsty subjects drank less water than slightly thirsty subjects following an hypnotic induction of bloatedness, was interpreted in terms of dissonance theory. Bloatedness is a barrier against further water consumption, and acceptance of such a barrier was considered more inconsistent with high than with low thirst. When bloatedness was induced, the resulting high and low magnitudes of dissonance were reduced by corresponding decrements in need for water. In view of the control data, it seemed unlikely that either the hypnotic procedure or the nature of the suggestion somehow accounted for the results. The critical factor was acceptance of the feeling of bloatedness as "literally true" (Barber, 1958). As in Glass and Barber (1961), such acceptance did not characterize the role-playing subjects.

The results might be explained in terms of contrast or reinforcement notions rather than dissonance reduction. High Thirst subjects, on being told they had drunk a great deal and were bloated, would feel that they had drunk more than Low Thirst subjects and might, on awaking, feel they should drink very little. This account is similar to one in which the bloated induction is considered reinforcing. The greater the drive, the greater the effect of a reinforcer; consequently, High Thirst subjects would drink less. This alternative explanation requires assumptions that appear doubtful, and if accepted, it entails a further difficulty. Observation of the subjects suggested that the probable locus of the bloated sensation, the stomach region, was not the site of the thirst drive in the present experiment; drinking by control subjects showed that the appropriate reinforcement was to assuage the "hotness" of mouth-throat tissue. Bloatedness was an impediment to such reinforcement because it created intolerance for further water consumption. A more serious difficulty with the proposed alternative can be seen in the water consumption of experimental subjects *after* the bloated suggestion, the alleged reinforcer, was removed (Table 2). That High Thirst subjects continued to require less water than Low Thirst subjects was an outcome not implied by the contrast-reinforcement explanation here examined.

Awareness of Inconsistency

A major objective of this study was to decide whether or not the subjects were at all aware of inconsistency (dissonance). If awareness of the bloated sensation was limited or absent, then it would be implausible to assert that the subject was fully aware of inconsistency between the bloated sensation and his knowledge concerning his thirst. Awareness undoubtedly has many levels and meanings: in this study the criterion was the translation of a feeling into a verbalizable cognition. Of course, in special circumstances, a person can be aware of a sensation or feeling without being able to "cognize" it; but bloatedness was not considered so bizarre, threatening, or uncommon as to require dispensation from cognitive representation.

However, there are grounds for doubting that the subjects were unable to verbalize their bloated or tired feelings. First, the operator did not tell the subjects that they would be unaware of the critical sensation: amnesia was induced for the suggestion but not for the content of the suggestion. Second, it can be argued that more intensive probing would have elicited reports of bloatedness or fatigue. For example, the experimenter might have inquired: "Do you have any particularly strong sensations now?" and/or "When you think of how you feel physically, what do you think of?" A related possibility is that the bloated and tired feelings were not particularly strong and that consequently subjects failed to report them.

The present subjects, unlike those in other research employing hypnotic inputs (for example, Blum, 1961, and Zimbardo, Rapaport, & Baron, to be reported in the next section of this text), did not undergo hours of intensive training in hypnosis. Inducing amnesia for the critical suggestion and telling subjects they would be able to remember only that the hypnosis was relaxing and pleasant may have impaired recoverability of the content of the suggestion. It is questionable that a naïve hypnotic subject easily distinguishes content from process; being told "you will not remember my telling you this" might well affect awareness of content as well as of induction. This effect was obtained by Blum, who also mentions the possibility of "spontaneous" posthypnotic amnesia (1961, pp. 35, 162).

Both the experimenter and the questionnaire asked the subjects to report what they were told, what happened, and how they felt during hypnosis, and both the experimenter and the operator inquired about the subjects' current feelings.

If more intensive questioning were necessary to elicit reports of feeling bloated and tired, this would be congenial with assuming that the sensations were not *readily* verbalizable. Precise determination of the strength of the bloated sensation was not possible, but the data are some indication that the somatic experience of bloatedness was not so weak or obscure that it would only be verbalizable after very intensive interrogation (the test of the difference in water consumption between "bloated" and "tired" subjects was significant well beyond the 0.001 level). If further questioning had elicited verbalization of the critical sensations, this could also have been misleading, for there is some evidence that awareness can be enhanced or artificially induced by a post-experimental interview (Spielberger, 1962, pp. 93–94).

If the subjects' failure to verbalize bloatedness was not due to inadequate probing by the experimenter, then a tentative conclusion is allowable: awareness, defined as the verbalization of experience, is unnecessary for response to inconsistency. The present study is comparable to one by Blum (1961) in which the subject was confronted by inconsistency between affects (anxiety and contentment) hypnotically attached to letters of the alphabet. Blum assumed posthypnotic unawareness of inconsistency:

> [The] *S*, placed in a dilemma by the appearance of conflicting stimuli to which he was required to react, unconsciously resolved the task by reasoning to himself that anxiety can [not] legitimately accompany . . . contentment (1961, p. 70).

There is, of course, no evidence that the present subjects were unconscious of the posthypnotic suggestion. If future research supports the possibility that one of the elements contributing to a dissonance relation may be unconscious, then psychoanalytic and dissonance theories, which are both concerned with resolution of intrapsychic conflict, might be addressed to the same evidence. Such a convergence, though it entails formidable methodological difficulties, would seem especially fruitful (for example, Bramel, 1962).

It is also of interest to note that the present approach does not conform to Miller's conflict model (1959, p. 207, Fig. 2). If the drinking of water is the goal behavior and bloatedness can be represented as a gradient of avoidance which has a constant slope within an experimental treatment, then the two levels of manipulated thirst, high and low, can represent, respectively, strong and weak approach gradients. It follows then that greater approach and consummatory behavior should occur among the High than the Low Thirst subjects. The present data reveal a contradictory pattern; water is refused (avoided?) by 80 per cent of the High Thirst subjects and only 20 per cent of the Low Thirst subjects. Perhaps such a conflict model is not adequate when extended to human motivation where expectancies can modify the relationship between approach and avoidance gradients in ways not possible among infrahuman species.

Editor's Comments

If we accept the assumptions posed by Brock and Grant, then indeed the data are quite compelling and add considerably to the evidence for our thesis that drives like thirst may be brought under cognitive control. Thirsty subjects (of both sexes) in the Dissonance group not only drank significantly *less* water than less-thirsty subjects, but most of them drank no water at all. In fact, there is no relationship between self-estimates of thirst and cubic centimeters of water consumed for Dissonance subjects, while there is a significant correlation between these measures for the Control subjects; as expected, the thirstier they felt, the more water they drank.

Thus, the effect of dissonance resolution on water consumption was not an effect mediated by changes in subjective feelings of thirst or prior self-reporting (and therefore need for response consistency) of thirst. This finding, as well as the discovery that it is possible to create dissonance without awareness, does not support Bem's recent (1967) reinterpretation of dissonance phenomena in terms of a conscious process of self-observation.

From data on self-ratings of thirst, it seems clear that for both sexes the experimental manipulation of thirst in the laboratory was effective. Subjects who ate the hot sauce perceived that they were more thirsty and experienced less enjoyment than subjects who ate the diluted catsup. The experience of eating the hot sauce mixture is one of an initial burning sensation of the tongue, lips, and lining of the mouth which, although diminishing over time, persists for at least an hour. As the primary sensation of heat lessens, the mouth begins to feel very dry and the throat parched.[1] It is probably the burning feeling that produces the "unenjoyable quality" of the experience, while the local dryness in the mouth produces the perception of thirst. Given this awareness by the subject, it is then inconsistent for him to feel that his stomach is bloated with water, since these two sensations are not normally experienced simultaneously.

King (1878) describes the unusual conditions under which these usually dissonant sensations might occur together—in the reactions of men suffering from severe thirst following exposure in the desert: "Although water was imbibed again and again, even to repletion of the stomach, it did not assuage their insatiable thirst." These men may have experienced water bloatedness of the stomach and local dryness in the mouth without any concomitant dissonance; they also continued to be thirsty even when their mouths were wet *and* their stomachs full.

Thus, it is likely that the subjects in the present study had an experience (local dryness of the mouth) that was similar to one they had in the past when they were thirsty and that they experienced cognitive dissonance when this sensation was accompanied by one that typically occurred when they were not thirsty (feeling a stomach full of water). Although dry mouth and throat have been designated "false thirst," as distinguished from "true thirst" caused by

1. This is a first-hand account, since I was a guinea pig in testing this manipulation in the next experiment by Helge Mansson.

dehydration of the tissues (Wolf, 1958, p. 53), Brock and Grant have isolated one of the many factors that play a complex role in thirst. From among the hormonal, mechanical, neural, and oral factors that influence thirst, they have chosen to manipulate one, which although it may not produce "physiological thirst," is an important and usually correlated component of thirst—laryngeal mouth dryness. While it is true that there are a number of reports of human subjects who do not feel thirsty even when their mouths are dry, nevertheless, for most people the two sensations are associated. That the association is not stronger only serves to make the differences obtained by Brock and Grant even more dramatic and helps explain why the mean self-ratings of thirst are only about 35 on a 60-point scale and why the correlation between these ratings and drinking for the Control subjects is not higher than +0.45.

The authors' assumption that water consumption is an accurate index of thirst level appears to be valid insofar as stimulation from dryness in the mouth or throat becomes, through conditioning over the lifetime of the organism, a conditioned stimulus for drinking. On the other hand, if thirst is viewed in terms of body-water loss, then drinking in humans (unlike dogs, whose drinking almost precisely meters their water loss) "may fail completely as an index of need" (Wolf, 1958, p. 9).

Another problem with using water consumption in man as a gauge of thirst arises from the fact that drinking is in part a socially learned response; thus, some people characteristically sip while others take large gulps. In the next study, Mansson avoids this source of variability (not due to motivation) simply by having subjects drink through a straw. The increased constancy in the response and the additional effort required by drinking this way appear to reduce some of this error variance within groups and yield statistically significant effects even with smaller mean differences than those observed in Brehm's thirst experiment (Article 4), where between-group effects were not statistically significant.

On the matter of amount of water consumed, the reader should have noted that the Low Thirst Dissonance group with the suggestion for bloatedness drank less than half as much as the Low Thirst Control subjects. This also points to the effectiveness of the hypnotic induction since in the thirst literature, gastric distention is considered a possible source of cues for termination of drinking. In man, this is not a major factor, since he typically drinks only small amounts of water, but when gastric distention is excessive, it does serve an inhibitory function.

It is also interesting to see that this effect, as well as the dissonance-inhibited drinking of water, is not transitory, but persists even when the hypnotic suggestion is removed. The Low Thirst Dissonance subjects still drink less than half as much as their relevant Controls, while the High Thirst Dissonance subjects drink less than a tenth the amount consumed by their Controls!

In using water consumption, both Brehm, and Brock and Grant attempted to supplement their self-report measures of the cognitive aspect of motives with a behavior that has been utilized in animal experiments as a noncognitive index of thirst. However, it is obvious that in man, drinking may at times simply reflect the same cognitive processes operative in the self-ratings of thirst. A person might choose to drink or not for a variety of reasons that have little to do with his level of thirst. Therefore, it seems that in studying human motivation, a good strategy is to extend the approach used so effectively by Neal Miller (1957) with animals. He advocates use of multiple task and response measures at several levels of analysis, since our measures of drive may be "impure and hence affected by factors other than the drive." In addition, he cautions against thinking that given drives like thirst are necessarily single, unitary intervening variables, when they may in fact be heterogeneous clusters involving a number of neural centers which are "differentially affected by various regulators and have differential effects on various response systems" (1957, p. 1275).

Operationally, this would require an approach to our current problem that would not rely upon the functional relation between a given drive and a single response (as thirst and drinking, or even hunger and FFA release). Rather, we should choose multiple response indicators of drive, each of which correlates with magnitude of drive but taps a different aspect of its functioning. In the next experiment, Helge Mansson utilizes this research strategy in a carefully controlled experiment to obtain highly reliable data that satisfy many of our reservations about the results of some of the previous studies. Of interest also is his use of three levels of dissonance arousal and his treatment of the data of those who refuse to commit themselves to additional deprivation.

6. THE RELATION OF DISSONANCE REDUCTION TO COGNITIVE, PERCEPTUAL, CONSUMMATORY, AND LEARNING MEASURES OF THIRST

Helge Hilding Mansson

Although the influence of hunger on the behavior of human beings has been dealt with in a variety of experiments (Atkinson & McClelland, 1948; Keys, et al., 1950; Epstein & Lewitt, 1962; and Wispe, 1954), surprisingly little research has focused on the behavioral correlates of thirst in man. In the research that has been done on thirst (e.g., Klein, 1954), like that on hunger (e.g., Levine, Chein, & Murphy, 1942; Sanford, 1936), the interest has been in relating current drive level to perceptual and cognitive aspects of behavior. Little research has attempted to deal with the effects of anticipated food or water deprivation when the person is already hungry or thirsty. To wit, what happens when a thirsty person knows that he will not be able to drink for a

---

SOURCE: Mansson, Helge Hilding, "The Relation of Dissonance Reduction to Cognitive, Perceptual, Consummatory, and Learning Measures of Thirst," adapted from *The Cognitive Control of Thirst Motivation: A Dissonance Approach*, unpublished doctoral dissertation, New York University, 1965. Reprinted by permission of the author.

long time? Is it possible that a person's expectation of future deprivation influences his present level of felt thirst as much as do his current physiological deficiencies, and perhaps even more? Or do the two interact in such a way that the individual reduces the motivational impact of his physiological deficiency *more* the greater that deficiency and the more severe the anticipated deprivation? It is to this general problem that the present study is directed.

The primary focus of the previously reported studies in this volume has been on the variable of justification supporting the discrepant commitment to future deprivation. However, postcommitment dissonance processes should also be influenced by the anticipated extent (severity) of the future deprivation. The present study, therefore, will examine the interaction of these two cognitive variables in their effects upon modifying the experience of thirst.

The thirst drive seems particularly well suited for testing the dissonance formulation proposed in this text. It is one of the least conventionalized of the basic needs, and it is not overwhelmingly affected by social norms in its manner of gratification; thus, the drive and its goal behavior are rarely implicated in psychoneurotic developmental processes (as hunger and eating are). It is also a relatively easy drive to induce and satisfy quickly within a laboratory setting. Finally, in human subjects the reduction of thirst by water consumption can be better assessed quantitatively than can hunger by food consumption.

It is assumed here that dissonance reduction will be achieved by a reduction in the level of felt thirst. Therefore, the necessity of delaying gratification for a long period without adequate justification should no longer be dissonant if the person no longer feels thirsty (or is less thirsty than when he made the commitment). We will reserve until later in this paper the issue of whether dissonance reduction actually lowers the drive itself or only suppresses it.

We can gauge the magnitude of dissonance aroused only indirectly, of course, through the measures we assume reflect attempts to reduce dissonance. Water consumption and self-estimates of thirst obviously should be included, but what other dimensions of thirst can we explore?

1. *Learning Measures.* Epstein and Lewitt (1962) found that hungry subjects were faster at learning a set of 12 paired-associate words (word pairs, the first member of each pair being a cue for the second, associated member), which included food words. They found not that hungry subjects learned the specifically food-related words faster, but that the overall learning rate was faster. In the present study, then, we may expect that this might be true as well for thirst: high thirst might result in faster overall learning. If so, and if thirst is then reduced through cognitive re-evaluation, this reduction should be accompanied by a corresponding reduction in overall learning rate (slower learning). We may thus employ a learning task and, extrapolating from Epstein and Lewitt's study, predict that learning will vary as a function of experimentally produced thirst and dissonance-produced variations in level of that thirst.

Another experiment by Spence and Ehrenberg (1964) on the effect of hunger on the recall of words associated with cheese (cheese associates) in a subliminal stimulus condition showed that neither hunger alone nor food stimulus alone had any effect on the number of words recalled. When both conditions were present, however, the interaction resulted in a significant recall of cheese associates. The indication is that the drive by itself does not always have a direct effect on learning unless drive-related stimuli are present. This latter study points out the importance of controlling both the drive state and the stimulus conditions in which the drive state is experienced. Thus, as Jack Brehm's study on thirst (Article 4) also demonstrated, it is important to make salient the goal substance as well as the drive.

2. *Perceptual Measures.* Atkinson and McClelland (1948) have shown that increased length of initial food deprivation is related to an increase in the frequency of need-for-food themas as measured on TAT responses to a picture depicting an old man and a young man and another picture representing a piece of meat with a knife next to it. Using this approach, the expectation would be that differences in thirst drive would be reflected in need-for-water themas. In addition, if the thirst drive became changed or reduced through cognitive re-evaluation, we would expect a corresponding reduction in projected need-for-water themas.

Klein (1954) found that thirsty subjects who, on the basis of the Stroop (1935) color-word test, were divided into groups varying in the degree to which their task performance was disturbed (interfered with) by cognitions discrepant with the task response (e.g., to read aloud the word *blue* when it was written in red), differed in their ability to perceive stimuli arranged concentrically around a thirst-related symbol. The subjects who scored high on the color-word test (i.e., who could not avoid having the irrelevant stimulus influence their task response) were not able to disregard the thirst-related symbol and did not perceive and learn the surrounding stimuli as well as the low-scoring subjects.

On the basis of this evidence, we might predict that thirsty subjects would choose more thirst-related words when faced with having to choose one out of each of several pairs of words simultaneously presented (one word in each pair being thirst-related and the other, neutral). We might also predict that thirsty subjects would respond faster when selecting a thirst-related word. If then an initially high drive level is decreased through the cognitive resolution of dissonant elements, fewer drive-related words would be chosen and the decision time should be the same as for subjects with an initially low thirst drive. We might add here that if dissonance reduction is effected through suppression of the experience of being very thirsty, then the presence of this suppressed cognition might act as a high-interference cognition, in the sense that Klein uses the concept. This should result in a longer delay in decision time for High Dissonance subjects than for even Low Thirst Control subjects.

Since the validity of these measures for studying thirst has not been established, it will be necessary first to establish reference points for thirsty and nonthirsty Control subjects before examining the effects of dissonance manipulations on these presumed indicators of thirst drive.

DISSONANCE PREDICTIONS

In summary, the reduction of thirst-related dissonance should be reflected in: lower self-estimates of thirst, reduced fantasy expressions of thirst, poorer performance on a learning task that involves thirst-associated words, fewer preferences for thirst-related words, longer relevant reaction time, and less actual water consumption. This should be true of High Dissonance subjects in comparison with those who experienced less dissonance, as well as with those who experienced no dissonance (made no commitment to discrepant behavior) but were initially thirsty.

Two additional predictions should be included before we turn to the experiment itself: first, since dissonance-reduction attempts are linearly related to magnitude of dissonance, a Moderate Dissonance group should on all measures be intermediate in performance between the Highs and Lows; second, subjects who refuse to commit themselves to future water deprivation should show results on dependent measures that are different from the High Dissonance subjects and similar to the Low or Moderate Dissonance subjects.

OVERVIEW OF EXPERIMENTAL DESIGN

The design required to test these hypotheses was a two-by-two factorial in which the degree of justification for commitment to deprivation and the length of anticipated deprivation were the main manipulated variables. Eighteen subjects were randomly[1] assigned to each of these four cells, yielding three levels of dissonance: (1) High Dissonance—minimal justification and long anticipated deprivation (24 hours); (2) Low Dissonance—high justification and short anticipated deprivation (4 hours); (3) Moderate Dissonance—minimal justification and short anticipated deprivation; (4) Moderate Dissonance—high justification and long anticipated deprivation. All Dissonance groups made a voluntary commitment to a period of future water deprivation after thirst was experimentally aroused. In two Control groups (each with 18 subjects), which did not make this voluntary commitment, level of thirst was varied: it was high for one group and low for the other. The research design enabled data to be collected on subjects who refused the discrepant commitment, and they constituted an additional group of 33 subjects. A series of dependent measures was taken of learning time, thema projection, reaction time, water consumption, and subjective thirst.

PROCEDURE

Subjects

A total of 141 male undergraduates were recruited as volunteers for this study from an admissions list of incoming freshmen at Washington Square College of New York University.

---

1. Random assignment was disturbed by the unequal refusal rate between cells; these subjects being replaced in round-robin fashion between the various groups. Subject assignment then only closely approximated random distribution.

Preparation

The subjects, who were usually tested in groups of four, were isolated from each other by partitions between the tables at which they sat. A large EEG machine in front of them, electrodes, and miscellaneous other equipment helped to create a "scientific atmosphere" and make the experimental instructions plausible. Also in view of the subjects were five glasses (each capable of holding 300 cc. of water), a pitcher full of water, a box of straws, and covered paper plates, each of which contained five saltine crackers (to be used for the thirst manipulation).

After the subjects were seated and given a chance to visually explore the laboratory, they were told they were participating in a study measuring physiological changes and their relation to thirst (for the No Thirst Control group, their relation to certain tasks). The experimenter then attached electrodes to each subject with adhesive tape, one to the subject's throat and a second near the corner of his mouth. This was done to increase the subject's sensitivity to his mouth region (as in the Sarnoff & Zimbardo, 1961, study) in order to enhance perceived differences in thirst.

Thirst Arousal

Thirst was aroused under controlled laboratory conditions by having the subjects eat crackers with a specially prepared sauce that created a sensation of a hot, dry mouth. The recipe for the sauce was modified from Brock and Grant's (Article 5) and consisted of two parts catsup, one part tabasco, and one part horseradish. Subjects in the Low Thirst Control condition were given only crackers with peanut butter, and the directions were altered accordingly. After eating, all subjects rated their degree of thirst on a 71-point scale (ranging from "extremely" to "not at all" thirsty).

Dissonance Arousal

The dissonance manipulation then followed with these instructions [which were adapted from those used by Zimbardo et al. in Article 7].

Low Justification for Commitment

> Now, after we have finished with the next few tasks you will be finished with the experiment for which you came today. We appreciate the help that you have already given us; however, since you are here anyway, it occurred to me to ask you to help out with another experiment when you are through with this one today. I wish I could give you a whole spiel on how valuable this second experiment would be. But I'm just trying something out and to be honest, I'm

not at all sure anything will come of it. I'd like to try it with you and see how things go. It may not add anything more to what I will already have learned here today. Obviously, as you know, it's completely up to you whether or not you want to be a subject in this second experiment, especially since it involves deprivation of liquids for some time.

High Justification for Commitment

Now, after we have finished with the next few tasks, you will be finished with the experiment for which you came today. We appreciate the help that you have already given us; however, since you are here anyway, it occurred to me to ask you to help out with another experiment when you are through with this one today. It would be especially valuable to me if you would participate. Since you were in the first experiment, it gives me the opportunity to use you as your own control. This doubles the value of the data in the second experiment. If my predictions work, I'll be in a good position to get a National Science Foundation grant to develop some new methods for the telemetering of physiological information in the government's space program. Obviously, as you know, it's completely up to you whether you want to be a subject in this second experiment, especially since it involves deprivation of liquids for some time.

High and Low Future Deprivation

However, I would like you to participate in this other experiment. It involves your going without drinking any fluid whatsoever, or eating food which contains water, such as soups, cereals and fruits for another 24- (or 4-) hour period.

Control Against False Compliance

After that period you will call me on the phone, at which time I'll ask you a series of questions. It is very important that you rigidly observe the water restrictions I mentioned. I'll also attach to your arm a small band-aid which has in it a special kind of litmus paper, which will absorb your perspiration and give a measure of your reaction in the water deprivation. After you talk to me tomorrow (or later in the day) on the phone, you may then remove the band-aid and return it to me by mail. I will furnish you with the necessary stamped and addressed envelope for that purpose. We realize that it will not be very pleasant to go without water and fluids. As I said before, you are completely free to decide yourself. I'll give you a statement to sign if you are willing to help out. Read it first, please.

The rationale for including this procedure was to make the subjects feel that they would not be able to cheat on the liquid-deprivation restrictions without being detected.

Control for Experimenter Bias

Each subject agreed to or refused the commitment by responding on a prepared form. Since the experimenter did not look at this form at this time and since the subjects were tested in groups, in no case was he aware of the nature of any subject's commitment while the subsequent dependent measures were being administered.

Response Measures

The experimenter had the subjects re-estimate their thirst on the 71-point scale and then continued with the presentation of the three experimental tasks previously outlined.

Thirst Words Perceived and Preferred. Subjects were led to believe that one member of each of 15 separately presented pairs of words had previously been exposed at a subliminal level, and their task was to detect which member of each pair it was. In actuality, the words previously presented for the brief (1/10 second) exposure bore no relation to the test pairs and were, in addition, mirror images of words not related to liquids (e.g., icon, lemma, ginkgo). The test pairs contained one liquid-related member (e.g., lake, wet, soup, dew) and one unrelated word (e.g., mountain, plate, cheese, solid). Five additional pairs served as fillers to lower the salience of liquid items (e.g., love—hate, sorrow—music). Chance performance would result in an average of 7.5 liquid-related words "perceived" to have been shown subliminally. Scores greater than this were thus presumed to reflect the operation of thirst motivation (i.e., the prepotency of responses related to liquids or drinking).

Learning of Paired Associates. After the following list of paired words was exposed to the subject one pair at a time, subsequently he had to anticipate the second word when shown only the first until he could correctly make all of the appropriate pairings: coffee—tea, beer—ale, soda—milk, cola—juice, lamp—light, carpet—rug, window—sofa, bed—hall, nectar—house, seltzer—ceiling, screen—water, stair—lemonade. The measure taken was the number of trials the subject took to learn and anticipate all the correct associations.

Fantasy Projections on TAT. Each subject was shown two TAT pictures—one water-related and one motivationally neutral—and was asked to write a story about what was happening in each picture. The stories of each subject were scored according to the following three categories. The first category was the presence of "need-for-water" thema, i.e., mention made in the story that somebody wanted, needed, offered, or expressed a desire for water or liquids. The second category was the "presence of water" thema, i.e., mention of water or liquid, whether or not there was any consummatory behavior associated with it. The third category was the "presence of trouble" thema, reflecting a worry or problem for the persons in the story. If a subject mentioned a need for water at least once, he was included in the category of need-for-water thema for that picture. This was done for the other two categories as well. Consequently, the measure used was the frequency of subjects in each condition who had incorporated the above-mentioned themas into their two TAT stories. Two judges, who did not know in which condition the subjects belonged nor had any knowledge of the design of the experiment, independently rated each subject's stories. A reliability check on the consistency of the two judges' ratings yielded a correlation of .87 ($p < .001$).

Water Consumption and Conclusion of Experiment

The experimenter then allowed all subjects to drink through a straw as much water poured from the pitcher in front of them as they wanted, explaining that even if they had committed themselves to participating in the second experiment, they were allowed to have a last drink before the period of deprivation began. After they had drunk, they were again requested to rate their degree of thirst. Finally, a postexperimental questionnaire was administered to assess several aspects of the procedure. Then the subjects were told that because of some scheduling problems that had just arisen, they would not have to undergo the further liquid deprivation after all.

RESULTS

Success of Thirst Arousal

The initial inducement of thirst by eating the cracker-sauce combination was quite effective. The subjects in the experimental groups and the High Thirst Controls rated themselves as significantly more thirsty than did the Low Thirst Controls ($p < 0.01$).[2] On a 71-point scale, the mean for the Low Thirst Controls was 15, while the means for the experimental groups and the High Thirst Controls ranged from 41 to 52 (none significantly different).

Ratings of Choice

The Dissonance subjects rated themselves as having much free and voluntary choice to participate in the experiment (all means, including Refusal groups, varied only slightly around a mean value of 50 on a 71-point scale). In addition, they felt only a slight obligation to agree to the request to participate in the deprivation (all means varied around a mean of 25, again on a 71-point scale). Thus, the essential conditions for assuming the presence of dissonance were met.

Perception of Deprivation, Experimenter, and Value of the Experiment

When asked to rate how unpleasant they estimated it would be for the average person to go without water for the period of time that they themselves had

2. All analyses employed the statistical computer test known as General Linear Hypotheses with Contrasts (BMDO6V), except where otherwise noted.

agreed to, the subjects in the various Dissonance conditions showed no significantly different reactions. There were also no significant differences among the Dissonance conditions on the direct evaluation of how unpleasant they themselves found the prospect of going without liquids (the mean rating was "somewhat unpleasant"). There was, however, a significant difference between the ratings of "projected" unpleasantness and those of "direct" personal unpleasantness, with all subjects perceiving that others would be *more* bothered by the future thirst deprivation than they themselves were ($p < 0.05$). More will be made of this point in the discussion.

In line with the role behavior designed for the experimenter, he was perceived as being mildly positive but close to neutral on a 71-point, "anonymous" rating scale measuring his pleasantness (the means for all groups varied from 35 to 43, and were not reliably different).

In evaluating how worthwhile they felt the future deprivation experiment would be, the subjects should have been influenced by the manipulation of verbal justification for participating in the next experiment; and so they were. Those given the High Justification treatment reported that the experiment was more worthwhile than did those given the Low Justification treatment (significant beyond the 0.02 level). This effect was true for both the 4-hour and 24-hour future-deprivation conditions.

Rationale Behind Commitment or Noncommitment

The major reason given for commitment to deprivation by those in the High Justification condition was that the experiment was "very important," perhaps "crucial." Such answers were given by 24 subjects, while 12 others gave a variety of different reasons, such as a personal interest in being in experiments. By contrast, in the Low Justification condition, only 4 subjects stressed the importance of the research, 17 indicated that they committed themselves solely to help out the experimenter, while 15 gave no answer at all. Clearly, then, on this free-response item, subjects responded according to the experimental treatment to which they had been exposed.

Of the 33 subjects who refused to make the commitment to go without water for a period of time following the experimental session, 24 came from the 24-hour deprivation condition while only 9 were in the Low Deprivation condition. This difference in rate of refusal was statistically significant ($p < 0.01$ by chi square), as would be expected from the degree of severity of the deprivation. The refusal rates for the justification conditions—15 for High and 18 for Low—were not significantly different.

It is interesting to note that all subjects who refused gave as their reason either conflicting prior commitments or special diets that didn't allow them to go without liquids. None gave answers that directly implicated the unpleasantness of the anticipated experience, the "forced compliance" nature of the volunteering, etc. It should be remembered that all subjects indicated their decisions to continue or drop out on a form that the experimenter could not see;

thus they were able to complete the alleged "first experiment" despite their decision not to continue with the "second experiment."

Baseline Effects of Thirst Arousal on the Experimental Tasks

As mentioned earlier, it was necessary to determine the effects of thirst arousal on the various tasks without any dissonance in order to have a baseline against which any cognitive reevaluation via dissonance could be compared. Control subjects made thirsty by eating the sauce-cracker combination behaved differently on a number of experimental tasks from the nonthirsty Controls, who had eaten their crackers with peanut butter.

1. *Thirst Ratings.* Immediately after the thirst arousal, the mean self-rating of thirst for the High Thirst Controls was 50 ("quite thirsty"), as compared with only 15 ("not at all thirsty") for the Low Thirst Controls ($p < 0.001$). After the dissonance arousal (in the other groups), the mean ratings of the Controls remained divergent—(40 for High Controls and 18 for Low Controls; $p < 0.001$). These differences were eliminated once the groups were given the opportunity to consume as much water as they wanted (the mean ratings for both groups declined to about 12).

2. *Water Consumption.* The High Control group drank more water than did the Low Controls—a mean of 151.0 cc. compared with 105.4 cc. ($p < 0.001$).

3. *Thirst Words Perceived and Preferred.* While the mean number of thirst words chosen on this test by the Low Control subjects was 7.7 (indicating an equal frequency of choosing each type of word), the High Control subjects showed a definite preference for thirst words. These thirsty subjects selected an average of 9.7 thirst-related words to 5.3 neutral words. This choice is significantly different from that made by the Low Controls ($p < 0.05$).

Incidentally, reaction times in choosing one or another type of word did not differentiate among any of the groups, either Control or Dissonance, and thus will not be discussed again.

4. *Learning of Paired Associates.* While the difference between High and Low Thirst Controls on this test was in the expected direction of the former learning the 12 thirst-related paired associates faster than did the latter, the effect only approaches statistical significance ($p < 0.10$). The mean number of trials required to learn the list perfectly was 4.9 for the High Controls, while it took one more trial (5.9) for the Low Controls.

5. *Fantasy Measures—TAT.* There were no significant differences among any of the conditions (Control or Dissonance) in frequency of need-for-water or water themas written to describe the neutral TAT picture. Thus there was no generalized difference among groups in utilization of fantasy responding. However, there was a quite specific effect when shown the drive-related TAT picture; the High Thirst Controls wrote significantly more need-for-water themas than did the Low Controls (10 vs. 3; $p < 0.05$). Over both fantasy measures, on the drive-related TAT picture, the High Controls composed twice as many drive-related stories as the Low Controls (26 vs. 13; $p < 0.05$).

The results on the frequency of trouble themas for both pictures were again in the expected direction, but they were not statistically significant; the thirsty subjects gave a total of twice as many stories which were scored as indicating some trouble.

Not only can we now be assured that the thirst manipulation employed in this study was effective in influencing a wide variety of experimental behaviors, but we also have some guidelines against which to estimate the extent and direction of dissonance effects.

Cognitive Re-evaluation of Thirst via Dissonance Reduction

Since the High Thirst Controls ate the same thirst-inducing sauce-cracker combination as did the Dissonance subjects, the only differences between the groups were the expectation about future events and the decision to commit oneself to them. It would be expected that the High Dissonance subjects would generally be similar in relevant responding to the Low Thirst Control and that the Low Dissonance subjects and the High Thirst Controls would be comparable.

1. *Thirst Ratings*. The self-ratings of experienced thirst are presented in Figure 1. Immediately after the arousal of thirst, all groups except the Low Controls rated themselves as "quite thirsty" (means from 41 to 52—none statistically different). A few minutes later, after dissonance had been aroused, there were only slight (nonsignificant) changes in thirst ratings in all groups—except the High Dissonance group. While some of the other groups reported feeling a little more or less thirsty (mean differences from -9.7 to $+5.2$), the High Dissonance group reduced their self-evaluation dramatically by 23.5 scale units!

This change in thirst ratings makes the High Dissonance group significantly different not only from the Low Dissonance group ($p < 0.01$), but also from the Moderate Dissonance group ($p < 0.01$), the Refusal group[3] ($p < 0.05$), and the High Thirst Controls ($p < 0.05$). In fact, the previously thirsty High Dissonance group rated itself at 28.1 after dissonance arousal, while the group that was initially not at all thirsty (the Low Control) was fewer than 10 scale points less thirsty (mean = 18.3; $p < 0.10$).

After all groups drank, the ratings of experienced thirst declined to very low levels where all the means were within 5 scale points of each other (and, of course, none was statistically different).

2. *Water Consumption*. The results for the amount of water consumed by the subjects during the opportunity to drink are presented in Figure 2, where several findings are obvious. First, the High Dissonance subjects drank less water than any group except for the Low Thirst Controls. The 128.4 cc. of water consumed by the High Dissonance group was greater than the 105.4 cc. drunk by the Low Controls, who were not thirsty ($p < 0.05$), but it was significantly less than the 151.0 cc. drunk by the High Controls ($p < 0.05$), less than the

3. The Moderate Dissonance groups did not differ significantly on any measure and were therefore combined, as were the Refusal subjects from the various treatments.

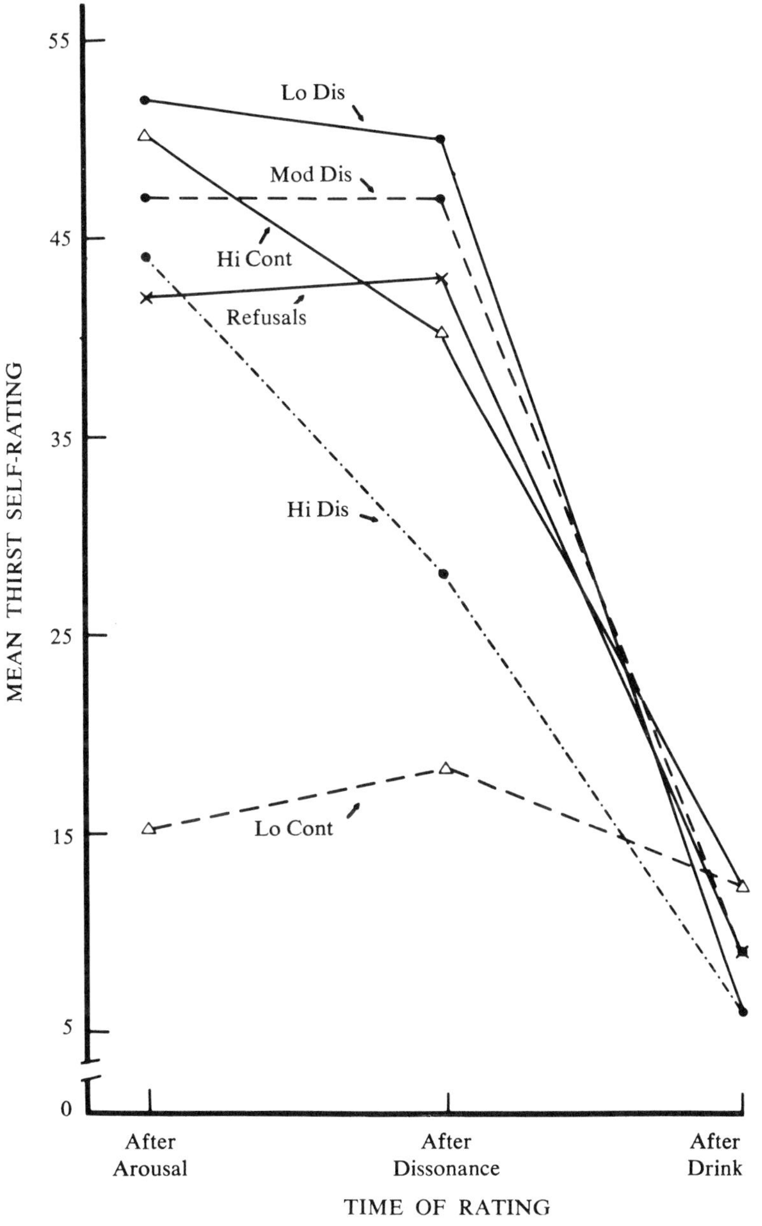

FIGURE 1

Mean thirst self-ratings after thirst arousal, after dissonance arousal, and after water consumption; presented for the Low and High Control, High Dissonance, combined Moderate Dissonance, Low Dissonance, and combined Refusal groups.

138.4 and 155.6 cc. drunk by the Moderate and Low Dissonance groups, respectively ($p < 0.05$), and also less than the Refusal group (150.0 cc., $p < 0.05$).

The linear decrement in drinking as dissonance arousal increased is also statistically significant, with each of the three groups being different ($p < 0.05$) from the others. The Refusal group resembles both the Low Dissonance subjects and the High Thirst Controls, but certainly not the High Dissonance group.

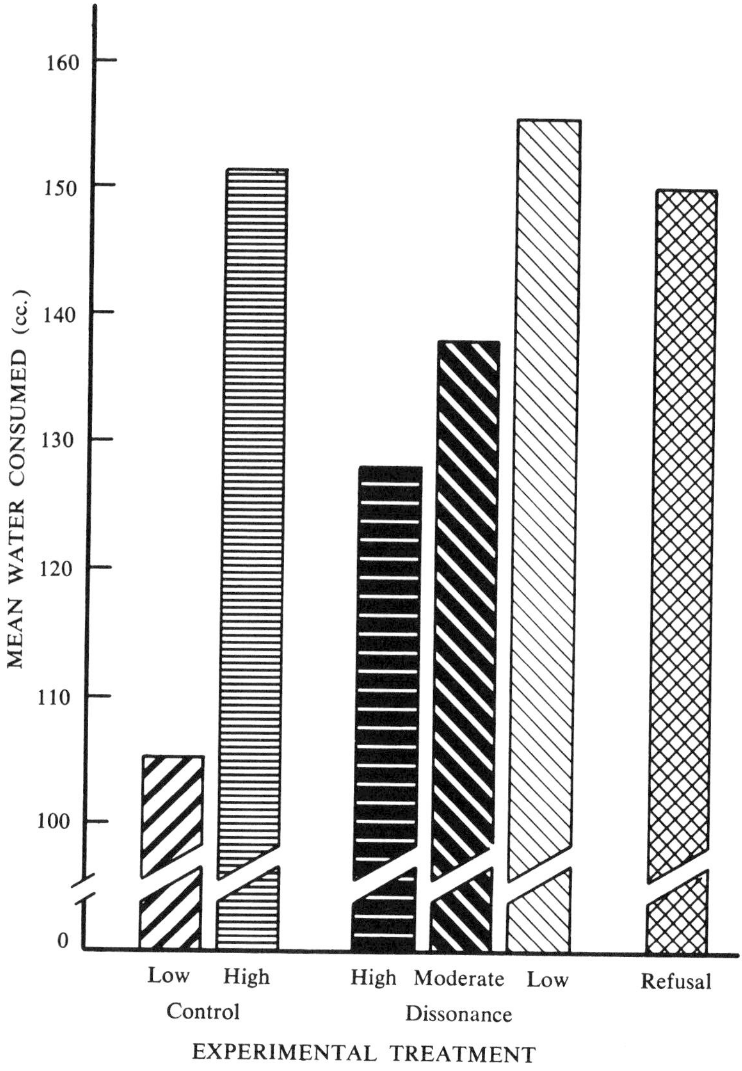

FIGURE 2
Mean water consumption in cubic centimeters (cc.) for the Low and High Control, High Dissonance, combined Moderate Dissonance, Low Dissonance, and combined Refusal groups.

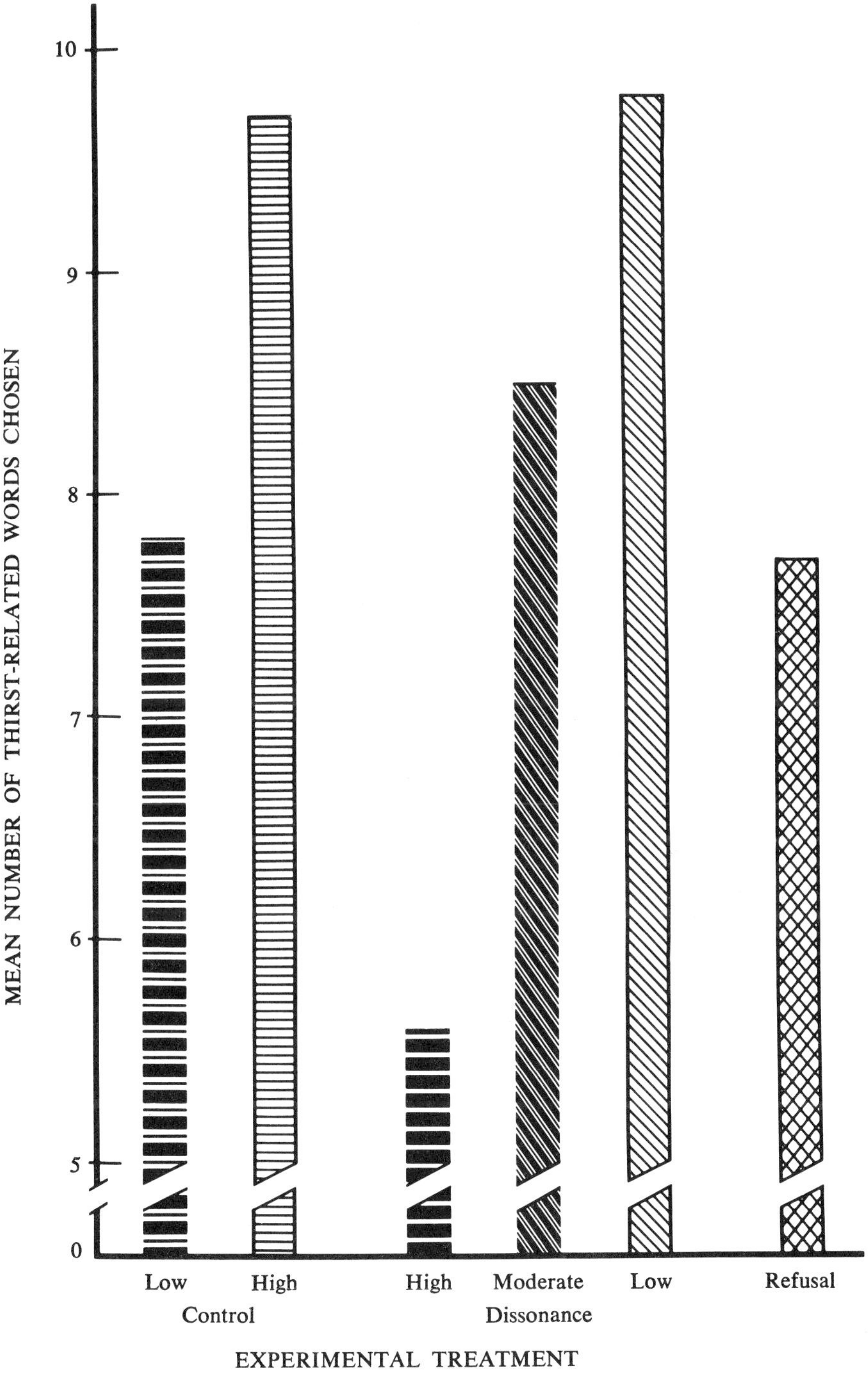

FIGURE 3
Mean number of thirst words chosen by subjects in the Low and High Control, High Dissonance, combined Moderate Dissonance, Low Dissonance, and combined Refusal groups.

3. *Thirst Words Perceived and Preferred.* It will be recalled that when Control subjects had to choose one word out of each of 15 word pairs that he had supposedly been shown before, the High Thirst Controls chose more thirst-related than neutral words, while the Low Thirst Controls did not show a preference for either type of word, choosing each with equal frequency.

The results for this measure are presented in Figure 3 and fit the pattern of results already obtained, with the exception of the High Dissonance group, which in a sense overdoes it. Again, there is a linear decrement in response as dissonance arousal increases, with the Low Dissonance group (mean = 9.8) again behaving like the High Thirst Controls (mean = 9.7), the Moderate Dissonance group (mean = 8.5) being intermediate, and the High Dissonance

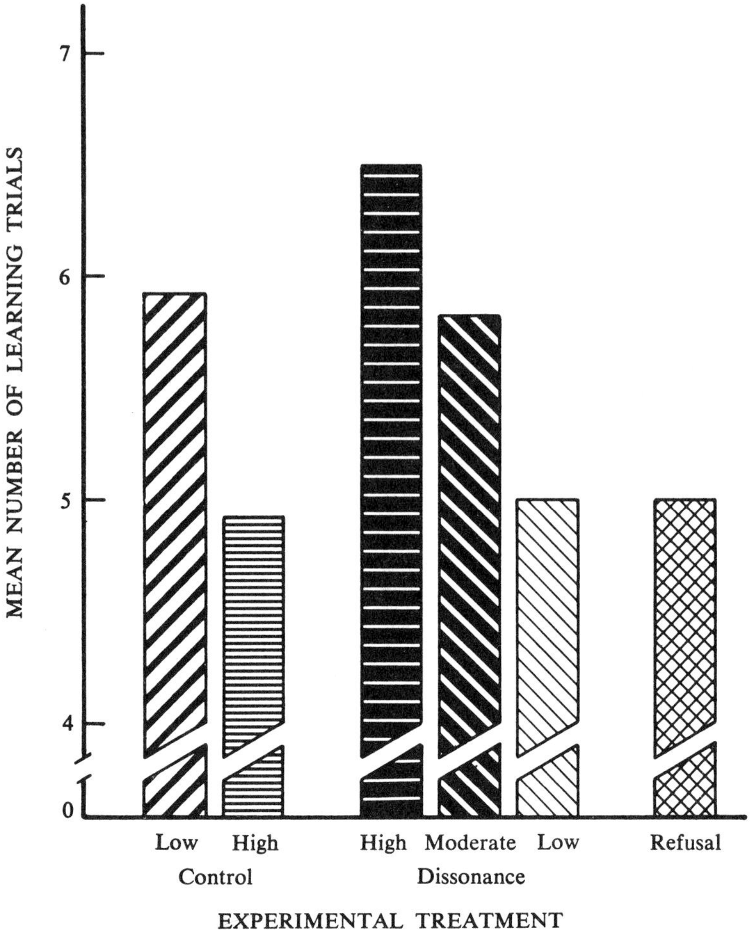

FIGURE 4
Mean number of trials required to learn correctly 12 paired associates by subjects in the Low and High Control, High Dissonance, combined Moderate Dissonance, Low Dissonance, and combined Refusal groups.

group choosing the fewest thirst-related words of any group (mean = 5.6). The High Dissonance group differs from these others by 0.01 and 0.05 levels of confidence, respectively.

That the High Dissonance subjects chose even fewer thirst-related words than the Low Thirst Controls ($p < 0.10$) indicates something more than a simple lowering of thirst motivation—perhaps an avoidance or denial phenomenon. We shall attend to this possibility in the remainder of the data.

4. *Learning of Paired Associates.* Figure 4 presents the data for the mean number of trials required to learn correctly the 12 paired associates. As reported earlier, the Control groups demonstrated a tendency for thirsty subjects to learn faster than nonthirsty ones.

Once more, there is a linear effect of dissonance arousal on this behavior—only this time, the response measure goes up as dissonance increases. Again, the Low Dissonance and Refusal groups behaved comparably to the High Thirst Controls, learning the list most quickly, in fewer than five trials.

On the other hand, the High Dissonance subjects took longer than any other group to learn the list (a mean of 6.5 trials), significantly longer than either the Low Dissonance or High Control groups ($p < 0.05$) and somewhat longer (although not significantly so) than the Low Thirst Controls. This last result is in agreement with the avoidance or denial process postulated to explain why the High Dissonance group chose fewer thirst-related words than the non-thirsty subjects.

5. *Fantasy Measures—TAT.* The last set of data to be presented is a behavioral check of the effects of dissonance arousal on projections of thirst motivation. Figure 5 graphically presents group differences on the measure of frequency of need-for-water themas on neutral and drive-related TAT pictures.

On the neutral TAT picture, there were no differences between the High and Low Dissonance groups in their use of need-for-water or water themas. However, on the drive-related TAT picture, fewer High Dissonance subjects wrote stories projecting either type of the water-related themas than did the Low Dissonance subjects ($p < 0.10$).

While 12 subjects in the Low Dissonance group wrote stories expressing need-for-water themas, only 3 subjects in the Low Control did (a significant difference—$p < 0.05$). The High Dissonance group was not different from the Low Control group on this measure, and although fewer subjects in this condition ($n = 6$) wrote need-for-water themas than in the High Control group ($n = 10$), that difference is not statistically significant.

In Figure 5 we can again note the inverse linear effect of dissonance upon the thirst-related behavior of interpreting the drive-related TAT picture. However, an interesting finding emerges when one compares the relative frequency of need-for-water themas when they are inappropriate (i.e., in response to the neutral picture) to when they are appropriate (i.e., in response to the drive-related picture). Obviously, the frequency of need-for-water themas should be greater where the stimulus characteristics of the materials call forth such responses, and this is the case for all groups except one—the High Dissonance group. The High Dissonance group gives more need-for-water themas to the neutral than to the drive-relevant TAT picture!

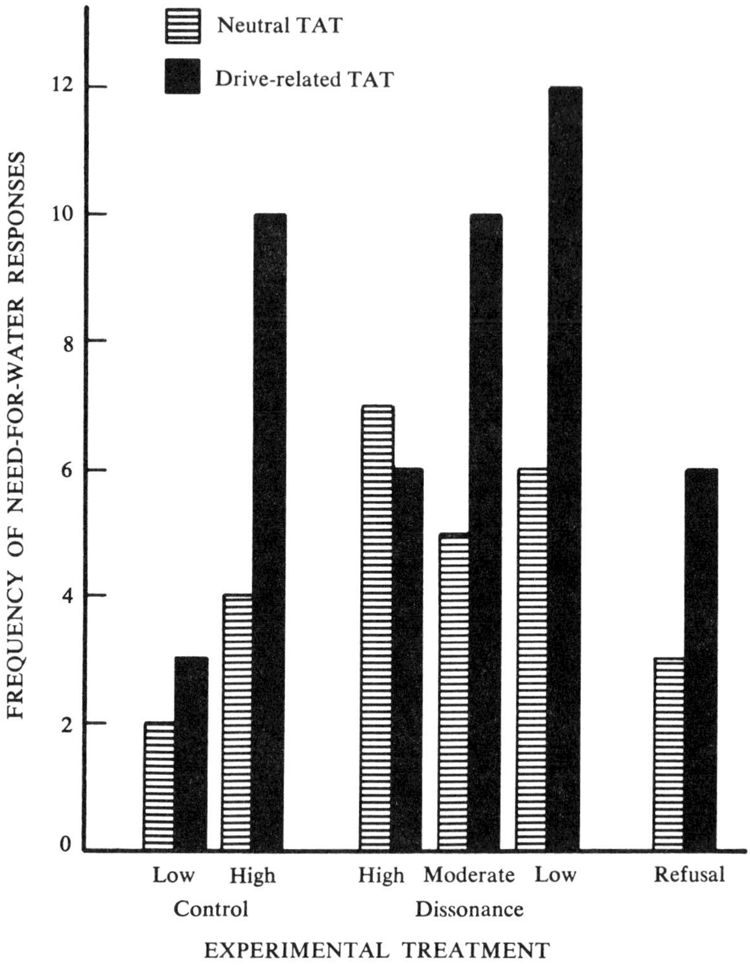

FIGURE 5
Frequency of subjects with need-for-water themas in their TAT stories, presented for the Control, Dissonance, and Refusal conditions.

This interesting finding receives additional support when we consider the final scoring category, the frequency of themas depicting trouble. The High Dissonance group had more subjects who gave trouble themas to the neutral picture than any other group. The frequency of trouble themas on the neutral picture is significantly greater for High Dissonance group ($n = 13$) than for either the Low Dissonance ($n = 6$) or the Low Thirst Control groups ($n = 4$; $p < 0.05$ in each case). Thus, the High Dissonance subjects were bothered by something, not only more than the Low Dissonance subjects, but also more than the Low Thirst Controls. They reacted to the neutral picture as the Thirsty Controls did to the drive-related picture.

DISCUSSION

This study has shown that the arousal of thirst can be induced experimentally in human subjects and that its effects on a wide variety of behaviors can be clearly delineated. However, the major concern of the research was to assess whether the reduction of thirst motivation could be accomplished by purely cognitive manipulations. All available evidence points to the conclusion that subjects in the High Dissonance condition behaved on a series of tasks as if they were not thirsty, although they should have been as thirsty as any of the other experimental groups since they were exposed to identical thirst-arousing operations.

It is assumed that the behavior of these High Dissonance subjects reflected their attempt to reduce the dissonance occasioned by voluntarily committing themselves to future water deprivation for a long period of time with rather minimal rational justification. These attempts at dissonance reduction then led them to experience less thirst, to drink less water, to perceive fewer thirst words, to learn thirst-related paired associates more slowly, and to give fewer need-for-water themas and more trouble or disturbance themas in response to TAT pictures. In general, this group differs significantly from both the Low Dissonance group and the High Thirst Control group. On most measures, the High Dissonance group closely resembled subjects who were not thirsty (the Low Thirst Control subjects).

Thus, this study both substantiates and extends the provocative findings of Brehm's earlier thirst study (Article 4). The trends he obtained with self-ratings of thirst and water consumption are statistically supported here. In addition, since our design created three levels of dissonance, it was possible to examine the functional relation between magnitude of arousal and behavior change. As predicted by the theory of cognitive dissonance, the effect was linear, with the Moderate Dissonance group experiencing a thirst intermediate between the Low and High Dissonance groups. Moreover, the predicted effects were obtained at several levels of analysis (on very different tasks): consummatory, behavioral, and fantasy.

At this point let us consider briefly several interesting findings worthy of further investigation. It will be remembered that all the subjects rated the anticipated deprivation as more unpleasant for the average person than they rated it for themselves. While there were no differences among the conditions on each of these ratings, the difference between the two ratings suggests that the subjects did reduce some dissonance through convincing themselves that it would *not* be as bad for them as it would be for others. Thus, the use of projection as a technique for altering the basis of social comparison may be considered a mode of dissonance reduction that has not been treated extensively (cf. Bramel, 1962). When it is difficult to deny the reality of the environmental conditions (external and/or internal), one can achieve some dissonance reduction by perceiving that it would be much worse for others, or that relative to persons to whom the subject usually compares himself, he is not reacting too badly.

There is much in the present data to suggest that in addition to, or perhaps even rather than, thirst reduction through cognitive re-evaluation, what took place among the High Dissonance subjects was an active process of denial of thirst motivation. On three measures they behaved even more extremely than did the Low Thirst Control group: they chose fewer thirst-related words, required more trials to learn a list of paired associates which had liquid-related members, and gave more fantasy themas with a troubled content to a neutral TAT picture. The question then arises as to whether the dissonant individual is actually resolving the state of motivation created by cognitive inconsistency, or whether he is suppressing the cognitions associated with the conditions of deprivation.

Festinger's position on the issue clearly favors the former alternative: "The dissonance reduction process is not one of distortion, but mainly one of reevaluation in that experimental situation" (1964, p. 59). However, the work of Klein (1954) and his associates stresses the role of cognitive interference in the solution of various tasks. In fact, some individuals can be characterized by the extent to which their performance is hampered by habitual patterns of interference.

Other researchers (Silverman & Silverman, 1964), in a study on subliminal perception, have pointed out:

> If a drive-related stimulus is presented, some of the activated ideas may be threatening to the subject and a defensive need may arise. Such a need can influence the subsequent cognitive act in a number of ways: (a) it can play a role in determining *which* specific traces of the schema the subject "selects" for use in the cognitive act. For example, it may lead him to verbalize a symbolically related idea rather than a drive-dominated conceptually related idea, the latter being too threatening.

This may well have been what happened when our High Dissonance subjects responded to the drive-related TAT picture. Here they projected less of a concern for water than they did in response to the neutral TAT picture. To the latter, however, there was more projection of trouble themas. This may mean that while a direct admission of thirst was too threatening, the thirst could become symbolically verbalized through the trouble themas—an indication that something was indeed bothering the High Dissonance subjects. Thus it would appear that the subjects in the High Dissonance condition resorted to a denial of their level of motivation and of the deprivation conditions associated with it.

Further evidence supporting the interpretation that dissonance reduction may have resulted in a denial or avoidance process comes from the task in which the subjects had to select the one word in each pair of words that supposedly had been presented in a prior "subliminal" stimulus slide. We had expected that thirsty subjects would select more thirst words than nonthirsty subjects and that subjects who reduced their thirst in the High Dissonance condition would select fewer thirst words than those in the Low Dissonance and High Control conditions. The results confirmed these expectations. The

Moderate Dissonance subjects chose significantly more thirst words than the High Dissonance subjects, and the Low Dissonance subjects chose more than the Moderate Dissonance subjects, although not significantly more. Still, the trend is clear. The higher the dissonance, the fewer the thirst words chosen. A separate linear analysis of this trend shows it to be significant at less than the 1-per-cent level. While the High Thirst Controls and the Low Dissonance subjects selected more thirst words, consistent with their drive level, the High Dissonance subjects less frequently chose thirst words—perhaps in order to avoid a possible thirst-associated threat. There is one more result to support this contention: the High Dissonance subjects selected even fewer thirst words than did the Low Thirst Controls. These findings are consistent with an avoidance hypothesis.

The central role of cognitive controls is most clearly demonstrated in the learning task. It was expected (following Epstein and Lewitt's 1962 work) that differences in thirst motivation would be reflected in differential learning rates of thirst-specific stimuli. While the effect obtained with the Controls was in the predicted direction—i.e., the High Thirst Controls learned faster than the Low—this difference only approached statistical significance. On the other hand, the difference between the two Dissonance treatments (under equal deprivation conditions) was large and quite significant. On this task, also, the performance of the High Dissonance subjects was even more extreme than that of the Low Thirst Controls. Thus it appears that this learning performance can be brought under finer control by manipulation of relevant cognitive variables than by the manipulation of the physical state or biological variables usually associated with drives like thirst.

A person whose mouth is hot and dry (as from the cracker-sauce combination) and who expects to go without water for a relatively long time ought to drink a lot when given the opportunity to do so before the start of the deprivation period. The High Thirst Controls did exactly that. However, the High Dissonance subjects—who were under the same physical stimulus conditions—drank much less. This is what we would have expected from the self-ratings of experienced thirst—if they were valid. A correlation across all conditions (which were relatively consistent) between the thirst ratings and the amount of water consumed revealed a highly significant ($p < 0.01$), positive value of $r = +0.41$. When a person convinces himself that he is not very thirsty, he drinks less water. Thus, motivation is not a simple function of the "basic drive level," but it also depends somewhat on the cognitions associated with the motivational state.

We drink for a number of reasons, and we satisfy our needs in a variety of ways. Social drinking is not like drinking in order to satisfy a specific motive state. Having another drink when not actually thirsty, or foregoing another drink when thirsty, is tied up with our expectations of future demands. This may be kept in mind when the next Martini is put in front of us.

SKOAL and L'CHAIM

Editor's Comments

Mansson's study borrows some techniques, manipulations, and approaches from earlier research presented in this volume, and it incorporates previously validated response measures and integrates them in a carefully thought-out and rigorously executed study. Inductions of choice and justification are comparable to those established in the study on control of pain by Zimbardo et al. reported in the next section (Article 7); the thirst manipulation is based upon that of Brock and Grant (Article 5); the basic dissonance paradigm follows that of Brehm (Article 4); and the work of Epstein and of Klein on cognitive controls is evident throughout. What is added are the appropriate control groups, the manipulation of anticipated severity of future deprivation, three levels of dissonance arousal, controls against biasing the decision to accept or refuse deprivation, as well as a procedure for collecting data from the refusal subjects. Thus this study provides a body of sound data that certainly increases our confidence not only that expectancies can modify motivation but that the interaction of choice, justification, and anticipated deprivation can modify thirst motivation and a host of behaviors related to thirst in predictable directions.

Of greatest theoretical interest, of course, are the findings indicating that the High Dissonance subjects did not reduce their level of motivation in a direct and simple fashion, resulting in behavior exactly like that of subjects who are not thirsty. Rather they appear to be protesting too much that they are not thirsty! On several measures they score as less thirsty than even the Low Thirst Controls, and on the TAT measure their need-for-water responses are suppressed when the cue value of the stimulus clearly ought to elicit such themas and are more frequent when the cue value is ambiguous. This, in addition to the finding that these subjects projected more trouble or general conflict themas in response to the neutral picture than the other groups, suggests that they are indeed in a state of active coping with the reality of a persistent burning sensation in the mouth and the cognitive demands to be internally consistent with the overt, public commitment to forego drinking water. It is likely that a temporal factor is involved here and that after a while there would be a less conflicted resolution in which attempts at cognitive consistency would override moderate-intensity levels of the drive stimulus, resulting in a functional lowering of the drive itself. Unfortunately, none of the research in this series incorporates repeated measurements over time, but such an approach is clearly demanded by these results as well as others soon to be reported. Walster (1964) has shown that dissonance-induced changes in attitudinal ratings vary over time in a complex way, and we would expect the motivational effects of concern in the present research to be influenced by temporal considerations as well.

While the correlation between thirst ratings and amount of water consumed is similar to that in Brock and Grant's study (+0.41 and +0.45, respectively), in the latter study this positive relation held only for the Control groups and not for the hypnotized Dissonance groups. In the present study, the correlation is similar for all groups; therefore, the lower water consumption by the High

Dissonance subjects may be reflecting an overt attempt to be consistent with their self-ratings of thirst rather than being an independent or direct measure of changes in thirst motivation.

The behavioral profile of the Refusal subjects offers little support for the criticism that such subjects are the high-sensitivity dropouts from the High Dissonance treatment. Their subjective ratings of thirst immediately after the manipulation of thirst arousal were more similar to those of the High Dissonance (to-be-committed) subjects than to the ratings of any other group. Even after the dissonance arousal attempt, their thirst ratings were still lower (although not significantly) than either the Low or Moderate Dissonance group. With regard to water consumption and learning, the Refusals behaved more like the Low Dissonance group, while on the word-preference task they were equivalent to the Low Thirst Control, as they were on the frequency of need-for-water themas to the neutral TAT. To the drive-related TAT, they reacted more like the High Dissonance group than like any other. This variability in their relative position across tasks contrasts with the stable ordering from measure to measure of the other groups. Thus it appears that refusing this type of commitment to deprivation is not a simple function of sensitivity to or severity of deprivation but is influenced by a complex of motives.

The evidence presented thus far strongly supports our basic thesis in showing that the effects of hunger and thirst cannot be predicted simply knowing the extent of deprivation or the arousal operations since cognitive variables may substantially alter expression of these drive states and enable man to exercise considerable control over them. But have we been dealing with truly aversive stimulus states? How much hunger or thirst is induced in healthy college students as a consequence of missing several meals, or going without liquids for part of a day, or even having a hot, dry mouth for a short period of time? Would we expect the same cognitive control if the drive stimulus induced high levels of repeated, unavoidable pain? The next study suggests that if dissonance increases with degree of aversiveness of the discrepant behavior, then *greater* motivational control is possible as the initial drive stimulus is more intense.

Section C

Pain

7. THE CONTROL OF EXPERIMENTAL PAIN

Philip G. Zimbardo, Arthur Cohen, Matisyohu Weisenberg, Leonard Dworkin, and Ira Firestone

> Every feeling person knows from personal experience what pain is, yet scientists have found it extraordinarily difficult to agree on a satisfactory definition for it. The question is not a metaphysical one. It has profound bearing on the search for ways to relieve pain and on basic human fears. Probably no subject in medical science interests people more than this one.
>
> W. K. Livingston, 1953, p. 59

In contrast to the drives of hunger and thirst, the natural incidences of which decrease with affluence and technological advancement, pain remains a universal experience. Although pain *relief* may be facilitated by modern drugs and surgery (sometimes equally well by the witch doctor's remedies), susceptibility to pain is part of every man's inheritance. Therefore, there is more than theoretical interest behind the question of whether man can control his pain in the way the previously presented studies have shown he can modify his hunger and thirst.

Pain can be described (after Barber, 1959) as a complex response to a nociceptive stimulus that typically includes four major components: (1) a sensation of pain, (2) discomfort, (3) muscular withdrawal movements, and (4) measurable alterations in physiological systems (e.g., blood pressure or galvanic skin response).

If pain is the sensory accompaniment of a protective reflex that is obviously important for survival, to what extent can cognitive factors be involved? According to some investigators (Hardy, Wolff, & Goodell, 1952), there is a mathematically specifiable relationship between physical-stimulus intensity and pain intensity. Such psychophysical evidence is presented in support of the

SOURCE: Zimbardo, Philip, G., A. R. Cohen, Matisyohu Weisenberg, Leonard Dworkin, and Ira Firestone, "The Control of Experimental Pain," unpublished.

assumption that pain is a primary sensation arising from a physiological system that directly interconnects skin receptors and the pain center.

The perceptive analysis of Melzack and Wall (1965) makes apparent the inadequacies of such a "specificity theory of pain" (cf. Sweet, 1959) and its opposing theory of "patterning" (i.e., that pain is determined by stimulus intensity, input patterning, and central summation rather than by physiological specialization; cf. Sinclair, 1955). Their review of the relevant evidence leads to the conclusion that the amount and quality of perceived pain are determined by many psychological variables as well as by sensory input. Observations by Beecher (1959) and Pavlov (1927) indicate that "activities in the central nervous system may intervene between stimulus and sensation which may invalidate any simple 'psychophysical law'" (Melzack & Wall, 1965, p. 972). Beecher noted that most American soldiers wounded in the bloody battle at the Anzio beachhead in World War II "entirely denied pain from their extensive wounds or had so little that they did not want any medication to relieve it" (1959, p. 165). Pavlov demonstrated that when electric shocks, burns, or cuts were used as conditioned stimuli preceding the unconditioned stimulus of food, his trained dogs responded to these noxious stimuli only as signals for food, and they never showed "even the tiniest and most subtle" signs of pain (1927, p. 30).

Melzack and Wall contend further that the existing theories of pain cannot account for the finding that the threshold for pain in response to shock on one arm can be raised by giving a second shock to the other arm as long as 100 milliseconds *later* (Halliday & Mingay, 1961). Accordingly, they propose a "gate control" theory of pain, which integrates the valid aspects of physiological specialization and patterning theory with what is now known about central control of afferent input and spinal mechanisms. The reader is referred to their article for a fuller account of the physiological and mechanical functioning of the model, since for our present, rather limited purpose it is sufficient to consider only their central mechanism.

Melzack and Wall propose that when pain occurs, selective brain processes are activated that exert control over sensory input via a central control trigger. This system makes it possible for central nervous system activities—subserving attention, emotion, and memories of prior experience—to alter afferent input. Both the dorsal column-medial lemniscus system and the dorso-lateral are candidates for this role because they carry precise information about the nature and location of the stimulus and they conduct very rapidly; either of them could influence (through activation of selective brain processes) information being carried over slower conducting fibers or pathways.

> The model suggests that psychological factors such as past experience, attention, and emotion influence pain response and perception by acting on the gate control system. The degree of central control, however, would be determined, in part at least, by the temporal-spatial properties of the input patterns. Some of the most unbearable pains, such as cardiac pain, rise so rapidly that the patient is unable to achieve any control over them. On the other hand, more slowly rising temporal patterns are susceptible to central control and may

> allow the patient to "think of something else" or use other stratagems to keep pain under control (Melzack & Wall, 1965, p. 978).

If pain is one of the relevant cognitions in a dissonance-arousing situation, then we propose that the experience of pain can be modified (brought under some degree of control) by stratagems involved in the process of reducing cognitive dissonance. It was the goal of this investigation (and of the two related studies that follow) to develop an elegant experimental design to study whether the variables of choice and justification could be implicated in the complex process of controlling pain. In addition, we hoped to determine the extent to which such cognitive control was possible and the nature of the specific psychological stratagems that could be employed. In so doing, we examined several components of pain response: subjective experience (i.e., self-reports of pain); overt behavior known to be influenced (motivated) by pain intensity (i.e., learning); and finally alterations in a physiological system (i.e., changes in the electrical conductance of the skin, or galvanic skin response).

OVERVIEW OF EXPERIMENTAL DESIGN

We used a simple before-after nonfactorial design, with shock level varied in three Control groups, with justification for commitment (to a series of additional shocks) manipulated within two Dissonance groups, and with choice varied between Dissonance and Control treatments. The relative effectiveness of specifiable physical manipulations of shock intensity in the Controls was contrasted with cognitive alterations produced in the Dissonance groups on three dependent measures.

The experiment involved three phases: (1) precommitment, during which all subjects were treated similarly and measurements were taken of subjective, behavioral, and physiological reactions to shock; (2) commitment, during which the manipulations of choice and justification were introduced; and (3) post-commitment, during which shock level was varied in the Control groups and "after" measures identical to the "before" measures were taken. The subject's view of the experiment can be coordinated with the sequential procedural execution of the experiment with the aid of the flow diagram presented in Figure 1. Each step in the following procedure has been keyed to this diagram.

PROCEDURE

Each subject[1] was seated in a sound-resistant cubicle and told only that he was about to participate in a study involving the effects of electric shock on learning

1. A sample of 80 male undergraduates was used, after first pretesting 100 different subjects in order to minimize error variance by empirically determining the best incentives to use and the best wording of the rational justifications, testing different learning tasks and shock procedures, and familiarizing ourselves with the techniques of physiological recording. The subjects were required to participate in order to fulfill an introductory psychology course requirement at New York University.

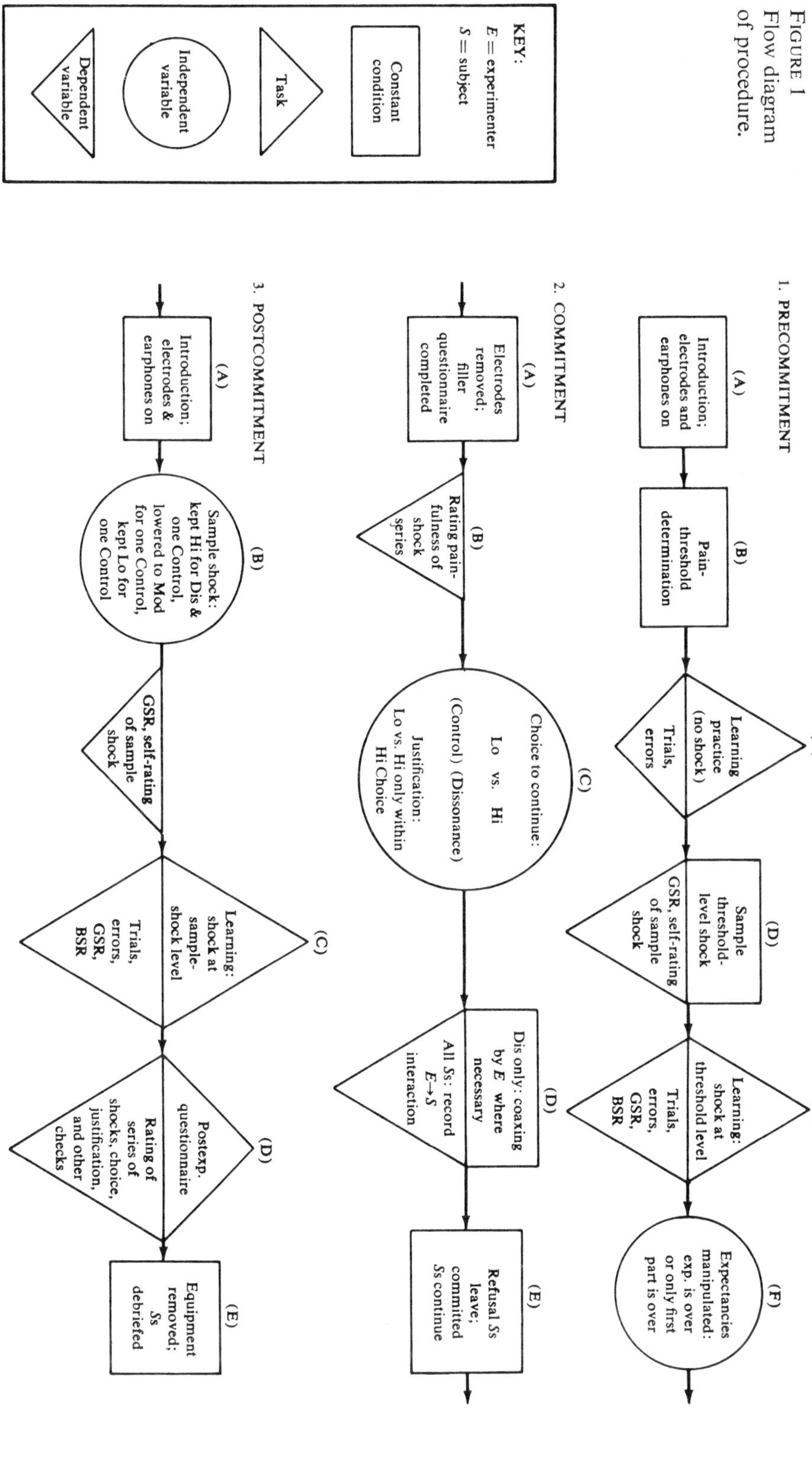

FIGURE 1
Flow diagram of procedure.

and physiology. Interaction between the subject and experimenter was kept minimal; after attaching shock electrodes to one of the subject's hands and GSR (galvanic skin response) electrodes to the other, the experimenter left the subject alone. All subsequent instructions were delivered to the subject through earphones by a standardized tape recording, and all the subject's verbal responses were relayed by means of a microphone (see Figure 1, 1A).

The subjects heard that this experiment was part of a research project being conducted by their psychology professor (Dr. Z.) and was being run by his assistant (Dr. M. W.). After hearing about the general nature of the experiment, the subject's threshold for painful shock was determined. It was necessary that the stimulus be painful since the presumed cognitive effects of a weak stimulus might not be appreciable. This was determined by the threshold procedure and observations of muscular movements to be described.

Determination of Threshold for Painful Shock (1B)

Shock was presented by means of a Grass SD5 stimulator. Frequency and duration of the shock were held constant for all subjects at 120 cps and 4.5 milliseconds, respectively. Voltage was varied for each subject on the basis of the perceived painfulness of the shock, as determined by threshold measurements. During the threshold procedure, the experimenter administered a 5-volt shock and increased it in increments of 5 volts to determine (in this order) the level at which the subject perceived the stimulus,[2] the level at which he was uncomfortable, and the level at which the shock became painful. After this point was reached, several shocks slightly higher and lower in voltage were administered and comparative judgments were obtained to validate the initial "painful" response. The painful-shock level used in the rest of the experiment was this final threshold level.

Since many New York University students are quite sophisticated, they realized that if they said the shocks were painful before they actually were, they could avoid being given really painful shocks. To counteract this effect, a second crude criterion of painfulness was employed: the shock had to be of sufficient intensity to produce an unconditioned arm withdrawal strong enough to break a rubber restraining strap. So that the jolting of the subject's arm would not disturb his line of vision during the learning task, his fingers were taped to the shock electrodes, the shock electrodes and his arm were strapped to a cotton-padded board, and his hand was secured to the board. There is little question that each subject did receive a series of painful, unavoidable shocks.

Learning Practice with No Shock (1C)

Th subject was then shown a list of nine words (see Table 1) presented in serial order and told that his task was to learn the words so that he could correctly

2. Subjects in one control group, who were given low-level shocks throughout the experiment stopped at this point in the threshold procedure and never received any painful shocks.

TABLE 1

EXPERIMENTAL WORD LISTS

	List I (Practice)	List II* (Precommitment)	List III (Postcommitment)
1.	Boy	Gentle[a]	Quick[e]
2.	Girl	Small[b]	Merry[f]
3.	School	Tiny[b]	Joyful[f]
4.	Work	Moist[c]	Fast[e]
5.	Country	Rare[d]	Gay[f]
6.	House	Mild[a]	Rapid[e]
7.	Grass	Scarce[d]	Swift[e]
8.	Green	Wet[c]	Happy[f]
9.	Young	Little[b]	Speedy[e]

* Adjectives with same letter designation are members of a semantically similar group.—Ed.

anticipate each one when the preceding word in the list was shown. He was also told that there would be no shock, and he was instructed to continue until told to stop.

The criteria for learning this and the subsequent lists were two successive errorless trials. The controlled rate of exposure for each practice word was 2 seconds on and 2 seconds off. The practice list was used to familiarize the subject with the general nature of the learning task and to provide him with some easily earned positive reinforcement.

Sample Shock and Initial Subjective Response (1D)

Before the next learning task was presented, the subject received a sample shock, "so that you will be able to get an idea of what the rest of the series will be like, and so that we may calibrate our recording instruments." After a 1-minute waiting period, the subject received a shock at his threshold for painfulness. He gave his subjective reaction to it by calling out a number from 0 to 100 to indicate how painful it felt. Projected on the screen was a scale with the following labels: 0 = not painful at all, 25 = slightly painful, 50 = moderately painful, 75 = very painful, and 100 = extremely painful. Most reactions varied around a score of 50, with none below 30 and a few as high as 80.

Serial-Anticipation Task with Shock, GSR, and BSR (1E)

Our major behavioral measure was verbal rote-learning performance as influenced by shock level. Again the serial-anticipation method was used, but this time the subject was told that he would receive a series of electric shocks while learning the words and that

> . . . these shocks will *not* follow a regular pattern, but will be entirely at random. You will not be shocked for guessing a word either right or wrong, but the shocks will come at random, predetermined intervals regardless of what you do. Let me make it clear that the effect shock will have on you varies from person to person. Some are disrupted by it, others are facilitated by it. Obviously, because of these individual differences we are interested in this problem, and this is one of the reasons for conducting this study.

Two shocks were delivered on each trial according to a prearranged, random sequence that was, in fact, independent of the subject's performance.

The word lists were specially selected from an interesting study by Carson (1958). One list was used in the first part of the study (precommitment) and a parallel list in the second part of the study (postcommitment). Both lists were composed of groups of adjectives that were semantically similar to each other but dissimilar to members of the other clusters (see Table 1).

The assumptions underlying the use of these word lists were based upon Gibson's (1940) formulation of the nature of verbal rote learning and the effect of drive level on generalization. Carson clearly describes (1958, p. 99) the learning process involved:

> To the extent that the stimuli are similar (formally or in meaning), the response to one stimulus tends to generalize to (be evoked by) other stimuli in the list in proportion to the degree of similarity between them. This generalization results in the occasional blocking of correct responses by interference from other responses with a consequent retardation of performance. Obviously, the extent to which generalization tendencies of this type develop (and hence, other things being equal, the difficulty of the list) is a function of intralist stimulus similarity. This interpretation of the verbal learning process has held up well experimentally and many observations are integrated by means of it (cf. Underwood, 1949).

The addition of aperiodic electric shock raises drive level, increases generalization (flattens the generalization gradients), produces interference responses, and thus impairs learning. Learning in this situation should be negatively related to the intensity of shock employed.

Each subject was encouraged to guess if he was unsure of the correct response and to continue to call out answers until he was told to stop (after the two successive errorless trials).

During the entire learning sequence, galvanic skin response (GSR) to each shock was recorded, as well as continuous basal skin response (BSR) to determine nonshock-specific reactions. These data were recorded on an Offner type R dynograph from silver-silver chloride cup electrodes (O'Connell & Tursky, 1960). Electrode jelly ensured a good contact on the surface of the index and middle fingers.

Manipulation of Expectancies

Up to this point in the procedure, all subjects had been treated similarly; but in order to manipulate the independent variables of choice and justification, differential expectations were now induced by leading half the subjects—the Controls—to believe that they had completed only the first part of a two-part experiment (1F). The second part was to begin in a few minutes, after the electrodes were removed, allegedly "to allow for depolarization and for the measuring instruments to be recalibrated." During this time, the Controls remained disengaged from their electrodes and headsets (2A) while they filled out a brief questionnaire on the painfulness of the entire series of shocks and on general background (2B).

No-Choice Controls

Without being given any choice, justification, or further reason (2C), each of these No-Choice Control subjects was rewired and told that part two of the experiment—dealing with some of Dr. W.'s work on shock, learning, and physiology—was about to begin (3A). The Controls were then subdivided into three groups, depending on the shock intensities they received (3B): Low-Low Controls—the same low level of shock ("slightly painful") in parts one and two; High-High Controls—the same high level ("painful") in both parts; High-Moderate Controls—a high level in part one but a moderate level in part two (individually determined during the threshold procedure as each subject's "uncomfortable" level). These subjects, then, were not given an explicit choice in whether to participate in either part of the study.

Dissonance Manipulations

Choice to Continue (2C). The other half of the subjects were led to believe that the entire study was over after they had learned List II (1F). Their electrodes and headsets were removed (2A), and they filled out the same short questionnaire on painfulness of the series of shock (2B)—usually accompanied by audible sighs, assumed to indicate relief. Just as the subject was rising to leave, however, the experimenter made this request:

> Look, before you leave *I'd* like to ask you something. I'm asking some of Dr. Zimbardo's subjects to give me some time for a similar experiment of *mine* which does involve electric shock. It's completely up to you, of course. If you agree, it will take place right now and it won't take very long.

Thus, each Dissonance subject was given an explicit choice of whether to commit himself to more of the same stimulation just experienced as painful—for no extra course credit or money.

Justification (2C). Before these Dissonance subjects could respond (and while most subjects were still in a semicrouched position of disequilibrium), the experimenter continued by giving half of them a lot of reasons for making the commitment; that is, he provided extrinsic, rational justification for engaging in behavior discrepant with the assumed motivational state of pain avoidance (similar to the kind of justification previously described in Mansson's study, Article 6). Such justification, by adding elements consonant with commitment to further shock, is designed to lower the total magnitude of the dissonance occasioned by such commitment. Accordingly, it is called the *Low Dissonance treatment.*

For the other half of the Dissonance subjects, we deliberately attempted to minimize the extrinsic justification for participation (i.e., benefits to experimental design, science, the experimenter, N.S.F., America's space program, etc.). To achieve this end, the experimenter said:

> I wish I could really give you a whole spiel on how valuable this second experiment would be. But, I'm just trying something out and to be honest, I'm not at all sure anything will come of it. I'd like to try it with you and see how things go. I may not add anything more to what Dr. Zimbardo's study has already found. Obviously, as you know, it's completely up to you, whether or not you want to be a subject in this second experiment, especially since it involves electric shock.

This treatment, where subjects were given a choice to continue with minimal justification for doing so, is called the *High Dissonance* condition.

Coaxing (2D). If a subject hesitated, or was uncertain or negative, a standardized probe[3] was used to try to coax the commitment. If he still refused (most did not), the subject was allowed to leave, after the purpose of the experiment was described to him in more detail and any questions he had were answered (2E). The duration and content of the subject-experimenter interaction during this commitment phase between Parts 1 and 2 of the study were observed and recorded for all subjects.

Phase Three: A Replication

The final part of the study began for the Dissonance subjects after choice, justification, and commitment; for the Controls, it began immediately after the first part. It was identical to Part 1, except that List III was used for the serial-anticipation task. Each subject gave his subjective evaluation of a sample shock (3B) and then learned the list of words while receiving two unavoidable shocks per trial and having his GSR and BSR recorded during learning (3C).

3. (1) "It won't take very long" (used for 21 subjects); (2) "Since you were in the first experiment, I can use you as your own control" (used only once); or (3) "Well, I might get *some* information that might be worth-while" (used only once).

Finally, all subjects completed a postexperimental questionnaire to evaluate the manipulations and possible channels of dissonance reduction (3D).

ANALYSES POSSIBLE

First, we can analyze the effects of shock-produced pain on the three major dependent variables (subjective estimates of pain, learning, and GSR) during Part 1, when all subjects were treated comparably. (The one Control group given low shock was employed only to evaluate the effects of two levels of shock on learning in Part 1—Low vs. High—and three levels in Part 2.) This should enable us to establish a base line for estimating the effects of our experimental treatments. Then, we can analyze the data from the last phase of the study for the No-Choice Control subjects to determine the effects of lowering (by about half) the physical intensity of the shock (High-Moderate Controls), the effects of continued high shock (High-High Controls), and the effects of three different levels of shock (these two groups compared with the Low-Low Controls). Finally, by examining the data for the Dissonance subjects, we may determine whether the cognitive manipulations had any effect on pain-related behaviors. The Low and High Dissonance groups are similar to each other (and to the High-High Controls) in terms of physical level of shock, but they differ in cognitive inputs.

DISSONANCE ASSUMPTIONS

Theoretically, dissonance should be aroused by choosing to endure pain with minimal (barely adequate) justification for such a commitment. This dissonance should then be reduced by perceiving that the sensory input is less intense than it really is. Agreeing to be shocked is not so irrational if one expects that "the shocks will not hurt as much this time." It is assumed the High Dissonance subjects will say the shock hurts less, and if subjectively it does, their learning performance should be less disrupted by it. Finally, if we are studying more than a process of verbal rationalization and if the central nervous system is being implicated in an effort to control the experience of pain, there should, as Melzack and Wall suggest, be corresponding physiological alterations, specifically in galvanic skin response.

Thus, we assume that for the No-Choice Controls and the Low Dissonance group (where adequate justification has undercut choice), there will be a relatively direct relation between level of stimulus input and behavioral output. For the High Dissonance group, behavioral output will not be predictable from knowledge of sensory input but will instead be mediated by the cognitive variables that are expected to exert a controlling influence on the experience of pain. For this group then, there should be a functional lowering of pain motivation as a consequence of dissonance-reducing processes.

PREDICTIONS

1. For the No-Choice Control subjects, as shock level increases, subjective estimates of pain will increase, serial-anticipation learning will deteriorate, and GSR to shock will be greater.
2. For the High-Moderate Controls, when the physical intensity of shock is lowered, the reported sensation of pain will be lowered, learning will be improved, and GSR to shock will be smaller.
3. The Low Dissonance group should react on all measures similarly to its relevant control group, the High-High Controls.
4. The High Dissonance group should react on all measures similarly to its relevant control group, the High-Moderate Controls.

RESULTS[4] AND DISCUSSION

Establishing the Conditions for Testing the Hypotheses

Assessment of the experimental manipulations by means of the postexperimental questionnaire reveals that we were successful in creating the impression that the Dissonance groups had considerable choice in whether to commit themselves to the discrepant behavior (mean of 55 where 70 = maximum choice), while the Controls experienced significantly less choice (mean of 15). This highly significant difference ($p < 0.001$) between treatments can be viewed against a no-difference effect within the two Dissonance and three Control groups.

Also in line with our induction procedure, only the Low Dissonance group perceived the relative importance to the experimenter of the "second part" of the study to be significantly greater than that of the first. On a 6-point rating scale, the mean for the Low Dissonance group was 4.2, while it was 3.2 for the other groups ($p < 0.05$). In addition, the Low Dissonance group perceived their participation in the second part to be relatively more important than did the High Dissonance group ($p < 0.05$). Thus, the choice and justification conditions necessary for testing the dissonance theory hypothesis were satisfied.

Obviously, dissonance could have been reduced in ways other than modification of cognitions about the shock—for example, by adding "extra attractions" to the experimental situation (after Lawrence & Festinger, 1962). Our attempt to minimize the use of alternative avenues of cognitive reorganization—by means of the standardized, minimal subject-experimenter interaction and the highly structured testing procedure—was effective. There were no significant differences among any of the groups in how pleasant they perceived the experimenter to be (mean of 48 where 50 = "quite pleasant"); how important it was for them to do well on the learning task; how absorbed they were in the task, or how satisfied they were with their performance (all means varied around

4. All data were first analyzed by the experimenters, using manual desk-calculator techniques, then reanalyzed independently, using IBM program BMD062 (general linear hypothesis with contrasts—a quite conservative statistical test).

a score of 40 where 35 = a moderate level). In addition, all groups believed that they could not avoid the shocks and felt that the shocks were in fact random.

The appropriateness of using Carson's word lists was independently established with a sample of 10 subjects, who demonstrated that performance was interfered with as intralist similarity increased under a constant high level of shock intensity ($p < 0.02$). In passing, it should be mentioned that a serial-order position effect (bow-shaped curve) was found among all experimental subjects for List II, but not for List III. For List III, the errors were not concentrated in the middle of the list but were more evenly distributed.

Tests of the Hypotheses

Perception of Pain. Although the data on the subjective estimates of pain are in the predicted direction, the effect is weaker than on our other measures. It can be seen from Table 2 that the Low Dissonance group behaved like the High-High Controls, exhibiting only a minor adaptation to shock and thus perceiving the second, identical sample shock to be about 2 units weaker than the first. The High-Moderate Controls responded veridically, changing their estimate of perceived painfulness by 26 units. The High Dissonance group falls in between—saying the precommitment shock was more than "moderately painful" while the second sample shock was less than "moderately painful" (a reduction of 9.2 units). The difference between the Control groups is highly significant ($p < 0.001$), while the predicted difference between the Dissonance groups fails to meet the acceptable level of significance ($F = 3.07$, $p < 0.10$).

In addition to estimates of the single sample shock, the subjects had estimated the painfulness of the entire series of shocks after Part 1 and again after Part 2. The net proportions of subjects who felt the shocks in Part 2 were less painful than in Part 1 were: 67 per cent for the High-Moderate Controls, 53 per cent for the High Dissonance subjects, only 26 per cent for the Low Dissonance subjects, and 20 per cent for the High-High Controls. The difference between the Dissonance groups, however, still only approaches statistical significance ($CR = 1.71$, $p = 0.09$). We can conclude, then, that our hypothesis

TABLE 2

MEAN PERCEIVED PAIN AND PHYSICAL SHOCK LEVEL OF SAMPLE SHOCKS

Group	n	Mean shock (volts)	Perceived pain		
			Precommitment	Postcommitment	Difference
Control:					
High-Moderate	15	45–22	46	20	−26
High-High	15	44	50	47	−3
Dissonance:					
Low	20	38	49	47	−2
High	20	49	46	37	−9

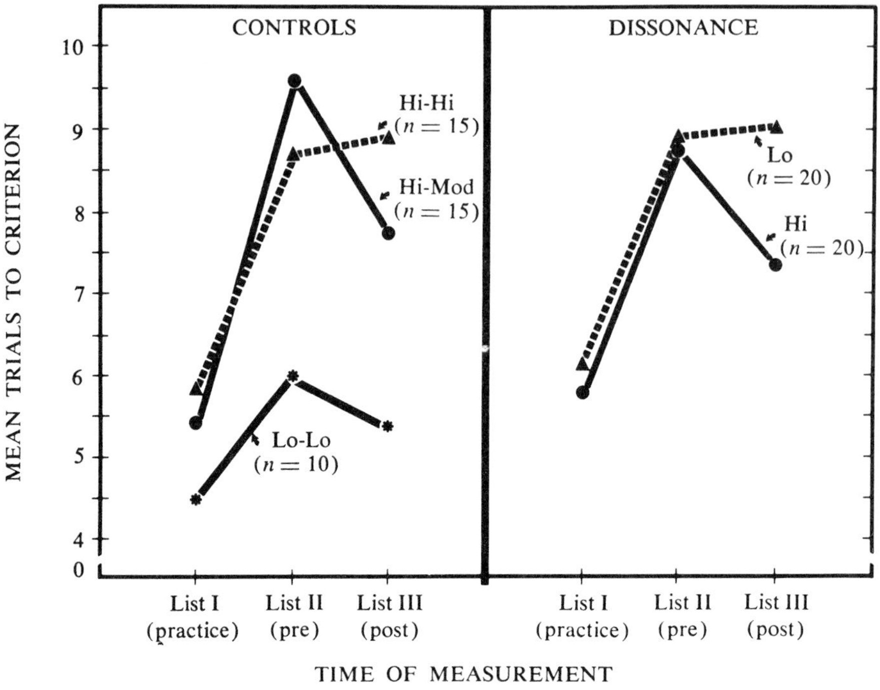

FIGURE 2
Mean number of trials to reach criterion in the serial-anticipation learning task. The greater the number, the slower the learning.

—that the conditions of High Dissonance lead subjects to feel that constant-level shocks[5] are somewhat less painful—is tentatively supported. But were the subjects only saying they experienced less pain, or were the shocks *really* less painful, as reflected by the subjects' performance? Examination of the learning data should help illuminate this point.

Learning. As shock intensity increases, learning should be more interfered with and more trials should be required to reach criterion. Figure 2 clearly demonstrates this effect for the Control conditions. Subjects given low shock required fewest trials while those given high shock required most trials to learn the list. Learning time improved when the physical intensity of the shock was reduced (High-Moderate), and it deteriorated slightly when a high level was maintained (High-High). When the trials to criterion on List III were adjusted by statistically covarying the scores on both List II and the List I (practice), the adjusted means revealed a systematic effect of shock level on performance: Low-Low (10 volts) = 6.4 trials, High-Moderate (22 volts) = 7.3 trials, and High-High (44 volts) = 8.9 trials; $p < 0.01$.

5. It should also be noted from Table 2 that although the mean shock voltages received varied slightly among groups (the High vs. Low Dissonance difference was not significant), the threshold procedure resulted in almost identical initial subjective estimates. Data for the Low-Low Control group is excluded because its relevance is limited to providing a baseline on the learning task.

The results for the Dissonance groups are dramatically similar to their relevant control groups. Starting from virtually identical performance base lines during the no-shock practice list and the precommitment shock list, the two Dissonance groups diverged on the postcommitment learning. Although both Dissonance groups received high shock throughout, the High Dissonance group responded in a manner indistinguishable from the High-Moderate Control group, while the Low Dissonance group responded in accordance with the physical characteristics of the shock level, as did the High-High Control group.

Since it was difficult for us to believe at first that such unequivocal results could be real, we reanalyzed the data, using many different learning measures. Regardless of the analysis used, the same pattern of results emerged. If one considers the percentage of subjects who learned faster or slower on List III compared to List II, the majority of those in the Low Dissonance and High-High groups did worse, while 70 per cent of the High Dissonance and 60 per cent of the High-Moderate groups improved. When mean number of correct anticipations, instead of trials, is used, the adjusted means on List III (covaried for List II scores) become: Low-Low = 172.1, High-Moderate = 166.3, High Dissonance = 165.5, Low Dissonance = 161.7, and High-High = 160.9.

Two more stringent tests of learning were then devised for these data. First, speed and thoroughness of learning were evaluated by computing for each word individually the number of trials required before the word was never missed again. These scores were then combined over words, and a measure of trials prior to an errorless run was computed for each subject. Table 3 presents these data. Again the High Dissonance group reacted like the High-Moderate Controls, while the Low Dissonance and High-High Control groups were similar.

Finally, a measure called "shock-specific errors" was applied to the data. Since there were two words on each trial that were associated with shock, errors on only these specifically shocked words were compared in the pre- and post-commitment phases of the study. As can be seen from Table 4, only the High-Moderate and the High Dissonance groups made relatively fewer errors on words accompanied by shock after the commitment; the Low-Low group made

TABLE 3

MEAN NUMBER OF TRIALS PRIOR TO AN ERRORLESS RUN

Group	Mean trials			Subjects who improved, %
	List II (Precommitment)	List III (Postcommitment)	Difference	
High-Moderate Control	5.2	3.9	−1.3	73
High Dissonance	5.0	3.9	−1.1	65
Low Dissonance	4.6	4.8	+0.2	50
High-High Control	4.3	4.6	+0.3	40

TABLE 4

SHOCK-SPECIFIC-ERROR DIFFERENCE FROM PRE- TO POSTCOMMITMENT*

Group	Difference
High-Moderate Control	−1.05
High Dissonance	−0.25
Low-Low Control	0.00
Low Dissonance	+0.23
High-High Control	+0.43

* Mean change in number of errors on specific words accompanied by shock. A negative difference indicates a decrease in errors from pre- to postcommitment; a positive difference indicates an increase.

an equal number in both parts of the study, while the Low Dissonance and High-High groups made more shock-specific errors in Part 2. The differences on each of these measures are significant beyond the 0.05 level. Fewer of the High Dissonance subjects took more trials to learn these words on List III than on List II (30 per cent). For the other groups, the values were 40 per cent for the High-Moderate and 60 per cent for both the Low Dissonance and the High-High.

The consistent,[6] significant pattern of these results enables us to feel confident that we were able to modify the motivational state of the High Dissonance subjects and thereby minimize the effects of shock on their learning performance. We have therefore demonstrated one kind of equivalence between the physical parameter of shock intensity and the verbal-cognitive manipulations of choice and justification.

Physiological Data: Galvanic Skin Response (GSR). Next we turn to the physiological data to determine whether the changes noted above in cognitions and learning extended to the noncognitive components of pain. Figure 3 presents mean GSR data for each of the four main groups, subtracting a subject's GSR to each of the first three shocks in List III (postcommitment) from each of the first three shocks in List II (precommitment). This measure was used because the number of shocks each subject received obviously varied depending upon his rate of learning, which, as we have seen, was a function of the experimental treatment. We wanted, therefore, a physiological measure that was uncontaminated by differential exposure to the pain stimulus. It might be mentioned that there was no relationship between the number of shocks received and subjective rating of the painfulness of the series of shocks.

6. In four separate replications of this experiment with five to ten subjects in each of the two Dissonance groups, we varied the difficulty of the learning task (by shortening the interword interval or the stimulus-exposure time) and always got the same results as noted above.

The High-High Control group showed an increase in physiological responsiveness to the shocks, while, as expected, the lowering of the shock for the High-Moderate group produced a decrement in GSR. What is dramatic, however, is the fact that the Low Dissonance group again mirrors the High-High Controls, while the High Dissonance group behaves physiologically as if the shocks (of constant intensity) were not as painful after the commitment as they had been before. Again these differences are statistically significant ($p < 0.05$).

Two related physiological findings are also of interest, although they are not statistically reliable because of rather considerable within-group variability.

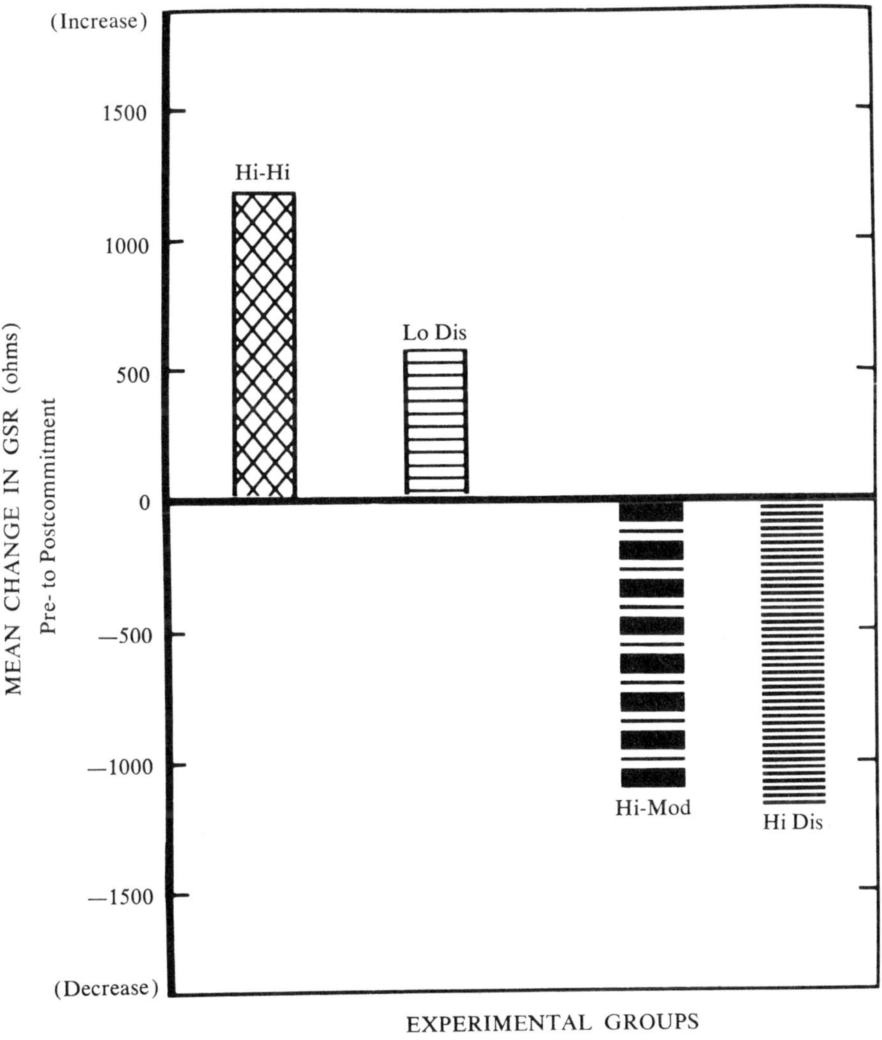

FIGURE 3
Mean differences in galvanic skin response (ohms) between the first three shocks in List II (precommitment) to the first three shocks in List III (postcommitment). Negative values indicate reductions in GSR, while positive ones indicate increases.

During the one-minute waiting period of Part 2 (prior to the sample shock) *both* Dissonance groups lowered their GSR (pre- to postcommitment shock-anticipation period), while the average GSR of the Control groups was elevated. The reduced average GSR value of the High Dissonance group was, however, more than twice that of the Low Dissonance group (2865 ohms to 1140 ohms).

Once the Part 2 sample shock was actually given, the pattern changed: the High-Moderate subjects lowered their GSR (from its average value in response to the sample shock in Part 1) by 30 per cent; the High Dissonance, by 23 per cent; the Low Dissonance, by only 1 per cent; while only the High-High group increased their mean GSR, by 7 per cent.

As we have seen from Figure 3, after three more shocks during learning, the Low Dissonance subjects increased their GSR, as did the High-High subjects, while the High Dissonance and High-Moderate groups maintained their reduced GSR levels.

Physiological Data: Basal Skin Response (BSR). Changes in BSR from

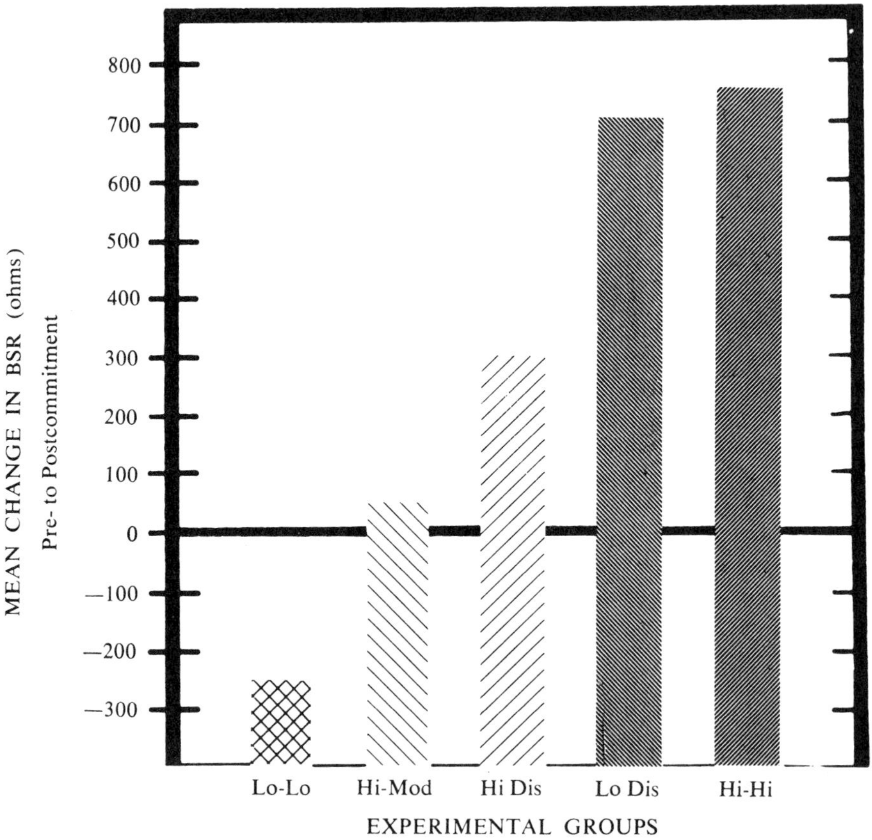

FIGURE 4

Mean differences in basal skin resistance (ohms) during the learning tasks from pre- to postcommitment. Negative values indicate decreases in BSR, while positive values indicate increases.

the first to the second shock-learning task were examined from samples taken every 20 seconds, excluding GSR measurements to the shocks. It was expected that the groups showing reduced GSR would show an elevated BSR. In a sense, the individual shocks would have less effect because the entire basal responsiveness had been raised (comparable to an increase in threshold level). Similarly, those groups with increased GSR ought to have shown a lowered BSR. The results presented in Figure 4 indicate, however, that just the opposite actually occurred! The greatest increase was demonstrated by the High-High and Low Dissonance groups, with the High Dissonance and High-Moderate groups significantly lower ($p < 0.05$).

Apparently, changes observed in GSR are independent of these BSR effects, since they remain the same (still significant) even when differences in BSR are statistically covaried. In fact, the GSR data are all the more striking in the light of the BSR effects. Lowered physiological responsiveness in the High Dissonance and High-Moderate groups was specific to the sensory input of the shocks rather than part of a general pattern of reduced physiological (BSR) lability.

These mean data over all trials do not allow for an analysis of changes in basal skin resistance during the course of the learning tasks. In order to examine whether there was any systematic relation between BSR changes and the learning sequence (and whether there is any orderly relationship between groups), the subjects' total BSR scores were refined into four separate scores. The BSR for each quarter of the postcommitment learning trials of each subject was subtracted from the BSR for the comparable quarter of his precommitment learning trials. (For example, if a subject took 12 trials in pre- and 8 trials in postcommitment, then his BSR for the first 2 "post" trials would be subtracted from his BSR for the first 3 "pre" trials.) Figure 5 presents a family of parallel functions revealing the same group ordering as in the previous analysis for each of the four data points, but in addition it shows a lowering of BSR over the course of learning for all groups.

BSR Variability and Performance Feedback. Perhaps, then, the BSR data are not simple indicators of pain sensitivity or responsiveness but have been influenced by other variables in the situation. A spectral analysis of these data[7] in Table 5 does provide some indication that these physiological effects may in part be a consequence of psychological factors correlated with the learning task and not a direct consequence of the shock. Using the spectral-analysis technique to provide an estimate of individual cyclical *variations* in skin resistance (given a fixed power input) for cycles of 40, 80, and 160 seconds, we find that while there are no group differences prior to commitment, there are significant effects following commitment. The High Dissonance and High-Moderate groups reduced their spectra least (continued to be most variable), while the spectral estimate for each of the other groups was significantly smaller—in fact, reduced by twice as much.

7. A computer program for the preliminary estimation of the spectral analysis of our physiological data was developed by Edward Haupt of New York University from Blackman and Tukey (1959, esp. pp. 45–47, 135–139).

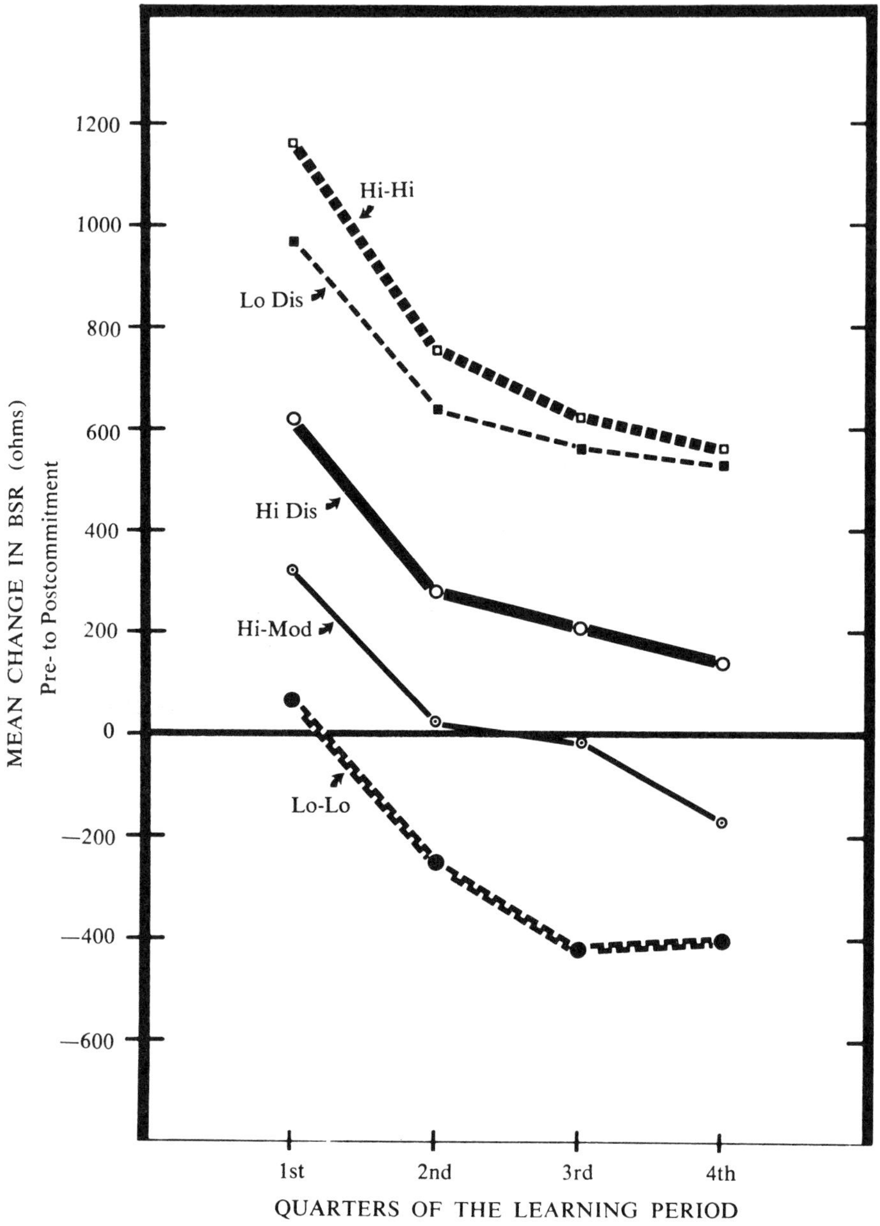

FIGURE 5
Mean differences in basal skin resistance (ohms) for each quarter of the total learning trials, postcommitment levels subtracted from precommitment levels. Negative values indicate decreases in BSR, while positive ones indicate increases.

These group effects are clearest when the cyclical variation is taken over a 40-second interval. One of the events in this study that had a 40-second periodicity was the duration of one learning trial of presenting nine stimulus words and a cue word (each for 2 seconds on and 2 seconds off). Since BSR decreased over trials as the subject's learning obviously improved and since the spectral data may be related to something occurring during the course of each trial, it may be that these physiological data are reflecting an emotional reaction to success and failure in learning more than to shock sensitivity. Perhaps there is an attentional or expectancy factor operating to a greater extent in the High Dissonance and High-Moderate subjects so that they are more affected by feedback from their learning performance than are the other groups. Some support for this interpretation comes from internal analyses (see Table 6) that show a significant relationship between decreases in BSR and improvement in learning performance only for the High-Moderate and High Dissonance subjects. Moreover, even within these groups, 90 per cent of those subjects who improved most (three or more trials) *decreased* their BSR, while of those who improved slightly, only 30 per cent showed this decrease ($p < 0.05$). Apparently, then, although these findings are not directly relevant to our experimental hypothesis, they should be provocative for further research on physiological correlates of psychological feedback during learning.

Before presenting some auxiliary data, it may be appropriate to state the conclusion that can be drawn from the evidence already presented—that the perception of pain, its impact on behavior, and its alteration of physiological processes can be brought under cognitive control.

Auxiliary Data

Finally, we would like to present some additional data that have an indirect bearing on some of our underlying assumptions and implications.

Subject Refusal to Continue. During the commitment phase of the study, the experimenter presented the Dissonance subjects with a choice of whether or not to receive more painful shocks. Four High Dissonance, two Low Dissonance, and no Control subjects refused to continue (the refusal subjects were

TABLE 5

SPECTRAL ESTIMATE OF BSR*

Group	List II (Precommitment)	List III (Postcommitment)	Difference
High Dissonance	56,268	36,070	20,198
High-Moderate Control	53,561	26,299	27,262
Low Dissonance	53,513	17,495	36,018
High-High Control	48,164	15,247	32,917

* The larger the spectral estimate, the greater the cyclical variation in Basal Skin Resistance over a 40-second interval.

TABLE 6

RELATION OF CHANGES IN LEARNING TO CHANGES IN BSR*

Combined groups	Learning change	BSR change: Decrease		BSR change: Increase
Low Dissonance / High-High Control	Worsen	1	<	15
	Improve	3	<	10
High Dissonance / High-Moderate Control	Worsen	2	<	5
	Improve	13	>	10

* Subjects whose learning or BSR values did not change are excluded from this analysis.

not represented in the reported total of 80 subjects). A similar percentage refused among our pretest subjects. These figures reveal that the choice was meaningful, that there was no differential self-selection between the two Dissonance groups, and that the overall drop-out rate was rather low. This low refusal rate was probably due to the fact that the senior experimenter was also a professor in a required course for the subjects and the fact that some of the subjects who wanted to exercise their choice to leave were coaxed into staying.

Effects of Coaxing by the Experimenter. Observation of the experimenter-subject interaction indicated that more than half (54 per cent) of all Dissonance subjects required some coaxing by the experimenter, while only 2 out of 40 Control subjects did ($p < 0.05$). For both Dissonance groups, the experimenter was perceived as less pleasant (on the postcommitment questionnaire) by those who required coaxing than by those who did not, and the effect was quite significant ($p < 0.01$).

Three other interrelated findings are vital for an understanding of this crucial aspect of the only "social" part of this entire investigation:

1. It was rated *less* important to be successful on the learning task in Part 2 for the High Dissonance subjects who had to be coaxed than for those not coaxed, but *more* important for the Low Dissonance coaxed subjects than for those not coaxed ($p < 0.05$).
2. Subjects who had to be coaxed felt they were more able to ignore the shock ($p < 0.05$), and the High Dissonance coaxed subjects felt they were able to ignore it to a greater extent than did any other subgroup ($p < 0.05$).
3. Improvement in learning was related to being coaxed by the experimenter. The Low Dissonance subjects who had to be coaxed did *worse* on Part 2 (mean decline of 0.92 trials), while the opposite held for the High Dissonance coaxed subjects, who improved most (mean increase of 1.88 trials; $p < 0.10$).

This pattern of results may be understood if we assume that those subjects needing to be coaxed were more bothered by the aversiveness of part one and/or had greater feelings of autonomy and independence. The experimenter's coaxing becomes a salient cognition, since the coaxed subjects liked him less for this "harder sell," but the High and Low Dissonance subjects interpreted his coaxing differently, according to their justification condition. Under Low Dissonance conditions, the coaxing was an additional cognition consonant with the commitment since it bolstered the other reasons the experimenter had already given. Thus, their dissonance should have been lowered still further. For the High Dissonance subjects, however, the coaxing added further dissonance by increasing the irrationality of the decision: although the experimenter had supplied few rational reasons for continuing in the experiment, he was nevertheless exerting pressure on the subjects to endure more pain without clarifying the basis for commitment (since his most often used probe was, "It won't take very long, it will take place right now"). In contrast to Low Dissonance, these High Dissonance subjects perceived that their participation in the next part of the study was less important, and by being better able to ignore the shock (through dissonance-reducing stratagems), they learned faster.

Time Required for Commitment. The amount of time elapsed between the pre- and postcommitment phases of the study varied significantly ($p < 0.001$) between groups. As would be expected, the Dissonance groups required more time during the commitment phase than did the controls. However, the mean of 8 minutes required by the Low Dissonance group was significantly longer than for any other group, while the High-High Controls took about 6 minutes, which was significantly shorter than for any other group. The 7 minutes required on the average by the High Dissonance group was not reliably different from the 6 1/2 minutes required by the High-Moderate and Low-Low groups. Thus these commitment-time variations were not systematically related to our Dissonance-Control group pairings (Low Dissonance and High-High; High Dissonance and High-Moderate).

Interrelations Among Variables

All that remains at this point to bring our thesis to a convincing conclusion is the documentation of significant correlations between the variables of change in pain perception, learning, and GSR. Unfortunately, this cannot be done, since the pattern of correlations does not reveal the expected relationships in the Control groups. The within-group correlation between pain perception and learning is -0.01 for the High-High Controls and $+0.11$ for the High-Moderate Controls, and it is virtually zero for both groups between GSR and learning performance. The correlation between pain perception and GSR of $+0.51$ makes sense for the High-High group (GSR is less when pain is less) but doesn't make sense for the High-Moderate group where the weak correlation of -0.14 is a trend for lower GSR to be associated with more pain.

Although we have demonstrated that learning is affected by shock intensity and that the lowering of shock intensity produces corresponding changes in pain perception, learning, and GSR, apparently either these reactions to pain are not interdependent or there is some peculiarity about the measures or distribution of responses in this study that obscures such relationships. Only further parametric study can clarify this issue.

The results of this investigation provide some experimental confirmation for the position of Melzack and Wall (1965) that central nervous system activities may intervene between sensory input and the pain response and that pain may be controlled by psychological stratagems. Verification of the predictions extrapolated from Festinger's theory of cognitive dissonance suggests that one set of such stratagems may arise from successful attempts to reduce dissonance.

Editor's Comments

Only three of the many issues that could be discussed in relation to this study will be considered here (although others will appear in the Conclusion to this book): (1) How might the study have been improved by utilizing different measures and tasks? (2) Can one generalize from results on experimental pain produced in the laboratory to chronic pain occurring in normal life? (3) How is it possible to increase our understanding of the theoretical mechanisms involved in the dissonance effects on pain control and enhanced learning?

(1) The choice of serial-anticipation learning as the behavioral task for the subjects appears to be justified in light of the stable base lines and the relatively small variability in performance within groups that it provided. It made possible the detection of fine as well as gross differences in performance attributable to the experimental treatments (e.g., shock-specific errors and trials to criterion). However, because the duration of the task varied with success on it, measures other than speed of learning (perhaps GSR, perception of the painfulness of the series of shocks, and some postexperimental measures) may be biased because of time differences and differences in shock-frequencies between groups. Moreover, because of differential feedback from performance on the learning task, other response measures may be contaminated (perhaps the BSR measure). If the primary concern is with these nonlearning measures, then a performance task with a constant number of trials is preferable.

The use of GSR as an indicator of pain reactivity also leaves much to be desired, since it is sensitive to a host of psychological factors that could have been operating, such as attention, orientation, test anxiety, and emotional excitation from sources irrelevant to experimental pain. Future research that takes into account the intra-individual specificity in physiological channels of responding (cf. Engel, 1960; Lacey & Lacey, 1958; Schnore, 1959; White, 1965) would benefit from a design that initially established each subject's unique pattern of physiological response to pain. Then the effects of cognitive variables could be evaluated more precisely by means of a discriminant-function analysis, which would empirically determine the set of weighting coefficients for a multiple-regression equation in order to discriminate maximally between treatments (cf. Cohen, 1967).

Because commitment to endure pain in our laboratory situation not only involved the cognition of aversiveness of the shock but for many males also became a personal challenge, or a test of masculinity, the theoretical interpretation of any future results would be clearer if a testing situation were employed where such "artifacts" could be eliminated or controlled.

Wolff and Jarvik (1963) have shown that deep, visceral pain can be similar to skin, cutaneous pain. They found a significant correlation ($r = 0.49$) between pain thresholds for radiant heat on the forehead and hypotonic saline solutions injected into muscle. Although the locus of pain was different, the action of the pain was similar since a hypotonic saline injection produces a sharp, well-localized pain of short latency and duration, similar to the cutaneous pain from radiant heat. When hypertonic-saline-induced pain was compared to cutaneous pain, the correlation between the thresholds dropped to 0.15, due to the latter's different pain action (dull, poorly localized, of long latency and duration). Since Melzack and Wall's (1965) gate-control model specifies speed of pain conduction as a critical variable in central nervous system control of pain, it would be well to test the model by investigating the relative extent of cognitive control of pain under different types of pain that vary in spatio-temporal characteristics (as shown in this work of Wolff and Jarvik).

Although Wolff and Goodell (1943) reported that suggestion, autosuggestion, attitude, and distraction raised pain threshold, there is some controversy in more recent literature as to whether thresholds are susceptible to influence by such psychological factors. Gelfand (1964) has summarized the results of these studies in a formulation that postulates different factor loadings of physiological and psychological components for pain threshold and tolerance. Psychological variables influence pain tolerance to a greater extent than pain threshold (Wolff, Krasnegor, & Farr, 1965), while pain threshold should be more related to physiological variables (this is not yet established). Any further work on cognitive control of pain would therefore profit by studying these experimental pain parameters at different behavioral levels.

(2) The introduction to the present study alluded to the possible practical significance of the results for understanding pain control. Can we generalize from findings on experimental pain to effects of naturally occurring pain? I believe so, as long as we are aware of the multiplicity of factors that may exist when people suffer from chronic pain.

That attitudes formed as a consequence of subcultural experiences can influence reaction to pain has been clearly demonstrated by Zborowski (1952). He was able to categorize differences in responses to pain among Old American, Jewish, Italian, and Irish male patients suffering from neurological diseases (treated at the Kingsbridge, Bronx V.A. Hospital). While Jewish and Italian patients emotionally exaggerated the intensity of their pain, the Irish and Old Americans had a phlegmatic, detached reaction toward theirs. But the similar demonstrativeness of the Italians and Jews originated from different basic attitudes: the Italians focused on the immediacy of the pain while the Jews were concerned about the future implications of the pain.

Recently, a laboratory study employing experimental pain induced by electric shock (Sternbach & Tursky, 1965) revealed similar differences in pain response among housewives varying in ethnic background. Italian women had significantly lower thresholds (tolerance) for shock than women from the other ethnic groups (using as a measure the shock level at which the subject did not want to receive higher shock even when coaxed by the experimenter). Jewish women were able to take a greater increase in shock when motivated to do so by the experimenter than women in the other groups. Yankee women (Protestants of British origin whose grandparents were born in America) had a significantly faster and more complete adaptation of diphasic palmar skin potential than the other women. This skin potential is a unique, qualitative feature of sympathetic nervous system reactivity to sudden strong stimulation. The action-orientation, matter-of-fact attitude toward pain of this ethnic group thus characterizes equally well the reactions of males to chronic pain and of females to experimental pain. Similarly, undemonstrative Irish subjects suffered in silence but did not exert the kind of cognitive control over automatic reactivity that the Yankee subjects did. Finally, it is important to observe the contrast between Jewish patients and Jewish subjects. They displayed similar distress when in pain, but their concern for its future implications was not activated in the laboratory situation where the pain bore no possibility of future impairment. Thus, the Jewish subjects had pain thresholds similar to the normally less responsive Irish and Yankee subjects.

The effects of culturally conditioned attitudes toward pain have also been demonstrated by Lambert, Libman, and Posner (1960, 1963). In the latter Posner study, pain tolerance, but not pain threshold, was influenced by suggestions to different ethnic groups. A good research site for further study of this problem would be a mobile innoculation lab unit vaccinating children in different urban neighborhoods. One could then investigate in a natural field setting both ethnic and developmental age differences in reaction to pain induced by needle puncture and then impose dissonance-type commitment procedures.

Attempts to generalize from the laboratory to real life situations (or vice versa) might therefore have to take into account some of the following differences between the two situations, especially where they may be related to attitudinal predispositions in the populations studied:

	Experimental Pain	*Chronic Pain*
1. Source	The subject is aware of the experimenter as the external agent of pain.	May be known and external, as in an accident, or unknown and internal, as in migraine or abdominal pain.
2. Onset	Usually predictable within a short time interval, and sudden.	May be unexpected, unpredictable, and gradual.
3. Duration	Finite, self-limiting.	Usually prolonged, may be indefinite.
4. Localization	Usually clearly defined.	Often diffuse, vaguely defined.
5. Preparatory set	The subject must be told about stimulus, and may thus prepare for it.	Usually no preparatory set for initial symptomatic pain.

	Experimental Pain	*Chronic Pain*
6. Attending persons	Usually only a researcher whose interest in the subject is limited.	Physician, nurses, etc., and/or family whose interest in the patient is extensive.
7. Secondary gains	May not be very appreciable, but primarily approval from the experimenter, money, or mastery of feared stimulus.	May be quite extreme, involving dependence, manipulation of others, attention, sympathy, excuse for failure, punishment for guilt.
8. Future implications	None, except where pain tolerance is perceived as a challenge and self-esteem is at stake.	Patient's normal life routine may be interrupted, pain may be a symptom of worse pain or fatal disease.
9. Interpretation of pain	Subject has allowed himself to experience a pain that is under the control of a scientist (assumed to be benign and rational).	Patient *may* feel victimized by a hostile environment (assumed to be irrational or perhaps responsive to religious ritual or magic); may feel a need to suffer.

(3) To narrow our focus and return to the basic concern of this monograph, there are two ways in which we can increase confidence in the validity of the theoretical underpinnings of this experiment. The dissonance interpretation would be strengthened if the same model could predict opposite effects on learning where the relationship between drive level and performance was the reverse of the present study. Here, high drive (shock) interfered with learning (they were negatively correlated) and voluntary commitment to more shock for minimal justification improved learning, presumably by lowering the pain response to the shock. However, in a situation where high drive normally *facilitates* learning (they are positively correlated), then a dissonant commitment to endure more of the aversive stimulus should result in poorer learning if the drive level is functionally lowered via dissonance reduction. The next study, a recently completed dissertation by Joël Grinker (1967), was designed in part to evaluate this line of reasoning.

It has been tacitly assumed by us that the primary psychological stratagem of the High Dissonance subjects was akin to convincing themselves that "the shocks will not hurt so much this time." However, other alternative nondissonance explanations of the learning data could be (and have been) advanced. For example, achievement motivation can be postulated as the causative factor. The third study in this series (Article 9, by Zimbardo, Rapaport, & Baron) attempts to provide a direct test of several of the alternative mechanisms that could have produced the present set of results. In that study, we tried to convert intervening variables into independent variables by means of hypnotic induction. But before we get to that study, let us see how Grinker has employed an apparently simple experimental paradigm and design to clarify a complex issue.

8. COGNITIVE CONTROL OF CLASSICAL EYELID CONDITIONING

Joël Grinker

Classical eyelid conditioning has traditionally been assumed to provide a simple paradigm for studying the effects of physical and temporal stimulus variables on behavior. This model of learning is one of a unitary response developing out of the paired presentations of an otherwise neutral stimulus and an unconditioned aversive stimulus (see Kimmel, 1965; Prokasy, 1965). The paradigm, of course, is the same for a salivary response to an appetitive stimulus.

More recent research evidence has suggested that this supposedly simple process may involve complex attitudinal, cognitive, and emotional variables, which make the eye-blink response a multiply determined learned response. Frequency and magnitude of response have been manipulated through instructional set (cf. Fishbein, 1965; Miller, 1939; Moyer & Lindley, 1962; Norris & Grant, 1948), through discriminability of experimental conditions (Spence, 1966a, 1966b; Spence, Homzie, & Rutledge, 1964), through the "attitudinal effect" produced by a ready signal (Kimble, 1967), and through the experimental history of the subject (Moore & Gormezano, 1961), to mention a few representative examples (see Grinker, 1967, for a full presentation of the role of cognitive and noncognitive factors in eyelid conditioning).

Spence (1963) specifically includes cognitive or perceptual variables as determinants of conditioning that can affect the level of drive by changing the level of emotionality. Conditioning performance has been shown to be a regular function of unconditioned stimulus (UCS) intensity and drive level by both Spence (1953, 1958a, 1958b) and Passey (1948), leading to the conclusion that where there is but a single and highly dominant response tendency, an increase in drive strength will increase the probability of response and result in a higher level of conditioning. According to Spence's most recent analysis (1964), the fundamental mechanism in determining the level of drive in the case of aversive stimulation is an internal, emotional state or response of the organism. Since this emotional state is assumed to be aroused differentially with varying intensities of the aversive stimulus, it follows that emotionality level and thus level of conditioning in humans can be modified through instructions that arouse anticipation of the feared or noxious stimulus.

This line of reasoning led Spence and Goldstein (1961) to hypothesize that verbal threat could lead to increased strength of conditioning. Thus, if the threat of a more intense unconditioned stimulus (e.g., a stronger air puff to the eye) produces an emotional arousal in the subject, conditioning level (e.g., the number of eye blinks in response to a conditioned stimulus) should be elevated.

Source: Grinker, Joël, "Cognitive Control of Classical Eyelid Conditioning." Adapted from "The Control of Classical Conditioning by Cognitive Manipulation," unpublished doctoral dissertation, New York University, 1967. Reprinted by permission of the author.

They found that subjects who were threatened with the fact that the UCS was going to become more intense and unpleasant than it had been on the first 20 trials but who were not actually given the increase showed the same increase in responding as subjects who actually received the increased UCS immediately following the threat. Both of these groups, one expecting pain and the other experiencing pain, showed significantly higher mean percentage increases in responding than did a nonthreatened control group. One interpretation then is that classical eyelid conditioning is enhanced by anticipation of aversive stimulation and that it is the correlated rise in anxiety that mediates the effect.

The present experiment, therefore, was designed first to offer additional empirical validation of the proposition that the level of conditioning performance can be experimentally increased by emotional arousal or emotion-elevating instructions during the course of the conditioning—but only when subjects have little or no choice in whether to endure the anticipated aversive stimulation. Where choice is provided but where maximal or adequate justification is also provided, the level of conditioning performance will be similarly increased. However (as suggested in the editor's comments preceding this article), the experiment was primarily designed to show that where choice and minimal justification are provided, the effect of the threatening instructions is reduced and the level of conditioning performance is correspondingly lowered.

DISSONANCE PREDICTIONS

Thus, our prediction is: Given a relevant drive state (the impact of the threatening instructions on the subjects), the process of dissonance reduction should lead to significantly less eyelid conditioning for subjects given choice and minimal justification. This prediction is obviously predicated upon the assumption that the dissonance aroused by voluntary commitment to a painful stimulus will be reduced by lowering pain-avoidance motivation—that is, by perceiving the UCS to be less threatening or painful—and thus the conditioning level will not be as affected by the independent variable of verbal threat.

OVERVIEW OF EXPERIMENTAL DESIGN

The major dependent variable was the change in percentage of conditioned eye-blink responses during acquisition from before to after threat. All three groups employed in the study were threatened that the UCS would be intensified (after an acquisition level had been established for the first 20 trials). One of these groups was given no choice in the commitment to further stimulus exposure (a replication of Spence and Goldstein's 1961 experimental treatment), while the other two were given an explicit choice in whether or not to continue. As in the previous study by Zimbardo et al., one of these groups received adequate justification for this discrepant behavior, while the other group was given minimal justification. The methods of inducing choice and manipulating justification were almost identical to those used in the preceding study.

APPARATUS[1] AND PROCEDURE

The apparatus was similar to that described by Moore and Gormezano (1961) and Gormezano (1966); a complete description is presented in Grinker (1967). The subject sat in a dentist's chair with his head supported while looking ahead at a fixation point. The conditioned stimulus (CS) was a tone (800 cps., 70 db., 550 msec. duration), and it preceded the air puff (the UCS) by an interval of 500 msec. The initial intensity of the air puff was sufficient to support a 100-mm. column of mercury (weak UCS, 1.93 psi). For the last ten trials, the intensity was increased to support a 400 mm. column of mercury (strong UCS, 7.72 psi). The air puff was delivered from an air jet attached to a head band. Eyelid movements were recorded in analog form on an Offner Dynograph from a potentiometer signal induced by mechanical movement of a wire taped to the eyelid.

Randomly ordered, inertial intervals averaging 20 seconds were used between occurrences of the CS, and all timing, delivery of stimulation, and recording of responses were standardized by automatic programing equipment. The response was defined as an eyelid closure of at least 1 mm. deflection (on the Offner chart record) from an established individual base line. To qualify as a conditioned response, the response had to follow the CS by a latency of not less than 150 msec. nor more than 500 msec.

Commitment to Increased Intensity of UCS

After 20 acquisition trials, the Control subjects were told that the first part of the experiment was over and that there would be a short break so that they could rest their eyes. Dissonance subjects were led to believe the entire experiment was completed at this point. Until now, the experimenter had been a male, who presented himself as an assistant of Dr. Zimbardo; for the second part of the experiment, a female experimenter appeared and was presented simply as "one of the graduate students." This experimenter proceeded to describe what was termed a "second experiment" to the Dissonance subjects and the "second part" of the experiment to the Controls: the intensity of the air puffs would be increased, there would be more trials, and "some subjects find this increase quite unpleasant." The Dissonance subjects were then offered the choice of whether or not to continue with this second experiment, and they were given differential verbal justification, depending on whether they were in the High or Low Dissonance treatment. The Control group, of course, was given neither choice nor justification.

On the 10 trials immediately after the threat (trials 21–30), the UCS was

1. Since no eyelid-conditioning apparatus was available at New York University when this study was initially proposed, the author spent a summer at the University of Massachusetts learning the experimental procedures and techniques under the supervision of Dr. John Moore. A pilot study conducted during this "apprenticeship" provided the occasion for both replicating the basic Spence and Goldstein effect (threat vs. no threat under no choice) and learning how to instrument our own conditioning laboratory. Conditioning data obtained using the apparatus built at N.Y.U. proved to be both reliable and comparable to the data obtained at the University of Massachusetts.

not increased; on trials 31–40, it was increased; and then without warning, on trials 41–50, it was discontinued entirely (i.e., there were 10 extinction trials).

Subjects

The data to be reported were taken from 125 subjects who participated to satisfy an introductory psychology course requirement at N.Y.U. (Washington Square College). Of these, 70 were males and 55 were females, a proportion similar to that (56 : 44) used by Spence and Goldstein (1961). Actually a total of 192 subjects were tested; but 42 refused to continue, the data for 21 were discarded for technical failure of the Offner early in the study, and 4 were discounted for failure to condition.

Refusals

Since the experimenter for part two was a young graduate student and the subjects were not familiar with the alleged senior experimenter, there was little pressure on the Dissonance subjects to comply with the request to volunteer for the second experiment out of considerations of status, personal relations, or fear of the influence of nonparticipation on a professor's evaluation of them (as may have been true in the previous study). Accordingly, a relatively large percentage of subjects refused to continue—25 per cent of the 167 subjects with analyzable records. While none of the Control subjects refused, 24 per cent of the Low Dissonance and 41 per cent of the High Dissonance subjects did. Obviously, the manipulations produced a meaningful difference in volition, as well as physical discomfort.

Checks on the Manipulations

Questionnaire data indicate that Dissonance subjects perceived that they had almost complete freedom of choice in their decision to participate in the second study (average of 60 on a 70-point scale)—more than twice as much as the Control subjects ($p < 0.01$). In addition, the Low Dissonance subjects (given the extrinsic justifications) found the "second experiment" more important to participate in than the first, while both the Control and High Dissonance subjects found both parts equally important (the difference is significant beyond the 0.05 level). Incidentally, there were no differences between the three groups in their perception of the experimenters (both "quite pleasant"), of the general scientific value of the experiment ("moderate"), and of the general value of their participation (also "moderate"). Thus, the manipulation appeared to work successfully, and since possible alternative modes of dissonance reduction were not used to a greater extent by any group, we are in a good position to assess the validity of our prediction that the increased conditioning performance shown by the Control and Low Dissonance subjects following threat would be inhibited under conditions created by High Dissonance.

RESULTS

There were no differences in conditioning level on trials 11–20 (pre-threat) among the groups (Duncan Multiple-Range Test). However, on trials 21–30 (post-threat), the Control group ($n = 44$) increased its level of conditioning by 19.1 per cent, the Low Dissonance group ($n = 40$) increased similarly by 14.3 per cent, while the High Dissonance group ($n = 41$) increased by only 2.7 per cent.

After a significant Conditions-by-Trials effect was established, a comparison of the difference between the Control and the High Dissonance groups yielded a (multiple comparison) t value significant at the 0.001 level. The High Dissonance group also differed from the Low, by a value significant at the 0.01 level. The Control and Low Dissonance groups were not different, but the increase in conditioning of both of these groups was significant. The increased conditioning

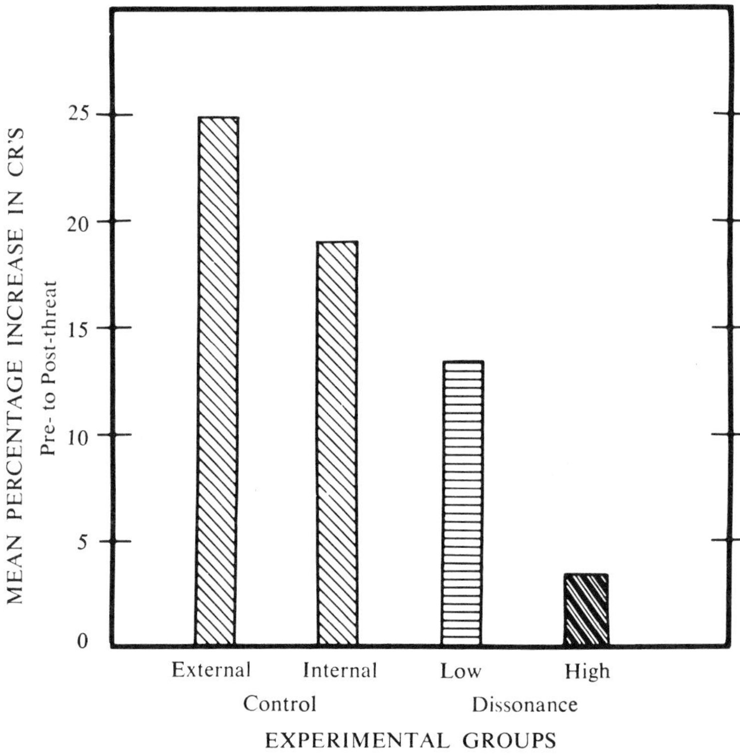

FIGURE 1
Mean percentage increase of conditioned responses from trials 11–20 to 21–30 (pre- to post-threat) for Control and Dissonance groups. The data for the External Control group are taken from Spence and Goldstein (1961).

effect raised the mean percentage of Conditioned responses (CRs) to about a 75-per-cent level for both these groups.

Figure 1 shows the mean percentage increase of conditioned responses on trials 21–30 over trials 11–20 for the Dissonance and Control groups compared to the data from Spence and Goldstein's (1961) Threat-No Choice group. The inclusion of this group provides an External Control for the complete experimental procedure—i.e., to see how subjects run in the N.Y.U. laboratory compare with those at Iowa under equivalent experimental conditions (with minor changes: an auditory rather than visual CS, and the omission of ready signal). Only the data for the High Dissonance group are significantly different from the others; the two Control groups do not differ significantly from the Low Dissonance group.

The predicted effect for the High Dissonance group is even more striking for the males in that condition: threat had virtually no effect on their conditioning performance, since it increased their percentage of CRs by only 1.7 per cent.

The differential effects of the cognitive manipulations on conditioning during the post-threat trials disappeared on trials 31–40 when the UCS intensity was actually increased. In addition, the group curves were also similar to each other during extinction.

External validity was established not only through the comparison shown in Figure 1, but also by obtaining absolute levels of responding comparable to other conditioning studies, a comparable effect of sex of subjects (females about 10 per cent higher), and a similar absolute conditioning-level effect of actually increasing the stimulus intensity (see Spence & Platt, 1966).

DISCUSSION AND CONCLUSIONS

These findings clearly support the prediction that the level of conditioning performance of subjects immediately after being threatened with a strong, unpleasant puff of air to the eye is markedly increased unless subjects are given a choice about continuing under conditions of low justification. The condition of cognitive dissonance renders this increased drive state ineffective for enhancing conditioning (through a blocking or functional lowering of the drive). Thus, we have established one source of data that contradicts the assumption that where there is a single and highly dominant response tendency (like the eyelid CR), an increase in drive strength will increase the probability of responding and thus lead to a higher level of conditioning.

The results of this investigation, therefore, have the value of underscoring the necessity for the recent trend among experimental psychologists to reconsider the significant role of attitudinal, cognitive, and emotional factors in even as "simple and direct" a response as eyelid conditioning. Moreover, when these results are viewed in conjunction with the results of Zimbardo et al. (Article 7), the theoretical structure of the relationship of dissonance orientation to the cognitive control of motivation is considerably strengthened. The same model was shown there to predict both improved learning or inhibition of learning knowing only the direction of the relationship between drive level and learning (or performance) in the given situation. Such a research strategy was also employed to rule out alternative explanations that could account only for *either* facilitation or deterioration of learning under the specific experimental conditions employed.

One possible alternative explanation for these experimental findings is that subjects could have adopted the strategy of blinking *before* the receipt of the air puff, thus minimizing its noxious effect. If subjects had adopted this strategy, it would seem there should be more "voluntary responders"[2] discernible in the Dissonance groups than in the Control group. This is in fact not the case. By the conservative latency criterion of 300 msec. (since there was no ready signal), there were 9, 14, and 13 voluntary responders in the High Dissonance, Low Dissonance, and Control groups, respectively. There was no difference even with a more liberal criterion of 350 msec.; the totals were 8 males and 9 females in the High Dissonance group, 14 males and 9 females in the Low Dissonance group, and 12 males and 10 females in the Control group. The opposite strategy of inhibiting responding should serve to produce many very late responses in the High Dissonance group. There is, however, no evidence that the latency of CRs differed among the groups.

Although the predicted effects on the behavioral measures are significant and sizable, there were no significant differences between any groups on self-report measures of perceived pain, irritability, eye tearing, or apprehension, or on other questionnaire items designed to measure subjective response to the aversive aspects of the situation. It may be that failure to find expected effects is attributable to taking these measures at the end of the entire conditioning procedure, when differences in perception and cognitive orientation may have been minimized by the comparable treatment all groups received on the 10 increased-UCS trials and 10 extinction trials. On the other hand, it may be that dissonance reduction can influence motivation and performance directly and still not be at the level where it can be verbalized (as suggested in the earlier study by Brock and Grant, Article 5).

The convergence of all group conditioning effects when the UCS was actually increased can possibly be best understood in terms of the proposal of Block and Bridger (1962) relating change in stimulation to the Law of Initial Value (as noted in the Introduction to this text). More severe stimulation is assumed to produce greater constancy of response. While the Law of Initial Value expresses a strict relationship between the stimulus and response level, both the prelevel and the arousal function of the stimulus can be modified effectively by cognitive functions up to some given level of stimulus intensity. When the UCS is increased above that level (for a given subject in a given sense modality), cognitive controls are overpowered and variance in behavior is drastically reduced. At such values of stimulus intensity, cognitive factors and individual differences can account for little of the variance that must be largely attributable to the parameters of the physical stimulus being applied.

2. Subjects were identified as voluntary responders if 50 per cent or more of their conditioned responses had a latency of less than 300 msec. (after Spence & Ross, 1959).

Finally, what can be said about the large percentage of refusals? Are the present results either biased or of limited generalizability as a consequence of this high rate of self-selected dropouts? The answer would clearly be "yes" if it could be shown that these subjects were more responsive to or disturbed by the UCS or the conditioning procedure and that their refusal thus represented a loss of subjects with lower sensitivity thresholds. There is no suggestion of this in any of our own data, however; and, in fact, there are no differences in either pre-threat conditioning or in perceived painfulness of the air puff or the entire procedure between subjects who accepted and refused the discrepant commitment. The mean percentages of CRs for the first ten trials were 44 per cent for the Refusals and 46 per cent for the committed subjects. On the second ten trials (pre-threat), the values were again not different: 57 per cent for the Refusals and 60 per cent for the committed subjects. On questionnaire data gathered after part one (during the "break" before the commitment attempt), there were no differences between these two populations in how painful they thought the UCS was, in their reactions to the experimenter, or in any aspect of the experimental procedure. Thus, there is no basis in the data we have available to assume that the decision of some subjects not to volunteer for exposure to an anticipated painful stimulus is related to differential initial drive level, threshold levels, or perception of the experimental procedures. Most important is the fact that they showed no differences in overall conditioning performance compared with those who made the commitment. Obviously, they must differ on some dimension, but it may not be one related specifically to the theoretical variables investigated in this study.

Editor's Comments

The value of this study lies not only in its unequivocal support of the dissonance hypothesis, nor in its extension of the concept of the cognitive control of motivation, but almost equally in the rigor and sophistication of its methodology and execution. The number of subjects assigned to each condition and the sex ratio were determined a priori by a statistical power analysis on data collected during extensive pilot testing. A total of 265 subjects were run during the two years required to develop the necessary skills, pretest the procedures and manipulations, and test the hypothesis. External validity was established between results obtained in the laboratory at New York University and those in eyelid-conditioning laboratories at the Universities of Iowa and Massachusetts. This was possible because of the degree of standardization attained in the conditioning procedure and in the objective assessment of the critical response—conditioned eye blinks. In addition, the inducements used to manipulate the cognitive variables were almost identical to those developed by Zimbardo et al. in the previous study and used by Mansson in his study on thirst (Article 6) and by Firestone in his study on aggression (Article 15). Therefore, the success of this study reflects back upon, and offers further validation of, the dissonance-arousing procedures developed in these related studies.

Without such a degree of methodological control over the many situational and stimulus variables operating, it would have been impossible to advance such a stringent test of the dissonance hypothesis, resting as it does on differences in percentage of CR increase for two data points (mean of trials 21–30 over trials 11–20).

Thus, the best features of the behaviorists' empirical approach have been used to demonstrate the weakness of any approach to human motivation that does not adequately account for the cognitive variables of choice and justification.

In neither this study nor the previous one was the distinction between learning and performance clearly articulated. Descriptions of the results, although phrased in terms of the effects of dissonance on verbal learning and classical conditioning, should more rightly be limited to effects on performance.

Learning is the consequence of a given history of reinforcement, while performance is a function of the variables that maintain the behavior. In the theoretical models used to generate the predictions in both of these last studies, drive was assumed to affect performance either negatively (shock decreases speed of rote learning) or positively (threat of pain increases eye-blink responses). Attempts to reduce cognitive dissonance were assumed to operate through the drive variable and to modify performance by lowering the drive. Thus, it should be clear that we have demonstrated only that dissonance can exert a powerful control over performance, but we have not shown whether, or in what ways, it could influence the learning of a new habit.

It has been suggested (by A. C. Catania of New York University) that if one is concerned with the effect of a stimulus on maintained behavior, the best research strategy to employ is the Skinnerian approach of superimposing a manipulation on stable behavioral (i.e., asymptotic level) output rather than on the variable output characteristic of acquisition responding. This is an approach some of our current research is taking (cf. Zimbardo, Dworkin, Ebbesen, & Fraser, 1966).

Data comparing the subjective reactions of the committed subjects to the refusal subjects (17 males and 12 females in High Dissonance; 7 males and 6 females in Low Dissonance) reveals an interesting, though complex, pattern of results. Contrary to the obvious expectation, those subjects who subsequently refused to continue experienced *less* anxiety during the first part of the study than did the committed subjects. On questionnaire reactions taken after the entire study for those committed and after the justification manipulation for those refusing, no differences were shown in perception of the experiment as anxiety arousing, of the air puffs as unpleasant, or of the procedures as annoying. However, refusal subjects felt less interest in the experiment, more choice to remain or go, relatively less value for the second than the first experiment, and less willingness to return again to serve as experimental subjects. Surprisingly, the committed Dissonance subjects were significantly more suspicious about being "tricked in some way in this experiment" than were their counterparts who refused to go on. The reactions of the refusal group were by no means homogeneous, they varied on different items according to sex of the subject, justification treatment experienced, and content of the item.

Pursuing our present, limited concern of clarifying the "self-selection artifact" has led us to see how little we understand of the process of social compliance in general, and how badly we need an appropriately sophisticated program of research to investigate the complex network of interacting predispositional, perceptual, and cognitive variables.

It is easy to talk on a theoretical level of dissonance lowering drive and pain perception or of anticipation of pain being minimized, but it is difficult to conceptualize the phenomenological view of the individual subject responding in these situations. Our self-report data provide few leads as to how the subject translates the impact of the cognitive manipulations into a response to the aversive stimulus or the experimental task. In the last study, data on perception of pain were weak and correlations between pain perception and the other dependent variables were low.* In the present study, there were no reliable differences among groups on any of the cognitive measures.

Perhaps we must then concur with the assertion of Verplanck (1957) that people don't have cognitions! Or is it that they may sometimes be unaware of them or unable to verbalize them, or that the questionnaire techniques used to elicit them are too insensitive or reactive?

An alternative approach to the problem is to consider what the average subject might have thought or said to himself in order to generate the behavior we observed in these studies. What is the psychological stratagem that is most probable when a subject volunteers to endure a painful, aversive stimulus with little extrinsic justification for doing so? He ought to try to minimize the unpleasantness of the stimulation by saying (hoping) that it will not be so bad: "The shocks won't hurt so much this time," and "The increase in the air puff won't make it much worse than it was before."

Such a cognitive interpretation is consistent with the obtained pattern of data and supported by the theoretical model we have been using. Unfortunately, the subjects won't tell us what we want to know. We certainly would feel more comfortable about the cognitive orientation of the subjects if *we* could temporarily control their cognitive input. If they perceived the situation according to verbal formulations provided by the experimenter, then we could determine the cognitive conditions required to reproduce the behavioral effects we have already demonstrated. Reasoning by analogy, then, we might be able to infer that the psychological stratagem most probably employed by the subjects is similar to the induced stratagem that yields the same behavioral consequences. The technique of hypnosis appeared to offer promise as a means of inducing, in more clearly defined, intensified form, the analog of several different motivational sets that might be the causal mechanisms involved in the pain control and modification of behavior we have shown here. The next study was designed to explore alternative cognitive orientations that the subjects might have developed as consequences of the experimental inductions used in the previous studies.

---

* In a study on the effects of competition, Church (1962) also found that a stimulus can influence each of three variables at the same time that the variables themselves are not interrelated. Competition was shown to increase reaction time, self-reports of "alertness," and skin conductance; however, the correlations between the dependent variables were negligible.

9. PAIN CONTROL BY HYPNOTIC INDUCTION OF MOTIVATIONAL STATES

Philip G. Zimbardo, Chanon Rapaport, and John Baron

This study was specifically designed to test two of the cognitive strategies that could have been responsible for the results of the earlier study by Zimbardo et al. (Article 7). These two strategies were thought to be the most likely ones that subjects in a High Dissonance condition could adopt to cope with the experimental demands of a verbal learning task under electric shock: (1) the self-induction of anesthesia to minimize pain and (2) the adoption of a heightened state of achievement motivation to enhance task performance.

The first strategy would follow as a natural consequence of the cognitive realignment produced by voluntary commitment to a situation in which the most salient consideration was the anticipated painfulness of the shocks. More rapid learning and lowered GSR (galvanic skin response) would occur if the subject could convince himself that the shocks would not hurt as much the second time around and if, in some unknown way, this self-persuasion modified the non-cognitive component of the pain-avoidance motive.

On the other hand, our results (in Article 7) could have been generated by an entirely different intervening process that has little or nothing to do with dissonance reduction. It is conceivable that some unexpected aspect of the experimental treatment used in the Low Justification condition (to create high dissonance) aroused achievement needs and made success on the learning task the most salient consideration. The wording used in this treatment might have been perceived as a challenge to the subject: he might have felt that since the second part of the experiment was not likely to add anything new to what was already known, by implication the experimenter expected the subject to behave on the second part as he had on the first. The subject might have thought, then, that a radical improvement in learning would make the experiment worth while and significant. Thus, by focusing his attention on improving his performance, he might have thought he could (1) help make the assistant's experiment "better" than the professor's, (2) show up the assistant's presumed lack of faith in the subject's ability, or (3) prove to himself that he could do better in a situation where other students apparently had not. Regardless of the object of this motivation, its operation would be quite different from the supposed dissonance-created pain-reduction strategy. Concentration upon the learning task might lead to improved performance in spite of the shock, whose distracting effects would then be overridden by this heightened state of achievement motivation.

The reasonableness of this strategy is supported by data not previously presented. The correlation (in the first study) between feelings of being absorbed in the task and being able to ignore the shocks was positive and relatively high ($r = +0.40$) for both the High Dissonance group and the High-Moderate

---

SOURCE: Zimbardo, Philip G., Chanon Rapaport, and John Baron, "Pain Control by Hypnotic Induction of Motivational States," unpublished.

Controls. Thus, being absorbed in the learning may have enabled these groups to ignore the shocks more. (Interestingly, the correlation between these variables for the other groups was in the opposite direction: Low Dissonance, $r = -0.44$; High-High Control, $r = -0.07$).

Evaluation of these alternative explanations of the results ought not to be by the sophistry of post hoc analyses but rather by means of a direct, empirical test. The test that was devised forms the basis for the present study. Basically, it involves the hypnotic induction of the two cognitive states—pain anesthesia and achievement motivation—in order to see if the subjects under either induction would react the same way as the High Dissonance subjects in the previous study. Obviously these are only two of the many processes that could have been operating in this complex situation, and if we are not able to reproduce our previous results through the induction of either of these two states, then we will be forced to re-examine other possibilities. If, however, we can replicate the entire pattern of earlier results by inducing one of these processes, we will have a more substantial basis for hypothesizing the cognitive strategy that was dominant in generating those results. If induction of the pain-anesthesia mechanisms lowers pain perception, improves learning, and lowers GSR to the shocks, then there is support (reasoning by analogy) for the assumptions underlying the dissonance interpretation. If, instead, the induction of the achievement mechanism produces this pattern of results, then the application of the dissonance formulation would appear to be entirely gratuitous.

OVERVIEW OF DESIGN

This experiment was identical in every way to the previous one by Zimbardo, Cohen, Weisenberg, Dworkin, and Firestone (Article 7), with the following exceptions: (1) Subjects were given up to 12 hours of prior hypnotic training until all had achieved a deep level of trance (somnambulistic state). (2) Following initial training in hypnotic relaxation and standard motoric and hallucinatory phenomena, subjects received either pain-anesthesia training (Hypnotic Anesthesia group) or achievement-orientation training (Hypnotic Achievement group). (3) For all subjects, the two-part shock-learning experiment involved the same instructions, tasks, and measures as the original study did for the High-High Controls—i.e., none of the subjects was given any choice as to whether he wished to participate in the second part of the experiment, and all subjects received the same (pain-threshold) level of shock in both parts of the experiment. The only changes were that respiration measures and checks (via TAT) on the arousal of achievement motivation were added. (4) There were two Control groups: one was used only in the training phase, to help evaluate the success of the hypnotic achievement induction; the other went through the entire procedure, but the motivational state (anesthesia) was induced through role playing rather than hypnosis. (5) During the pause between the two parts of the experiment, hypnosis was induced in the Hypnotic subjects and they were given either the achievement or the pain-anesthesia instructions. At this same time, the Role-Play Anesthesia Controls were instructed to role play pain-anesthesia.

FIGURE 1
Flow diagram
of procedure.

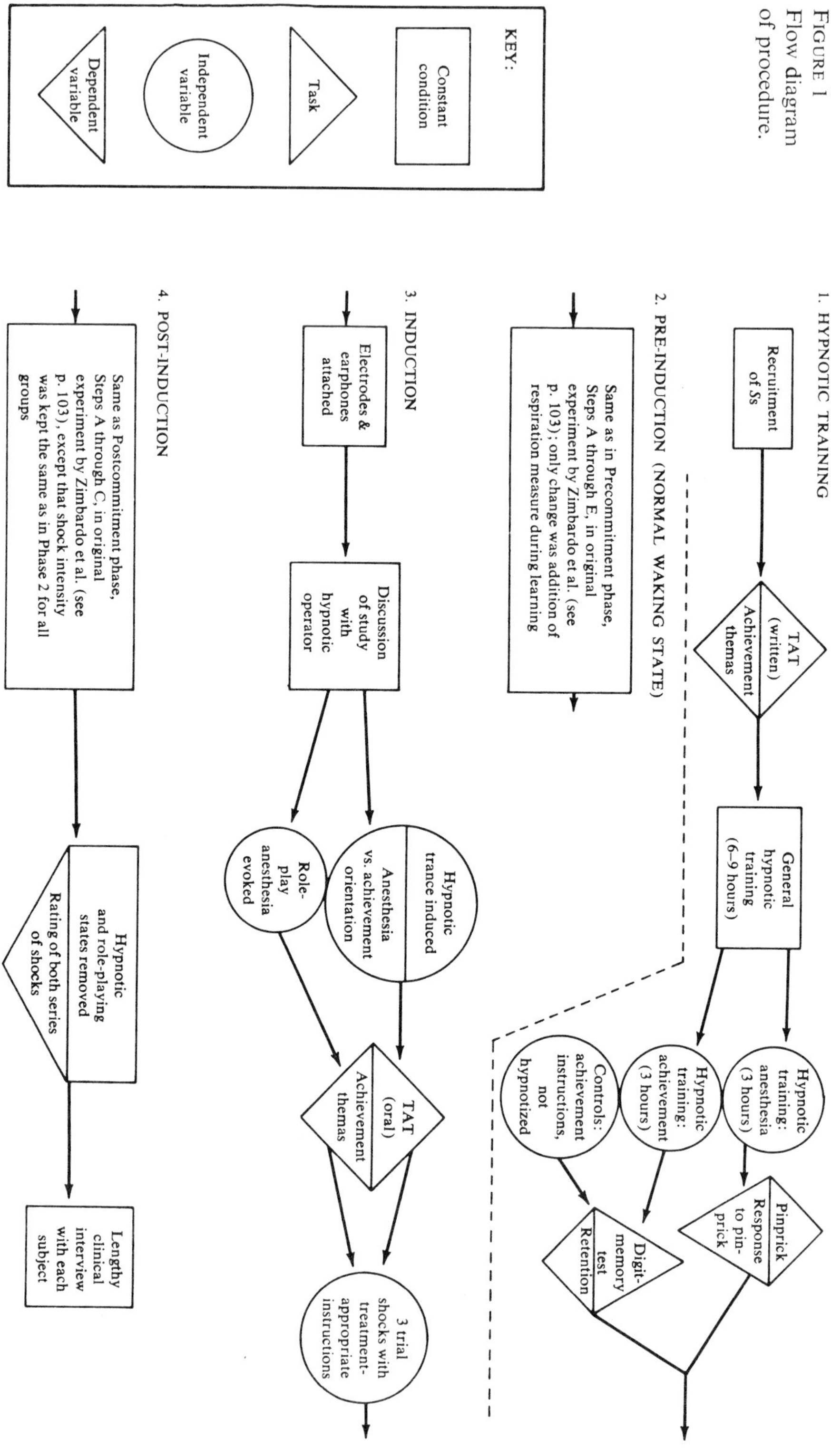

PROCEDURE

The sequential development of the procedure can best be seen in the flow diagram of its components in Figure 1.

Subject Selection

The subjects were graduating seniors from the Bronx High School of Science and freshmen from University College of New York University. They had previously been in a verbal-reinforcement experiment (unrelated to the present study) and were individually contacted by telephone to request their participation in another study, involving hypnosis. They were told that participation involved not only willingness to be hypnotized but a commitment to a training program of a minimum of three 3-hour sessions and a 2-hour experimental session, for which they would be paid $25.00.

Of 54 subjects contacted, only 4 refused[1] because of the hypnosis aspect, while 18 felt they could not meet all the required appointments because of jobs, school commitments, and religious reasons (we held sessions even on Saturday). Of the 32 assenting subjects, 26 actually showed up for the first training session (the others gave various reasonable excuses). Only one subject who went through the entire training procedure could not reach a deep state of hypnotic induction. The final data to be reported for the Hypnotic subjects are based on 19 subjects who experienced between 9 and 12 hours of hypnosis training and were able to achieve a somnambulistic state. Data for six subjects were discarded because of apparatus failure during critical stages of the procedure. The trained subjects were randomly assigned to the two motivation treatments.

An additional 25 subjects were contacted by phone and asked if they would be willing to be in a hypnosis experiment. The 19 who were willing were then told that although they might actually be used in such a study in the future, first they were to participate in an experiment in which they would not have to be hypnotized[2] (for the same hourly rate of pay that the Hypnotic subjects received). Of these subjects, 10 were assigned to the Role-Play Anesthesia group, while 9 were Controls for the effect of achievement instructions on performance during training.

Hypnotic Training

The training procedure was designed to accomplish the following: (1) to correct misconceptions about hypnosis (through counter-information); (2) to dispel

1. In one case, the student's mother paid her son $25.00 not to be hypnotized, and he accepted hers as the better proposition.

2. We had intended to have these subjects go through the same hypnosis training procedure as the others but could not because Dr. Rapaport had to return to Israel before the training could have been completed. Their comparability is limited, therefore, to coming from the same population and being willing to be hypnotized.

fears about hypnosis (by eliciting the fears and then discussing them and by letting the subjects question a "model" student who was hypnotized while they observed); (3) to make the subjects feel relaxed and confident about what might happen and how they would react (they were tested in small groups composed of their friends; the hypnotist and senior investigator tried to be warm, reassuring, and personally concerned about their individual welfare); (4) to achieve a deep enough state of hypnosis so that amnesia, posthypnotic suggestion, and various hallucinatory phenomena were possible; and (5) to induce pain-anesthesia and achievement effects that were unequivocally demonstrable and reliable.

The first training session consisted of repeatedly inducing a hypnotic relaxation state, having the subjects experience some reaction or stimulation, bringing them out of it, and then discussing the experience. The session stressed motoric phenomena (arm levitation, catalepsy, etc.) as well as deep relaxation. The second session stressed auditory, olfactory, and visual hallucinations (e.g., all the subjects saw a "good movie") and time distortion. All subjects were subsequently given training in reducing pain sensitivity in one hand and then increasing it in the other, as well as training in concentration. In the final session, the subjects received *either* the anesthesia training ("glove anesthesia") or achievement training, along with further deepening of the level of relaxation. Some subjects required an additional session prior to this final one in order to achieve as deep a state of hypnosis as the others.

Pain-Anesthesia Training. During the last training session, the Hypnotic Anesthesia subjects were told that their right hand was growing numb, that it could feel no sensation, that it felt as if it were covered with a thick impenetrable glove. This general set was amplified until the subject indicated that his hand indeed felt numb; then he was told that he would not feel any pain from a pinprick. The back of each subject's hand was then pricked with a pin until a drop of blood appeared. In no case was there any muscular reaction or change in facial expression. When "awakened," subjects reported feeling either pressure only or a momentary pain that rapidly dissipated.

Achievement-Motivation Training. During the final training phase, the Hypnotic Achievement subjects were given intensive training in concentration, focusing their attention, and avoiding distractions under hypnosis. The external criterion for the success of this training is not as immediately obvious as the pinprick was for the anesthesia training. However, it was determined in the following manner: Prior to being hypnotized, the subjects were given the digit-memory test of the Wechsler Adult Intelligence Scale (WAIS). They were then hypnotized and told, "You should try hard to concentrate on the new set of numbers you will hear, and *you will* be able to remember them better." A parallel form of this test was then administered, and any difference between the two scores was attributed to the hypnosis-achievement training.

So that we could assess the effects of the instructions alone and the contribution of hypnosis on this test of memory, the Control group of nine subjects was given the same two tasks, with instructions and temporal factors held constant, but they were not hypnotized. Table 1 presents the test results for these two Achievement groups. Eight of the nine Hypnotic Achievement subjects

TABLE 1

EFFECT OF ACHIEVEMENT-MOTIVATION TRAINING ON DIGIT-MEMORY TEST

Group	*n*	Score*			Subjects who improved, %
		Before instructions	After instructions	Difference	
Hypnotic Achievement	9	117.1	134.0	+16.9	89
Achievement Control (nonhypnotized)	9	110.5	108.3	—1.8	44

* Scores have been converted to full-scale Wechsler IQ.

improved their memory scores, and they did so by almost 17 IQ points (using a conversion of the subscale to full-scale Wechsler IQ). The only subject who did not improve was one who did exceedingly well in the prehypnosis test (IQ = 143). In contrast, those subjects given the same achievement-oriented instructions but not the hypnotic training and induction actually did slightly worse. The difference between these groups is significant at the 0.01 level.

Motivation Manipulation

Pain-Anesthesia Induction. After Part 1 of the shock-learning experiment (during which all subjects were in a normal, waking state), the Hypnotic Anesthesia subjects were hypnotized and told, "You will again receive shocks, but they will not be as painful as they were before." They then received three trial shocks equal to one third, one half, and the full intensity of the pain-threshold level of shock received in the first part. Before each of these trial shocks, the hypnotist said, in sequence, "This one will not hurt much," "This one will not be painful," "This one will not hurt as much as before." (These gradually increasing trial shocks were given to the Achievement subjects also, but without comment.) Then the final learning list was presented—accompanied, as in the earlier study, by painful, unavoidable shocks.

Achievement-Motivation Induction. Between Parts 1 and 2 of the shock-learning experiment, the Hypnotic Achievement subjects were hypnotized and told, "*You will* try hard to learn the word list, and *you will* do very well—better than you did before."

To assess specifically the effectiveness of these hypnotic instructions in arousing achievement motivation, responses made to TAT cards before and after the manipulation were examined. Prior to the first training experience, all the subjects wrote stories according to the standard TAT instructions to four TAT cards (#7BM, 8BM, and—from McClelland, Atkinson, Clark, and Lowell, 1953, p. 375—#1b and 1H). Immediately after the experimental manipulation of anesthesia and achievement, all subjects again responded to the same four

TAT cards. Interscorer reliability was +0.87, and all stories were analyzed by a rater who did not know the experimental status of the subjects.

There were no initial group differences in frequency of themas depicting achievement; but after the manipulation, while the Hypnotic and Role-Play Anesthesia groups maintained the same mean rank of achievement imagery, the mean rank of the Hypnotic Achievement group increased (showed more achievement imagery) by almost twice as much. These data are in the predicted direction, but they fall short of our established level of significance ($p = 0.07$).

Anesthesia Role-Playing Induction. These 10 Control subjects were not given any experimental training, but they participated in the first part of the shock-learning experiment as usual. Before Part 2, they were told:

> The second part of this experiment also involves electric shock and learning. However, this time I want you to act *as if* the shock does not hurt much. In other words, your task now is to role play or pretend that the shocks you receive are not as painful as in Part 1. Try to do so during the learning trials and also whenever you are asked to answer any questions which you feel are relevant to the intensity of the stimulation.

After the completion of the experiment, these Role-Play Anesthesia subjects were asked how well they thought they were able to maintain the prescribed role. Three of them felt that the intensity of the shocks made it impossible for them to act as if they didn't hurt, while the others felt they were able to role play "often" or "almost always."

Post-induction Procedures

After the subjects had been hypnotized and the differential sets induced, they were relaxed further and then told to open their eyes and look at the screen in front of them. On this screen were projected, successively, the TAT cards, the subjective-pain scale, and the words in List III to be learned. They were further told they could talk (call out answers) without disturbing their hypnotic state. They were reassured that the hypnotist would at all times be present in the adjacent booth and would observe their reactions. The first part of the experiment had been presented as Dr. Zimbardo's study of learning and physiology, while the second part was allegedly Dr. Rapaport's independent study of hypnosis and memory.

When the subjects had learned the words in List III perfectly (i.e., had two successive errorless trials), the experiment was terminated, the GSR electrodes, shock electrodes, and respiration belt were detached, and the experimental manipulations (i.e., the role playing or hypnosis) were removed. Under these "normal" conditions, the subjects then rated the perceived pain of both series of shocks. A lengthy postexperimental interview discussed the subjects' reactions to all phases of the study. The Hypnotic subjects were invited to describe their general reactions to the hypnotic experience and training on a questionnaire to be mailed to us after they had time to evaluate their feelings critically. In return for this, each subject received a complete report of the study as well as feedback on his individual performance.

RESULTS

On all measures, the Hypnotic Anesthesia group was more comparable to the High Dissonance group in our original study than was the Hypnotic Achievement group. In addition, the Hypnotic Anesthesia treatment was more effective in modifying pain response than was the Role-Play Anesthesia condition.

Pain Perception

Although there were no differences between groups in their initial subjective responses to the sample shock, after the motivation manipulation there were sizable and significant differences. The Hypnotic Achievement group felt the second sample shock was only slightly less painful than the first—a difference identical to the average 2-scale-unit adaptation shown previously by the High-High Controls and the Low Dissonance group. The Role-Play Anesthesia subjects were successful in playing that the shocks did not hurt, thus lowering their second estimate by 15 scale units. However, this simulation effect was only half as large as the reduction in pain perception of the Hypnotic Anesthesia group. The difference between the two types of anesthesia induction is significant at the 0.05 level, while that between the two hypnotic inductions is significant beyond the 0.01 level. When the role-playing orientation was removed and the subjects were asked to compare how the two series of shocks (Part 1 versus Part 2) "really" felt, they reported there was no difference—they were equally painful. On the other hand, we can see from Table 2 that the Hypnotic Anesthesia subjects internalized their motivational orientation; even when they were no longer

TABLE 2

MEAN SELF-RATINGS OF SHOCKS

Group	Shock level (volts)	Sample shock			Entire series*
		Pre-induction	Post-induction	Difference	Difference
Hypnotic Anesthesia	43	50	20	—30	—1.7
Role-Play Anesthesia	42	49	34	—15	0.0
Hypnotic Achievement	40	56	54	—2	—0.1

* The ratings of both shock series were made while the subjects were neither hypnotized nor playing a role.

TABLE 3

MEAN LEARNING-PERFORMANCE CHANGES*
(pre- to post-induction)

Group	Trials	Errors	Errorless runs
Hypnotic Anesthesia	—1.5	—4.2	—0.8
Hypnotic Achievement	+0.6	+1.6	+0.5
Role-Play Anesthesia	—0.3	+0.9	—0.1

* Negative values reflect improved learning following the motivation manipulation, while positive values indicate poorer learning (i.e., more trials and errors).

hypnotized, they felt that the second series of shocks was really less painful than the first (a change of 1.7 units, from "slightly painful" to "somewhat annoying," on a 6-point scale; $p < 0.05$).

Learning

The Hypnotic Achievement subjects, who had shown dramatic memory improvement during hypnotic training, did worse on List III (after motivation manipulation) than on List II! As can be seen in Table 3 and Figure 2 they

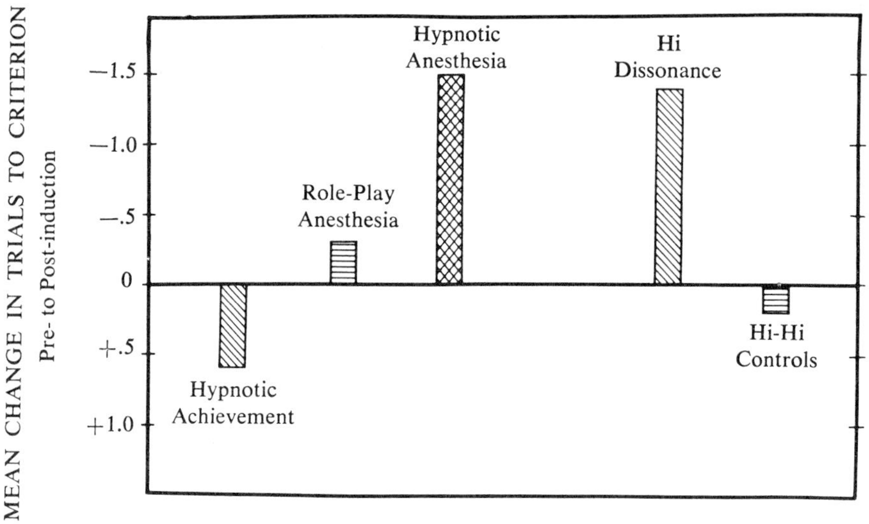

FIGURE 2
Mean change in learning performance from Part 1 to Part 2 of the experiment, expressed in number of trials required to reach criterion. Negative values reflect improved learning, and positive values reflect poorer learning. (All groups were given threshold-level shocks throughout.)

made an average of 1.6 more errors and required about half a trial more in Part 2 of the experiment than in Part 1. The change in trials to criterion is not different from zero, although the change in mean number of errors approaches significance ($p < 0.10$).

Role-Play Anesthesia subjects showed virtually no change in verbal learning performance, making more errors on List III than on II but requiring slightly fewer trials (−0.3) to learn the more difficult list. Neither difference is significantly different from zero.

Only the Hypnotic Anesthesia subjects (who were given pain-reducing instructions while they were hypnotized) significantly *improved* their learning performance in Part 2. They made an average of 4 fewer errors and required fewer trials on the more difficult List III than on List II. Both of these means are reliably different ($p < 0.05$) from those of the other two groups.

Results of the measured *errorless runs* (see Zimbardo et al.) are similar to those obtained on the other two indices of learning (see Table 3).

Comparisons with Groups from the Original Study

Figure 2 also presents some trials-to-criterion data from the earlier study, in order to make graphic the extent of comparability between the earlier High Dissonance group and the present Hypnotic Anesthesia group, as well as between the earlier High-High Controls and the present Hypnotic Achievement group.

This comparison is extended in Table 4 to include changes in pain perception, as well as other learning data. The physical-stimulus conditions for both the Hypnotic Anesthesia and the High Dissonance groups were the same as for the High-High Controls. Nevertheless, the cognitive differences had more impact on behavior than the similarities in sensory input. The Hypnotic Anesthesia and

TABLE 4

COMPARISON OF HIGH-DISSONANCE AND HYPNOTIC-ANESTHESIA GROUPS WITH CONTROLS IN WHICH PHYSICAL SHOCK WAS REDUCED OR HELD CONSTANT

Group	Shock level (volts)	Changes in pain perception		Trials to criterion			
		Sample	Series	Pre-induction	Post-induction	Difference	Subjects who improved, %
Hypnotic Anesthesia	43	—30.0	—1.7	9.2	7.7	—1.5	80
High-Moderate Control	45–22	—26.2	—1.8	9.6	7.7	—1.9	60
High Dissonance	49	—9.2	—0.9	8.8	7.4	—1.4	70
High-High Control	44	—2.9	—0.1	8.7	8.9	+0.2	33

High Dissonance groups show a remarkably similar pattern on all the learning data—extent of improvement from virtually the same Part 1 level as well as a similar percentage of subjects who improved. Moreover, their learning is more similar to that shown by the group in which shock intensity was physically reduced (High-Moderate Controls) than it is to that of the High-High Controls.

The cognitive control of pain by the hypnotic induction of anesthesia had an even more impressive effect on modifying perception of pain than did the physical control of pain produced by an average 23-volt reduction in the original study. For the Hypnotic Anesthesia group, a sample shock twice as intense as the one received by the High-Moderate group was felt by them to be even slightly less painful. The changes in pain perception produced by this hypnotic technique are clearly much greater than those produced in the previous experiment by the dissonance manipulation.

Physiological Data

GSR. We were able to perform more extensive analysis of the GSR data from this experiment than we had earlier, through the use of a semi-automatic Gerber digitizing apparatus and the use of a specially written (by John Ricci of New York University) IBM program for handling these data. Therefore, we were able to look at GSR changes not only on the first three shocks in each list but also on the last three and on all the shocks during List III minus List II.

On each of these measures (see Figure 3), the Hypnotic Anesthesia group was physiologically less reactive to the shocks after the induction than they were before. Moreover, the absolute value (in ohms) of the GSR reduction on the first three shocks mirrors the values shown previously by the High Dissonance and High-Moderate groups.

Although the role playing, or simulating, of an anesthesia effect resulted in lower self-reports of perceived pain, this reaction was not internalized in any way that affected either learning or GSR. There was a slight but nonsignificant *increase* in GSR for the Role-Play Anesthesia subjects on all measures; and the difference between these means and those for the Hypnotic Anesthesia subjects is significant ($p < 0.05$).

The pattern of GSR data for the Hypnotic Achievement group is somewhat less orderly; considering all shocks, there is no difference in GSR to the shocks accompanying either list. This mean value is significantly different from that of the Hypnotic Anesthesia group ($p < 0.05$) but not from the Role-Play Controls. However, on only the first three and last three shocks, this Achievement group showed a slight reduction in GSR—just enough to render the difference between it and the Hypnotic Anesthesia group on the first three shocks not quite significant ($p < 0.10$). This may be due to an initial generalized effect of the deep relaxation produced by the hypnotic induction.

Respiration. Respiration data was not available for all subjects because some of the required technical components were not ready at the start of the study. Thus, data for only 8 Controls and 8 Hypnotic subjects (2 Achievement and 6

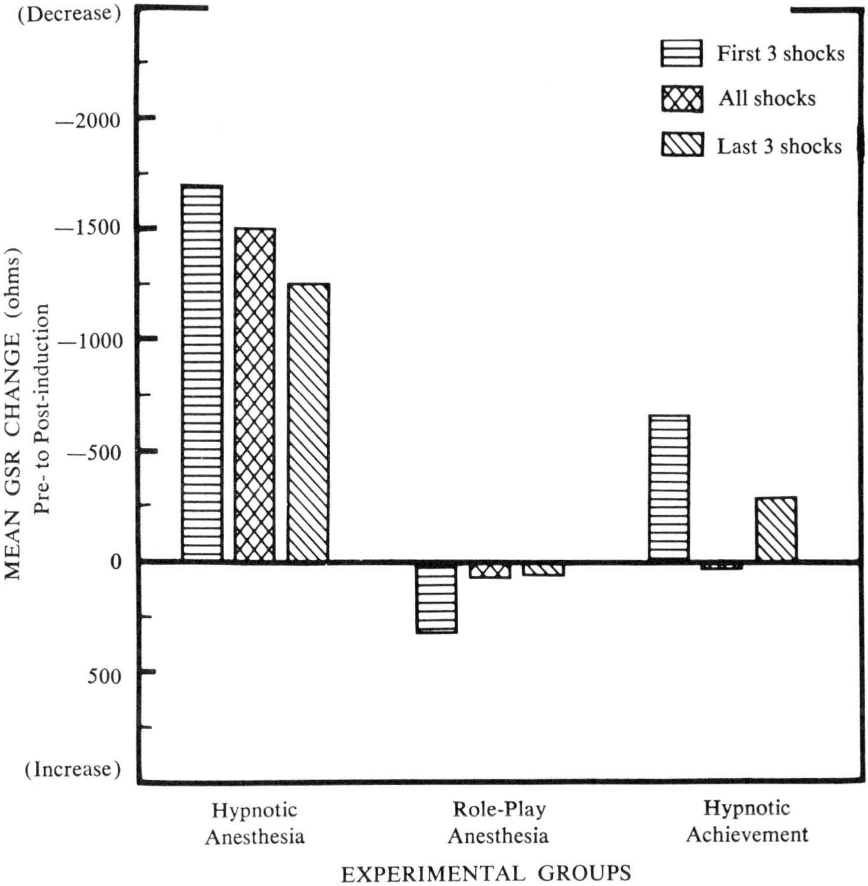

FIGURE 3

Mean differences in galvanic skin response to discrete shocks from Part 1 to Part 2. Three GSR samples were analyzed: reaction to all shocks, to first three only, and to last three only.

Anesthesia) could be used in evaluating whether the hypnotic relaxation effect apparently observed in the subject's overt behavior was systematically manifested in more regular breathing.

Two minute samples before and during hypnosis (during a no-task period) were selected, and frequency as well as variability in amplitude of respiration were recorded. There were no differences in rate of breathing between hypnotized and nonhypnotized subjects, but there was a difference in variability of amplitude. The average *variability* from a subject's largest inhalation to exhalation was the same for the Hypnotic and Control groups before the induction (both means about 51 on a 50-units-to-1-inch scale). After the induction, the Role-Play Anesthesia Controls were slightly more variable (mean = 55, increase = 4) while the Hypnotic groups were much more regular in their respiration (mean = 37, decrease = 14; $p < 0.10$).

An Example of Complete Cognitive Control of GSR

The data presented thus far are average group data and show relative differences which, though theoretically quite meaningful, may have little importance at the practical level of the management of pain. To what extent can an individual suppress his physiological response to a noxious physical stimulus? The data from one of our subjects, shown in Figure 4, provide a strong argument for rather complete control of pain-related physiological responding. Before hypnosis, each shock elicited a sizable response with rapid recruitment. After the Hypnotic Anesthesia induction, the response to the first shock was ten times smaller than the response to the first shock in the prior state (with shock intensity constant and basal skin response unchanged). After the second shock,

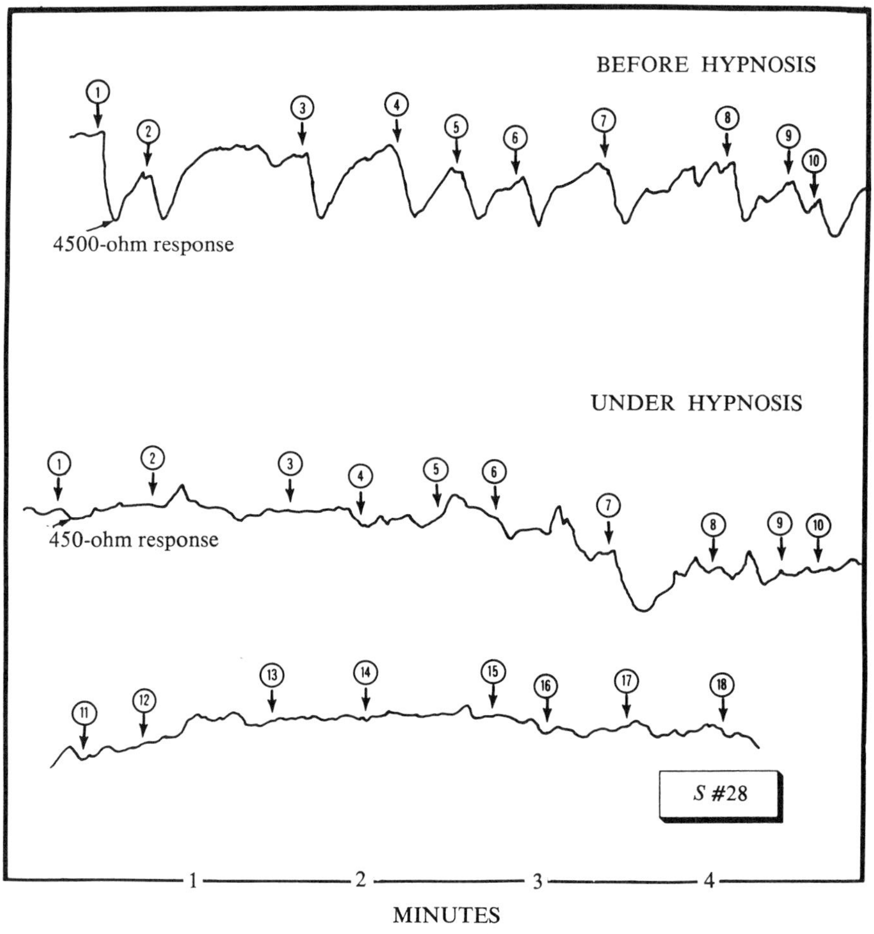

FIGURE 4
Continuous recording of GSR for an individual subject (#28) before hypnosis and while under the pain-anesthesia hypnotic induction. The numbered arrows indicate the successive shocks.

the subject shows absolutely no GSR to any of the shocks until #6 and #7, where he started to "come out of the trance" and his hand flinched. The hypnotist relaxed him and told him that the shocks would not hurt, and from then on he never responded physiologically to the shocks again. Although only several other subjects demonstrated this complete suppression of physiological response to one or more shocks, it is evident that such fine cognitive control of pain is possible. The next step is to discover the physiological mechanisms that mediate such a phenomenon.

CONCLUSIONS

It seems reasonable to conclude at this point that the hypnotic procedures utilized were effective in creating a general state that was different from that produced by the suggestion to role play an anesthesia-like reaction to the shocks. Within the Hypnosis condition, achievement orientation was aroused (as shown on the WAIS subtest scores and on the TAT data) and pain anesthesia was effective (as observed from the lack of reaction to normally painful pinpricks).

It is worth while to mention that the reason the Hypnotic Achievement group's task performance improved in training but not during the experiment was precisely because of the disrupting effects of the shocks. Some subjects told us that they believed the hypnotist completely, that they expected to do better and to do so immediately, and that when they began to make errors because the shocks distracted them, they became even more upset than previously. Others said that because the induction did not tell them anything about the shocks or *how* to improve their performance, they were unable to give themselves the instructions to ignore the shocks—without the hypnotist's permission. This reaction was clearly demonstrated during hypnotic training by an engineering student whose arm would not levitate when he was told to imagine a rising balloon tied to his wrist. He was able to have his arm levitate only after being taken out of the hypnotic state and requesting that the hypnotist *tell him* that the balloon was filled with helium and that it was tied to the last joint of his finger, which provided the necessary mechanical advantage. He knew this was how his arm could be made to rise, but while under hypnosis he felt he could not move the balloon without permission.

The entire pattern of results generated by hypnotized subjects who were told the shocks would not hurt as much is remarkably similar to that of the High Dissonance subjects. Since the data for neither of the other groups provide nearly as good a "fit," we may conclude (given the faults of reasoning by analogy) that the psychological stratagem employed by the High Dissonance subjects is likely to have been one that focused on cognitive control of shock intensity and involved a process of internalizing a self-persuasive communication to the effect that the shocks (and perhaps the air puff in Grinker's study) would not hurt as much. Such a cognitive realignment is in accord with the dissonance interpretation advanced earlier and increases our confidence in some of the assumptions we had advanced about the mechanisms by which dissonance arousal was translated into the behavioral consequences observed.

Editor's Comments

Three conclusions can be drawn from this present study and the original one (Article 7) on dissonance and reaction to electric shocks:

1. Subjects in a hypnotic state given anesthesia instructions reacted behaviorally and physiologically like nonhypnotized subjects in a condition of high cognitive dissonance when exposed to the same stimulus treatment.
2. Hypnotized subjects given anesthesia suggestions reported significantly less subjective experience of pain, improved their learning, and, given the same suggestions, showed reduced GSR to shock in comparison with role-playing controls simulating analgesia.
3. Hypnotized subjects given task-motivating instructions improved their performance in a digit-memory task significantly more than nonhypnotized controls given identical motivating instructions.

Surprisingly, evidence both supporting and contradicting these conclusions comes from the same series of studies by Barber and his associates (who have attempted to isolate the effective variables in results presumed to be produced by hypnosis). First, let us use this impressive array of research findings to document our basic conviction about the extensive degree of control exercised over psychological and physiological processes by cognitive mechanisms. According to Barber (1965a, p. 218), under hypnosis allergic reactions can be minimized, physiological reactions to cold stress can be minimized, labor contractions can apparently be induced and inhibited in some women at term, some features of the narcotic-withdrawal syndrome and some narcotic-like drug effects can be produced in postaddicts, water diuresis (increase in urine flow) can be elicited in some hydropenic female subjects (hypnotically hallucinating water ingestion while fluid intake was restricted), ichthyosis (fishskin disease) can be mitigated, and wheals can be produced in patients suffering from urticaria (hives).

In addition, the major thrust of Barber's methodological critique of hypnosis studies has been to explode the myth of special hypnotic phenomena by demonstrating that the effects attributed to hypnosis can be produced in nonhypnotized control groups given the same motivating instructions. From our point of view, accepting the null hypothesis between the experimental (hypnotized) and control groups can be a source of comfort if it is valid or it can provide the occasion for examining procedural differences between our study and his work.

If the hypnotic procedure is really irrelevant, then the only difference between our critical groups—High Dissonance and Hypnotic Anesthesia—is that the analgesia instructions were explicit in the latter and presumed implicit in the former. Such a state of affairs would allow us to draw the theoretical analogy we have proposed without concern for hypnosis as a source of confounding. In fact, Barber and Hahn (1962) have demonstrated that an appreciable number of subjects can reduce their responses to pain in a manner like hypnotized subjects, even without being hypnotized.

How can it be that hypnosis is ineffective and task-motivating instructions extremely effective? The most parsimonious answer lies in the impotency of the hypnosis procedure used and in the potency of the motivating instructions. In general, experimental purity was retained in these studies by the use of standardized tape-recorded instructions. Tapes are usually more authoritarian than permissive in tone, and they pose many challenges to the subject in a short time period—such as eyelid and arm catalepsy, inability to unclasp hands or to say one's name, regression to age six, hallucinations, and amnesia. A study by Parker and Barber (1964) may be used to illustrate the induction of the two experimental conditions. Hypnosis was created by "a standard hypnotic induction procedure which subsumed a period of approximately 10 minutes" (p. 501) and included 10 tests or challenges during that time. (Other studies by Barber have used longer training sessions—of 15 minutes, [cf. Barber & Calverley, 1964]. In a recent study by Klinger [1968] of the effects of length of induction on hypnotic responsiveness, the "long" induction was only 10 minutes while the "short" was less than 60 seconds, and there were no differences found between them.) It is the opinion of Parker and Barber that such a procedure was adequate for these subjects to attain "what investigators in this area generally view as a medium or deep 'trance'" (p. 501; see also Parker, 1963).

On the basis of our experience with hypnosis, we would be surprised if such a standardized, brief, one-shot procedure, not tailored to the individual subject's ongoing reactions, and utilizing repeated challenges, could produce more than what was designated as "light trance" in our study. Thus, one difference between these results and ours may be that the hypnotic-induction procedures in our study were too strong.

The reasons why the task-motivating instructions had such potent effects in the studies by Parker and Barber may perhaps be gleaned from the following description of them:

> In this experiment I am testing your ability to perform better on equivalent forms of the three tasks you have completed. How well you do depends entirely upon your willingness to try. If you try real hard, you will do better. Everyone who has tried harder on these tests has done better the second time and I'm sure you can, too. You'll be surprised how well you can really do, if you really try hard. I want you to score as high as you possibly can, because we are measuring the maximum ability of people who have really tried. I am asking for your cooperation in this experiment to try to the best of your ability. If you don't try the experiment will be worthless, I'll feel disappointed, and it will have been a waste of your time and mine. On the other hand, if you really try hard to the very best of your ability, you can and will do much better. Are you ready? Now try to do the very best you can, try real hard, really try (Parker & Barber, 1964, pp. 500–501).

Thus, the other source of difference between these studies and our own is that our motivating instructions were, by comparison, too weak. It may be that we could have replicated some of the findings of Barber and his associates by minimizing the difference between hypnosis and motivated role-playing conditions through superficial training procedures for hypnosis and intensive motivation instructions for the Controls; but then we would have been faced with the problem well articulated by Barber himself in his recent (1965a) review of this literature: "Whether or not subjects who have received only motivational instructions are in a hypnotic state remains to be demonstrated" (p. 202).

Our study was not designed to assess whether hypnosis alone was the effective variable (or state) in producing the results, and therefore it did not adequately control for all of the many variables that could confound such an interpretation. We did, however, heed Hilgard's (1965) methodological suggestion in our evaluation of the achievement training procedure: "The correct comparison would be between the effect of task-motivating instructions in the waking state and the same task-motivating instructions in the hypnotic state; only then could it be ascertained whether or not hypnosis made a difference" (pp. 165–166).

Although some researchers have failed to find any effect of hypnotic analgesia in laboratory studies (cf. Shor, 1962, and Sutcliffe, 1961), Hilgard concludes his review (1965) of the available research reports by noting that evidence of hypnotic analgesia in surgery is so widespread that "the possibility of reducing subjective pain by hypnotic-like procedures cannot be questioned" (p. 163). But here again we are dealing with the difference between clinical hypnosis and the management of chronic pain on one hand and experimental hypnosis and reactions to induced pain on the other—a problem we discussed earlier, in the notes following Article 7.

If hypnosis is viewed simply as a powerful technique for modifying motivational states and cognitive processes, even though the process by which it operates is not yet understood, then it can be a valuable adjunct to other forms of manipulation employed by those interested in studying human behavior in a controlled, laboratory setting. With regard to the central problems raised in this text, hypnotic techniques might be used to arouse drives, to create cognitive inconsistency or lack of awareness of inconsistency (as Brock and Grant did in Article 5), to alter temporal aspects of anticipation of events through time distortion (can dissonance exist if one has no awareness of the past?), to modify perception of choice and the significance of specific forms of justification, and to limit available channels of dissonance-reducing behavior through appropriate instructions.

This study, in directing our attention to the role of socially learned needs such as the need for achievement, provides a transition point from our studies on hunger, thirst, and pain control to those on a variety of social motives. On the one hand, it is more convincing to be able to demonstrate cognitive control over biologically and physically based motivation than over social motivation, but it is also empirically easier because of the relative clarity of the operations required to arouse and reduce such drives. In the next section, we will be dealing with more complex manipulations designed to induce certain social motives and with less obviously direct response reflections of those motives. Can cognitive control of social motives be unambiguously demonstrated using the same theoretical model and methodological strategy shown to be effective in the previously presented research?

Part II

Social Motives and Personality Variables

10. DISSONANCE AND THE NEED TO AVOID FAILURE

A. R. Cohen and P. G. Zimbardo

> Essential to survival as the physiologically [based] motives are—fascinating and exotic as may be the ways in which we gratify them—their actual indulgence occupies surprisingly little time among most people of the world. Even people in the least technologically advanced societies do not spend most of their waking moments in eating, drinking, and sexual activities. Instead, people in both modern and preliterate societies bend the bulk of their energies toward the attainment or expression of states of mind and qualities of experience that are not stirred by the innate imperatives of their biological functioning but, instead, by the values they have learned as members of their society (Sarnoff, 1966, pp. 15, 16).

Sarnoff's provocative analysis of the social-psychological foundations of our society demonstrates the extreme importance most men place upon the values of aggrandizement (wealth, prestige, and power) and how we come to develop a self-concept, a definition of our purpose and place, in terms of such values. Finally, he points out the manner in which such a value system is transformed into powerful motives that come to guide, direct, and even to compel our behavior toward limitless achievement (see also McClelland, 1967).

Although this focus on achievement is most characteristic of the American enterprise system, it can be found in an even more pernicious form in our citadels of higher learning. The procedures for competitive testing, evaluation and comparison, and the use of grades as keys to higher levels of further competition or for their own sake rightly deserve the students' characterization of the whole endeavor as one big rat race with only a small piece of cheese in the trap. Nevertheless, the need to succeed, to achieve, to perform well (or rather, better than everyone else) does become dominant in the motivational hierarchy of all but a select few college students.

Let us suppose that a success-oriented student is induced to commit himself to performing in a situation that promises failure. His initial motivation to achieve success (and to avoid failure) should not logically lead to his commitment to a probable failure experience. But if he does make this commitment under conditions where the pressure or justification is just sufficient to induce such a discrepant behavior but where he perceives that the decision was nevertheless voluntary, then he ought to experience a high level of dissonance motivation; and his dissonance should be increased the more certain the prospect of failure and the more serious its consequences.

SOURCE: Cohen, A. R., and Philip G. Zimbardo, "Dissonance and the Need to Avoid Failure." Adapted from "An Experiment on Avoidance Motivation," from *Explorations in Cognitive Dissonance* by J. W. Brehm and A. R. Cohen (New York: John Wiley & Sons, Inc., 1962), pp. 143–151. Reprinted by permission of the publisher and the editor.

How can such dissonance be reduced? First, the student might disavow personal responsibility for the decision by pointing to coercive forces that determined his decision (e.g., "My advisor insisted that I take the risk"), or he might be able to generate new justifications for the probable failure by redefining the failure as a risky choice (e.g., "It's necessary sometimes to take a step backward before you can take two forward," or "Nothing ventured nothing gained," or "I didn't think I could win, but the prize was too big to pass up," etc.). However, if the circumstances associated with his commitment do not permit such ready rationalizations, we might expect to see the process of dissonance reduction influence his behavior in a more dramatic fashion. Commitment to failure would not be dissonant if the motive to succeed was itself lowered or eliminated. Thus, it is likely that our subject will behave in a manner contrary to the value system he has learned from his success-oriented culture—by actually lowering his achievement motivation. Rather than attempting to avoid failure, such a person should behave in ways to guarantee it.

DISSONANCE PREDICTIONS

Given people with high success motivation who voluntarily commit themselves to a task promising failure, greater dissonance will be aroused the more probable or extreme their anticipated failure. Dissonance reduction will take the form of lowering success motivation (or lowering motivation to avoid failure[1]). This motivational change will be reflected in task-relevant behavior that makes improvement in performance unlikely. More specifically, if given the opportunity to select a difficulty level for the anticipated task, Low Dissonance subjects should choose a level likely to promote success, while High Dissonance subjects should choose a more difficult level, one promising failure.

The ambitious aim of attempting in a brief laboratory experience to reverse a subject's history of cultural reinforcement for achievement and success represents an admittedly exploratory attempt to extend the dissonance formulation into the area of social motives and the behaviors generated by such motives.

OVERVIEW OF EXPERIMENTAL DESIGN

Subjects were first given task instructions designed to arouse achievement needs, after which they were given a 5-minute failure experience on an extremely difficult task. They were then asked to commit themselves to a subsequent, much longer experience (50 minutes) under the same conditions. Compliance was expected to create dissonance because, while being voluntary and only minimally coerced, it represented exposure to failure for subjects who had wanted to be

1. No explicit distinctions are made here between motivation to achieve success and to avoid failure. For our present purposes, these presumably separate motivational strands can be viewed within one framework, although they have, of course, been explicitly separated and shown to have different implications for behavior (see Atkinson, 1957).

successful on the task. The magnitude of dissonance was manipulated by varying expectations of the degree of anticipated failure. Accordingly, half the subjects were told that it was likely they would not do too badly in the next session (Low Dissonance), while the other half were led to expect they would probably do "very poorly" (High Dissonance).

After committing themselves to this prospect of moderate or extreme future failure, subjects were allowed to adjust a dial on the apparatus that controlled the stimulus presentation. Reducing the dial setting from the level employed in the 5-minute task would be expected to improve future performance, while maintaining or increasing its level would not. This was the major dependent measure, on which we predicted that High Dissonance subjects would choose higher dial settings than Low Dissonance subjects. Auxiliary measures of motivation and evaluation of the experimental manipulation and perception of choice were also taken.

PROCEDURE

Each of the 21 subjects (12 male and 9 female New York University undergraduates, participating to fulfill an introductory psychology course requirement) was taken individually into a sound-resistant room where the study was described to him (through earphones) as relating verbal behavior to memory processes under special conditions.

A generally high motivation to succeed was induced by instructions that stressed the creativity, sensitivity, and general ability required to perform well on the experimental task, involving disruptive speech conditions. The task was to memorize a short poem in 3 minutes, then recite it aloud from memory and discuss its psychological implications. The poem read:

> Who when looking over
> Faces in the subway
> Each with its uniqueness
> Would not, did he dare,
> Ask what forms exactly
> Suited to their weakness
> Love and desperation
> Take to govern there.

This task was made exceedingly difficult by the requirement that it be performed under conditions of delayed auditory feedback. A delay of 0.2 seconds was mechanically interpolated between the subject's speaking (which he could not hear directly) and the return of his speech over the earphones. Delayed auditory feedback (DAF) of this duration usually produces speech, emotional, and thought disturbances, and, because of the novelty of the experience, subjects do not have established standards for a "good" performance on this task (Smith, 1962; Yates, 1963; Zimbardo, 1965).

None of the subjects was able to perform this task without considerable effort, and most had difficulty even making themselves comprehensible.

Dissonance Arousal

After this initial failure experience, subjects were asked to commit themselves to a second, much longer session with the DAF apparatus. All subjects were told:

> In a second session for which we are asking our subjects to volunteer, we will be studying the same phenomenon, but for a full 50-minute period, not for only 5 minutes as in the initial session. Although participation in this initial session is part of your course requirements, volunteering for the second session is entirely up to you. Since it will be *after the regular term is over*,[2] we are giving all of our subjects $2.00, a nominal fee, for returning for the second session. Now, before I ask you whether you wish to return at a time convenient to you, let me tell you that from our experience and analysis of several response measures obtained from you today, we can tell you that, compared to all of the other students we have tested, *next time* you will:
>
> (High Dissonance:) perform very poorly—among the worst subjects we have ever run.
>
> (Low Dissonance:) perform not too badly, about average or a little less than the average subjects we have run.
>
> In spite of this, we would like you to return for a second session. Will you be able to come?

At this point the subject's freedom of choice was stressed several times. If he agreed, he was then scheduled for the alleged second session and committed himself by signing a petty cash voucher. (Only one High Dissonance female subject refused the commitment.)

DAF Dial Setting

After agreeing to return, the subjects—tested individually throughout—were told that the initial testing was over and the experimenter pretended to relax his previously formal (scientific) composure (by removing his white lab coat, smiling more, inviting the subjects to smoke if they wished, etc.). The subjects were then taken into the apparatus room so that they could see the DAF equipment. They were shown the recorder and the dial indicating the delay interval, and they were told that in the initial session the interval was extreme but constant at point 13 on the 15-point scale. *It was stressed that the size of the delay determined the amount of speech disruption and presumably the amount of failure each subject experienced and that a shorter delay would result in a better performance.* The subjects were then told that since they knew their own subjective reaction to the situation, the experimenter would like *them* to choose the

---

2. The experiment was purposely conducted during the last weeks of the school term in order that the subjects' decision to commit themselves to the discrepant future behavior would not be bound by "involuntary" participation requirements, but would involve a meaningful choice.

point on the dial at which they would like to begin the next session (and would keep for at least half the session). Each subject then physically adjusted the dial in response to the request that he select the DAF level he wanted to experience at the second session. The subject could see how the tape loop changed speed as a function of the direction and extremity of the dial setting.

Auxiliary Measures

Approach to and avoidance of the failure task were also measured by: (1) offering the subjects—after they had reset the dial—an opportunity to switch to a different, nonevaluative, nonfailure task; (2) having them list all the advantages and disadvantages of DAF research they could recall from a prepared report they had read before the experiment; and (3) asking them to rate their desire to perform well on the future task. Checks on their perception of the likely degree of failure and of the voluntariness of their choice to undergo the future session were also taken.

All subjects were then assured that they had actually performed rather well on this very difficult task, that the second session could not be conducted, but that they would receive the $2.00 anyway.

RESULTS

Behavioral Measures

Table 1 presents the data for the mean dial setting selected by the subjects in the two experimental groups. As predicted, the majority of those in the High Dissonance condition (80 per cent) chose to maintain the interval of delay at its initially high level (13 on a 15-point scale) or to make it even higher, while most of those in the Low Dissonance condition (90 per cent) chose to reduce it ($p < 0.05$). The Lows attempted to minimize their anticipated difficulty in speaking and thinking in the expected second study by lowering the setting by more than 3 units, while the average setting for the Highs was unchanged from its initial value. Even with the small size of the groups ($n = 10$), this difference is significant beyond the 0.05-per-cent level (by t-test). There were no differences attributable to the sex of the subjects.

TABLE 1

MEAN DAF DIAL SETTING FOR ANTICIPATED-FAILURE TASK

Group	n	Initial level	Adjusted level	Change	Subjects who lowered level, %
Low Dissonance	10	13.00	9.58	—3.42	90
High Dissonance	10	13.00	13.03	+.03	20

None of the other results is statistically significant, although they form a pattern consistent with the dissonance expectations. While 4 of the 10 Low Dissonance subjects preferred to change to a nonfailure task (allegedly, to help the experimenter score GSR records accumulated from this study), none of the High Dissonance subjects chose to avoid failure by changing to this task. Similarly, the Lows had better recall of the disadvantages of DAF research than did the Highs, who recalled more of its positive attributes. The recall of more disadvantages indicates greater avoidance motivation toward this task for the Low Dissonance subjects, while the High Dissonance subjects revealed greater involvement with and approach toward this failure task

Cognitive Measures

On cognitive measures, too, the results do not reach acceptable levels of significance, so that we may refer only to the consistent *trend.* The High Dissonance group expected more failure on the second DAF task than did the Low Dissonance group (mean of 4.5 vs. 5.5, respectively, on an 8-point scale), and they wanted to do *less* well compared to the Lows (mean of 5.0 vs. 6.1 on an 8-point scale).

Even though choice was not experimentally manipulated in this study, the High and Low Dissonance groups differed in the degree to which they felt "coerced." Dissonance in the high-arousal treatment was reduced in part by exaggerating (in comparison to the low-arousal treatment) the degree to which the commitment was forced. The High Dissonance subjects perceived they had slightly less free choice (mean of 4.9 vs. 6.7 for Low Dissonance, out of 8.0) and were slightly more obliged to continue (mean of 5.0 vs. 6.8 for Low Dissonance, out of 8.0).

CONCLUSIONS

Subjects appeared to reduce the dissonance occasioned by commitment to a prospect of failure (after being motivated to succeed) by two strategies: decreasing the proportion of cognitions arguing against their discrepant commitment (e.g., lowering task-success motivation) and increasing the proportion of obligation to accept the commitment. It may well be that the subjects' use of this second strategy served to minimize the observed differences between the two Dissonance groups and attenuated the large effects found on the first response measure (DAF-dial setting).

Although interpretation of these results is far from unequivocal without additional control measures and control groups, nevertheless, it appears that subjects who commit themselves to greater failure in the future show a greater willingness not to avoid that failure. The behavioral data on adjustments of the DAF-dial setting are taken as evidence that avoidance of failure motivation has been significantly reduced for subjects given an experimental treatment assumed to create high cognitive dissonance.

Editor's Comments

This preliminary study in our research series (actually the first we conducted) is provocative because of the sizable behavioral difference obtained by using a small, mixed-sex sample and a dissonance manipulation that objectively might not seem capable of yielding such effects. However, the limited nature of its design raises many questions of interpretation, which can only be answered by reference to other research. A recent study in our laboratory at New York University provides some information about perception of the DAF task and anticipation of future performance on it, while the next study presented in this section attempts to clarify the dissonance explanation of the change in motivation.

Performance on reading and memory tasks under delayed auditory feedback (DAF), reduced auditory feedback (RAF, or white noise), and normal feedback conditions was tested on 72 subjects in a Latin Square design, i.e., with each subject exposed to all treatments in a counterbalanced order (Mahran, 1966). DAF produced the most speech errors, required the longest durations for reading, and resulted in poorest recall (all p values < 0.001). In addition, self-report measures revealed that subjects perceived they expended most physical effort under DAF ($p < 0.001$), were most distracted by it ($p < 0.005$), did "worse than other students at this college" on DAF ($p < 0.001$), could improve only slightly even with longer exposure or additional practice, and would consider it intolerable to have to perform under DAF for a long period of time. Thus, there is little question that this task is aversive, produces a feeling of failure, and does not create a high expectation of improvement with practice (in fact, this last is a veridical perception, since adaptation is minimal on this task).

It is interesting to speculate upon what might have resulted if subjects in the present study had been allowed to repeat the same task immediately after the dissonance commitment with the same DAF interval as they experienced initially. On the one hand, motivation to succeed should have been lowered, but on the other, the aversiveness of the stimulus situation should have been lessened by the agreement to endure more of it. Combining these cognitions, dissonance reduction might have taken the form of a result in which subjects would perceive they did poorer on a task they judged to be easier. Such a subjective interpretation would certainly be damaging to one's self concept and could, if repeated, produce low self-esteem and eventually result in academic dropouts.

In the next study, Peter Schlachet clarifies some of the ambiguities about the dissonance interpretation of the results of this study versus a level-of-aspiration interpretation (seeing the selection of more extreme dial settings as reflecting raised levels of aspiration produced by the experimenter's "challenge"). He combines a less complex failure manipulation with a previously validated manipulation of dissonance (different incentives for commitment) and includes the relevant control group. However, his study focuses on the issue of selective recall. In the present study, the main interest was in the DAF-dial-setting behavior, and only tangential interest was directed to the recall of attributes of the task. The problem of motivational influences upon selective recall is, however, a more generally important one to psychologists than the behavior scrutinized in the present study. If a dissonance commitment to failure results in reduced motivation to succeed, then there should be a change in the affective quality of stimuli associated with the failure. If so, this should lead to demonstrable changes in the recall of such stimuli.

11. THE MOTIVATION TO SUCCEED AND THE MEMORY FOR FAILURE

Peter J. Schlachet

One of the most interesting and complex problems faced by both experimental psychologists and clinicians involves the dynamics of selective recall. What are the conditions that increase the probability that one event will be easily recalled, another will be difficult to remember, and a third will be repressed and thus not available for recall except under very special conditions (e.g., hypnosis, truth serums, prolonged therapy, etc.)?

The principle of selection in memory was recognized as early as 1873 by Spencer who defined *pleasure* as a " a feeling we seek to bring into consciousness." Thorndike's "law of effect," according to which an experience followed by a satisfying state is "stamped in" while one followed by an unpleasant state is "stamped out," may well have been inspired by such a concept. In fact, one early study sought to classify people into "memory optimists" and "memory pessimists" on the basis of whether pleasant or unpleasant life experiences were most readily recalled (Kowalowski, 1904). According to this view and the results of many early studies, recall was guided by emotion, with a stimulus of positive hedonic tone having a greater likelihood of being recalled than one of negative hedonic tone (cf. Diven, 1937, and McGranahan, 1940, for studies demonstrating poorer recall for shock-related stimuli).

The effects of failure on recall are somewhat more complex. The original work by Lewin and his students revealed the "Zeigarnik" effect of better recall for interrupted tasks (Zeigarnik, 1927; McKinney, 1935). However, it was later shown that the subject's interpretation of the interruption was a critical determiner of recall (Rosenzweig, 1943). Recall was poorer when the interruption was perceived of as task failure than when it was perceived of as part of an informal, nonevaluative condition. This general conclusion was subsequently modified by research (Ito, 1957) that found that recall was better for tasks associated with

Source: Schlachet, Peter J., "The Motivation to Succeed and the Memory for Failure." Adapted from "The Effect of Dissonance Arousal on the Recall of Failure Stimuli," *Journal of Personality*, 1965, *33*, pp. 443-461. Reprinted by permission of the author and Duke University Press.

success under stressful conditions, while nonstressful conditions resulted in better recall of failure tasks.

While this line of reasoning posits memory selections on the basis of association of an affect with a "neutral" stimulus, another approach suggests that affect may provide an interference to recall by interpolating an unpleasant experience. Zeller (1950, 1951) showed that a frustrating interpolated task significantly depressed recall, while Merrill (1954) found that a combination of experimentally induced failure and anxiety-related words led to a sizable decrement in recall. In like manner, Worchel (1955) demonstrated that both recall and relearning were poorer for failure-associated words than for nonfailure ones. Truax (1957) extended these general findings by utilizing an individual-differences variable with which he showed that hysterical subjects tended to relearn anxiety-laden words (associated with failure) more slowly than neutral words. However, quite unexpectedly, obsessive subjects showed the opposite effect; they relearned the anxiety words slightly faster on the postfailure trials.

Speculation upon the implications of this finding leads one to question whether different predictions could be made if one considered the cognitive elements of the recall situation rather than seeing recall as dependent on previous association of affects. Although the Zeigarnik conception of forgetting as one version of "closure" is a cognitive one, it appears that the affective qualities of the experimental conditions are the causal agents in forgetting, i.e., the stress, ego-involvements and perceived failure. As early as 1911, Henderson drew the distinction between the thought of a disagreeable state and the affective state itself:

> When thought cannot cure the situation, we instead cure the thought by forgetting it. We forget not so much disagreeable ideas as useless ideas, ideas the distasteful quality of which stimulates us to know devices that modify their object. . . . To forget the disagreeable would mean that we would be deprived of one of the principal sources of thinking (quoted in Rapaport, 1961, pp. 70–71).

He indicates that there is no necessity in the prediction that a disagreeable state will lead to the forgetting of its accompanying circumstances. Cognitions about affective states and the affective states themselves may vary independently, and forgetting, or selective recall, may be a function on either class of variables depending on the general task conditions.

FAILURE AND DISSONANCE

If failure is imminent and yet for one reason or another a subject chooses to undergo it, the resulting cognitive circumstances necessitate a distinction between the negative affective response to failure and the cognition of that response. If we consider the plight of a typical subject in the preceding experiment by Cohen and Zimbardo, it is clear that he has committed himself to a task with a high certainty of failure at the same time that he is motivated to succeed. He wants to understand the poem, to recite it well, and to offer a perceptive analysis of its meaning, and he wants to do as well on the related tasks in the future, which apparently will also assess his creativity, sensitivity, and intelligence. However, he agrees to perform under conditions that will obviously prevent his success. Under such circumstances, the process of dissonance reduction can make this "irrational" commitment acceptable if the cognitions associated with task failure are realigned in such a way that failure no longer has aversive connotations, at least in this specific case. The High Dissonance subjects in that experiment chose not to change the conditions of the task to make it easier (as did the Lows); and since the higher dial settings that they chose to keep made performance more difficult and failure more probable, their behavior is assumed to reflect a lowered need to avoid failure. However, it may be argued that the High Dissonance subjects perceived that success at the next session required performing well at the same extreme level used in the initial session. Doing well at a lowered level would not change the experimenter's impression of their inability to meet this more difficult challenge.

If the dissonance interpretation advanced is valid for motivation to succeed as it has been shown to be for other motives, then perhaps a more appropriate behavioral test would focus on recall of specific stimuli associated with failure.

DISSONANCE PREDICTIONS

The discrepancy between one's motivation to succeed and one's voluntary commitment to failure should create greater dissonance the higher the probability of failure, the less the incentive for commitment, and the higher the individual's level of need for achievement. Highest dissonance should result when a high need achiever commits himself to a task that has a high probability of failure and does so with minimal external incentives.

This dissonance can be reduced either by lowering the motivation to succeed on the task (or perhaps in general) or by not reacting to failure as if it were an aversive ego-threat. If these strategies are employed, then we can predict that as dissonance increases: (1) there will be less negative affect associated with failure stimuli; (2) stimuli that are part of the failure task will be recalled *better* (in contrast with their usually greater incidence of being forgotten); and (3) motivation to succeed in the experimental situation will be reduced, and this effect can be assessed independently of the recall measure.

OVERVIEW OF EXPERIMENTAL DESIGN

After having engaged in an initial task, subjects were asked to commit themselves to another task. Both the nature of the commitment and anticipated performance on that task were experimentally varied. The Experimental subjects were given an explicit choice of whether to undergo the second task, half of them with a high reward* (HR) for making this commitment (the Low Dissonance group) and half with a low reward (LR, and thus the High Dissonance group). Control subjects, given neither choice nor the justification of a monetary reward, were

* Actually, "high incentive" for anticipated monetary payment.—Ed.

tested under conditions identical to those of the Dissonance groups. Expectations about the probability of failure on the second task were varied by informing one half of each of the Dissonance groups that there was a high probability of their failing the task (HPF), and leading the other half to expect that the probability of failure was low (LPF). This basic 2×2 factorial design, with the added control, was supplemented by inclusion of a subject-selection variable that separated subjects into High-Need Achievers and Low-Need Achievers.

The failure task consisted of a "judgment" task on which all subjects received the same falsified feedback regarding their performance. Incidental recall of the stimuli used in this task was the major dependent measure. In addition, affect and motivation were also assessed on several other instrumental measures.

SUBJECTS

The sample was composed of male undergraduates ($n = 101$) from Washington Square College of New York University, who participated to fulfill an introductory psychology course requirement. They were assigned to the various treatments in round-robin fashion.

PROCEDURE

The need-for-achievement scale from the Edwards Personal Preference Schedule (EPPS—Edwards, 1957) was completed by all subjects prior to their arrival for the experiment. The study was described as dealing with personality and judgmental ability under stressful conditions. To make the judgment process more focal and increase personal involvement, subjects were asked to make an initial rating of how good they felt their judgment generally to be.

The subjects were then given an association task, in the guise of a personality test, on which they had to call out the first three words that came to mind when each of 18 nonsense words was presented on a screen. The experimenter pretended to score the subjects' responses in order to create a plausible justification for the failure manipulation that was interpolated between this task and the next one.

The subjects were then told that the main part of the experiment was a dot-judgment task, which was related to one's ability to appraise a situation "quickly, accurately, and on first impression." The task consisted of estimating the number of dots that formed a given nonsense word flashed on a screen for 2 seconds. The same 18 words previously employed in the association task were used again, but this time each was formed by a pattern of small dots.

Dissonance Arousal

Probability of Failure. Before the second task was begun, the subjects were told that there was a statistical relationship between the first task they had completed, word association, and the judgmental task. In fact, it was alleged that the correlation between performance on these tasks was adequate to permit valid predictions of performance on the dot-judgment task from knowledge of performance on the association task. The experimenter then attempted to create different expectations of probable failure on this task with these instructions:

> I suppose you'd like to know what the prediction would be for you. (Pause) Well, judging by the way you did on the word associations, let's see . . . . (Here the experimenter referred to an elaborate dummy table that had been in full view of the subject throughout the procedure.) You got a score of 24 (or 51 depending on the subject's group assignment) so that your percentage is about 10 (or 50). That means that the likelihood that you'll do well on the dot-judgment task is only about 1 in 10 (for High Dissonance subjects; "slightly better than 50–50" for Low Dissonance subjects).

Incentive for Commitment. To increase the clarity of the dissonance interpretation, an additional monetary-incentive manipulation was introduced (the subjects who received the least money for commitment were expected to experience the greater dissonance). For this induction, the experimenter said:

> Now, we know that this is not too pleasant a task to go into. So, to go on to this task and the ones after it is really up to you. If you like, we will consider your participation completed as of now, and I'll make sure you get your course credit for your assistance. However, if you do decide to go on to this task and the ones after it, we are prepared to offer you a token fee. Since we need your help, we feel that your participation is worth something to us, I'd say at least $7.50, and we'd like to be able to pay you that. But I'm afraid that because of the limitations of the grant we are on we can't be quite that generous. However, we are prepared to pay you a token fee of $1.00 (for the High Dissonance subjects; $5.00 for the Low Dissonance subjects) to continue with the experiment and finish it. We'll appreciate it if you do, but remember it's up to you.

All subjects except one in the High Probability of Failure-High Reward group, agreed to continue. As each subject agreed, the experimenter made out a voucher in the amount promised, and the subject countersigned it, thereby committing himself to a given likelihood of failure for that amount of reward. (The subjects were told that the value of the participation was $7.50 in order to equate the financial value assigned to the task by all groups).

When these dissonance manipulations had been completed, the task instructions were finished and the dot-judgment task was presented. Each subject received the same feedback from the experimenter, in the form of an announcement of whether the number of dots estimated was correct (within three of the actual number) or incorrect (and greater or less than the actual number). Of the 18 judgments, 13 were labelled incorrect and 5 correct regardless of actual performance, to give all subjects the overall experience of having done poorly on this task.

A card-sorting filler task (lasting 7 minutes) was interpolated between the dot-judgment task and the subsequent assessment of memory for failure words, in order to allow some time for the forgetting effects to take place.

Dependent Measures

First, the subjects' *recall of nonsense words* was measured by asking them to list all the nonsense words they could remember within 4 minutes. Accurate recall received full credit, and half credit was given for exact reversals or words with two of three letters in their correct positions.

Reaction times (RT's) were measured in response to each of the 18 nonsense words on a second administration of the word-association test (each RT being the elapsed time from the presentation of each word to the subject's calling out his first association to that word). Slower RT's were assumed to reflect more negative affect (according to Woodworth & Schlosberg, 1954, pp. 67–68).

Finally, to measure the subject's general level of motivation after failure and incentive manipulations, a *tallying task* was presented. After a minute-long practice trial, the subject was informed of an arbitrary " passing score " for a second trial, of 4 minutes' duration. Since this score was easily attainable (all surpassed it readily) and could be freely exceeded if the subject were motivated to achieve a high score, this test could be used to evaluate motivation not specific to the failure task. The task itself was a modification of one used in previous studies (Kipnis, 1962), on the basis of which it was expected to be an instrumental measure of motivation to succeed. If Dissonance subjects lowered their need to succeed, they would be expected not to persevere beyond the "passing score" on this test to as great an extent as other subjects.

To check on the manipulations and on the alternative ways of reducing dissonance, each subject completed a questionnaire at the end of the procedure. Each was then carefully informed of the actual nature of the study.

RESULTS

Assessment of Dissonance Arousal

The conditions necessary for dissonance arousal were that the subjects must feel a high degree of free choice to continue on to the failure task and they must be aware of the odds against their success, as well as of the fact that they are being underpaid for their commitment.

The Dissonance subjects, who were offered the choice to continue the experiment by taking the probable-failure task, did perceive this decision to be largely of their own volition (median rating for all groups was 60, where 70 = maximum free choice). None of the experimental groups differed significantly from each other on this rating; the Control group, of course, did not make the rating.

Subjects given the High Probability of Failure, or HPF, treatment perceived less likelihood of their success than those in the Low Probability of Failure, or LPF, condition (medians of 10 and 19, respectively, on a 40-point scale). Over 70 per cent of the HPF group were below the common median, while 85 per cent of the LPF group were above the median ($p < 0.001$, by chi square). However, the HPF group perceived their chances of success as being not 10 per cent, as they had been told, but closer to 25 per cent.

The monetary incentive was seen as less than appropriate for the Low Reward (LR) subjects and as more than appropriate for the High Reward (HR) subjects (medians of 27 and 40, where 35 = appropriate payment). In the LR group, over 80 per cent of the subjects were below the common median, while in the HR group over 70 per cent were above it ($p < 0.001$, by chi square).

A mild, though equal, degree of suspicion was shown by all groups on a questionnaire item asking whether they felt they had been deceived at any point in the experiment (a median value of 31 on a 60-point scale). Every subject indicating more than slight suspicion was extensively questioned, but none was able to identify the specific source of deception. Rather, they confessed to a general suspicion about the alleged purpose of any psychological experiment.

Recall for Failure Stimuli

The Control group and the group given the Low Probability of Failure treatment remembered relatively more nonfailure words than failure words—a result comparable to the previous research described earlier. In marked contrast, the subjects who committed themselves to the dot-judgment task with the anticipation of a high probability of failure remembered more failure than nonfailure words—a result predicted from dissonance theory.

The memory data for all groups is presented in Table 1, where positive scores indicate that proportionately more of the 13 failure words were remembered than of the 5 nonfailure words, while negative scores indicate the opposite

TABLE 1

MEMORY SCORES* FOR ALL GROUPS

Need for achievement	Probability of failure: High		Probability of failure: Low		Control group
	Low reward	High reward	Low reward	High reward	
Low	+0.44	+0.36	−0.54	−0.07	−0.46
High	+0.23	−0.01	−0.31	+0.06	+0.04
Group mean	+0.34	+0.18	−0.42	−0.01	−0.22

* A positive score represents more failure than nonfailure words recalled; a negative score represents the converse. The means represent fractions of words.

effect. Thus, scores approximating zero reflect the same proportions, respectively, of failure and nonfailure words accurately remembered.

The recall of failure words in the HPF condition was significantly greater than in the LPF condition ($p < 0.05$). This main-effect difference was intensified under the dissonant conditions of minimal incentive for commitment: the mean for the HPF-LR condition is $+0.34$, while it is -0.42 for the LPF $-$ LR ($p < 0.01$). In both failure conditions, the effect of High Reward was more veridical recall of failure and nonfailure words; Low Reward produced greater recall of nonfailure words when anticipation of failure was low, but the opposite effect, greater recall of failure words, when anticipation of failure was high. The Control group fell on the same side of the continuum as the Low Dissonance groups and differed reliably from the High Dissonance groups ($p < 0.05$).

The effects of individual differences in need for achievement were consistent but not in accord with our predictions. The dissonance effects are most clear for the Low-Need Achievers across all conditions: in the Control group and LPF condition there was more recall of nonfailure words, while in the HPF there was more recall of the failure words. High need for achievement attenuated these differences in every group. In fact, it appears that for High-Need Achievers a high incentive to engage in a future task overrides the dissonance manipulation of commitment to failure, since both HPF and LPF groups behaved like the Control group (with relatively accurate recall of both failure and nonfailure words). Nevertheless, the predicted dissonance effect was manifested under the Low Reward treatment even for High-Need Achievers.

Suspicion in the Control Group

If subjects in the Control group reported being suspicious about the experimental procedure, the suspicion was likely to be centered upon the failure induction, since they did not experience the choice or incentive manipulation. Thus, suspicious Control subjects should be likely *not* to attribute their failure to themselves, and if so, then failure would not be threatening. If the Control group were divided into those subjects who were and were not suspicious, there should be a greater recall of nonfailure words for the nonsuspicious subjects for whom failure would be perceived as the consequence of their own prior performance.

Accordingly, the Control subjects were separated on the basis of their postexperimental-questionnaire responses to the suspicion item, and the recall in the suspicious and nonsuspicious subgroups was compared. The nonsuspicious Controls forgot significantly more failure words than did the suspicious controls (means of -0.68 to $+0.12$, respectively; $p < 0.02$ by Mann-Whitney U-Test). Considering this as the appropriate base line Control, the dissonance effects of relatively greater failure-word recall were found in seven of the eight subgroups (in Table 1). Unfortunately, this refinement of the data cannot be made on the experimental groups, since they experienced several sources of deception and their suspicion could not be unambiguously attributed to a perceived specific locus of failure.

Reaction Times

Reaction times to the word association task that followed the failure manipulation were assumed to be an index of affective response to specific stimuli. Thus RT's to failure-related stimuli should be slower than to nonfailure stimuli, except under conditions of dissonance arousal, where the affective quality of the failure stimuli was presumably modified.

These data are presented in Figure 1 as group means based on RT differences between failure and nonfailure words for each subject. The scores were normally distributed across all groups, permitting an analysis of variance without transformations of the scores.

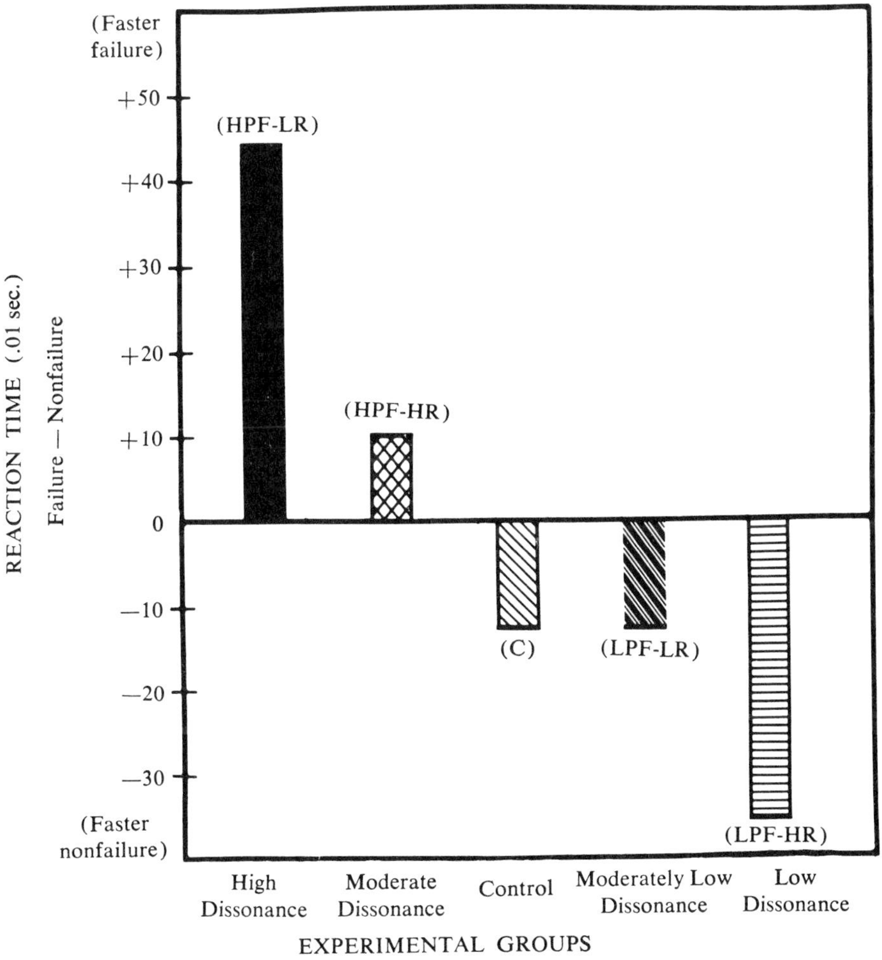

FIGURE 1

Mean group differences in reaction time to nonfailure words subtracted from failure words as a function of probability of failure and justification for commitment.

In contrast to the Control group and the LPF groups, those subjects committed to a high probability of failure reacted faster to failure than to nonfailure words ($p < 0.01$). Low Reward tended to result in faster failure than nonfailure reaction times, opposite to the High Reward effect ($F = 3.05, p = 0.07$). Need for achievement was not significant either as a main effect or in its interaction with the other variables. However, within the Control group, the High-Need Achievers responded faster to nonfailure (mean = −0.037 sec.) while the Low-Need Achievers responded faster to failure words (mean = +0.034 sec.). In general, it can be said that there was a progressive decrease in reaction times to failure stimuli (relative to nonfailure ones) from the lowest-dissonance groups on the right of Figure 1 to the highest-dissonance groups on the left.

Control for RT to Recalled Words

To demonstrate that these RT data are not biased by group differences in recall of failure and nonfailure words, a separate RT analysis was undertaken of each type of word as a function of whether it was remembered. No significant differences were found related to accuracy of recall. However, the interaction between experimental treatment and type of word (failure vs. nonfailure) was significant at the 1 per cent level of probability. For the Low Dissonance and Control groups,[1] nonfailure words had faster RT's, while for the High Dissonance group failure words were reacted to more rapidly. Thus, with recall differences controlled, only the High Dissonance group responded with significantly faster RT's to failure than nonfailure stimuli.

General Motivation to Succeed

The tallying task used to measure the general need to succeed is reported by Kipnis (1962) to be most valid for subjects who are *poor* general achievers. In the present study, the Low-Need Achievers scored significantly higher than the High ($p < 0.05$), i.e., they continued to work longer beyond the suggested minimum passing level.

The group that exhibited the weakest motivation to succeed was the group theoretically conceived of as the highest-dissonance group, the subjects with a high need for achievement who committed themselves to a high probability of failure for a low reward. Highest scores on this task were made by the lowest-dissonance group, the Low-Need Achievers given the LPF and HR treatments (significantly different, $p < 0.05$). The Control group was intermediate. Thus, the general motivation to succeed in this experimental situation was altered as a consequence of the dissonance arousal and the presumed attempts at dissonance reduction.

1. This analysis was done for only the extreme Dissonance groups (HPF-LR and LPF-HR) on reaction times converted to logs (because these distributions were not normal).

Self-Reported Failure Reaction

On the postexperimental ratings, the HPF subjects rated themselves as *less uncomfortable* during the failure task than did the LPF subjects. On a median test, 60 per cent of the HPF group were below the common median, while 65 per cent of the LPF group were above it ($p < 0.05$).

DISCUSSION

The potent need to achieve success and avoid failure can be significantly altered when people can be induced for minimal incentives to engage in a task that promises a high likelihood of failure. Such subjects show a reversal of the repression hypothesis of forgetting, i.e., they recall more failure stimuli than nonfailure ones. Moreover, they exhibit less negative affect to failure stimuli, as shown by their significantly faster reaction times to failure words. They are also made less uncomfortable by the failure experience than others not under the same cognitive set, and, finally, their poorer performance on a related task reveals that their general motivation to succeed has suffered a decrement.

Thus, under conditions specified by the theory of cognitive dissonance, selective recall was modified as were other behaviors that reflect motives to succeed and to avoid failure. The effects of monetary incentive (justification for commitment) and of the individual-difference variable of need for achievement were not consistent across all experimental tasks; the incentive differences emerged most clearly in the reaction-time data, while the need-for-achievement differences were clearest on the tallying task (measuring motivation to succeed).

Obviously, we have been assuming that dissonance was aroused in subjects who, though motivated to do well on the experimental task, volunteered in the face of imminent failure. There is one source of data not previously reported that supports this assumption. If subjects who rated their own likelihood of success prior to performing on the failure task as high are compared with those who predicted low success, there is a general tendency for greater recall of failure words for the high predictors (means of $+0.18$ to -0.14, respectively; not significant). Duncan's New Multiple-Range Test ($p = 0.05$) reveals that high predictors in both HPF-LR (mean $= +0.48$) and HPF-HR (mean $= +0.36$) groups differed from the low predictors in the LPF-LR group (mean $= -0.79$). Here the probability-of-failure induction and the self-generated predictions have a cumulative enhancing effect on selective recall of failure words in the High Dissonance subjects.

The important role of volition in this type of situation is supported by the results of a study by Green (1963) in which recall of failure tasks was significantly greater than recall of nonfailure tasks. Moreover, subjects who had volunteered performed better than those required to participate.

Although the achievement variable was not systematically related to the dissonance variables, nevertheless, one of the most intuitively compelling alternative explanations of the present data derives from Atkinson's (1957) position on failure and the need for achievement. Atkinson would hold that subjects lower their need for achievement in the face of overwhelming odds against success. The affect and memory effects found in the present study would naturally follow from such a change in motive state. His view should lead to the prediction of main-effect differences on all measures in favor of High-Need Achievers and to the prediction of an interaction on the instrumental measure of need to succeed (tallying task) such that High-Need Achievers would be more motivated to perform with a 50 per cent likelihood of success (LPF) but less motivated with only a 10 per cent likelihood of success (HPF). This interaction does not emerge. Further, the main effect is evident only on the tallying task and in the opposite direction. Finally, the need-for-achievement subgroups among Control subjects performed almost identically, leading to the inference that poorer performance among High-Need Achievers in the experimental groups is a function of dissonance reduction. The data thus do not seem to conform with this alternative view.

Those who believe that high need for achievement is essential to the progress of civilization may find little of practical consequence in these findings; however, critics who see our society as characterized by overachievement and limitless aspiration may derive some meaningful implications from this research in which adjustment to failure is seen as a vital part of the psychological development of any truly human being.

Editor's Comments

Our confidence in the results and theoretical explanation of the previously reported pilot study by Cohen and Zimbardo (Article 10) is increased by the supporting data obtained in the present study and by its methodological refinements, which help clarify the conceptual status of the major variables. Taken together, these studies point to a rather dramatic, immediate change in a motive that had been culturally elevated to a position of prominence in the lives of most, if not all, of the subjects studied. Thus, providing people with certain expectations and having them choose to behave in a manner discrepant with one of their salient motives can initiate a process of cognitive re-evaluation, the consequence of which is a reduction in the need to succeed, to achieve, and to avoid failure.

In the Cohen and Zimbardo study, failure was apparent to the subjects in the feedback from their own performance, while here, failure was dependent upon the experimenter's announcement of it. This latter effect may have helped to contribute to the suspicion felt by many of the subjects. Schlachet demonstrates that when this source of variability is removed from the Control group data, obtained group differences emerge even more clearly in line with the theoretical expectations. If suspicion is somehow correlated with differences in level of need for achievement, then interpretation of the need-for-achievement variable may be confounded by differential suspicion aroused by the various tasks. Thus, the inconsistency of the relation of need-for-achievement to the dissonance variables in this research may be due either to its unreliability or complexity (see Atkinson & Litwin, 1960, who interpret it as failure avoidance) or to subject differences in the interpretation of what each task was measuring. It would be preferable to manipulate experimentally the achievement needs rather than to rely upon a subject self-selection measure with its host of possibly confounding relations with various aspects of this research.

Two other points deserve mention in passing. Although subjects perceived a very high absolute level of free choice in whether to undergo the failure task, only one subject actually refused to make the commitment. This behavioral compliance is, however, in accord with the subjects' perception of being moderately obligated to continue. Although the subjects felt free to do as they chose, they chose to accept the commitment to a failure task because of pressures they felt which made dropping out difficult. Some of these pressures may be attributable to the experimental situation, while others may have been internally generated due to the kind of motive under consideration. In our society, quitting in the face of failure is an admission of failure itself, since "if at first you don't succeed, you must try again." On the other hand, although the motive to succeed and the achievement of success are valued, it is not socially acceptable to give the appearance that one is striving to succeed. This inconsistency could have resulted in the obtained low subject-dropout rate and may have weakened or complicated the dissonance effects.

Despite these problems, significant, specifiable dissonance effects on incidental recall of failure stimuli and on reaction time were noted. In Mansson's thirst study (Article 6), his only failure to show a dissonance effect was on the RT measure. In the present study, on the other hand, where the affective value of the failure and nonfailure stimuli were more clearly differentiated, the predicted effects emerged strongly. In the present study, then, lowering of the motive to succeed by virtue of the discrepant commitment resulted in better recall for failure stimuli and less negative affect toward them as measured by faster reaction times.

The next study focuses on a more "social" motive, the need for social approval from others, in an effort to explore whether a dissonance commitment to deprivation of this powerful motive can modify a continuous process of verbal conditioning that is influenced by such reinforcement.

12. COMMITMENT TO SOCIAL DEPRIVATION AND VERBAL CONDITIONING

Arthur R. Cohen, Charles W. Greenbaum, and Helge Hilding Mansson

That people have strong needs to be with, accepted by, and approved of by other people is certainly obvious to any student of human behavior. However, we often tend to minimize or even overlook this phenomenon when, as social scientists, we direct our attention toward biological and physical determinants of behavior, or as humanists, we take it too much for granted. When people serve as social stimuli for one another, then their absence or relative inaccessibility defines a condition of deprivation, which as a social drive is functionally equivalent to other drive states. Any behavior that is emitted under this condition and is followed by the opportunity to interact with, or receive approval from, a relevant social "other" will become conditioned and increase in frequency.

Thus when people act in a stimulus role as reinforcers for the behavior of others, their effectiveness in modifying, shaping, and controlling behavior is enhanced if it follows a prior history of social deprivation. (See Baron, 1966; Gewirtz, 1967; Gewirtz & Baer, 1958; Hill & Stevenson, 1964; Landau & Gewirtz, 1967; McCoy & Zigler, 1965; Stevenson & Odom, 1962; Walters & Karal, 1960, for examples of the many recent studies on this issue; see also Schachter's, 1959, pioneering research on the pervasive effects of the need for social affiliation.) A specific instance of this relationship among social deprivation, reinforcement, and behavior change is the increased frequency with which an individual will employ a particular verbal response class, such as plural nouns or personal pronouns, if the emission of that response class has been followed by some form of social approval (cf. Salzinger, 1959). This verbal conditioning effect is more pronounced if it follows a period of absence of such approval, while it is attenuated if the individual has been "satisfied" for social approval prior to the systematic reinforcement.

This motive for social reinforcement is not only a potent one in most of our everyday behavior but, because of its direct consequences for the conditioning of verbal behavior (Skinner, 1957), it is ideally suited to the experimental investigation of the effects of choice and justification upon human motivation. First, it permits the use of a simple paradigm for the experimental arousal and manipulation of antecedent conditions of motivation that can reasonably be assumed to affect verbal behavior. In addition, verbal conditioning provides a reliably measurable response that is stable and orderly. Finally, it offers us access to a behavioral *sequence* rather than merely a discrete event as the end-product of the process of our concern.

Given this motive, which has the virtues of being psychologically significant

SOURCE: Cohen, A. R., Charles W. Greenbaum, and Helge Hilding Mansson, "Commitment to Social Deprivation and Verbal Conditioning," *Journal of Abnormal and Social Psychology*, 1963, *67*, pp. 410-422.

and methodologically compelling, it is the aim of our research to determine whether there are some conditions under which the arousal of such social motivation *does not* lead to greater responsiveness to social reinforcement. The theory of cognitive dissonance directs our attention toward those conditions involving the person's expectations of what social deprivation he will experience in a future deprivation situation. Through the dissonance formulation we can see how these cognitions affect the strength of the initial social motive and thereby determine the degree to which the person's behavior will subsequently be maintained by social reinforcers. To carry out our aim, research strategy demands that we at least demonstrate that a motivation for social reinforcement does exist and does have effects, i.e., that it can be instigated in a laboratory situation. We will then have to show that when a person freely commits himself to further deprivation of that social motive, dissonance is aroused that can be reduced by lowering the intensity or the importance of the need for social reinforcement. Behaviorally, such a process should be reflected in a lessened response to social reinforcement and thus, in this case, in a lower level of verbal conditioning.

Past research on these issues (e.g., Gewirtz & Baer, 1958; Walters & Karal, 1960) indicates that the best experimental approach to the creation of social deprivation is to first establish a maintenance schedule of social approval and then interfere with it, i.e., cut it off differentially. In effect, limiting access to an event that sometimes acts as a reinforcing stimulus will increase attempts to obtain that stimulus, whereas increasing access to that particular event will reduce such attempts. If we are successful in producing higher social responsivity in a high-deprivation condition than in a low one, we can assume that our deprivation operation does in fact result in stronger motivation towards, and more consequent behaviors leading to, social reinforcement. We can then compare the reactions of such a High Deprivation Control group to the behavior of other groups who receive the same high-arousal treatment but experience different amounts of dissonance. Dissonance will be created by having the subjects voluntarily agree to undergo an experience which promises the frustration of their needs for social support, approval, recognition, etc. Differential levels of dissonance will be produced by varying one type of extrinsic justification for engaging in this discrepant behavior—namely, a monetary incentive.

DISSONANCE PREDICTIONS

Our predictions are therefore twofold: First, among the Control groups, there should be a higher level of verbal conditioning following high social-need deprivation (High Deprivation Control) than following low-deprivation conditions (Low Deprivation Control). Secondly, High Deprivation subjects who voluntarily commit themselves to further social deprivation for minimal financial incentives (High Dissonance) should behave as if they were not so motivated and thus show only weak conditioning effects in response to social reinforcement. This prediction assumes that a high magnitude of dissonance will result from a decision to behave contrary to one's most salient motivation at the time for justifications barely sufficient to induce such a commitment. This dissonance can then be reduced by lowering the original social motive (in a sense, by not "needing" social reinforcement) and thus by becoming insensitive to relevant social reinforcement when it occurs. Where no choice to engage in the deprivation condition is allowed (Control conditions) or where the justification for the discrepant behavior is sufficient to "force" the decision (Low Dissonance), then such cognitive realignment will not occur and verbal conditioning should directly reflect the original level of social deprivation experienced.

OVERVIEW OF EXPERIMENTAL DESIGN

The study consisted of four main stages: (1) Each subject's operant level for emitting personal pronouns was determined during a standardized verbal learning task: (2) Deprivation of social approval was manipulated by maintaining one group on a consistent schedule of verbal reinforcement during an interview (Low Deprivation), while abruptly terminating the interviewer's approval for a second group early in the interview (High Deprivation). (3) Dissonance was aroused by giving 40 of the 60 High Deprivation subjects choice in whether to expose themselves to a second interviewer who was likely to be disapproving, for a small or large monetary incentive (High and Low Dissonance, respectively). Twenty of the High Deprivation and the twenty Low Deprivation subjects were not given this part of the experiment and are considered base-line controls for the effects of deprivation and subsequent reinforcement. (4) Conditioning was assessed in terms of emission of personal pronouns, " I " and " we, " followed by verbal reinforcement for 100 trials and then by silence for 80 trials (extinction) for all subjects. Verbal conditioning rate was thus the major dependent variable of this research.

SUBJECTS

Of the 80 male undergraduates who served as subjects, 40 were recruited from a New York University fraternity (paid a lump sum for sending their members) and were randomly assigned to the two Control groups. The additional 40 subjects were recruited from classes at New York University, paid $2.00 each for their participation, and randomly assigned to the two Dissonance groups.

PROCEDURE

Subjects were told they were participating in a study of verbal behavior and physiological responsiveness. They were led to believe that during an initial adaptation period their basal physiological responses would be recorded, a verbal task would be administered, then a second adaptation period consisting of an interview would follow, and finally their verbal behavior would be studied again in another longer session on the verbal task.

Operant Level

Each subject's operant level (OL) was determined by a procedure similar to that described by Taffel (1955) and Kanfer and Karas (1959). Twenty stimulus cards were presented one at a time to each subject. In the middle of each card, a verb in the simple past tense appeared, and below it were typed the pronouns *I*, *We*, *You*, *He*, *She*, and *They*. The order of the pronouns for any given card was chosen randomly. The verbs used were reported as "neutral" in a study performed by Binder, McConnell, and Sjoholm (1957). Each verb appeared once in a block of 20 trials, and its order of appearance within each block was chosen at random.

The subject was told that his task was to construct one sentence upon the presentation of each card, using "the word at the top" (verb) "and one of the six words toward the bottom" (pronoun). He was also told to attempt to say the first thing that came to mind, to construct simple sentences, and to speak as clearly and distinctly as possible. The experimenter then presented the subject with the first block of 20 cards. He did not reinforce any responses made on this block of trials and later tallied only the sentences using *I* or *we*; it is this count that constituted the operant level of responding.

Manipulation of Deprivation

The second "adaptation" period followed, during which each subject participated in an alleged unrelated interview study with "Dr. Mansson, a Danish sociologist, temporarily at the Research Center as part of his cross-society research on the effect of education on student life."

Dr. M. informed the subject that during the interview he, the interviewer, would sit behind and to the right of the student (in order to minimize any nonverbal reinforcement effects) and would hand him cards, one at a time, on which were typed questions concerning university life. The questions were fairly general, such as "Explain your purpose in coming to college," and "What do you think of the Peace Corps?" The subject was to respond at length to each question and when finished put the card down on the table. Dr. M. would then hand him another card and so on until the 15-minute interview was terminated.

Low Deprivation Control. For the 20 subjects assigned to the Low Deprivation Control condition, Dr. M. said "Good" at the rate of 5 times per minute *throughout* the 15-minute interview period, a total of 75 times in all. Reinforcement was administered usually at the end of a sentence or phrase without regard to the particular content of the subject's responses.

High Deprivation. For the 60 subjects assigned to the High Deprivation condition, Dr. M. said "Good" at the same approximate rate of 5 times per minute for the first 5 minutes of the interview, for a total of 25 times. After that, Dr. M. said nothing for the remaining 10 minutes of the interview. Thus the two Deprivation conditions differed in total number of reinforcements, 75 versus 25, as well as in consistency of reinforcement, uniform throughout vs. disjunctive.

A third of these subjects constituted the High Deprivation Control condition, and like the Low Deprivation Controls they received no further experimental treatment before being given the reinforcement and extinction procedures. The remaining 40 High Deprivation subjects were randomly assigned to the two Dissonance conditions.

Manipulation of Dissonance: Monetary Incentives

Voluntary commitment to a future period of social deprivation was expected to create dissonance in the subjects who were already in a state of high social deprivation from the preceding interview treatment. The experimenter therefore asked these subjects if they would participate in another interview study being conducted at the Research Center. The topics discussed would be similar to those used by Dr. M., and they would be paid (by Dr. Zimbardo, the alleged researcher) either \$1.00 (High Dissonance) or \$5.00 (Low Dissonance) for their half-hour's participation.

Expectations about this future task were guided by the following instructions from the experimenter:

> Before you decide, "Dr. Z." has asked me to tell you something about the nature of this interview. First, it is one in which you can expect a great deal of disapproval for your views. The interviewer has asked me to tell you that he is extremely skeptical with regard to views of the sort that are usually expressed in these interviews. He has been known to become somewhat disapproving in these interviews, so you can expect him to be extremely critical with regard to the statements that you make. We are making this information available to you because we know that interviewers differ in various ways and it is our policy to let students know just what to expect.

At this point three subjects refused to commit themselves to the interview with Dr. Z.; they are not included in the experimental sample.

Reinforcement and Extinction

Next the experimenter administered 100 trials of verbal reinforcement to all subjects on the same task that was used to establish the operant level of responding. In this set of trials, however, every sentence beginning with *I* or *we* that the subject constructed was reinforced by the experimenter's saying "Good" in a flat, unemotional tone of voice. This was followed without interruption by 80 trials of extinction, where, as in the operant level, the experimenter did not reinforce any of the subject's responses. These 180 trials were administered in nine continuous 20-trial blocks.

Self-Report Measures

A postexperimental questionnaire probed for subjects' awareness of the contingency between reinforcement and response in the preceding sessions (using questions similar to those developed by Dulany, 1961). This questionnaire also attempted to assess alternative modes of dissonance reduction and to evaluate the efficacy of the experimental treatments.

In a postexperimental interview, suspicion on the part of the subjects was also probed, and two subjects were eliminated from analysis of the data—one who didn't believe Dr. M. was really a visiting dignitary, and one who didn't believe Dr. Z. was "real."

RESULTS

Anticipation of Social Disapproval

The manipulation of anticipated social disapproval in the interview with Dr. Z. was quite successful, and equally so, for both Dissonance groups. For example, on the question, "How supportive do you expect Dr. Z. to be," the High Dissonance group mean was 2.2 while it was 1.9 for the Low Dissonance group (0 = not at all, while 8 = very supportive). On a question about how unpleasant the subject thought the interview would be, the mean was 3.5 for High Dissonance and 3.4 for Low (on an 8-point scale), indicating slightly more unpleasantness expected by High Dissonance subjects. In addition, subjects in both groups felt they could not bypass this future deprivation of approval by actually getting Dr. Z. to give them approval. There was also no difference between the two Dissonance groups in their positive perception of Dr. M. or in their unfavorable orientation toward Dr. Z.

Effects of Social Deprivation on Conditioning

Deprivation of social approval during the interview stage of the experiment apparently did create a motivation that resulted in a significant increase in responding to verbal reinforcement. Figure 1 presents a composite graph that averages conditioned responses over the 100 reinforcement trials and subtracts that value from the averaged 20 OL trials (to yield a measure of change in response strength). It also compares the 80 extinction trials with the OL trials.

The Controls started from an identical OL but diverged markedly as soon as their verbal responses were reinforced. Those given the Low Deprivation treatment increased only weakly, +0.55, while those given the High Deprivation treatment increased five times as much, +2.59 ($p < 0.05$ by Duncan's New Multiple-Range Test). During extinction, the Low Controls decreased in their responding (to −0.41) while the High Controls actually increased slightly (to +3.25, $p < 0.01$).

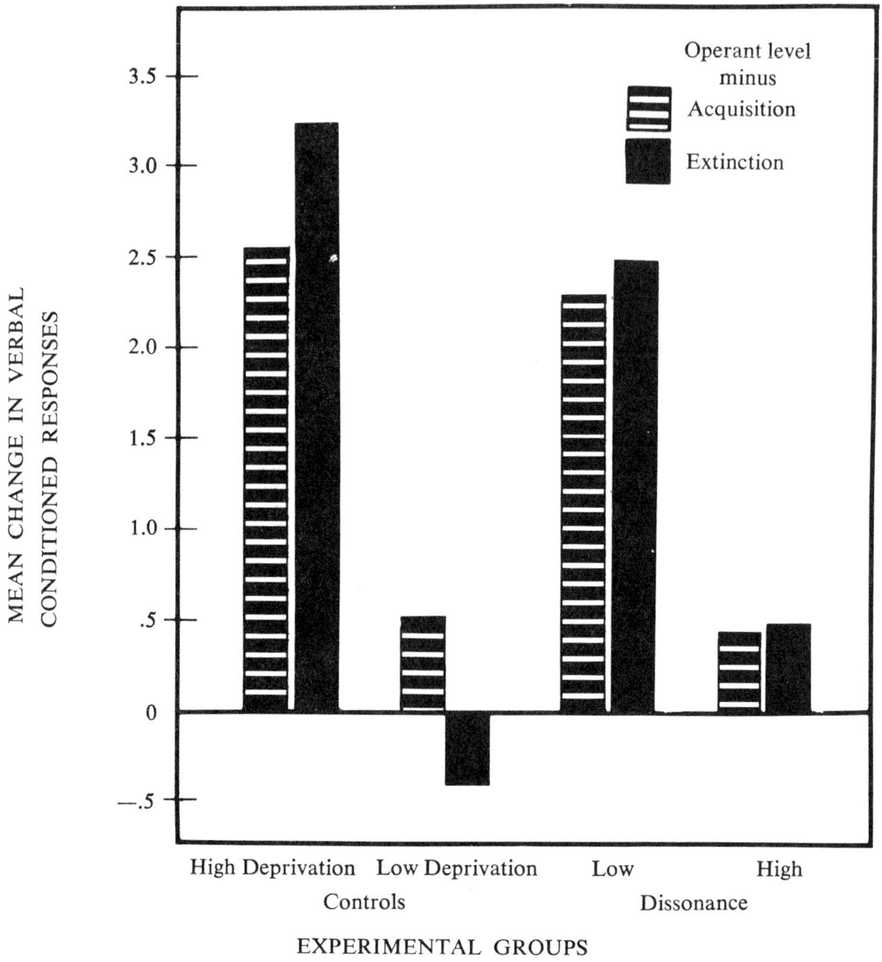

FIGURE 1

Mean-response-strength changes for all groups from operant level (without reinforcement) to acquisition (with reinforcement for *I* and *we* responses) and to extinction (again with no reinforcement).

Effects of Dissonance on Conditioning

If we now consider the data in Figure 1 for those subjects given the dissonance arousal superimposed on high deprivation, it is obvious that the High Dissonance group did not condition like either the Low Dissonance group or the High Deprivation Controls. From their conditioning performance, one would conclude that they most resembled subjects in the Control group that had not been deprived of social approval. In acquisition, the High Dissonance group (mean of 0.45) differed significantly ($p < 0.05$) from both the High Deprivation Control and the Low Dissonance groups (mean of 2.29); in extinction, the differences were also significant. In fact, the mean increase in verbal conditioned responses is slightly less (although not significantly so) for the High Dissonance group than for even the Low Deprivation Controls. However, unlike this Control group, the High Dissonance group showed a slight increase rather than a decrement in responding during extinction.

Internal Evidence Bearing on the Dissonance Formulation: Awareness. It seems clear, then, that the existence of dissonance in the presence of motivation for social reinforcement can produce a decrement in social responsivity. It is our assumption that this effect is mediated by an actual change in the subject's motivation for social reinforcement once he commits himself to further social deprivation. Let us now examine some additional evidence bearing directly on the validity of our line of reasoning. Earlier studies (see Eriksen, 1962) have shown that, in the absence of commitment, subjects who are aware of reinforcement contingencies are more likely to respond to reinforcement than subjects who are not aware of them. We should, therefore, expect our Control subjects to reflect such a general effect; and, in fact, they do (see Table 1). During both acquisition and extinction, within both High and Low Deprivation Control conditions, aware* subjects responded more than unaware subjects (all four p values, derived from Duncan's Multiple-Range Test, are significant at least to the 0.05 level).

For the Dissonance conditions, the differences between awareness subgroups are not significant. In the Low Dissonance group, the size and direction of the scores are comparable to the High Deprivation Controls. However, the High Dissonance group responded quite differently. Like the unaware Low Deprivation Controls, unaware subjects in this Dissonance group show little conditioning, but unlike any other group, aware High Dissonance subjects show even less conditioning than their unaware counterparts (mean of 0.23 to 0.57, p = n.s.). Thus, although awareness generally tends to increase reinforced responding—in this case, responding to gain social approval where that motive is salient—under conditions of High Dissonance, awareness leads to the least responding for social approval.

TABLE 1

MEAN-RESPONSE-STRENGTH-CHANGE SCORES* FOR *I* AND *we* RESPONSES FOR AWARE AND UNAWARE SUBJECTS IN ALL GROUPS

Awareness	Control		Dissonance	
	Low deprivation	High deprivation	Low	High
Aware	2.93 (n = 6)	3.69 (n = 7)	2.80 (n = 5)	0.23 (n = 7)
Unaware	−0.47 (n = 14)	2.15 (n = 13)	2.16 (n = 15)	0.57 (n = 13)
Difference	3.40	1.54	0.74	−0.34
p value of difference	$p < 0.01$	$p < 0.05$	n.s.	n.s.

* From operant level to acquisition.

* In the present study, "aware" subjects realized that the experimenter's reaction to their choice of specific personal pronouns was intentional.—Ed.

Internal Analysis: Conditioning and Perceived Deprivation. On the post-experimental questionnaire, High Dissonance subjects reported that the prior deprivation interview was *less* socially depriving (less unpleasant) than the Low Dissonance subjects felt it to be (means of 5.3 to 4.4, respectively, on an 8-point scale; $p < 0.05$). Although the manipulation was constant for both groups, the High Dissonance subjects perceived it to be not so bad as did the Lows. Clearly, this would be one mode of reducing dissonance occasioned by commitment to further social deprivation. However, subjects who used this technique of reducing their dissonance should be less likely to reduce their need for social approval; i.e., they ought to condition more to verbal reinforcement than the High Dissonance subjects who did not so alter their perception of the severity of the initial deprivation state.

An internal analysis was performed to examine this possibility. Subjects in the High Dissonance group with scores above the median for the rating of pleasantness of the prior deprivation were compared to those below the median on the measure of mean response change from OL to acquisition. Those who committed themselves to future deprivation while feeling that the initial deprivation was unpleasant responded significantly *less* to reinforcement than those who felt that it was not so unpleasant ($p < 0.05$). There was no such relationship within the Low Dissonance group.

This internal analysis therefore provides an additional source of verification for the theoretical model we have utilized in this research, since the predicted group differences occur both between experimental conditions and also within the High Dissonance group between subsets that should have either experienced different levels of dissonance or coped with it differently.

DISCUSSION

The data support the hypothesis that individuals will reduce their motivation to respond to social reinforcement after committing themselves to forego such reinforcement in a future situation. Such reduction in social motivation is dependent upon the amount of dissonance created by the commitment, and it will affect conditioning to social reinforcers. This dissonance formulation of motivational change received some additional support from an internal analysis that made use of the awareness-of-conditioning variable. The fact that subjects who were aware conditioned *more* under Control conditions but not under Dissonance conditions shows that awareness may be a mechanism whereby the subject can increase or inhibit his responding depending upon his motivation to respond. Aside from the support given to the present theoretical formulation, these results offer some insight into the role of awareness in verbal operant conditioning, which remains a controversial topic (see Eriksen, 1962; Farber, 1963; Dulany, 1962, 1968; Spielberger & De Nike, 1966).

Perhaps the best support for our assumption that processes of dissonance arousal and reduction were at work in the present experiment comes from the data just presented on retroactive perception of the deprivation interview. The greater perceived pleasantness of the deprivation interview on the part of the

High, contrasted with the Low, Dissonance subjects (and a nonsignificant tendency to feel less choice and more obligation to continue) coupled with the obtained internal relationship between conditioning and this perceived pleasantness are difficult to explain in other than dissonance terms. Thus, dissonance reduction may lead to those cognitive changes (also reported previously by Brehm, Cohen and Zimbardo, and Schlachet in this volume) as well as to the behavioral changes observed. For some subjects, use of one mode of dissonance reduction may weaken the other, as in the internal analysis reported here, while under some circumstances there may be positively correlated response outcomes on several measures.

A final issue concerns the mechanisms postulated by the present dissonance formulation to account for the relationship between commitment and decreased social responsivity. We know from prior research (reported in this volume) that cognitive components of motivation can be changed by dissonance pressures; people can identify the magnitude of their needs and say that they have less need than they did at some previous time, e.g., for social reinforcement. But, how does this relate to less conditioning?

It is possible that changes in cognitive aspects of motivation lead to changes in noncognitive aspects and that it is through these latter changes that behaviors such as learning are then affected. On the other hand, it is also possible that it is *only* via changes in cognitive aspects of motivation that effects on behavior can be obtained; underlying noncognitive aspects of motivation may affect behaviors like learning only to the degree that they have cognitive representation. In effect, it may very well be that it is only what the subject knows about his motivational state that affects learning, performance, perception, and all of his motivated behavior.

Editor's Comments

Although the general research strategy and the data obtained in this experiment are among the most convincing we have presented, this study would, of course, have been more satisfactory if it had employed a reinforcing agent who was a different person from the experimenter who induced the subjects to commit themselves. Similar results under such conditions would have increased our optimism about the validity of the dissonance approach to motivational change. However, the authors note that the sheer mechanics involved in having a third experimenter made such an obvious procedural control (see Rosenberg, 1965) inexpedient in the present experiment.

A more serious problem is the lack of comparability between Control and Dissonance subjects, since they came from two different populations and were randomly assigned to subgroups only within each of these treatment conditions and not across them. Control subjects were recruited from a fraternity paid a lump sum for participation while Dissonance subjects were recruited from classes and paid small sums individually. This recruitment procedure could have produced differences in initial level of motivation toward being in the study that may have weakened the obtained differences between Dissonance and Control subjects, as apparently occurred in the previously reported study by Brehm, Back, Bogdonoff (Article 2).

Although the Control condition provides a base line for the effects of deprivation and subsequent reinforcement on learning, it should have been augmented by an additional group that expected the future deprivation interview but was given no choice in whether to undergo it. Thus, choice differences were not clearly created in this study.

However, a recent study by Epstein (1968) replicates the basic finding of the present research while utilizing a clear manipulation of choice in exposure to future deprivation. Epstein defined deprivation in terms of a social isolation operation, making it more comparable to previous verbal conditioning studies reported earlier than is the anticipated disapproval used to define deprivation in this study.

The subjects were elementary-school girls who, after their operant level of imitating the experimenter (also female) was established, were deprived of the presence of the experimenter for 15 minutes while she "tried to fix the apparatus" (social isolation). They were then given a choice or required to remain for an additional isolation period, after which they were given 60 more learning trials with a consistent schedule of reinforcement for imitation behavior. Dissonance arousal via voluntary commitment to future (actually experienced) deprivation by subjects already socially deprived resulted in significantly *less* effect of social reinforcement on learning than that which occurred in the group exposed to social isolation without a choice.

Thus, despite many methodological differences between these two studies, the same basic dissonance paradigm resulted in comparable learning effects in both; and this fact alone greatly extends the range of generalizability both of the findings and the model used to generate the predictions.

One final point should be made regarding the extinction data in the present study. With one exception (Low Deprivation Controls), the groups did not extinguish their conditioned verbal responding during the 80 trials of nonreinforcement. Although all groups began to show decreased responding toward the end of extinction and might have shown the expected decrement with additional trials, nevertheless the failure of the response to extinguish is surprising. Perhaps in this study the extinction procedure was enough like the original deprivation procedure to directly raise the drive level still higher and in some way interact with the previous reinforcement effects to maintain response persistence in the absence of subsequent reinforcement.

Although the acquisition data for the High Dissonance group look like those for the Low Deprivation Controls (who were not socially deprived), their extinction data are more in line with the pattern shown by the High Deprivation group. Such a finding complicates the interpretation of the effects of dissonance reduction on motivational control and may reflect another instance of the suppression of the need for social approval rather than a reduction in the need itself, a finding reminiscent of Mansson's TAT data (see Article 6).

In these last three studies, dealing with social motives, the subjects committed themselves to situations in which they were on the receiving end of an unpleasant experience. In a sense, even though some of them had a choice in the commitment, they committed themselves to accept passively failure or social disapproval. In the next paper, Brock and Pallak summarize a series of experiments in which each subject was on the giving end of an interpersonal relationship in which he believed was an active agent. However, he had to act toward another person in an aggressive manner that was inconsistent with his socially learned motives of not expressing aggression overtly, especially toward a helpless, nonprovoking victim. In such a situation, how will the process of dissonance reduction affect these motives?

13. THE CONSEQUENCES OF CHOOSING TO BE AGGRESSIVE: AN ANALYSIS OF THE DISSONANCE MODEL AND REVIEW OF RELEVANT RESEARCH

Timothy C. Brock and Michael S. Pallak

Dissonance theory has been extended to conflicts created by inducing aggressive responses in individuals who are opposed to such aggression. The study of post-aggression dissonance is an engaging inquiry because it concerns two salient and universal aspects of human behavior—the propensity to injure others and the tendency to experience discomfort when values and behavior come out of joint. Why persons engage in certain behaviors to which they are opposed is an interesting question not formally dealt with by dissonance theory. A tentative general answer is suggested by calling attention to the conflicting personal values and inconsistent social demands that beset us all. The world unfortunately is not ordered in such a way that each need can be instantly satisfied and every nascent whim immediately fulfilled. Hence, delay, forced redirection, and overt behavior that belies private values and needs characterize the human condition. Given the inevitability of discrepant acts and the aforementioned ubiquity of aggressive behavior, it became apparent that dissonance theory was a useful framework within which to increase understanding of this problematic and socially troublesome dimension of human interaction.

Unlike the other papers in this volume, the present article is not an experimental report but a review of a series of studies on the dissonance-induced

SOURCE: Brock, Timothy C., and Michael S. Pallak, "The Consequences of Choosing to Be Aggressive: An Analysis of the Dissonance Model and Review of Relevant Research," unpublished. Adapted by permission of the authors.

consequences of behaving aggressively. Five of the studies involve physical aggression, and two of them are concerned with verbal aggression.

Aggression, defined operationally as the delivery of noxious stimulation to another person, may be physical or verbal or both. In the two laboratory paradigms to be examined here, a victim, who is always the experimenter's confederate, is the ostensible recipient of electric shock or verbal derogation from the subject. Dissonance theory makes no distinction between verbal and physical aggression, and, indeed, we shall see that results with verbal aggression tend to corroborate those obtained using physical aggression.

PHYSICAL-AGGRESSION PARADIGM

According to this experimental procedure, subjects who are opposed to the use of electric shock on humans in scientific research are induced to deliver a series of what they believe are painful shocks to another subject (actually an experimental accomplice, here called the *victim*). The apparatus typically employed is an "aggression machine," a device invented by Buss and fully described in his monograph (Buss, 1961). Each subject is told to act the part of an experimenter studying concept formation. In that role, he has to shock the other person whenever the latter makes an incorrect response. The subject is told how to train the victim and how to deliver the stimuli and the shocks. Although there is no direct visual or verbal communication between the two people, the victim's reactions (i.e., gasps) to the presumably painful shocks are audible to the subject.

On slightly more than half the learning trials, the victim-accomplice responds incorrectly to the stimuli presented by the subject and therefore has to be shocked. The subject believes that the magnitude of shock administered depends upon which of 10 shock switches he depresses. The victim, of course, is not really shocked but merely pretends to be.

To preclude ambiguity or doubt about the noxiousness of the stimulation, each subject is actually made to experience some shock from the aggression machine. In some of the studies to be reviewed, the subject experienced the stimulation from four shock buttons (numbered 1, 2, 3, and 5). To acquaint him with "what will be felt by your subject," the subject got a mild shock, painful shocks, and, at the value of 5, an extremely noxious shock. He was told that the shock intensity continued to climb above this 5 value until the maximum of button 10, but the subject never received a shock above 5. In one of the other studies, the subject experienced a 40-volt shock during the instruction phase and believed he was administering a constant level of 100-volt shock to the victim (Glass, 1964, reported in detail in Article 14). Other procedural details in the Glass investigation also served to increase the believability of the shock procedure (such as the auditory and visual feedback to the subject in the form of clicks and flashing light produced by the depression of the switch).

A second important feature of this paradigm is that all subjects be on record as being opposed to the use of electric shock on humans in scientific research. In our experience, roughly one third of the undergraduates typically employed meet this theoretical requirement, and subjects are screened on this basis. The importance of this initial attitude against using shock was manifested in unpublished results obtained in conjunction with the Buss and Brock (1963) experiment. In that study, returns from subjects who *favored* using electric shock were uninterpretable in terms of dissonance theory or any other reasonable explanation.

The studies to be reported which utilized this general physical-aggression approach (with only minor variations) are those of Brock and Buss, 1962, 1964; Buss and Brock, 1963; Glass, 1964; and Pallak, 1966.

VERBAL-AGGRESSION PARADIGM

In another set of studies (Davis & Jones, 1960; Perry, 1965), the subject believes that in his role as experimenter he is verbally to derogate another subject on the basis of his answers to a standard set of questions. After hearing a tape recording of the victim's responses on ethical and ideological topics, the subject reads aloud a (prepared) insulting script, which he thinks is being heard by the victim.

The intensity of the verbal aggression administered can be appreciated by excerpts from the scripts used in these studies. Subjects in the Davis–Jones study told the victim:

> As I understand it, my job is to tell you in all honesty what my first impression of you is. . . . My overall impression was not too favorable. To put it simply I wouldn't go out of my way to get to know you. . . . I'd guess you have some personal problems that would make it hard for us to get along very well. Your general interests and so on strike me as those of a pretty shallow person. . . . Frankly, I just wouldn't know how much I could trust you as a friend after hearing your answers to those moral questions. You took the easy way out every time. I guess that I should point out some of the things you said that made a good impression on me, but that would be a kind of a waste of time since the general impression I have is not too good (p. 405).

Even more extreme was the attack delivered by subjects in the Perry study:

> I think that was a stupid way to answer the question. You're doing just as badly as you did in the last talk—terribly. You silly ass! Every time you open your mouth you show how dumb you are. What the hell are you doing in college? I've had the feeling all throughout this that you haven't been honest at all. Why don't you grow up and stop evading questions? How did I ever get paired up with a character like you? You don't give straight answers, you don't make any sense, and you sound like you have no idea what to do next. I really can't believe it! How can ordinary people put up with you? You're a coward who doesn't know what to believe! What a pile of manure you turned out to be. I wouldn't trust you with a thing, you creep! Anyone who would talk the garbage you talk and expect to be taken seriously must be crazy! (pp. 175–176).

The subject received no feedback from the victim during the Davis–Jones derogation, but in the Perry experiment each thrust of the aggressor elicited a preprogramed reaction from the victim. To illustrate:

> (Sharp intake of breath. Hesitantly: Wa— . . . was that for real? (Sighs.)
> Phew!
> (Heavy breathing. Under breath:) God! (Coughs, sniffs once, sighs again.)
> Damn!
> (Breathing pronounced, but words mumbled:) . . . it was terrible, it . . .
> (More audibly:) I'll be all right. . . E. . . (sniff).

And so forth.

The verbal attacks are always quite discrepant with the subject's own personal reaction to the victim. In the Davis–Jones study, this conclusion was supported by the number of subjects who balked at the commitment, coupled with evidence that practically all subjects regarded the prepared derogation as less favorable than their real evaluation of the victim.

The data to be reported here from the Perry (1965) study concern subjects who, prior to the experiment, expressed opposition to "stressing the human subject by insulting him or by deliberately lowering his self-esteem." In addition, Perry's description of the behavior of his subjects makes it clear that concern and resistance attended their aggressive impersonations.

SUMMARY OF ANTECEDENT CONDITIONS

The five independent variables manipulated in these studies are schematically displayed in Table 1, along with the sex of the subjects and victims.

Although research on postaggression dissonance has not proceeded in a neat, systematic fashion, it can be noted from Table 1 that specific variations are frequently repeated among experiments, often by different investigators. Experimental social-psychological research could benefit extremely if current experiments always included the reproduction of effects from preceding experiments. Although it is occasionally tedious, such replication ensures that the current investigator is attuned to the same phenomenal and empirical realms as his predecessors and enables conceptual comparison among experiments. This point is emphasized to highlight the value of the particular studies under review here as well as to indicate an avoidable source of foundering and apparent contradiction in the contemporary literature of personality and social psychology.

1. *Volition*

It is clear from Table 1 that all but one of the experiments included a manipulation of choice. Brehm and Cohen (1962) and Cohen (1960) have persuasively

TABLE 1

ANTECEDENT CONDITIONS IN SELECTED STUDIES OF DISSONANCE AND AGGRESSION

	Physical aggression					Verbal aggression	
Antecedent conditions	Brock & Buss, 1962	Buss & Brock, 1963	Brock & Buss, 1964	Glass, 1964	Pallak, 1966	Davis & Jones, 1960	Perry, 1965
1. Volition:							
High choice	×		×	×	×	×	×
Low choice	×			×		×	
Not manipulated		×					
2. Level of aggression:							
High	×	×	×	×	×	×	×
Low	×		×		×		
3. Further interaction with victim:							
Anticipate interaction			×		×	×	
Anticipate non-interaction			×		×	×	×
Not manipulated	×	×		×			
4. Justification for aggression:							
Positive		×	×				
Negative or none		×	×				
5. Self-esteem:							
High				×			
Low				×			
Not manipulated	×	×	×		×	×	×
6. Sex of participants:							
Aggressor	M & F	M & F	M & F	M	M	M	M
Victim	M & F	M & F	M	M	M	M	M

discussed the importance of volition to dissonance arousal (and this basic approach is reflected in the studies presented in this monograph). When a person feels obliged to perform a discrepant act, dissonance is minimized.* Consequently, postaggression dissonance is more likely to occur when subjects are given an explicit option to forego the discrepant aggressive act if they choose. Attempts at dissonance reduction, therefore, are more likely to be observed under these conditions.

It may be that dissonance can be produced without explicit presentation of an option to the subject (e.g., see Buss & Brock, 1963), but this is a theoretically complex issue involving the subject's perception of choice even when it is not explicitly delineated by the experimenter. The major point is that derivations from dissonance theory are more clear-cut and outcomes are less ambiguous

* That is, when the obligation is a consequence of external pressures. When, however, the obligation results from internal pressures—e.g., repressed motives, as in compulsion—dissonance may be quite intense.—Ed.

when the investigator has seen to it that subjects feel that it is up to them whether or not they engage in the discrepant behavior. In three studies (Brock & Buss, 1962; Davis & Jones; Glass), half the subjects were given a choice to aggress and half were simply instructed to aggress—that is, they were given no choice. In order to heighten overall dissonance, all subjects in the studies by Brock and Buss (1964), Pallak, and Perry were allowed to leave the experiment if they desired.

This perception of a high degree of choice was created by the following kind of instructions (in the Brock and Buss, 1962, and Pallak studies) to the subject:

> Although you came up here today and have learned what this experiment is all about and how to do it, I want to emphasize that there is no obligation to continue if you don't want to. You can leave if you want to—some students have preferred not to act as experimenters in this research and have left. Do you want to continue? Are you sure?

Even if the subjects agreed at this point, the experimenter re-emphasized their free choice:

> You know that it's entirely up to you whether or not you stay and give the shocks. Are you willing to do it?

Evidently, the option to leave was effectively communicated since up to 15 per cent of the subjects accepted it.

2. *Magnitude of Aggression*

Other things being equal, the greater the magnitude of the discrepant behavior, the greater should be the resulting dissonance. Hence, the greater the intensity of discrepant aggression, the greater should be the attempts at postaggression dissonance reduction. The posited effect of magnitude of aggression upon amount of postaggression dissonance reduction should be particularly clear under High Choice.

As Table 1 indicates, all the studies here reviewed included a High Aggression treatment—although, admittedly, the verbal-aggression study by Davis and Jones employed a derogation (previously quoted) that does not seem as noxious as Perry's.

The subjects assigned to the High Aggression condition in the Brock and Buss studies were instructed to use shock values higher than 5 (on the 10-value apparatus). In the Glass experiment, the subjects thought they were administering twice as much shock as they had felt (40 volts) during the instruction period. In the Pallak study, the subjects under High Aggression were told to use the "high" shock levels—"8, 9, and 10 and under no circumstances to go below number 8."[2]

2. To engender realism, the victim reacted by gasping to all shock values greater than 5 in the Brock-Buss and Pallak studies and to all shock values in the Glass investigation.

Under Low Aggression, the Pallak subjects were told to use shock levels "1, 2, and 3, and under no circumstances to use levels above number 3." Thus, the Pallak manipulation of High versus Low Aggression strove for more extreme effects.

In the Perry verbal-aggression study,[3] the subjects' perception of the magnitude of aggression they delivered was manipulated by providing differential feedback from the victim after the derogation. Subjects were assigned to one of the three feedback conditions immediately after their derogation of the victim. In the Positive Response condition, the subjects heard the victim say:

> I don't understand what just happened here, uh, why you feel the way you do about me, but I admire your honesty. I think that you must be a very straightforward and honest person—always on the level. It's too bad there aren't more people around who have the courage, uh, to speak their mind. . . I want you to believe me that I. . . respect you for being so frank about your feelings. . . It's not every person you can trust.

In the No Response condition, no feedback to the verbal aggression was received from the victim. In the Negative Response condition, the subjects heard the victim say:

> You . . . louse! . . . If you'd treat *anyone* . . . the way you treated me . . . and . . . and . . . be in the same room . . . huh! I'd pity you, *buster*! You *knew* that I couldn't get back at you, and that's the *only* reason you came out the way you did. . . The things you said to me, you wouldn't . . . well, you wouldn't get away with it if you weren't on the other end of this line, I'm telling you that right now. . . (More loudly:) From where I sit, buddy, you smell rotten !

On a postexperimental question asking, "To what extent do you believe that your partner was hurt by what you did to him?" those in the Positive Response condition estimated the victim's "discomfort" was half as much as in the other conditions (see Table 4).

3. *Anticipation of Subsequent Interaction with Victim*

The consequences of anticipated interaction with the victim can not be rigorously derived from dissonance theory. Davis and Jones speculated that persons enjoined to engage in derogation would subsequently attempt to revoke their discrepant aggression by making the appropriate explanations to the victim, if they had the chance to do so. Brock and Buss (1964) also predicted that subsequent interaction by physical aggressors would be consolatory. Hence, an

3. The writers' interpretation of Perry's (1965) data differs from the interpretation originally offered by Perry himself. However, in subsequent personal communications, Perry has acknowledged the merit of our position.

aggressor who could *not* interact with his victim would perceive fewer means of reducing his postaggression dissonance. Consequently, attempts at dissonance reduction should be observed in greater magnitude for aggressors who could not subsequently encounter their victims than for aggressors who anticipated a subsequent meeting (Davis & Jones, Pallak) or who were actually given an opportunity to communicate in writing with the victim (Brock & Buss, 1964).

The assumption that postaggression communication would be consolatory was borne out by a content analysis of letters written to the victim by the Brock–Buss (1964) subjects (see Table 2). In this study, half the subjects in each Aggression condition were instructed to communicate with the victim: "Write a short letter to him [the victim] saying whatever you would like. We should be able to get your letter out in this afternoon's mail." Expressions of sympathy and empathy for the victim's ordeal were most frequent under High Aggression. Brock and Buss thus concluded that the dissonant aggressor experiences a need to communicate specific personal feelings to his victim. To the extent that this communication is blocked, other modes of postaggression dissonance reduction will be employed.

For the three studies in which anticipation of further interaction was *not* manipulated (Brock & Buss, 1962; Buss & Brock; Glass), it seemed reasonable to suppose that subjects did not anticipate seeing the victim again. In the Perry experiment, subsequent communication with the victim was explicitly ruled out by the experimenter's instructions so that the prospect of interaction with the victim would not offer an alternative mode of dissonance reduction.

In their manipulation of anticipation of interaction, Davis and Jones told their Anticipation subjects:

> Of course, you realize that as soon as we have had time to study the effect of your reading of this negative evaluation on him [the victim], I shall explain to him that this was not your true opinion of him, and you will have an opportunity to meet him and to say anything that you like about your true impression of him. Of course, you don't have to say anything if you don't want to, but you will meet him as soon as we have gathered our data on his reaction (p. 405).

TABLE 2

FREQUENCY OF TYPES OF MESSAGES SENT BY AGGRESSORS TO THEIR VICTIMS*

Category	Treatment		Significance
	High Aggression	Low Aggression	
Neutral-informational	24	40	$p < 0.03$
Cordial-reinforcement	6	14	n.s.
Sympathy-empathy	47	19	$p < 0.001$
Total communications	77	73	n.s.

* A summary table from the data for 80 subjects presented by Brock and Buss, 1964, p. 410.

The Davis–Jones No Anticipation subjects were told that their identity would be protected and that the experimenters would "see to it that you get out of the building without having to meet him [the victim] and answer any embarrassing questions. Of course, he will never know your name just as you will never know his." Without exception, subjects in the Anticipation condition indicated a definite expectation of meeting the victim immediately after the experiment, while there was no such expectancy in the No Anticipation condition.

Pallak had a preliminary phase in his experiment (to be described in detail below) in which the subject and victim responded together to a TAT card. Expectancy for further communication was manipulated by the explicit separation of subject and victim in the No Anticipation condition: as soon as the subject and victim roles had been assigned, opportunity for communication, both visual and oral, was eliminated. Furthermore, each subject was instructed (1) that he was to return immediately to the experimenter's room once the concept-formation task was completed without communicating with the "learner," and (2) that he would be excused without seeing the learner again. In the Anticipation condition, the aggression machine was in the same room as the TAT materials, and the subject expected to be together again with the victim "to fill out several forms" after the concept-formation task was completed. Pallak also ran control groups that received only the manipulation of expectancy preceding the shock administration and found reliable differences between the No Anticipation and Anticipation conditions in subjects' expectancy for further interaction with the victim.

4. *Justification for Aggression*

It follows from dissonance theory (and from the bulk of studies previously reported in this volume) that postaggression dissonance should be less for subjects supplied with justification for their discrepant act than for those subjects not given prior consonant information.

In two studies (Brock & Buss, 1964; Buss & Brock), an attempt was made to vary the supportiveness of the cognitions accompanying the discrepant delivery of punishment. In the Positive Justification condition of the Buss–Brock study, the subjects read (before delivering the shock) an ostensible Medical Association report listing positive aspects of using electric shock on men and women in research: ready adaptation, benefits of stimulation, never serious damage, electrocution leads to *instant* death—no pain, no reason to fear shock, shock is exhilarating, scientific use of shock will increase knowledge. In the Negative Justification condition, the foregoing items were appropriately altered; for example, "Human beings cannot adapt to even slight amounts of electric shock" was the negative version of the first item.

The Positive Justification condition of the Brock–Buss (1964) experiment provided reasons for being the aggressor. Prior to the assignment to "trainer" and "trainee" roles, the subject and confederate completed an ostensible training aptitude test, which was then "graded." After the confederate was temporarily dismissed, the subject was told:

> Your score shows that your aptitude for training and supervising others is very high, higher than 90 per cent of others who have taken this test, according to national norms. Even though you may never have had any experience in training other people, the test clearly shows that you have definite aptitude to do so. Since the task today involves another person, I am going to ask you to be the experimenter. Are the reasons for choosing you completely clear?

In the No Justification condition, the subject and confederate simply drew lots rigged so that the subject would draw a slip saying "Experimenter." On a post-treatment measure, Positive Justification subjects indicated that they felt more qualified to be the trainer than the No Justification subjects. The manipulation was considered effective.

5. *Aggressor's Self-Esteem*

Only one of the studies here reviewed (Glass) manipulated a dispositional variable.[4] Glass reasoned that the higher the aggressor's self-esteem, the more dissonance would be aroused by the aggression since such behavior would be more discrepant with his self-image. "If the aggressor is led to believe that he has a preponderance of unfavorable characteristics (low self-esteem), the act of injuring another is consonant with his belief that he is an unpleasant person, or at the very least is less discrepant with his self-image than when he perceives himself as having predominantly favorable traits" (Glass, 1964, p. 532). Since this study and a more recent follow-up will be presented in detail in a separate article, further description of this procedure will be omitted here.

CONSEQUENCES OF BEHAVING AGGRESSIVELY

The investigations described above studied six outcomes of the dissonance created between the behavior of acting aggressively and the cognitions opposed to aggression (e.g., I do not like to hurt helpless victims). Table 3 summarizes the use of these dependent measures.

1. *Evaluation of the Victim: Victim Is Devalued*

One of the most interesting derivations from dissonance theory concerns the effects of postaggression dissonance on interpersonal evaluation. How a person behaves toward others may influence how he perceives those others. To the extent that dissonance accompanies the punishment of another, derogation of

4. See Perry, 1965, for mixed results pertaining to personality correlates of the aggressor's reaction to his derogatory behavior. (This study by Glass and a related one are presented in detail in Article 14, by Glass and Wood.)

TABLE 3

PRINCIPAL DEPENDENT MEASURES IN SELECTED STUDIES OF DISSONANCE AND AGGRESSION

Measure	Brock & Buss, 1962	Buss & Brock, 1963	Brock & Buss, 1964	Glass, 1964	Pallak, 1966	Davis & Jones, 1960	Perry, 1965
1. Evaluation of victim				×	×	×	×
2. Evaluation of pain	×			×			
3. Perceived obligation	×		×	×			
4. Self-evaluation (guilt)		×	×				
5. Repression of negative justification		×					
6. Situational attractiveness	×	×	×	×			

the other may follow as a means of reducing the dissonance. The cognitions "I've punished this person" and "This person is likable and worthy" are inconsistent when juxtaposed; hence, attempts may be made to reduce the dissonance by devaluing the victim.

Table 3 indicates that a postaggression rating of the victim has been one of the most often studied dependent variables in research on postaggression dissonance. The Davis–Jones subjects, who thought they were participating in a study of impression formation, evaluated the victim by rating his likability, warmth, conceit, intelligence, and adjustment, on a 20-item scale. Using a similar "first impression" guise, Glass had his subjects rate their feelings of friendliness toward the victim: willingness to admit victim to a circle of close friends, attraction to participating in another study with victim, and liking for victim as prospective roommate.

Davis–Jones and Glass found statistically significant derogation of the victim under High Choice—together with High Self-Esteem in Glass' study. There was no appreciable derogation of the victim in the other cells of these designs. Thus, when the aggressor expects an opportunity to revoke and/or explain his voluntary aggression or when the voluntary aggressor has low self-regard, there is less postaggression dissonance and less of a tendency to derogate the victim as a means of dissonance reduction.

Magnitude of aggression was held constant in the Davis–Jones and Glass investigations. The Perry and Pallak studies provided tests of the hypothesis that devaluation of the victim will increase with increased punishment, provided that the punishment is opposed and yet voluntarily administered. Perry's results are shown in Table 4. The mean change scores from before to after verbal derogation show most devaluation (that is, most reduction in perceived likability, warmth, modesty, and total favorability) under the condition in which the aggression was perceived as most severe—namely, Negative Response treatment.

TABLE 4

ADJUSTED MEAN CHANGE SCORES* OF SIX DEPENDENT VARIABLES (PERRY, 1965) IN RELATION TO VICTIM-RESPONSE TREATMENT†

Variable	Victim-Response Treatment			Alpha‡
	Positive	None	Negative	
Personal likability	−8.4	−15.1	−15.1	0.05
Desire to know better	6.5	−3.0	−2.5	0.05
Warmth	−2.4	−4.2	−5.5	0.05
Modesty	−1.3	−4.7	−10.0	0.001
Total favorability	−19.3	−27.0	−35.1	0.01
Estimated victim discomfort	11.8	5.9	5.9	0.075

* By removing variance attributable to "expressed aggressor discomfort" (see Perry, 1965). A negative sign preceding a tabulated value does not imply that the unadjusted value was of negative value. Each negative value indicates a decrease in favorability of the subject rating from before to after derogation of the victim; positive ratings indicate increases. On the estimated-victim-discomfort measure, the higher the mean, the *less* the ascribed discomfort.

† Data presented for subjects on record as being opposed to verbal derogation. Each mean based on $n = 15$.

‡ Estimated from Perry's data.

Scores are most favorable toward the victim in the Positive Response condition, where, it is recalled, the aggressor elicited appreciation for his honesty. The total favorability scores are intermediate for the No Response condition. Apparently, as would be expected from theory, the more the victim has appeared to suffer, the more *unfavorable* is the aggressor's evaluation of the victim. The crime is made to fit the punishment.[5]

It may be recalled that Perry's instructions explicitly ruled out the possibility of further interaction with the victim. When further interaction with the victim *is* anticipated, will magnitude of aggression still bear the same relationship to amount of devaluation of the victim? This question, as well as others, was posed by Pallak, who probed more deeply into the matter of punishment and altered evaluation of the victim.

Pallak raised an interesting issue by observing that punishment is often perceived as purgative, as serving a "cleansing" function, in some everyday situations. Punishment may lead to perceived enhancement of the victim when the victim is perceived as somewhat disreputable prior to the administration of

5. Our interpretation of Perry's data may appear questionable. In the first place, the check on the aggression-intensity manipulation, estimated victim discomfort, did not show more discomfort under the Negative than under the No Response treatment; secondly, the spread between No Response and Negative Response is not impressive for some of the dependent measures (likability, desire to know better, warmth); and, thirdly, the data might be explainable in reinforcement terms—the aggressor likes appreciative victims more than hostile victims. While the second objection is not easy to dismiss, the first and third difficulties are more apparent than real in that Perry's dissertation includes considerable observational evidence showing that (a) aggressors in the Negative Response treatment felt they hurt the victim more than aggressors in the No Response treatment and (b) the reaction of the victim in Negative Response treatment was perceived to be appropriate expression of the hurt he had just experienced and was never perceived as an inappropriate and/or gratuitous hostile evaluation. Negative feedback, when it is merited, does not necessarily have negative reinforcement value (Jones, 1964, pp. 28–29).

punishment. Little dissonance should be aroused by aggressing toward someone who is disreputable and who either "deserves" to be shocked or is the kind of person "anyone else would also shock in this situation." Thus, a purgation-enhancement hypothesis seems more appropriate than a dissonance-devaluation one.

After having established the victim as quite disreputable by means of an ingenious deception, Pallak was able to demonstrate support for the purgation-enhancement hypothesis: after the aggression, the "punished" victims were considered morally superior and more likable than the victims who were not shocked.

Figure 1 reveals not only this effect (comparing the No-Shock Control group

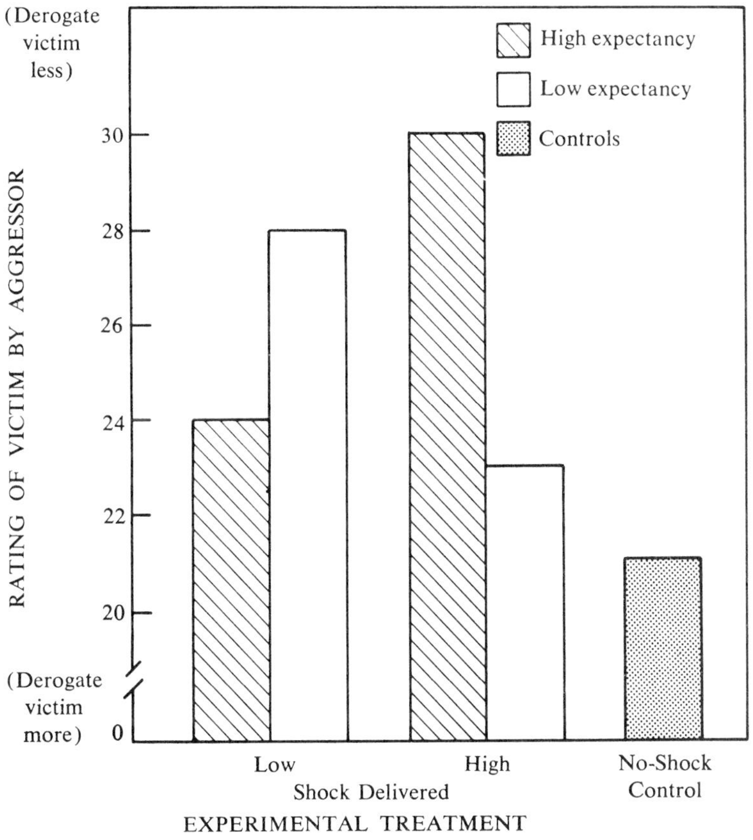

FIGURE 1

Effects of level of shock and expectancy of future interaction with the victim on the subject's postaggression evaluation of the victim. Each bar represents the mean of sums over four scales for that condition. The lower the mean, the lower the perception of the victim, i.e., the higher the derogation. The Control group is significantly different from all others; Low Shock-Low Expectancy is significantly higher than High Shock-Low Expectancy; and the interaction between expectancy and shock is significant. (From Pallak, 1966.)

and the experimental groups[6]) but also the relation of devaluation to both shock magnitude and expectation of future interaction with the victim. Subjects who expected to interact derogated the victim less the higher the level of shock. On the other hand, derogation is greater for High than for Low Shock for subjects who didn't anticipate future interaction. The results on each of the four separate rating scores from which the pooled data were graphed reveal the same results.

The studies of verbal aggression (Perry) and physical aggression (Pallak), taken together, firmly establish the effect of aggression magnitude on devaluation of the victim. For both neutral (Perry) and discredited (Pallak) victims, more injury by the aggressor led to more unfavorable ratings on a total of ten different measures, the bulk of which were not highly intercorrelated.

Further work is needed in which the aggressor's perception of the victim's character is varied along a "rotten-saintly" dimension prior to the instigation of aggression. Delivery of punishment to a saintly victim should intensify whatever dissonance has been aroused by traditional factors, since the goodness of the victim would be another cognition inconsistent with the discrepant aggression.

2. *Evaluation of Pain: Pain Is Minimized*

Another interesting avenue of postaggression dissonance reduction may be the altered perception of the noxiousness of the stimulation itself. The aggressor may reduce dissonance by judging the stimulus to be less noxious, saying in effect, "The pain I administered was really rather mild." In the Brock and Buss (1962) experiment, the subject was asked to rate each sample shock on a scale running from "can't feel a thing" to "extremely painful." At the end of the concept-learning routine, the subject was given shock values 3 and 5 again, and the before-after change in rating was the principal dependent variable. Pain minimization was greater under High Choice than under Low Choice. Under High Choice (when the victim was a male), High Shock led to more minimization of pain than Low Shock. These results were quite reliable and show that a rather unambiguous physical stimulus can be distorted in the service of dissonance reduction, a point amply demonstrated in the previously reported research by Zimbardo and his associates. Despite some procedural differences between the Brock–Buss (1962) and Glass studies, the strong and clear relationships between postaggression dissonance and pain minimization obtained by Brock and Buss are unequivocally reflected in the performance of the High Dissonance subjects in Glass' research.

3. *Perceived Obligation: Increased Obligation to Aggress*

The aggressor can also readily reduce postaggression dissonance by increasing his feeling of obligation to deliver the punishment. For this reason, in all but one

6. A better Control treatment would have required the Control subjects also to train the confederate by using, say, red and green signals (instead of electric shock). With such a control, it would have been possible to assess what contribution, if any, to victim enhancement in the experimental groups was made by the effects of training another person or time with victim.

of the studies here reviewed, the experimenter deliberately provided an explicit option to the subjects. The choice induction notwithstanding, it was still possible for the other independent variables to affect perceived obligation.

It follows from dissonance theory that the greater the amount and/or intensity of the discrepant behavior, the greater will be the attempt to reduce dissonance by saying in effect, "I was obliged to carry out this behavior." The hypothesized magnitude-obligation relationship was supported in the Brock–Buss (1962) study in which more obligation was reported under High Shock than under Low Shock. An interesting corroborative finding was the expression of greater obligation when the victim was female than when the victim was male. It seems very likely that the subjects' perceived intensity of the aggression was greater for female than for male victims because for female victims High Shock led to less pain minimization than Low Shock.

The strong effect of aggression magnitude on felt obligation was replicated in a subsequent experiment (Brock & Buss, 1964). This experiment also showed theoretically consistent effects upon obligation of anticipated communication with the victim and of justification for the aggression. More obligation was reported under No Justification than under Justification; more obligation under No Communication than under Communication. In other words, when subjects were given good reasons for carrying out the punishment and when they anticipated communicating with the victim, they were more willing to acknowledge that they were not obliged to aggress. The results for obligation[7] obtained by Brock and Buss (1962, 1964) lend strength to the view (Cohen, 1960) that volition is a major dynamic force when discrepancy occurs between a person's values and his behavior. Thus, denial of responsibility may be added to devaluation of the victim and minimization of pain as major consequences of postaggression dissonance arousal.

4. *Self-Evaluation (Guilt): Self Devalued*

The effects of postaggression dissonance arousal on guilt are more difficult to derive than the consequences that have been discussed thus far. The problem concerns the unclear theoretical status of guilt and the consequent lack of sound experimental manipulations. Self-attack might accompany acts or temptations, wishes, and intentions, both conscious and unconscious. Guilt may be a response to an act or a wish, or a defense against them. Some writers think of guilt only in connection with temptation while others see guilt largely as a response to social expectations and to class and sex norms.

Without further belaboring the point that conceptualizations of guilt are conflicting, we can simply ask what role self-devaluation might play in reducing postaggression dissonance. The reasoning behind the Glass experiment suggested that consonance can be increased for the aggressor to the extent he can entertain the following cognitions: (*a*) "Although I am opposed to shocking others, I did

7. Glass (1964) included a measure of obligation in his study that was sensitive to his Choice-No Choice treatment but was apparently unaffected by his manipulation of self-esteem.

so voluntarily," and (*b*) "I am a bad person." Cognition *b* is more consistent with *a* than is (*c*), "I am a good person." According to this rationale, more expression of guilt would occur under conditions calculated to produce greater post-aggression dissonance, i.e., negative justification for aggression, high aggression, and no anticipation of further encounter with the victim.

Some support for this hypothesis came from the Buss–Brock experiment in which it was predicted that subjects administering pain accompanied by negative justification would report more guilt than subjects administering pain preceded by positive justification. The hypothesis was supported when male aggressors shocked female victims and female aggressors shocked male victims, but not when same-sex pairing was used. Buss and Brock suggested that the positive justification may have been discredited under same-sex pairings since the aggressor would understand the reactions of a victim of his own sex *so well* that positive assurances would be unconvincing.

More impressive support for the dissonance–self-devaluation hypothesis came from the study by Brock and Buss (1964). Guilt reactions[8] were more extreme under No Justification than under Justification, under High than under Low Shock, under No Communication with victim than under Communication with victim, and when a female was the victim. These confirmations were reliable and seem to show rather clearly that postaggression dissonance can be reduced by means of self-attack.

5. *Repression of Negative Justification: Less Recall of Discrepant Elements*

Akin to the minimization of pain in postaggression dissonance reduction may be denial or forgetting of the discrepant aspects of the pain-administration situation. Danger, long-term injury, and permanent damage to many areas of functioning were some of the discrepant negative aspects that were underrecalled by the Buss–Brock subjects in the Negative Justification condition. Control subjects, who did not engage in aggression, did not underrecall when given the Negative Justification communication. Evidently, elements dissonant with the aggressive behavior can be forgotten as well as changed. The Buss–Brock study is the only one in which "repression" was recorded as a consequence of post-aggression dissonance.

6. *Situational Attractiveness: Situation Less Attractive*

Lawrence and Festinger (1962) have described as a generalized type of dissonance reduction increasing the attractiveness of relevant features of the dissonance situation. Therefore, it should follow that favorable re-evaluation of the aggression situation will occur in proportion to the magnitude of postaggression

8. The item read, "Concerning guilt over giving the shocks, I felt (None at all — An extremely great amount)."

dissonance. Attitudes toward using electric shock on humans in research were measured in the Brock–Buss (1962, 1964), Buss–Brock, and Glass studies, and in none of these did the attitudes change in ways that could be coordinated with dissonance theory. Mainly, the differences between experimental cells were unreliable. In the Brock–Buss (1964) experiment, subjects replied to an additional measure of situational attractiveness: "If I were asked to act as experimenter in this concept learning study again, I would be (Extremely opposed — Extremely willing)." Changes on this measure of situational attractiveness were reliably opposed to theoretical expectations: more attraction under Justification than under No Justification, under Low than under High Shock, and under Communication than under No Communication.

These failures to obtain favorable re-evaluation of the aggression situation cannot be attributed to measurement artifacts, such as initial scale position, nor to insensitivity of the measure itself. The measure is the same item that was used for the pre-experimental selection of subjects opposed to shocking humans. The measure is sensitive to the appropriate construct since there is evidence that subjects who are *not* opposed to shock administration have quite different postaggression reactions (unpublished data collected by Buss & Brock, 1963; Perry, 1965).

DISCUSSION

A new perspective on social perception and social interaction is offered by dissonance theory through its focus on the effects of behavior on cognition. Traditional models have tended to emphasize an opposite chain of causation, namely, how percepts, attitudes, and so forth, affect behavior. The dissonance flavor is captured in the way the studies reviewed here differ from many other experimental investigations of aggression (e.g., Berkowitz, 1962). Rather than employ common-sense and/or atheoretical explanatory constructs (for example, guilt), dissonance studies attempt to order postaggression reactions to a theoretical model (dissonance) found useful in accounting for a wide range of social and motivational phenomena. The confusing issue of "intent" in aggression (Feshbach, 1962) is bypassed in favor of volition, a variable which has clear theoretical meaning and which is susceptible to experimental manipulation.

The strength of empirical relationships can be gauged in terms of the likelihood of easy trans-situational replication. By this criterion, the studies of postaggression dissonance have supplied a number of solid findings that must be taken into account in any conservative "building-blocks" approach to the science of social behavior. Devaluation of the victim, minimization of pain, and increase of felt obligation have been shown to be well-established consequences of postaggression dissonance arousal. Choice in aggressing, magnitude of aggression, and expectancy of further interaction with the victim are antecedent factors that have been shown to affect the magnitude of postaggression dissonance. The role of certain consequences (self-devaluation, re-evaluation of the aggression situation, and repression of dissonant elements) and certain antecedents (personality factors and concomitant justification) is less clear, but they are, nevertheless, implicated in the process.

It appears that denial mechanisms take precedence over other possible types of postaggression reactions. The aggressor denies responsibility, minimizes the pain, and devalues the victim and/or himself. Situation and object enhancement, which are characteristic responses to dissonance in other empirical realms (Brehm & Cohen, 1962), are not obtained following discrepant aggression. The student of cognitive dissonance is reminded again of the persistent problem overshadowing further development of the theory: insufficient theoretical specification of the priorities of different responses when dissonance is alleged to have been aroused. Orthodox dissonance theory orders avenues of dissonance reduction in terms of the putative resistance to change of the pertinent cognitive elements: cognitions mapping social reality should be more easily changed than cognitions which map physical reality. Thus, attempts at dissonance reduction should more readily entail change of opinion about using shock than re-evaluation of the painfulness of a shock that has just been received. However, as noted already, Brock and Buss (1962) found that perception of the physical environment—i.e., judgment of painfulness—*was* modified while change in the presumably less resistant cognitive elements mapping opinion was not observed.

An alternative to the "least resistance" formulation may be advanced at this point. According to this alternative, dissonant individuals will bypass *easy* avenues of dissonance reduction in favor of those modes that provide the most *complete* reduction of the dissonance. The boulder is dislodged while pebbles are left unturned. Analogous behavior is exhibited by the very hungry driver who bypasses hot-dog stands and proceeds for ten more miles until he arrives at a steak house. A test is needed in which the maximum-reduction rule is pitted against the least-resistance rule. That test and, indeed, any attempt to order postaggression responses into the equivalent of a habit-family hierarchy requires methodological refinements that are not yet available. Thus far, there have been few serious attempts by dissonance theorists systematically to quantify independent variables (across three or more levels), to equate dependent measures for sensitivity and relevance, and to present avenues of dissonance reduction to the subject in balanced order.

This review of studies of dissonance and aggression ends on a note of caution. Although extension of dissonance theory to aggressive behavior has enabled discovery and verification of many interesting propositions, no claim is made that all the data gathered so far can be readily ordered to the dissonance model. Sex of victim and sex of aggressor complicate several of the relationships discussed here, and portions of the data in Buss and Brock (1963), Brock and Buss (1964), Pallak (1966), and Perry (1965) are explainable only by adducing extra-theoretical assumptions. The bulk of this material is already in print and can be consulted by the interested reader. It seems most likely that the introduction of new variables to the discrepant-aggression paradigm, such as pre-aggression perception of the victim's character (Pallak, 1966), may stretch the dissonance-theory framework beyond its range of applicability. For the moment, however, the theory does seem to provide the best means of understanding the relationships between the antecedents and consequences of discrepant aggression.

Editor's Comments

The studies reviewed in this paper focus on a social situation in which one person administers noxious stimulation to another person with the knowledge that it is causing pain. Such a behavioral analysis of aggression, while adequate for an application of the dissonance model, may be viewed by some as providing only a limited conception of aggression, with little generalizability to its natural occurrences. It is what the subject does and the consequences of his action that are the focus of attention here and not his intention to aggress or his need for aggression and catharsis. He responds not to provocation by the victim but to the demands imposed by the experimental task. Like the subjects in Milgram's (1963) studies of compliance to inducements to aggress, the subjects in these studies comply because they are expected to. The results here are even more striking than Milgram's findings because compliance occurs even under conditions of high choice and minimal justification, and these are the conditions that lead to the most extreme reactions (victim's pain is minimized, he is devalued, and blame is placed on external forces).

For dissonance to be aroused in the situations described in these studies, it is sufficient that the subject perceives that his behavior has hurt someone else and that he could have chosen to behave differently. In everyday situations, however, pain may be inflicted and be labelled by both victim and instigator as "accidental" and not be considered aggressive unless additional information increases the likelihood that the act was not a chance event but was motivated. Moreover, consider a parent who slaps his child's hand to prevent him from touching a hot stove, that is, inflicts mild pain to teach the child to avoid more serious pain. What are the conditions under which the parent would define this behavior as aggression toward the child? The complexity of any attempt to define unambiguously certain acts as instances of "real" aggression is seen in an extreme form when the hangman asks the victim's pardon before executing him, so that both realize that the agent of the aggression is a society and not the man performing the role of executioner.

The issue of intentionality may be a most important one for determining whether the entire process under investigation here can be understood as well in terms of guilt reduction as dissonance reduction. Surely the obtained outcomes could be explained as the consequence of guilt about behaving aggressively; if so, then why invoke an additional conceptual scheme?*

Guilt is traditionally seen as involving violation (in thought or action) of a norm that has become an internalized aspect of one's moral conscience. Guilt-producing behavior is assumed to be initially pleasurable, that is, motivated by needs for self-gratification. In fact, subsequent guilt reactions should be proportional to the pleasure experienced by transgression of the norm. According to some analyses of guilt (e.g., Sarnoff, 1962), complete guilt reduction can be

* The specification of the antecedent variables and consequent behavior derived from dissonance would not have been made a priori by existing "guilt" theories, but the main reason for distinguishing between them is that they refer to different psychological processes, although at points they converge.

achieved only through receiving punishment appropriate to the crime, while traditional views also stress the need for seeking the victim's forgiveness and for confessing to authority (see Reik, 1961).

In contrast, dissonance involves behaving in a way that does not follow from one's ego ideal (an aspect of the super-ego distinct from conscience, according to Freud). Dissonance should be aroused even if the discrepant act brings no gratification and is not motivated, but it should not be nearly as great from a discrepant thought as from a discrepant public action. Finally, dissonance-reduction processes should not necessarily involve moral retribution or penance but rather changes in self concept or the seeking of justification for the discrepant behavior.

An experimental distinction between guilt- and dissonance-reduction processes may be possible therefore by providing subjects who have behaved "aggressively" in the paradigms described in these studies with alternative behavioral choices (following a general strategy proposed by Sarnoff & Zimbardo, 1961, to distinguish fear from anxiety). For example, if given the option of waiting alone or with specific other people, a guilty subject should prefer to affiliate with others who are seen as punitive rather then be alone or be with permissive others. Since dissonance appears to be reduced most by denial mechanisms, however, dissonant subjects should have no need to expose themselves to someone likely to deliver punishment but should prefer instead to be alone. They should also prefer to affiliate with others who could be expected to facilitate denial processes by either distracting attention away from the aggressive act or by providing social support in the form of further derogationof the victim.

Dissonance arousal should be more sensitive to victim characteristics than guilt arousal. Thus, inflicting harm on another person should create less dissonance the more the victim deserves it (the more negative or disreputable he is), while morally it should make no difference whether the victim is good, bad, or neutral as long as he is helpless. Therefore, Pallak's results may be partially interpretable in terms of a guilt-purgation hypothesis: a disreputable victim who is shocked is seen as "morally superior" to one who is not shocked. Thus the victim enhancement found in that study may not be at odds with the dissonance-theory victim devaluation found in the other studies, but instead may be due entirely to guilt reduction unconfounded by dissonance processes. However, interpretation of this data must be tempered by the knowledge that victim characteristics were not manipulated between treatments and that the control and experimental groups differed in their degree of interaction with the victim.

The victim's reaction to the aggressive behavior ought to be a potent determiner of dissonance, and Perry's data appear to support such a notion. Dissonance should be greater the more the victim has been hurt by the subject. Perry varied the feedback his subjects received from the victims against whom they had verbally aggressed. When the feedback was a controlled, reasoned statement, understanding of, and complimentary to the subject, then such victims were evaluated as more favorable and in less discomfort. However, in the Negative Feedback condition, the subject hears that he has really upset the victim and the victim becomes quite insulting toward him. It would be natural to expect such victims to be perceived as less favorable and in more discomfort than those in the Positive Feedback condition. Attention should center upon the No-Feedback Control in order to evaluate the differential effectiveness of these extreme victim reactions. The data in Table 4 lead to the conclusion that the aggressor behaves toward the victim whose reactions *increase* his dissonance as if he has said nothing. The Control condition is like the Negative Feedback condition and unlike the Positive on every measure. In one sense, this is one of the most extreme instances of dissonance-predicted denial we have ever observed. What is needed in future research is a behavioral or autonomic measure of attention and immediate reaction to the negative feedback and a tracking of the process whereby the subject behaves as if he received no feedback.

Further research using verbal aggression might be better coordinated to the physical-aggression paradigm by developing a "verbal-aggression machine." By means of scaling techniques, one could obtain a set of hostile statements varying in judged aggressiveness and equally spaced along a continuum of hostility. Within each interval, there would be a number of statements differing in content but equivalent in scale value. Then, in the guise of a praise-reproof study, the subject would be asked to try to improve the victim's speech-making ability by criticizing him at selected points during the speech. Pressing one button (of perhaps 10 available) would deliver to the victim either a card with a written statement to be read or a prerecorded taped statement delivered directly by the machine. Feedback from the victim might be programed appropriately throughout the course of the aggressive attacks (as in the physical-aggression paradigm), and the severity of the aggression would be determined from the frequency of the scale values of statements chosen.

In suggesting that dissonance reduction may not follow the line of least resistance, the authors have advanced a novel principle which, though contrary to the original formulation of dissonance theory, may find support in some of the studies reported earlier in this volume. Brock and Pallak raise for consideration the idea that dissonance-reduction attempts may be directed toward the most central element rather than toward the one least bound by reality constraints, regardless of the degree of "cognitive work" involved in modifying that element. Thus, we need not always assume that cognitions about social reality are more susceptible to dissonance pressures than are cognitions about physical reality. An immediate change in the most central element may be less effortful in the long run than many change attempts directed at peripheral elements. Changing a single element that is bonded to many others in a cluster may result in the most total change in the system (borrowing concepts of centrality and bondedness from the attitude-structure approach of Peak, 1955, and Zajonc, 1955).

Thus, for example, in the pain-control study reported earlier (Article 7), the subjective estimate of pain would appear to be the element easiest to change, while behavioral and physiological reactions would seem much more resistant to change. The results indicated, however, that these latter reactions were more likely to be affected by dissonance reduction than were self-reports. The sizable changes in learning and GSR made the dissonance explanation not only more theoretically convincing to the researchers (and perhaps to the reader) but, by the same token, would logically seem to be more practically convincing to the subjects: "The shocks are not so bad, not merely because I *say* so but because I *feel* so."

One might extend this principle to predict sequential effects of dissonance reduction within individuals such that attitude changes follow and are mediated by changes in autonomic functioning, rather than the other way around, as we have assumed in our research. Such considerations demand an improvement in technical sophistication before they can be seriously evaluated.

Throughout this volume, we have been considering the consequences for an individual of behaving in ways that are inconsistent with his cognitions about a given drive state, value, attitude, or social need. While we have seen that this inconsistency influences postdecisional behavior only when the individual perceives he has made the commitment freely and with minimal justification, individual differences in self-concept should also influence how one reacts to cognitive inconsistency. In our Introduction to this volume, the dissonance paradigm was described as a face-saving approach; that is, it operates because individuals do not want to appear to have made a wrong decision. If, however, one's self-concept is not positive—if it includes cognitions about often being wrong, about not being seen by others as a "good" person, about ignoring the impression one makes on others, or about no longer evaluating oneself in terms of the outcomes of one's actions—then one ought to experience little or no dissonance.

The next paper, by Glass and Wood, presents two studies addressed to this point. Brock and Pallak have provided us with an idea of the research on self-esteem which Glass recently undertook. Roger Brown (1965) provides a more general framework within which we may reflect upon the implications of individual-difference variables in the processes of dissonance arousal and reduction:

> As one reads dissonance studies, it is interesting to try to identify the unexpressed premises upon which the dissonance depends. These turn out to be a curious set of ideas. Here are some of them: (1) I say what I believe; (2) I do what I want to do; (3) If I willingly endure something unpleasant it always turns out to have been worth it; (4) What I choose is better than anything I reject. Very many of the experimental manipulations that have been used would fail to generate dissonance in one who believed: I am a liar with bad luck, poor judgment, and no will power. Perhaps not many take this view of themselves. Still, since dissonance derives from premises about oneself and the world, it must vary with self-concept and world view. It ought to be possible, for example, to contrive situations that would be dissonant for authoritarians, but consonant for equalitarians . . . (pp. 597–598).

14. THE CONTROL OF AGGRESSION BY SELF-ESTEEM AND DISSONANCE[1]

David C. Glass and John D. Wood

The relevance of the dissonance paradigm for understanding complex phenomena in which personality and interpersonal variables interact has recently been shown by Bramel's research (1962, 1963). Bramel studied an area usually considered to be the exclusive domain of "personality theories," the relation of self-esteem to defensive projection. Projection of an undesirable characteristic onto others (as an ego defense mechanism) was found to occur when an individual was exposed to information about himself that was both unfavorable and dissonant with his self-image (specifically, that he had homosexual tendencies). However, little if any projection occurred when the individual had a negative self-image, and the new unfavorable information was consonant with that general image. Thus, projection may be viewed as a consequence of the desire to reduce discrepancies produced by information that is incompatible with a need for favorable self-evaluation and not simply as a consequence of guilt resulting from the transgression of superego precepts.

If one follows Bramel's line of reasoning, other processes traditionally viewed to be within the domain of personality theory may be seen to be amenable to a dissonance formulation. For example, increased dislike for the victim of an aggression has often been observed after a person injures another whom he does not necessarily want to hurt (as the previous review by Brock & Pallak clearly demonstrates). Given this "inappropriate aggression," the aggressor may be expected to experience dissonance. The higher his self-esteem, the more dissonant the aggression, since his behavior is more discrepant with his self-image the more self-esteem he possesses. On the other hand, if the aggressor believes that he has a preponderance of unfavorable characteristics (which we will define as low self-esteem), the act of injuring another is consonant with his self-image, or at the very least it is less discrepant than if he perceived himself as having predominantly favorable traits. So, the lower his self-esteem, the less dissonance will be aroused by the act of aggression. Assuming that the arousal of dissonance motivates the aggressor to reduce dissonance by, for example, *increasing* his dislike of the other person after the aggression, the prediction is that the higher

---

SOURCE: Glass, David C., and John D. Wood, "The Control of Aggression by Self-Esteem and Dissonance." Adapted from "Changes in Liking as a Means of Reducing Cognitive Discrepancies Between Self-Esteem and Aggression," *Journal of Personality*, 1964, *32*, pp. 531–550. Reprinted by permission of the authors and Duke University Press.

1. The present research was made possible by grants from the Development Fund of The Ohio State University and from the Research Division of Columbus Psychiatric Hospital. The assistance of Milton J. Rosenberg and the late Arthur R. Cohen in the design of Experiment I is gratefully acknowledged. Thanks are also due to Joël Grinker and Renée Bash for their assistance in the statistical analysis of data from Experiment II, and to Jack W. Brehm, Helge H. Mansson, Melvin Zelnik, Alfred Cohn, Seymour Giniger, and Polly Glass for their helpful comments on the original manuscript.

one's self-esteem, the more he will dislike the victim after aggressing against him, because he will have more dissonance to reduce.

The possibility exists that an aggressor will not feel responsible for his behavior because he perceives his aggression to be a consequence of situational pressures or coercion (e.g., Milgram, 1963). A number of recent studies (Brehm & Cohen, 1959; Brock & Buss, 1962; Davis & Jones, 1960) have shown that if a person has no alternative except to behave in a manner discrepant with his beliefs and values, little if any dissonance is created. If, on the other hand, he has the opportunity to behave in a manner consonant with his beliefs but he chooses to act in a discrepant manner, relatively great dissonance is created. Thus, in accord with these findings [and with those of the other studies in the present volume], we assume that choosing to engage in the discrepant aggressive behavior is a necessary condition for the arousal of dissonance, the magnitude of which is inversely proportional to justification for the act.

Two experiments are reported here. The first is both an extension of the preceding considerations on self-esteem into the domain of aggression and a further test of the importance of "choice" in arousing cognitive dissonance. It examines the effects of inducing aggressive behavior in an individual who is *opposed* to such aggression and who has a choice of withdrawing from the experiment. If such an individual chooses to aggress, then the higher his self-esteem, the greater his dissonance—since the act of injuring another is dissonant not only with his opposition to aggression but also with his self-image. The aggressor may attempt to reduce dissonance by increasing his dislike for the other person. If the aggressor perceives the other person in unpleasant terms, then the knowledge that he has aggressed against him would not be inconsistent with his self-image. Thus, the higher his self-esteem, the greater the increased dislike for the other person.

However, it has been recognized (Brehm & Cohen, 1962) that postaggression increments in dislike may also be related to the aggressor's initial perception of his victim, such that when the injured person is a good friend, for example, derogation of him is barred. If this mode of dissonance reduction is blocked, alternative means of coping with dissonance will be tried. Brock and Pallak's review has outlined a set of responses possible for an individual in such a dissonance situation. We would, however, concur with Berkowitz (1962) that there is strong resistance against the use of self-derogation and that in the absence of explicit influence pressures (Bergin, 1962) this mode of dissonance reduction is not likely to occur.

In the first study presented here, we focused on the individual's attempt to maintain a consistently positive self-image by disliking the *object* of his discrepant aggressive behavior. However, if a person cannot readily derogate the victim because the victim's likability or attractiveness are relatively "anchored," then a positive self-image may still be maintained by perceiving the *act* to be less negative (rather than the object of the act to be more negative). Dissonance may then be reduced by changing one's attitude toward the aggressive behavior (at least under the specific conditions in which it was expressed). In our second study, we expected that aggressors with high self-esteem who attack a liked victim should therefore resolve this inconsistency by enhancing the perceived value of the use of electric shock in scientific research on humans (the means of aggression to be studied).

EXPERIMENT I: OVERVIEW OF EXPERIMENTAL DESIGN

Choice and self-esteem were experimentally manipulated in a 2 × 2 factorial design with 15 subjects in each cell. Half the subjects were given the option of refusing (Choice), while half were directed (No Choice) to administer a series of seemingly painful electric shocks to another person (the victim), actually a confederate of the experimenter. All subjects were on record as being opposed to the use of electric shock on humans for scientific purposes. Within each of the experimental groups, the subjects were divided into High and Low Self-Esteem conditions based upon falsified feedback from a battery of previously administered psychological tests. Measured subjective levels of self-esteem prior to this manipulation were also obtained. The major dependent variable was change in liking for the victim. Evaluation of the experimental conditions and use of alternative dissonance-reducing responses were also recorded.

DISSONANCE PREDICTION

Only under conditions of Choice will differences in self-esteem affect the magnitude of dissonance aroused by engaging in an act of aggression, with High Self-Esteem subjects experiencing most dissonance. Thus, dissonance reduction will be reflected in a greater dislike of the victim following the (value-discrepant) aggressive act in the Choice, High Self-Esteem condition than in any other condition.

PROCEDURE

Subjects

From a large sample of students in introductory sociology classes at Ohio State University who responded to a questionnaire assessing their attitude toward "use of electric shock on humans for scientific purposes," 70 male volunteers were recruited who were opposed ("somewhat" or "extremely") to the use of shock; they were randomly assigned to the four experimental treatments. The final sample, however, was composed of 60 subjects, since the data for 10 subjects had to be deleted for various reasons.[2] Every precaution was taken to prevent the subjects from associating this study with the questionnaire.

2. These 10 Subjects were excluded from the analysis for the following reasons: 5 were suspicious that the confederate was not as presented, 3 did not believe they actually administered shock to the confederate, and 2 refused to administer shock when given a choice. Suspicious subjects were about evenly distributed across the four conditions, but the 2 subjects who refused to administer shock were both from the Choice, Low Self-Esteem condition.

Self-Esteem Manipulation

Approximately two weeks before the experimental session, the experimenter appeared in the subjects' classes and administered a series of psychological tests "designed to discover something about the personality and intelligence of college students." The subjects were told that these tests would be confidentially analyzed by three senior members of the Psychological Clinic as part of a nation-wide study being conducted by the Clinic. They were further informed that they could learn the results of these tests in a later interview, at which time they would take additional tests aimed at measuring their self-insight, their ability to form impressions, and related characteristics.

At the beginning of the actual experimental session, each subject was individually interviewed regarding his results on the previously administered personality and intelligence tests. Unknown to the subject, the results he received had nothing to do with his actual test performance. Only two test reports were used, one favorable and the other unfavorable. The reports were very similar to those used by Bramel (1962) and covered the following areas of personality and intellectual functioning: (1) general level of personality maturity, (2) mental alertness and intelligence, (3) concern for the feelings of others, and (4) egocentricity. Each section of the report discussed at length the test results bearing on a particular area, the tone of the report being consistently favorable or consistently unfavorable. Both reports were essentially the same but the contents were opposite in intent, one being designed to lower the subject's self-esteem (unfavorable report) and the other to raise it (favorable report). The reports and discussion lasted about 20 minutes.

High Self-Esteem. A sample section of the favorable report read to the High Self-Esteem subjects stated:

> This person shows a high degree of personality maturity, signified by a successful integration on the various levels of functioning. He reveals himself to be well-equipped for a productive and conflict-free adjustment to most environmental circumstances. In almost every respect, he presents a well-balanced and effective personality pattern, considerate and sympathetic, intellectually alert and flexible, and excellently qualified for a successful leadership role. . . . He stands above the average and presents one of the more favorable personality structures that has been analyzed by this staff.

Low Self-Esteem. The corresponding unfavorable feedback given to the Low Self-Esteem subjects stated:

> In general this person shows a low degree of personality maturity, signified by a failure to arrive at a really satisfactory integration of motivations on the conscious and unconscious levels. The pattern of his responses is generally poor indicating a weak personality, with evidence of inconsiderateness, lack of intellectual alertness and flexibility, and a lack of capability for successful leadership. . . . He stands below the average and presents one of the more unfavorable personality structures that has been analyzed by this staff.

Evaluation of the Self-Esteem Manipulation

As part of an alleged attempt to assess additional aspects of personality and intelligence, each subject then rated himself on 16 polar-adjective, 7-point scales (e.g., mature-immature, intelligent-unintelligent, considerate-thoughtless). An overall favorability score was computed, and it revealed that the manipulation of self-esteem was successful: the median score for the High Self-Esteem condition was 5.6 and for the Low Self-Esteem condition, 4.3. While 90 per cent of the High Self-Esteem subjects were above the common median, only 10 per cent of the Low Self-Esteem subjects were above the median ($p < 0.001$ by chi square). The mean difference in self-esteem between the two treatments was also significant ($p < 0.001$).

Initial Attitude Toward Victim

When the subject completed his self-ratings, the experimenter left the room and returned with an accomplice, who was introduced as another student waiting to take part in the study. The experimenter then explained that "the next test is concerned with how people make judgments of one another on the basis of first impressions" and that the subject and the confederate would therefore be required to make some personality judgments about each other. To aid them in forming their impressions, the experimenter suggested that they become better acquainted and that one way to do this would be for the confederate to administer some simple tests to the subject. Two tests were suggested: a picture-completion test and a task in which the subject had to count backwards from 99 to 1 by 2's as quickly as possible. The experimenter pointed out that the subject's responses would not be scored and that the whole procedure was designed only to help the subject and the other student "get acquainted with each other." He then quickly explained the method of administering the tests and told the two to begin. In administering the tests, the confederate consistently maintained a friendly attitude, although his remarks were restricted to the tests themselves and a final comment of "very good" when the subject finished both tests.

Upon completion of this phase of the procedure, the experimenter asked both students to fill out questionnaires that measured their degree of liking for one another. The questionnaire purported to assess the ability to make personality judgments on the basis of first impressions. A total "liking" score was computed based on the subject's responses to three intercorrelated items in the questionnaire (Berkowitz, 1960): (1) "Would you admit Mr. ——— (name of the confederate was written in here) into your circle of close friends?" (2) "Would you like to participate in another study with Mr. ———?" (3) "Would you like Mr. ——— as a roommate?" Each item was accompanied by a 7-point scale, where 1 = "Definitely yes" and 7 = "Definitely no." The subject's score was the sum of the scale points he checked for these items. These data represent the "before" measure of the subject's liking for the confederate.

Aggression Task

The technique by which the subject administered shock to the confederate was a modified version of the "aggression machine" developed by Buss (1961) and fully described in the paper by Brock and Pallak (Article 13). We will mention only those aspects of our procedure that departed from the physical-aggression paradigm presented in their review.

Immediately following the "liking" questionnaire, the subject and confederate were told that the next test was designed to study the ability to learn concepts—"more specifically, what effect the personality of an experimenter has on conceptual learning." The experimenter then selected—supposedly arbitrarily—the confederate to be the subject and the real subject to act as "experimenter" (delivering shocks on 24 incorrect response trials out of a total of 60 trials).

After completing his explanation of the concept formation test, the experimenter showed the subject what a 40-volt shock would feel like, ostensibly to acquaint him with what his "subject" would be experiencing. The experimenter emphasized that the confederate would receive more than twice that amount, i.e., 100 volts. After experiencing the 40-volt shock, the subject was asked to rate how much pain he thought the confederate would experience when receiving the 100-volt shock (on a scale from 1 = "No pain or discomfort at all" to 7 = "Extremely great pain"). At the end of the experiment, the subject rated how much pain he thought the confederate had actually experienced. The before-to-after change in his rating was used to assess whether the subject tried to minimize the painfulness of the shocks as a means of reducing dissonance.

Choice to Aggress

In the No Choice condition, the test was begun immediately after the instructions were completed, without the subject being given any option.

In the Choice condition, the experimenter made explicit the subject's high degree of volition to shock the confederate (adopted from the Brock–Buss, 1962, study [see Brock & Pallak, Article 13]). After emphasizing the subject's own responsibility in the act of staying to give the shocks or leaving and the fact that he should not feel any obligation toward the experimenter, the experimenter told all subjects who agreed to continue (only two refused) to begin the "learning task."

Postaggression Behavior

After the aggression experience, the subject indicated on self-report scales (1) his liking for the victim (measured with the same items initially used after becoming acquainted); (2) his attitude toward the use of electric shock in research (the same item used in selecting the subjects); (3) his judgment of the painfulness of the shocks he administered to the confederate (the same item given before the concept formation test); and (4) the effectiveness of the choice manipulations.

Debriefing

The postexperimental questionnaire was followed by an interview designed to determine whether or not the subject was suspicious of any aspect of the experimental procedure. An exhaustive explanation was given of the true purpose of the experiment, including the fact that the test reports were incapable of correctly evaluating a person's intelligence and personality. The importance of experimental deceptions was explained, and the experiment was not ended until the subject appeared to understand the necessity for using these procedures and seemed satisfied. The subjects were asked not to discuss the study with their friends, and there was no evidence to indicate that they did not comply with this request.

RESULTS

Perceived Choice

The manipulation of choice to aggress appears to have been generally successful: on a 7-point scale the mean perceived choice was 6.5 (almost "complete" choice) for those in the Choice condition, while it was only 4.5 for those in the No Choice condition ($t = 1.90, p < 0.10$). On a second related item, of perceived obligation to administer shock, the differences were highly significant: the mean rating was 5.3 for Choice subjects and 3.5 for No Choice (on a 7-point scale where 7 = "Not at all obligated"; $p < 0.01$).

Self-Esteem, Measured and Manipulated

We have seen that the between-group differences in manipulated self-esteem were significant, but we need to know whether there was any relationship between the initial self-reported measures of esteem and the experimental treatments. The scores on the adjective check list administered before the aggression provided data for this analysis. Although there was a significant mean difference in initial self-esteem between the two manipulated esteem treatments ($p < 0.05$), there was no difference in the relative *proportion* of high and low self-esteem subjects in the two treatments, i.e., there was an equivalence in median level of self-esteem. Moreover, as will be seen in the next section, the obtained effect between *manipulated* self-esteem and the major dependent variable (change in liking) was not affected by the initial mean difference (in which the High Self-Esteem subjects had more positive scores on the adjective check list).

Postaggression Changes in Liking for the Victim

Figure 1 presents data used to assess our prediction relating the dissonance-arousal treatment to change in evaluation of the victim from before to after the aggression. Under conditions where the subjects had no choice as to whether or not to be aggressive, differences in self-esteem did not influence attitudes toward

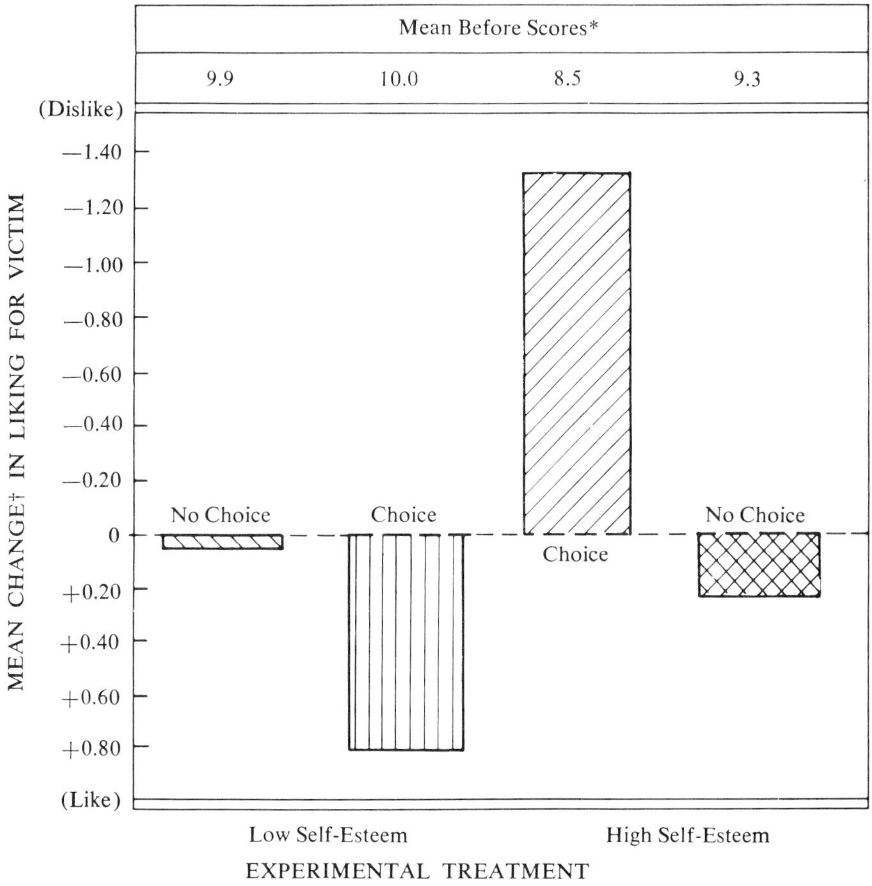

FIGURE 1

Change in liking for victim from before to after aggression for all groups. The lower the before score, the more the initial liking, the range running from a low of 3 to a high of 21. Since signs were reversed, a negative change score indicates a decrease in liking for the victim; a positive score indicates an increase in liking.

* High versus Low Self-Esteem, $F = 3.14$, n.s.; Choice versus No Choice, $F = 0.40$, n.s., interaction, $F = 0.54$, n.s. By the Duncan Multiple-Range Test, none of the before-score means is significantly different from any of the others at the 0.05 level.

† High versus Low Self-Esteem, $F = 8.15$, $p < 0.05$; Choice versus No Choice, $F = 1.30$, n.s.; interaction, $F = 10.48$, $p < 0.01$. By the Duncan Multiple-Range Test, the mean change in the Choice, High Self-Esteem condition is significantly different ($p < 0.05$) from the mean change in each of the other conditions.

the victim. However, the subjects who exercised their choice liked the victim less when their self-esteem was high but not when it was low. An analysis of variance of the change scores revealed a significant interaction between Choice and Self-Esteem treatments ($p < 0.01$). Moreover, the mean reduction in liking is significantly different from zero only for the Choice, High Self-Esteem condition ($p < 0.001$); the other mean change scores fail to reach the 5-per-cent level of significance. Our major hypothesis is thus clearly confirmed.

An analysis of covariance was performed in order to evaluate the effect of initial sampling differences in measured self-esteem on the relationship between changes in liking and manipulated self-esteem. After partialling out the variance associated with *reported* self-esteem, the adjusted mean change (in liking) scores were still virtually identical with those reported in Figure 1. Moreover, the within-conditions correlations between initial self-esteem and these change scores were uniformly nonsignificant. On the basis of these results, we may conclude that there is a causal relationship between the experimentally created cognitive state of high self-esteem and decreases in liking for the victim of aggression. That choice is a necessary condition for this relation is shown by the highly significant correlation between self-ratings of perceived choice and increased dislike in only the Choice, High Self-Esteem treatment ($r = 0.64$, $p < 0.01$).

In the Choice, Low Self-Esteem condition, the positive mean change score in liking (+0.80) indicates an opposite effect of greater liking for the victim after aggression, although it is not significantly different from zero. This finding is somewhat surprising, since one might expect that a subject's choice to administer shock would arouse some (minimal) dissonance even if he has low self-esteem. Apparently, however, the decision to administer shock was consistent with a negative self-concept, and the voluntary act of injuring another was not sufficiently discrepant to be dissonance arousing. Some support for this position can be found in the results of previous experiments. For example, Deutsch, Krauss, and Rosenau (1962) demonstrated that for an act to arouse dissonance it must be not only voluntary but also inconsistent with a positive self-image.

Alternative Dissonance-Reducing Responses

Table 1 presents data pertaining to the use of responses other than change in liking as possible means of reducing dissonance. Although individuals differed in the degree to which they employed various responses to dissonance, none of the alternatives was used significantly more by one group than by another. Apparently, then, the only systematic effect across conditions was the change in attitude toward the victim.

DISCUSSION

The results reported above support the main hypothesis of the present experiment, i.e., that the option of choosing to administer shock plus a positive self-

TABLE 1

ALTERNATIVE WAYS OF REDUCING POSTAGGRESSION DISSONANCE

Alternative	Experimental Condition			
	High Self-Esteem		Low Self-Esteem	
	Choice ($n = 15$)	No Choice ($n = 15$)	Choice ($n = 15$)	No Choice ($n = 15$)
A. Mean amount of perceived choice*	6.7_1†	4.5_2	6.3_1	4.5_2
B. Mean amount of perceived obligation‡	5.3_1	3.6_2	5.2_1	3.4_2
C. Mean amount of change in perceived painfulness of the shocks§	0.0	+0.1	+0.7	+0.4
D. Mean amount of change in attitude toward shock¶	+9.8	+5.0	+9.9	+3.7

* The higher the score, the greater the perceived choice. High versus Low Self-Esteem, $F = 0.62$, n.s.; Choice versus No Choice, $F = 35.29$, $p < 0.001$; interaction, $F = 0.36$, n.s.

† Within each row, the cells with different subscripts differ significantly from one another at the 0.05 level by the Duncan Multiple-Range Test. The only exception is in Row B where 5.33 is significantly different from 3.60 at the 0.10 level.

‡ The higher the score, the less the perceived obligation to administer shock. High versus Low Self-Esteem, $F = 0.08$, n.s.; Choice versus No Choice, $F = 8.77$, $p < 0.001$; interaction, $F = 0.004$, n.s.

§ A positive change score indicates an increase in perceived painfulness from before to after administration of the shocks. High versus Low Self-Esteem, $F = 4.47$, $p < 0.10$; Choice versus No Choice, $F = 0.08$, n.s.; interaction, $F = 0.85$, n.s.

¶ A positive score indicates attitude change in a direction favorable toward the use of electric shock on humans in scientific research. High versus Low Self-Esteem, $F = 0.04$, n.s.; Choice versus No Choice, $F = 2.59$, n.s.; interaction, $F = 0.03$, n.s.

image combine to arouse the greatest amount of dissonance when the administration of shock is contrary to one's attitudes or values. A direct consequence of this dissonance is an increased dislike for the person who has received the shock, a cognition that is consonant with the aggression and thus reduces dissonance.

In the analysis of changes in attitude toward the victim, it was shown that choosing to deliver shock did not by itself result in a reduction in liking. Earlier studies (e.g., Davis & Jones, 1960) have documented the importance of choice in postaggression re-evaluation of the injured person, but as with the Davis and Jones experiment, the present study suggests the need for specifying the conditions under which choice is made. It would appear that the choice to behave in an aggressive manner must be dissonant with a positive self-image in order for negative re-evaluation (e.g., increased dislike) to occur. In considering the consequences of choosing to aggress, therefore, it is essential to take account of personality factors, as in this study where we manipulated the aggressor's level of self-esteem. The combination of high self-esteem and choice appears to be the necessary and sufficient condition for the arousal of dissonance and the consequent negative re-evaluation.

This conclusion should not be construed as implying that choice in the absence of high self-esteem will produce only minimal dissonance. Since the present experiment involved only behavior that was discrepant with a positive self-image, the generality of our findings on the role of choice must await further experimentation. Specifically, a replication is needed in which the experimentally induced behavior is discrepant with a negative self-image, as, for example, where a person of low self-esteem performs an act of kindness and consideration. Under these conditions, choice may be both necessary and sufficient for the arousal of dissonance. On the basis of the results reported here, however, we can say only that in order to arouse postaggression dissonance, the commitment implicit in choosing to injure another must be a commitment that is also discrepant with a positive self-image.

EXPERIMENT II: OVERVIEW OF EXPERIMENTAL DESIGN

Forty subjects (male undergraduates from Ohio State University)[3] opposed to the use of electric shock in research administered a series of presumably painful shocks to a victim as part of the same task rationale used in Experiment I. In this study, however, *all* subjects were given a choice in the commitment to shock the victim, and the victim's attractiveness was experimentally manipulated at two levels. Self-esteem was again employed as the second independent variable in a 2×2 factorial design, but here it was a premeasured, dispositional variable rather than a manipulated variable. Data on alternative modes of dissonance reduction were collected, with theoretical emphasis focused on change in attitude toward the *act* of aggression.

DISSONANCE PREDICTIONS

It was assumed that if under the High Dissonance conditions used in Experiment I (Choice, High Self-Esteem) there were barriers to derogating the victim because he was initially attractive, then dissonance would be reduced by adopting a more favorable attitude toward the aggressive act, namely, toward the use of electric shock on humans in research. This consequent attitude change should therefore be a function of the self-esteem level of the aggressor and the initial degree of positiveness of the victim (given a constant high level of choice). We predicted a replication of our earlier findings under conditions where the aggressor does not have a strong initial attraction toward the victim, that is, a greater decrease in liking for the victim among High than Low Self-Esteem subjects. However, where the aggressor is positively attracted toward the victim initially, dissonance will be reduced not by re-evaluating the victim but by

3. A total of 57 subjects were tested, but 17 were excluded from analysis for the following reasons: 2 did not believe they actually administered shock to the victim; 6 were not convinced by one or more of the other experimental manipulations; 5 refused to administer shock when given the option of refusing; and 4 were generally uncooperative. These 17 subjects were about evenly distributed across experimental conditions, although the 5 who refused to administer shock all came from the Low Attraction treatment.

adopting a more favorable attitude toward using shock in research with human subjects.

PROCEDURE

Self-Esteem Variable

The subjects were randomly assigned to the two Attraction conditions after being categorized as High or Low in Self-Esteem, depending on whether they scored above or below the median (63.0 in this study) on Janis and Fields' Feelings of Inadequacy Scale (1959, pp. 55–68, 300–301).[4] Scores on this scale were obtained approximately one week prior to the experimental session, at which time the experimenter appeared in the subjects' classes and administered a series of psychological tests. Along with the Janis–Fields scale, the subjects completed a check list of personality traits on which they indicated the type of person with whom they would most like to work. The list of traits was preceded by the following questions: (1) "In conducting this study, participants will be paired with another student of their own sex. As we want people together who are congenial, . . . what characteristics would you desire in a co-worker?" and (2) "What characteristics would you object to in a co-worker?"

At the beginning of the actual experimental session, the procedure was introduced to the subject as a study of impression formation and learning. It was explained that the study was "trying to find out how people form impressions of one another and how this affects their ability to work together on learning problems." The subject was then reminded that he would be working with another student, who was due momentarily.

Attraction Toward the Victim

To induce the subject to feel strongly attracted to the other student[5] (High Attraction condition), the experimenter then proceeded to say:

> Remember the adjectives you checked on the sign-up blank? The ones which described the kind of person you'd like to work with? We try to put people together here who are compatible. It usually doesn't work out the way people want because of scheduling difficulties, but in your case we found a fellow who very closely matches the traits you described as desirable in a work partner. And even more, you seem to fit his description of a desirable partner. . . You two should get along exceptionally well.

4. Evidence indicated that the scale had acceptable reliability. A split-half correlation was carried out on the scores of the 40 subjects included in the study, where one half was composed of the odd items and the other half of the even items. The resulting coefficient was 0.83, corrected by the Spearman-Brown formula.

5. The procedure used for manipulating attractiveness in the present study is similar to one described by Back (1951) for manipulating cohesiveness.

In the Low Attraction condition, the experimenter gave these alternative instructions:

> Remember the adjectives you checked on the sign-up blank? The ones which described the kind of person you'd like to work with? We tried to find a partner with whom you could work best. Unfortunately, scheduling difficulties made this impossible. We couldn't find anybody who would fit your description of a desirable partner, but I do hope you get along with the person we scheduled to work with you.

Immediately following the attractiveness manipulation, the other student (again a confederate of the experimenter) arrived for his appointment. The experimenter introduced the two students and then explained that the first part of the session would be devoted to a study of "how people form first impressions of one another." The subject and the confederate were told that they would be required to make some personality judgments about each other. To aid them in this task, the experimenter proceeded to ask each one (in the presence of the other) a series of questions about his major field and extra-curricular activities. The confederate answered the questions identically in both Attraction conditions and tried to give the impression of being an "average" Ohio State University sophomore. At the conclusion of the interview, both students filled out a 20-item rating scale that measured the effectiveness of the attractiveness induction and also served as the "before" measure of the subject's liking for the confederate. Our concern, of course, was only with the subject's responses. We will have more to say about this rating scale later in the section.

The remaining procedure, including the concept formation task, was similar to that used in Experiment I. The following changes were made, which for the most part were relatively minor and were designed only to increase the plausibility of various inductions:

1. All subjects were given the option to leave, under the Choice instructions used in the first experiment.

2. The "aggression machine" was comparable to that used by Brock and Buss (1964), with 10 switches and with the subject experiencing shock from four of the lower levels while being told he should use only the upper levels (6–10) during the learning task.[6]

3. The number of trials was increased to 70, with shock on 34 "incorrect response" trials.

Postaggression Behavior

After the aggression, alternative modes of reducing dissonance were assessed by collecting self-report data on: (1) self-evaluation, on the Feelings of Inadequacy Scale; (2) evaluation of the victim, on five trait-clusters of likability, warmth, conceit, intelligence, and maturity; (3) evaluation of use of shock in research

6. Evidence indicates that the subjects did use only shock switches 6 through 10, as instructed.

on humans; (4) perception of the painfulness of the shocks at values 3 and 5 on the aggression machine; and (5) perceived obligation to administer shock. Changes in these scores from before to after the aggressive behavior constitute alternative ways of modifying the ratio of consonant to dissonant cognitions in this particular situation.

RESULTS

Attraction Toward the Victim

The manipulation of the degree of attraction toward or liking for the victim was quite successful. Those given the High Attraction induction gave the victim a mean rating (prior to the concept learning task) of +43.9, while those given the Low Attraction induction rated him only +29.5 (on a scale from −70 = "Extreme dislike" to +70 = "Extreme like"). This difference was significant beyond the 0.001 level.

What was the effect of this initially created difference in perception of the victim on liking for him *following* the dissonant behavior? The data for this relationship are presented in Table 2.

The results of an analysis of variance and Duncan Multiple-Range Test indicate that neither the Attraction manipulation nor the Self-Esteem difference had a significant effect upon change in liking scores. Moreover, none of the scores is significantly different from zero, and the small amount of change that

TABLE 2

MEAN BEFORE AND CHANGE SCORES OF ATTRACTIVENESS RATINGS*

Score	Experimental Condition			
	High Attraction		Low Attraction	
	High Self-Esteem (n = 10)	Low Self-Esteem (n = 10)	High Self-Esteem (n = 10)	Low Self-Esteem (n = 10)
Before†	46.0_1¶	41.8_2	26.7_3	32.3_4
Change‡	−1.6¶	−1.8	+1.4	+0.9

* The higher the before score, the greater the initial attraction to the confederate. A negative change score indicates a reduction in attractiveness of the confederate from before to after administration of the shocks.

† High versus Low Attraction, $F = 32.12$, $p < 0.001$; High versus Low Self-Esteem, $F = 0.08$, n.s.; interaction, $F = 3.72$, n.s.

‡ High versus Low Attraction, $F = 1.73$, n.s.; High versus Low Self-Esteem, $F = 0.03$, n.s.; interaction, $F = 0.01$, n.s.

¶ By the Duncan Multiple-Range Test, the cell containing subscript 1 in the first row is significantly different from the cells containing subscripts 3 and 4 at the 0.05 level. The cell containing subscript 2 is also significantly different from subscripts 3 and 4 at the 0.05 level. In the second row, none of the cell means are significantly different from one another at the 0.05 level.

did occur can probably be attributed to regression effects associated with repeated measurements.

Although we predicted that in the High Attraction condition there would be no change in liking for the victim because dissonance would be reduced in other ways, we did expect more of a decrease in liking for the victim in the Low Attraction condition. This failure to confirm our prediction will be treated in the discussion section of this paper.

Change in Attitude Toward the Use of Shock

Following the discrepant behavior of inflicting pain upon another person, the subjects in this experiment did not reduce their dissonance by changing their attitude toward the victim, but they did change their attitude toward the experimental purpose of the aggressive act. Figure 2 presents the data for the mean amounts of attitude change toward the value of using electric shock on humans. Evaluation of the before-aggression means and these attitude-change means was by analysis of variance followed by a Duncan Multiple-Range Test in order to make individual mean comparisons. While there were no differences between conditions initially, there were large, systematic differences in the attitude-change scores. The High Attraction condition, in contrast to Low Attraction, produced significantly greater positive attitude change toward using shock ($p < 0.05$). Also in line with our prediction was the greater positive attitude change in the High as compared to the Low Self-Esteem group, although this effect only approached significance ($F = 2.52$, $p = 0.10$).

It should be observed that all groups increased their belief in the value of using shock after having behaved aggressively. This increase is, however, systematically related to the several levels of dissonance presumably created by the experimental treatments. There is least change in the Low Dissonance condition (Low Attraction, Low Self-Esteem), twice as much in the Moderate Dissonance condition (Low Attraction, High Self-Esteem and High Attraction, Low Self-Esteem), and four times as much change in the High Dissonance condition (High Attraction, High Self-Esteem). This last group is significantly different ($p = 0.05$) from both Low Attraction groups and approaches a reliable difference ($p = 0.10$) from the Low Self-Esteem group given the same attraction manipulation.

Alternate Modes of Dissonance Reduction

The experimental procedures adopted to maximize the use of one mode of dissonance reduction—change in attitude toward the use of shock—at the expense of other modes of response was quite successful. The only significant effects obtained were on the attitude measure reported above. Thorough analysis of all the relevant data revealed that there were no significant differences between groups in (1) postaggression self-derogation, (2) minimizing the painfulness of

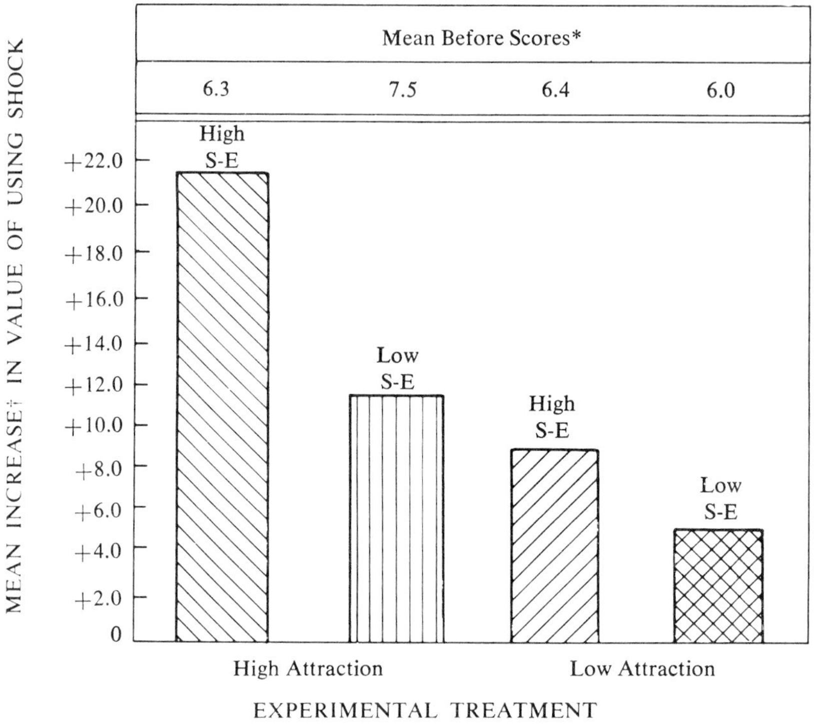

FIGURE 2

Change in the value of using shock in experiments on humans from before to after aggression for all groups. The higher the before score, the more favorable the initial belief in the value of using electric shock on humans for scientific purposes. A positive change indicates a shift toward a more favorable belief.

* High versus Low Attraction, $F = 0.23$, n.s.; High versus Low Self-Esteem, $F = 0.08$, n.s.; interaction, $F = 0.30$, n.s. By the Duncan Multiple-Range Test, none of the before-score means is significantly different from any of the others at the 0.05 level.

† High versus Low Attraction, $F = 4.34$, $p < 0.05$; High versus Low Self-Esteem, $F = 2.52$, n.s.; interaction, $F = 0.60$, n.s. By the Duncan Multiple-Range Test, the mean increase in the High Attraction, High Self-Esteem condition is significantly different from changes in the Low Attraction conditions at the 0.05 level and in the High Attraction, Low Self-Esteem condition at the 0.10 level.

the shock, or (3) increased feelings of being obliged to shock. We saw earlier that there were also no group differences in postaggression dislike for the victim.

DISCUSSION

We may conclude from these results that if a person chooses to carry out an aggressive act against a person toward whom he is attracted, the dissonance that is aroused leads him to adopt a more favorable attitude toward the aggression, without correlated changes in attitudes toward the victim, toward himself, or toward the severity of the aggression. This effect is greatest when the aggressive person perceives himself as having a high level of self-esteem. By becoming a less undesirable act, the aggression is less inconsistent with a positive self-image, and dissonance is thus reduced.

That dissonance arousal was a joint function of the subject's self-image and his initial perception of the victim (and not solely due to differences created by the Attraction manipulation) is shown by the similar reactions of the Low Self-Esteem subjects in the High Attraction condition and the High Self-Esteem subjects in the Low Attraction condition. Only in the High Dissonance condition, induced through combining High Attraction with High Self-Esteem, were the changes large and different from the other groups.

How can we interpret the failure to observe increased dislike of the victim under Low Attraction conditions? The two major reasons may have to do with the subject's interpretation of the Low Attraction manipulation and the operational definition of self-esteem. The Low Attraction instructions may actually have carried the implication that the confederate lacked the traits the subject considered desirable and therefore would be a poor co-worker. If this manipulation created initial negative feelings toward the victim, little or no dissonance would be aroused by shocking him. Although the subjects did not use the negative, or dislike, side of the rating scale in evaluating the confederate, ratings did fall as low as +18 (out of a possible +70). It is, however, difficult to interpret the absolute meaning of such scores because of the general tendency of experimental subjects to give more positive than negative evaluations ("warm is the norm").

The use of a response-measured definition of self-esteem in the second study compared to the standardized experimental manipulation in the first study may bear upon the failure to replicate the finding of greater dislike for the victim under Low Attraction. There is some evidence in the literature that self-esteem has a different impact on reactivity to dissonance-type situations depending upon whether it is measured or manipulated (e.g., Gelfand, 1962; McGuire, 1967). Even more important is the incidental finding of the first experiment that rated self-esteem was unrelated to changes in liking. These results suggest that chronic as opposed to acute variations of esteem may simply produce dissimilar results. This might begin to explain the failure to obtain dissonance effects between the two levels of esteem within the Low Attraction condition, except that predicted esteem differences *were* shown in the High Attraction condition, even though the variable was measured rather than manipulated here as well.

A possible explanation for the discrepancy in dissonance arousal may lie in the psychological significance of self-rated self-esteem. Thus, a high esteem score may reflect not a positive view of the self but rather a defensive attempt to protect a vulnerable self-image. By responding in a socially desirable way, the individual avoids the necessity of having to acknowledge that he considers himself worthless and, in consequence, presents a defensively enhanced picture of himself. Conn and Crowne (1964) have recently shown that subjects who respond in socially desirable ways have considerable difficulty expressing aggression. Cohen (1959) developed a similar analysis in his study of social influence; he reports that high-esteem subjects tend to use avoidant rather than expressive defenses to cope with threatening stimuli. Extending this reasoning to the present experiment, we might attribute the absence of increments in dislike under Low Attraction to defensive avoidance of this mode of dissonance reduction. The subjects who scored high on the Janis–Fields scale may actually have been defending their self-image by giving socially desirable responses. Since expression of dislike for the confederate would further threaten an already weak conception of self, these subjects may have denied their negative feelings and sought some other means of reducing postaggression dissonance. However, there is no evidence of appreciable pain minimization, perceived obligation, or attitude change among High Self-Esteem subjects in the Low Attraction condition. We can only assume, therefore, that they either found some other means of coping with dissonance (e.g., reducing the importance of the aggressive act) or managed to tolerate the tension occasioned by their aggression.

THEORETICAL IMPLICATIONS

The present research has implications for the role of dissonance theory in bridging the gap between personality and interpersonal aggression. Although much has been written about the cathartic virtues of aggression (Dollard, Miller, Doob, Mowrer, & Sears, 1939), a number of investigators have noted that an aggressor sometimes shows increased dislike for the victim of his attack (Davis & Jones, 1960; Feshbach, 1956; Berkowitz, 1962). Attempts to explain this increment in dislike have hypothesized an internal reaction in the aggressor that somehow enhances dislike of his victim. The specification of this internal reaction has remained unclear. Some researchers (e.g., Buss, 1961) have maintained that when aggression occurs in the *absence of anger*, there is an increase in dislike of the victim; when aggression occurs in the *presence of anger*, a decrease takes place. Others (e.g., Berkowitz, 1962) have suggested that the increment is a function of guilt feelings aroused by the aggressive behavior; since guilt implies frustration of the subject's need to think well of himself, dislike is aroused toward both himself and the victim, the latter being seen as at least partly responsible for the guilt-induced discomfort. Still others (e.g., Hokanson, 1961) have advanced an explanation closely related to the Berkowitz position, according to which the aggressor is said to become "anxious" about the consequences of his aggressive behavior; the anxiety is experienced as frustration and thus leads to increased dislike for the victim.

These explanations emphasize transitory emotional states of the aggressor and tend to overlook cognitive aspects of his personality as possible factors producing defensive increments in dislike. The results of the present research, particularly Experiment I, lead to a contradictory suggestion that the cognitive personality variable of self-esteem is an important determinant of such increments. Self-esteem, when viewed in the light of its role in arousing dissonance, leads to a derivation that specifies the nature of the psychological process giving rise to increased dislike. The dissonance formulation suggests that differences in level of self-esteem may account for postaggression increments in dislike without recourse to generalized internal reactions such as guilt. Of course dissonance itself is an intervening construct, but it appears to generate more specific predictions than these other formulations. A guilt or anxiety hypothesis fails to specify the conditions under which aggression will give rise to anxiety or guilt and thus to increased dislike.

The present research also has bearing on the issue of predicting the mode of dissonance reduction most likely to occur in specific situations. It has been repeatedly noted that very little is actually known about how dissonance is reduced or how different modes of reduction interact. Some investigators have concluded that unless variables other than dissonance are specified, the theory does not predict a given mode of reduction (e.g., Brown, 1962). The results of Experiment II suggest one variable that might be considered in attempting to specify how an individual will cope with at least postaggression dissonance. If the victim is not strongly attracted to the aggressor, increased dislike is a more probable consequence of postaggression dissonance. These results are of course limited to one type of dissonance, but they underscore the need for further research on the possibility of improving the predictive accuracy of the dissonance model by taking account of situational, personality, and related variables.

Editor's Comments

These studies demonstrate how dissonance predictions may be refined by considering the way in which social-stimulus variables interact with individual-difference variables. If the arousal of dissonance under some conditions depends upon an inconsistency between cognitions about how one is behaving and cognitions about the meaning of that behavior in terms of one's self-image, then it is important to understand what that image is. Glass and Wood have shown that the theory of cognitive dissonance can predict the consequences of value-discrepant aggressive behavior for subjects whose self-esteem is high, whether the latter is experimentally created or a response-measured disposition. When subjects perceived that they had volition in their commitment, they devalued the victim of their aggression, and when that response was made less probable because the victim was attractive, they increased the value of the aggressive aspect of the task, administering shock. However, it appears that there was no dissonance arousal among the Low Self-Esteem subjects. Even though they experienced the same social situation and engaged in the same behavior as the High Self-Esteem subjects, they did not significantly change their attitudes toward or perception of self, victim, task, or situation.

Since the arousal of dissonance cannot be determined independently of attempts to reduce it, it is only a matter of conjecture at this point whether dissonance is not experienced by these subjects, or it is aroused but can be tolerated without being reduced or it is reduced by means that are not typical of other subjects (i.e., the responses are not among those made available to them by the experimenter through the specific questions or task behavior he provides).

While a person with high self-esteem generally expects his behavior to reflect positively upon him, the person with low esteem expects negative consequences from his performance. In the situation under investigation here, performance is assumed to provide negative feedback—the subject hurts a helpless other—which, therefore, ought to be inconsistent only for the person with high self-esteem.

From another point of view, the high-esteem person, in contrast with the low, is more confident in the correctness of his own decisions; he sees himself as not making mistakes and is more certain of his ability to exercise control over even threatening situations (see Zimbardo & Formica, 1963). These differences would also make the person with high self-esteem less able to tolerate the dissonance of having made a discrepant commitment. He would have to show himself and others that his commitment was not a mistake, and he would have to do so by means of overt actions that justify the dissonant behavior and make it "right." In contrast, perhaps a person with low self-esteem is precisely one who defines himself as prone to making mistakes, deals that don't pay off, moves that backfire, and commitments that are premature, unwise, or plain stupid. It is likely that such a person will protect himself from excessive self-derogation by adopting a passive self-attitude in which personal commitment in decision making is avoided and responsibility for the consequences of action are nullified or minimal.

It may well be, therefore, that there are different motivational processes at work between subjects with high and low self-esteem in their *acceptance* of the aggression task itself, a task in which it is explicitly stated that the "responsibility is yours." One might argue that those with high esteem agree to shock the confederate largely to ingratiate themselves with the experimenter (see Jones, 1964, and Goffman, 1959), perceiving that volition in and responsibility for their actions are consistent with their self-image. This image then is violated only by the nature of the act itself in terms of the imagined or actual feedback from the victim. Those with low self-esteem agree with the request of an authority to shock another person not as much to gain his good opinion of them, but because they view his request as a persuasive communication that they are unable to challenge. For them, what may be dissonance producing is being "made to accept responsibility" and being given the important role of acting as the experimenter. Under such circumstances, these subjects with low self-esteem should behave cautiously and conservatively and should not change their self-report behavior markedly after the task.

These speculations are intended only to point up the multiple aspects of the experimental situation and the need for a more thorough analysis of the components of self-esteem. They lead to questions like: Would individuals with low self-esteem experience dissonance from unexpected *positive* feedback from their performance? Would they be willing to avoid responsibility by choosing a more effortful task with minimal responsibility rather than an easy one invested with responsibility? Would people with extremely high self-esteem, who were truly confident of their general ability and of their acceptance by others, be willing to admit making a wrong decision and thus experience little dissonance from situations that create much dissonance among persons whose high self-esteem is tenuous?

Despite such problems of interpretation, it is impressive to note that in these experiments by Glass and Wood the obtained predicted dissonance effects for the High Self-Esteem subjects were specific to individual response items embedded in a series of attitude statements. In passing, it should also be noted that the positive increase in the perceived value of shock for research found in the second experiment is one of the few instances of support we have seen in research with humans for the position of Lawrence and Festinger (1962) that dissonance can be reduced by finding "extra attractions" in the features of the situation itself.

We are somewhat limited in trying to understand the effects of the aggressive act per se on the subject's subsequent behavior due to the failure to include a nonaggressive control group in the experimental design. Such a group, which interacted with the confederate by merely recording his errors or signaling his incorrect responses, could have provided a base line for changes in evaluation against which to compare experimental groups that differed only in believing they inflicted pain on the victim. Without such a control, either it must be assumed that the base line is zero change or else the Low Dissonance group must be used as the reference point for the High. The first assumption may not be valid, however; and the second does not allow an independent evaluation of the Low Dissonance condition.

Is the task perceived by subjects in all conditions as aggressive? Putting aside the issue of the intent to be aggressive, there remains the issue of whether by disguising the aggression within a socially acceptable, intellectual task and by making the response dimensions only indirectly related to the fact that the *subject* hurt the victim, the significance of the behavior for the subject is diluted and thus the impact of the commitment to engage in such behavior is weakened.

In fact, once the task is started, the rules of the game take over, and it is they that determine when shock will be administered and how much will be delivered (either a constant "100 volts" or one of 5 shock switches from values "6 to 10"). In a second sense, then, dissonance may be weakened in all conditions because there is a suspension of individual, personal responsibility and a focus on perceived *role* responsibility. In this connection, it is instructive to note that none of the studies report any subjects quitting after the task had begun.

But let us assume that shocking another person *is* perceived as an aggressive act that is discrepant with the individual's self-image. Does dissonance arise only after final completion of the task, and are postbehavior response measures thus the best indicators of dissonance? It is much more reasonable to assume that *each act* of shocking the victim, followed by feedback of the resultant suffering, is dissonance generating. If so, then we should study attitudinal and behavioral change during this continuous process of repeated dissonance arousal. Our attention would then be drawn to the *pattern* of shocking over the course of the task. If No Choice conditions render an individual a passive subject (as argued in the Introduction to this volume), then the minimal task involvement and the compliance with external justification in Low Dissonance conditions should result in compliance with the demands of the task but with no systematic variance in the level of shock chosen to be administered. In contrast with this uniform level for the Low Dissonance and No Choice Control groups, we might expect a changing level of shock over the course of repeated shocking for High Dissonance subjects.

Each act of aggression ought to increase the dissonance or at least maintain its salience to the subject. If the subject employs the means of dissonance reduction observed in the studies reviewed in this and the preceding article, then he ought to change the intensity, duration, or frequency of shock (if they are available response dimensions) over the course of interaction with the victim as he minimizes the victim's pain, devalues him, or perceives the use of shock to be beneficial. But would this behavioral change be in response to the attitudinal changes adopted to justify the discrepant commitment, or would the changed attitudes develop as a consequence of changes in behavior?

Moreover, analysis of the pattern of aggressive behavior could perhaps offer more convincing evidence for the dissonance-versus-guilt interpretation advanced in the comments on the previous article. If guilt is produced by shocking a helpless victim, the subject should either use the lowest level of shock necessary to comply with the request of the experimenter or the level should decrease over the course of the task as guilt increased. At odds with this view is the prediction that under conditions of high dissonance, the shock level should not decrease systematically, or even that it should exhibit an increase over trials.

It should be obvious to the reader that the dissonant situation studied in this research on aggression does not fit the general model used in the earlier studies in this volume, namely, that of arousing a strong motive and then having the subject commit himself to further motive arousal or to deprivation of behavior that would reduce it. The individual's aggression here was not instigated by the victim, nor did it arise directly from any motive to be aggressive. The initial, primary motives of the subject are those of wanting to help science, please the experimenter, present himself as cooperative, and so forth. He is asked to participate in a task where one "subject" receives shock and one gives it, and arbitrarily he happens not to be on the receiving line. Under these conditions, High Dissonance subjects attempted to justify their aggressive behavior by various processes of denial ("The shock doesn't hurt so much"), dissociation ("I was obliged to shock because of my role; *I* didn't do it") or rationalization ("He deserves to be shocked" and "Shock is a valuable tool in research").

But what reactions would be forthcoming if the individual had ample intrinsic justification for aggressing against another person who had insulted and frustrated him? Clearly he ought to want to be verbally or physically aggressive toward such a person. However, suppose he is then induced (with free choice) to commit himself to a subsequent cooperative interaction with this antagonist. Suppose further that after making this commitment, which is discrepant with his motives to be aggressive, his "partner" is unnecessarily aggressive toward him. Let us then give our hypothetical subject-victim the opportunity to strike back, to retaliate under conditions where he is guaranteed the last laugh. Will he take it and aggress? Or is it conceivable that dissonance will inspire him to turn the other cheek?

The next provocative study by Ira Firestone presents the subject with this double dissonance-arousal situation and examines both his attitudes and aggressive behavior in response to it.

15. INSULTED AND PROVOKED: THE EFFECTS OF CHOICE AND PROVOCATION ON HOSTILITY AND AGGRESSION

Ira J. Firestone

> We know that, in the evolution of vertebrates, the bond of personal love and friendship was the epoch-making invention created by the great constructors when it became necessary for two or more individuals of an aggressive species to live peacefully together and to work for a common end. We know that human society is built on the foundation of this bond, but we have to recognize the fact that the bond has become too limited to encompass all that it should: it prevents aggression only between those who know each other and are friends . . . (Lorenz, 1966, p. 299).

The research to be presented in this report suggests that perhaps Lorenz' conception can be extended by considering the way in which dissonance may establish a bond between two people that prevents aggression.

If two individuals, O and P, have an antagonistic interaction, then "O harms P induces P dislikes O . . . P dislikes O induces P avoids O" (Heider, 1958, pp. 191–199). The breakdown in subsequent interaction and the buildup of barriers against communication will obviously limit the possibility of the development of a friendly working relation between the two parties and will increase the likelihood of aggression in such a dyad. Certainly the first step toward a reconciliation involves bringing the pair into contact again; but under what conditions? How can their mutual antagonism be most reduced?

Research into the effects of making such important decisions and personal commitments (stimulated by the theory of cognitive dissonance) points to the operation of choice as a prime consideration in any confrontation between potentially aggressive protagonists. When the choice to enter an interaction with another creates dissonance, the resulting process of dissonance reduction may have some consequences for postdecisional interpersonal behavior in the dyad. The person will attempt to justify his discrepant choice and will attempt to alter motives and attitudes that are inconsistent with his decision. These changes may then have considerable impact on subsequent social behavior.

As we have seen in the previous research in this volume, dissonance-arousing decisions made when the individual feels he is a "free agent," when his volition in the act is made explicit, result in major cognitive readjustments, and these, in turn, effect changes in behavior, presumably through modifying the relevant motivational structure. Accordingly, dissonance should be created

Source: Firestone, Ira J., "Insulted and Provoked: The Effects of Choice and Provocation on Hostility and Aggression." Adapted from *Insulted and Provoked: The Effects of Choice and Provocation on Hostility and Aggression*, unpublished doctoral dissertation, New York University, 1966. Reprinted by permission of the author.

if a hostile dyad is brought together and induced to interact through the use of subtle pressures that, nevertheless, still provide the individuals with the perception of choice. The dissonance created by disliking a person yet voluntarily choosing to work with him can be reduced by changing one's attitude toward that person to be consistent with the behavioral commitment—i.e., to like him more. This affective change should occur as a direct consequence of the decision, even prior to any actual interaction with the other person.

To demonstrate such an effect, it would be necessary (1) to have a group of subjects who dislike their coworkers enough not to want to continue interaction with them and (2) to require some of them to do so and provide the others with a choice to do so (with only minimal inducements). The efficacy of the choice procedure in reducing hostile interpersonal attitudes would be shown by an *increased* liking of the unpleasant coworker only in the choice treatment. But such a finding could not be unequivocally attributed to dissonance processes without a comparison provided by a control group given the identical choice to continue interaction with a coworker who was *not* antagonistic. By comparing the experimental group with this control condition given a nondiscrepant choice, which also equates for subtle cues in the choice procedure itself that might implicitly suggest to the subject that he should like the coworker, it should be possible to determine whether increased liking following the dissonant choice is indeed a function of dissonance reduction.

Supposing that this reduction in antagonism is found, what practical significance could it have? Is it a transient cognitive re-evaluation subject to easy reversal when buffeted by new hostility? If so, then its value in normalizing the relationship and providing the occasion for developing an aggression-preventing bond is nil. The question of consequence is whether the tension-reducing effects of the dissonant-choice treatment can restrain future aggression in the face of subsequent provocation.

This can be assessed only by systematically varying the intensity of provocation of the subject by his coworker after the two have begun to interact again. Those who were not previously insulted by their partner and chose to work with him (the Controls) should respond more aggressively to this provocation the more intense it is. Since those given no choice to work with an insulting partner already disliked him, further instigation by him should lead to even greater intensity of aggression than in the noninsulted-choice treatment. The most interesting behavior to observe, however, would be that of the insulted subjects who had made a dissonant choice to work with the partner. If the initial dissonance produced only temporary attitudinal change, additional provocation should cancel out all or most of this improved attitude, and subsequent aggression should be comparable to that expressed by the other groups.

If, on the other hand, dissonance reduction is conceptualized as a more dynamic, ongoing process than it usually is in its static, hydraulic descriptions, it may have relevance for more lasting behavioral change and the prevention of aggression. Consider that while the decision to continue interaction with a disliked partner arouses a certain amount of initial dissonance, the total amount of dissonance is indeterminate at this point because it will depend on the outcomes of the choice (Rosenau, 1964). The more unpleasant these outcomes, the greater the dissonance they will arouse. The subject has made his choice. It is an action that *cannot* readily be reversed, a commitment that cannot be reneged (Davis & Jones, 1960). He is thus continually responsible for its consequences. According to this view, the dissonance occasioned by the subject's choice remains in effect, motivating him to seek outcomes in the chosen interaction that are consistent with his decision to continue it. Cognitive re-adjustment in attitude, here the increased liking for the partner, is one component of dissonance reduction, but it alone is not sufficient to guarantee supportive outcomes. Concomitant changes in motivation and behavior are required to actually produce outcomes that will validate the choice and so maintain a reduced level of dissonance. Therefore, it is hypothesized that the consequences of choosing to work with a disliked partner will be twofold. The dissonant choice will generate not only a more favorable immediate evaluation of this person but also a continuing motivation to minimize the unpleasantness of this chosen interaction.

This analysis of dissonance as an ongoing motivational process leads to the following prediction about aggressive responses to provocation. Provocation by the partner instigates two response tendencies within the dissonant individual that are, to some degree, incompatible with each other. As per usual, strong provocation produces a strong instigation to aggression; but in the case of the individual who has chosen to continue working with the disliked partner, provocation also arouses dissonance. It is only by *not* being aggressive that this individual can keep the interaction from becoming unpleasant and, thus, from creating more dissonance. We expect that this incompatibility between the instigation to aggress and the need to keep to a minimum the unpleasantness of the chosen situation will serve as a restraint on the subject's aggressive responses.

DISSONANCE PREDICTIONS

Our basic assumption is that most persons do not willingly enter into, or long remain involved in, interactions with other individuals who are humiliating, anxiety provoking, or otherwise unpleasant. It follows from this assumption that choosing, for minimal incentives, to re-enter such an interaction will arouse dissonance. The prediction, then, is that there will be increased liking for this person following the dissonant commitment to continue association with him compared with groups given no choice and groups choosing to work with a noninsulting partner. We also expect that this change, alone, will not be sufficient to maintain a reduced level of dissonance. Specifically, subsequent provocation from the partner will instigate aggressive responses, and, where it follows a dissonant choice, this provocation will arouse further dissonance. Dissonance in this situation should instigate responses that are incompatible with retaliation. Our prediction is, therefore, that aggressive responses to high provocation in the Insult-Choice treatment will be less intense than those elicited by identical circumstances in the absence of choice.

OVERVIEW OF EXPERIMENTAL DESIGN

In Part 1 of the study, a standardized interaction between a subject and his partner concluded with the partner's publicly giving the subject either a favorable or insulting personality evaluation (randomly determined). After the subject rated the degree to which he liked or disliked his partner, half the subjects given the Insult treatment were required to take part in a second study that involved close interaction with the partner, while half were given a choice to re-enter interaction with the partner. Choice was also provided for all subjects in the No Insult treatment. Prior to the start of the "second" experiment and before any further interaction with the partner, all subjects re-evaluated their attitudes towards him.

In Part 2 of the study, each of the three treatment groups was given additional provocation by the coworker—at a high level for half the subjects and a relatively low level for the others. Each subject was then given the opportunity to aggress against his partner by inflicting him with a series of electric shocks. The subject was free to determine the frequency and duration of the shocks he would deliver, and he did so with the knowledge that the partner could not retaliate. The frequency and duration of the shocks are the major dependent behavioral measures of aggression.

SUBJECTS

Eighty-five male students from introductory psychology classes at University College of New York University participated in the "first" experiment as part of their course requirement. Subjects were not paid for their participation in either experiment, and they received no additional course credit for their participation, voluntary or involuntary, in the "second" experiment. The duration of the entire study was about 75 minutes, with the "first" experiment accounting for approximately three fourths of this time.

PROCEDURE[1]

The experimental procedure can be easily followed by referring to the flow diagram presented in Figure 1.

Part 1: "Personality Judgment"

The subjects were led to believe that as part of an examination of the process of personality judgment, Dr. Zimbardo was studying the "accuracy of the first impressions that people form of strangers." To this end, each subject would be

---

1. The conduct of this study was greatly facilitated by the resourceful contributions of Robert Mittenzwei who served with the author as experimenter.

FIGURE 1 Flow diagram of procedure.

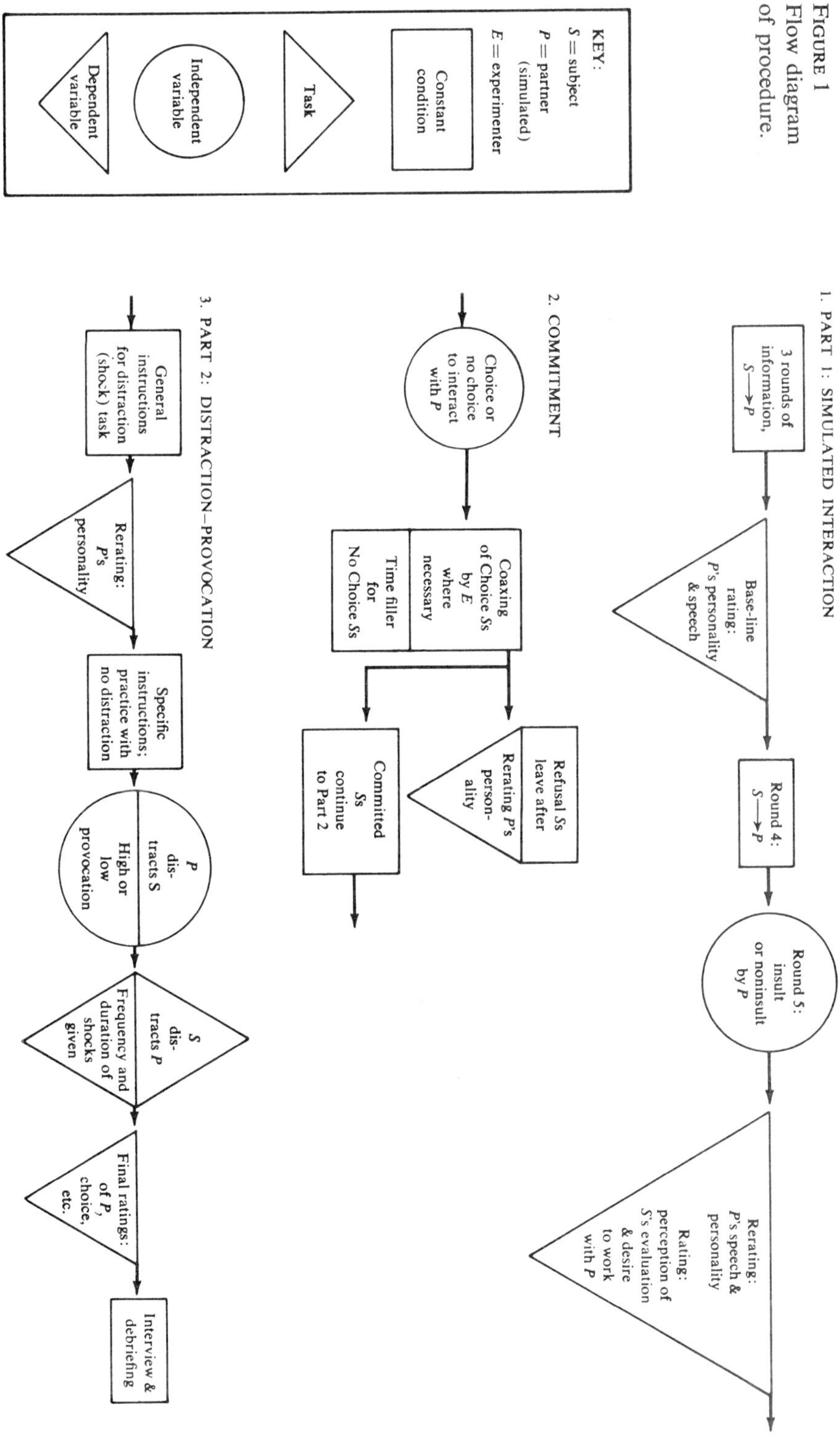
KEY:
S = subject
P = partner (simulated)
E = experimenter
Constant condition
Task
Independent variable
Dependent variable
1. PART 1: SIMULATED INTERACTION
3 rounds of information, S ⟶ P
Base-line rating: P's personality & speech
Round 4: S ⟶ P
Round 5: insult or noninsult by P
Rerating: P's speech & personality
Rating: perception of S's evaluation & desire to work with P
2. COMMITMENT
Choice or no choice to interact with P
Coaxing of Choice Ss by E where necessary
Time filler for No Choice Ss
Refusal Ss leave after
Rerating P's personality
Committed Ss continue to Part 2
3. PART 2: DISTRACTION–PROVOCATION
General instructions for distraction (shock) task
Rerating: P's personality
Specific instructions; practice with no distraction
P distracts S
High or low provocation
S distracts P
Frequency and duration of shocks given
Final ratings: of P, choice, etc.
Interview & debriefing

asked to exchange information with a student from a local college who was in an adjacent cubicle. The subjects were told that for "purposes of control" all instructions were tape recorded and that in order "to eliminate the influence of visual cues on your judgments" contact would be limited to a series of verbal communication rounds via an intercom system. They were further (speciously) informed that by varying the topics of conversation we could determine which ones yielded the most valuable information about personality and that although the procedure might seem artificial and unusual, it was in its basic elements similar to a number of real-life situations in which important judgments are made on the basis of limited information without direct contact with the person being judged.

To ensure the expectation that there would be no future interaction with the other subject and to increase the frankness of their responses, the subjects were assured of complete anonymity; they were told not to use their names, only code numbers 1 and 2, and that "it is against our policy to allow the two of you to meet each other, *even when the study is completed.*"

Simulated Information Exchange. In order to permit a precise realization of the conditions required to test the dissonance predictions, it was necessary to control various features of the interaction between the subject and his partner. This control was achieved by a deception, substituting a simulated partner with whom the subject believed he was communicating. The tape recorded pre-programing of the partner's contribution to the interaction standardized this aspect of the procedure and allowed for systematic variation in the presentation of the partner to the subject.

The personality-judgment task was adapted from a technique used by Rosenbaum and deCharms (1960) and deCharms and Wilkins (1963) to simulate a social interaction in their studies of hostility. In our study, the task of the subject during the first communication rounds was to describe himself to his partner and to form a clear impression of his partner's personality. The situation was structured so that the two did not interact freely as in an ordinary conversation. Rather, each of them was given an allotment of time (1 minute) to talk about himself. Further, the dummy control-panel setup indicated to the subject that he could not speak while listening to his partner. The instructions given by Dr. Z. at the beginning of each round defined the topic of communication and indicated the order of presentation. Timing was controlled by prerecorded signal tones.

The partner's presentation on the first four rounds was held constant across all experimental conditions. It was our intention to present a personality that was similar to the subject's and fairly likable. Briefly, the partner indicated that: he got along well with his parents and older brother; he came from a sociable middle-class home that was upward mobile; he was a sophomore at Hunter College (part of the New York City College system) with an interest in engineering; he was a good student without being a "grind"; he was a frank, fun-loving person who enjoyed good fellowship, sports, and girls, but not those who were overly coy; and he disliked single-minded students, braggarts, and people who cheat on examinations.

After the first three rounds of information exchange, the subject was asked to record his initial impressions of his partner. This rating provided a base line against which to evaluate the effects of the experimental manipulation of the subject's attitude. The subject also recorded his estimate of his partner's speech habits (a disguised evaluation of the partner).

Manipulation of Liking. On the fifth and final information round, the subject and partner were asked to evaluate each other's personality "based on what you have heard the other say and the inferences you can draw from this information." The order of speaking was arranged so that the partner always had the last word. Any uncalled-for replies to this evaluation could thus be prevented by the interruption of Dr. Z.'s voice a few seconds after the partner's speech had ended, requesting the subject to fill out some additional forms.

The subjects in the No Insult conditions received a fairly positive and friendly evaluation from their partners:

> Uh, well, your evaluation of me is really a pretty fair statement. I think that it . . . uh . . . that it shows that you're an intelligent person, and . . . uh . . . that you know quite a lot about people in that you can describe them accurately. I guess from that that your psych. prof will give you a good evaluation for this. From what you've said to me, and I admit that it hasn't been too much to go on, I think that I'd like to get to know you better. Uh . . . you seem to be the kind of guy who is bright, sociable, and who is uh . . . (cut off by tone).

The subjects in the Insult conditions received an extremely caustic and derogatory evaluation from their partners:

> You know, this is just what I'd expect from a typical NYU student. Your evaluation of me, it's . . . uh . . . so vague, so shallow, . . . it could describe almost anyone I know. I guess from this that you really don't know too much about people. Or . . . uh maybe you must be pretty thick or something. What you've said about yourself seemed inconsistent . . . you seem pretty confused, or, maybe you're trying to put me on. Really, I've never heard such crap, you're probably all wrapped up in that private little egotistical world of yours. I'm sorry, but I'd hate to give such a poor analysis in front of *my* psych. prof. . . . (cut off by tone).

The immediate effects of this manipulation upon the subject's evaluation of the partner were then assessed by questionnaire ratings.

Manipulation of Choice. In the Choice conditions, subjects were then told that the experiment was over and that they were to wait in their cubicles until the experimenter came in to conduct a brief interview with each of them. Each subject was then escorted out of the lab into a smaller interview room where the experimenter raised the question of further participation.

> Before we begin this interview, I'd like to ask you a favor. (Pause.) We are doing an experiment for a grad. course that we're taking and since our study also requires two subjects, Dr. Z. has given us permission to ask his subjects whether or not they would be willing to

> participate in it. If both you and the other subject agree to do it, we will be able to run it right here and now. I don't know whether you want to do it, but in any case it's completely up to you. Of course, before you make your decision, let me tell you what we're doing so that you'll know what it's all about.

A brief description of the study was then supplied as well as some information intended to control and minimize the subject's incentives for choosing to continue with the "second" experiment. He was told that this study would again involve interaction with his partner, but that it would not this time involve any verbal communication. He was also told that he would receive neither additional course credit nor pay for participation in the "second" study. If the subject agreed to go on, the experimenter went out, saying that he had to find out whether the partner had also agreed to continue; he returned a few moments later with an affirmative answer. If the subject was not so eager to continue, the experimenter tried again (using standard probes), telling him first that "our experiment won't take too long, it lasts only about 20 minutes." If the subject was still reluctant, he was told to wait; the experimenter departed, returned with the information that the partner was willing to continue, and then asked whether, since two persons were needed for the study, the subject would reconsider his decision. Finally, if this did not persuade the subject, a third probe was added, reiterating the short time interval required for participation. Subjects who agreed were then escorted back to their booths in the laboratory, where they received the same instructions about the "second" experiment given to the subjects in the No Choice condition. The 12 subjects who refused to continue were asked to re-evaluate their partners. The realities of the experiment were then explained to them, and they were dismissed.

The No Choice subjects were not taken out of the laboratory, and all references to the voluntary nature of participation in the "second" experiment were eliminated for them. Otherwise, the procedure was quite similar to that described above. The subjects were told that Dr. Z. had given the experimenters his permission to use his subjects for their graduate course experiment but that they (unfortunately) could not give them money or course credit for their participation. To equalize the amount of time (between Parts 1 and 2) spent in this condition with that required by the Choice condition, several minutes were taken by the experimenter to "collect the right forms," etc.

Part 2: "Distraction and Performance"

The "second" study was presented as an investigation of the effects of motivation and distraction on performance. First, each student would work alone on a task without external distraction; then the subject would work on a related task while his partner provided a source of distraction; after that, they would reverse roles and the partner would work and be distracted by the subject. The subjects were told that we were studying the effects of a variety of distractions and we would be using two that were qualitatively different but equally unpleasant. The subject's distraction would be loud white noise blasted in his ears, while his partner's would be electric shocks delivered to his fingertips.

After the task was described, the experimenter asked the subjects to re-evaluate their partners for "purposes of experimental control" before the second study was begun. This measurement provided a direct indicator of the effects of choice on the subject's liking for his partner prior to the possibly contaminating effects of the actual interaction.

Provocation of the Subject by the Partner. After rerating their partners, all subjects were told that part of the study was concerned with the effects of different *amounts* as well as different types of distractions on performance. This was done in order to provide the subject with some basis on which to perceive whether his partner was or was not being hostile and provoking and also to give him a wide latitude of aggressive retaliatory responding. These goals were achieved by the following instructions:

> Rather than specifying precisely the number of distraction stimuli that you should give to each other on this trial, we will just set up some rough guidelines for you. For example, 8 to 10 half-second stimuli during the 1-minute work period would be a fairly *small* amount of distraction, while 20 to 25 stimuli would be a very *large* amount. Any number of stimuli that you give in this range will be all right.

In the Low Provocation treatment, the subject received only 9 blasts of white noise (presumably initiated by his partner), suggesting that the partner was being rather considerate in going along with the minimum guideline established by the experimenter.

In the High Provocation condition, by contrast, the subject received 29 blasts of white noise, an amount of distraction beyond the upper limit suggested by the experimenter. This was to imply that the partner was adding some "for good measure" on his own, thus establishing him as punitive.

Opportunity to Aggress. The subject was then given the opportunity to retaliate by being allowed to choose the number and duration of electric shocks to be delivered to his partner while the latter was attempting to solve a problem.

After this came a final-reactions questionnaire, an interview to determine the credibility of the procedure,[2] and then a lengthy debriefing session in which all deceptions were revealed and the subjects' reactions elicited and discussed.

Summary of Dependent Variables

The reader should refer back to the flow diagram in Figure 1 to relate the various manipulations described above with the order in which the following dependent measures were obtained.

2. The data for three subjects, one from the Insult-Choice condition and two from the Insult-No Choice condition, were discarded prior to data analysis because it was revealed during our interview that these subjects did not believe in the "reality" of their partners.

1. *Speech-Habits Questionnaire.* This was a rather indirect measure, in that it focused the subject's attention on supposedly objective aspects of his partner's speech. It was explained that judgments of personality "might be influenced by some rather subtle speech habits and characteristics." They were asked to evaluate the partner's speech, "with regard to tone, style, and general communicativeness," by rating the presence or absence of several speech qualities on 5-step scales. A second measurement on the speech-habits scale was obtained after the subject had received his partner's evaluation, thereby allowing a check on the success of the insult manipulation in producing changes in evaluation of these supposedly objective, unchanging traits of the partner. Responses to the first scale were factor-analyzed, and a principal-components factor analysis of these ratings yielded two clear orthogonal factors that contained all but one of the speech qualities. The first factor consists of six negative qualities (caustic, confusing, insulting, inconsistent, irritating, and rude), and the second contains seven positive qualities (articulate, clear, logical, plain-spoken, pleasing, polite, and witty).

2. *Personality-Trait Evaluation.* Each subject evaluated his partner on a series of 14 bipolar adjective scales (e.g., sincere-deceitful, friendly-antagonistic, considerate-inconsiderate). These 7-point scales were arranged to minimize response set and were administered at three stages in the procedure—after information rounds 3 and 5, along with the speech-habits measurement, and again after the choice manipulation.

3. *Perception of Insult and Willingness to Work with Partner.* The subject's perception of the *content* of his partner's insulting or favorable evaluation was measured by scale responses from "overly favorable" through "fair" to "overly critical" on an item reading: "Considering the other subject's personality evaluation of you, do you think that he was (fill in) in his judgments." Willingness to work with the partner in another study was measured by responses on a 41-point scale anchored by the phrases "definitely want to" and "definitely not want to." Both of these measures were made immediately after the partner's evaluation of the subject in Part 1 of the study.

4. *Final-Reactions Questionnaire.* Willingness to work with the partner in the future on another study and perception of him as a possible friend were measured after Part 2 of the study. In addition, perceived choice and pressure exerted by the experimenter to participate in the "second" study were also measured on 41-point scales.

5. *Physical Aggression.* The aggression measures consisted of the number and the total duration of the shocks (which were recorded on automated frequency counters and timers) that the subject delivered to his partner as distraction stimuli while the latter was ostensibly working on a performance test. This procedure is quite similar to that used by Berkowitz and Holmes (1960), except that in their study the subject's delivery of shock was in the context of his evaluating a partner's performance. In our study, the shock data provided an assessment of the effects of the experimental manipulations—Insult, Choice, and Provocation—on the magnitude of the subject's "socially sanctioned" aggressiveness.

RESULTS

Single-classification variance and covariance analyses were used for much of the statistical evaluation of the data. Multiple comparisons of treatment means, using the method suggested by Scheffé (1959), were employed to provide greater precision than is obtainable from overall F-test. In all analyses, the Refusal subjects (all from the Insult-Choice group) are treated as a separate (seventh) group.

Premanipulation Comparability

Evidence that the subjects randomly assigned to the various groups came from the same population is shown in Table 1. There are no significant differences among the base-line evaluations of the partner's personality up to the point where the subjects stopped receiving identical treatment, and the mean base line rating of 44 is significantly more favorable ($p < 0.001$) than neutral (a score of 56).

Reactions to Being Insulted

Insulted subjects viewed the partner's evaluation as somewhat critical (mean = 33 for both Choice and No Choice groups) while the No Insult subjects regarded it as somewhat favorable (mean = 11, $p < 0.001$).

TABLE 1

SUBJECT ATTITUDE TOWARD PARTNER*

Measure	No Insult-Choice ($n = 22$)		Insult: No Choice ($n = 22$)		Insult: Choice ($n = 26$)		Insult: Refusal ($n = 12$)	
	Mean	(S.D.)	Mean	(S.D.)	Mean	(S.D.)	Mean	(S.D.)
1. Personality:								
a. Base line	44_a	(6)	46_a	(9)	46_a	(9)	40_a	(7)
b. Change† scores	$+5_a$	(6)	-12_b	(8)	-15_b	(13)	-14_b	(10)
2. Speech habits:								
a. Change† in negative traits	0_a	(4)	-5_b	(5)	-5_b	(6)	-9_c	(4)
b. Change† in positive traits	0_a	(3)	-3_{ab}	(4)	-4_b	(5)	-4_b	(3)

* Values have been rounded to integers for presentation purposes. Mean values in each row with a common subscript do not differ significantly (0.05 level) while those with different subscripts do.

† All "change" scores refer to changes in rating from before to immediately after the partner's insulting or non-insulting evaluation of the subject. Positive values indicate more favorable evaluation while negative values indicate less favorable evaluation.

In addition, compared to the No Insult group, the Insult groups rated the partner's personality more unfavorably than they had after information round 3, ($p < 0.001$) and they were more critical of his speech habits. On perceptions of his negative speech characteristics, all Insult groups differ from the No Insult groups by a probability value greater than 0.01, while two of the three Insult groups also differ from the No Insult groups ($p < 0.05$) in responding to his positive speech traits. The Insult-Refusal group is comparable to the other Insult groups on all measures except change in negative speech traits, where it responded more unfavorably than the others ($p < 0.05$).

Insulted subjects were also more reluctant to continue working with their partners in future experiments than were subjects who received favorable evaluations. The mean of 10 for the No Insult group differs significantly from that of the Insult-Choice group (mean = 19, $p < 0.025$), the Insult-No Choice group (mean = 22, $p < 0.01$), and the Insult-Refusal group (mean = 27, $p < 0.001$). The Insult groups do not, however, differ significantly among themselves.

A more impressive demonstration of the absolute degree of reluctance of these insulted subjects to work with their partners is provided by the behavioral data on the experimenter's greater coaxing of these subjects and their greater refusal rate than the No Insult subjects. Those insulted and given a choice to continue required twice as many probes (additional requests by the experimenter) than did those given a choice but not insulted ($p = < 0.05$). Furthermore, despite this coaxing, a third of the Insult-Choice group still refused to continue, while none of the No Insult-Choice subjects refused ($p < 0.01$).

Taken together, these findings indicate that the insult manipulation produced a strong dislike of the partner and a strong aversion toward further contact with him.

Manipulation of Choice

Subjective reactions to the manipulation of choice were in line with the intention to have subjects in the Choice conditions perceive the decision to work with

TABLE 2

THE EFFECT OF CHOICE ON SUBJECT EVALUATION OF PARTNER*

	No Insult-Choice ($n = 22$)	Insult		
		No Choice ($n = 22$)	Choice ($n = 26$)	Refusal ($n = 12$)
Attitude Change Score	-0.1_a	-0.9_a	$+5.0_b$	-2.5_a

* Scores are based on the difference between personality-trait-evaluation ratings made at the end of the "first" experiment and just before the beginning of the distraction tasks in the "second" experiment. In the case of the Refusal groups, the second rating was obtained immediately after the subject had decided not to continue. Positive change scores indicate more favorable evaluation. Cell entries bearing a common subscript do not differ from each other at the 0.05 level.

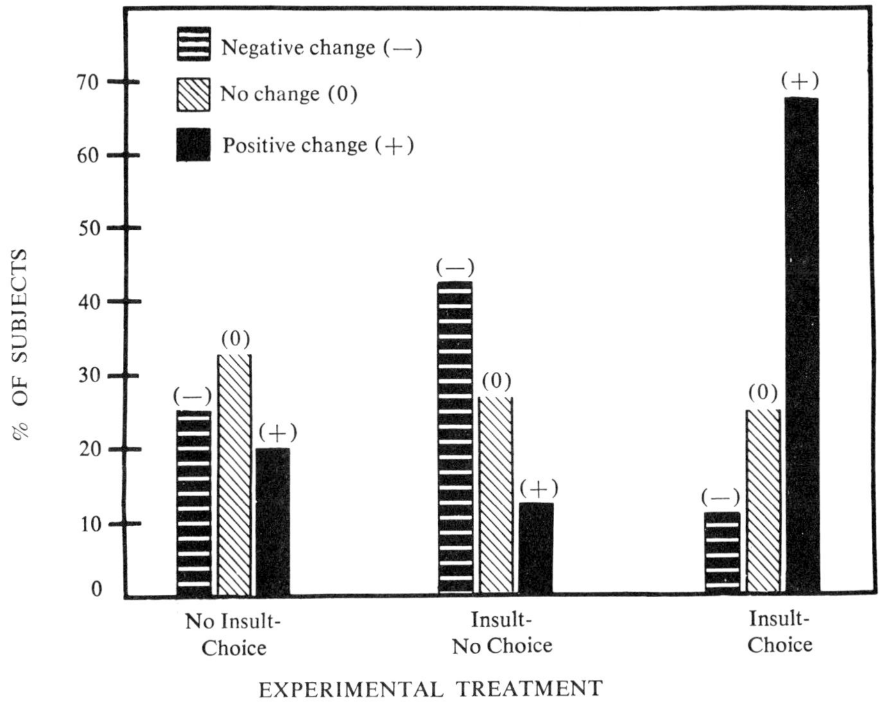

FIGURE 2

The effect of choice on subject evaluation of partner as measured by the difference between personality-trait-evaluation ratings made at the end of the "first" experiment and the beginning of the "second."

their partners as "very much" their own and those in the No Choice conditions perceive that they had "very little to say" about this required action (means of 10 to 36, respectively, on a 41-point scale; $p < 0.001$). In addition, all groups felt that the amount of pressure put on them by the experimenter in requiring or requesting them to participate in the "second" experiment was equal and on the average "very little" (of course, Refusal subjects, who were the most pressured, did not complete this questionnaire).

Tests of the Dissonance Predictions

Effects of Choice on Evaluation of the Partner. The impact of the choice procedure on the subjects' evaluations of their partners was assessed by examining the changes in the personality-trait evaluation between the rating made at the end of the "first" experiment and that made just prior to the beginning of the "second" experiment. The mean change scores are presented for all groups in Table 2; a positive score indicates a more favorable evaluation of the partner. The only change in evaluation that differs significantly from zero change is that of the Insult-Choice group. This change in evaluation is significantly more *favorable* than that for the Insult-No Choice group ($p < 0.01$), for the No Insult-Choice group ($p < 0.01$), and especially for the Insult-Refusal group ($p < 0.01$). These data provide strong confirmation of the prediction of increased liking for the partner following the dissonant choice of continued interaction with him. The absence of attitude change in the No Insult-Choice condition helps rule out the possibility that the increased liking results from some extraneous aspect of the choice procedure (e.g., direct suggestion) not related to dissonance.

Figure 2 shows in rather dramatic fashion how the distribution of changes in attitude toward the partner was affected by the experimental manipulations. For the No Insult-Choice group, the majority of evaluations were stable, with as many becoming more favorable as becoming less so. The Insult-No Choice subjects showed a skewed distribution of attitude change—few positive changes and many more negative changes. None of those who refused changed positively toward the partner. What is striking is the attitude change among those subjects who were insulted and then chose to continue interacting with the partner. The modal response (62 per cent) in this group was to like the partner more, while only a small percentage (8 per cent) changed to like him less.

The question we must now ask is whether this attitude change withstood the additional provocation and instigation to aggression by the partner in the distraction part of the study.

Effects of Provocation on Aggression. It was expected that the magnitude of the response to High Provocation would be greater than to Low Provocation, and the data in Table 3 reveal this to be the case both for the frequency of shocks administered ($p < 0.001$) and for their duration ($p < 0.001$).

TABLE 3

AGGRESSION TOWARD PARTNER: FREQUENCY AND DURATION OF SHOCKS*

Measure	No Insult-Choice (n† = 11)		Insult: No Choice (n = 11)		Insult: Choice (n = 13)	
	Mean	(S.D.)	Mean	(S.D.)	Mean	(S.D.)
1. Frequency‡						
Low Provocation	9.5_a	(4.3)	16.2_b	(7.5)	16.7_b	(7.4)
High Provocation	19.7_{bc}	(5.6)	24.7_c	(8.6)	19.1_{bc}	(5.7)
2. Duration§						
Low Provocation	46.7_a	(28.0)	68.8_{ab}	(41.9)	69.9_{ab}	(28.6)
High Provocation	88.9_b	(42.5)	122.0_c	(29.2)	73.2_{ab}	(40.4)

* Cell means on each *pair* of rows having a subscript in common do not differ significantly at the 0.05 level.

† n = number of subjects at each provocation level.

‡ Number of shocks per minute.

§ Seconds × 10.

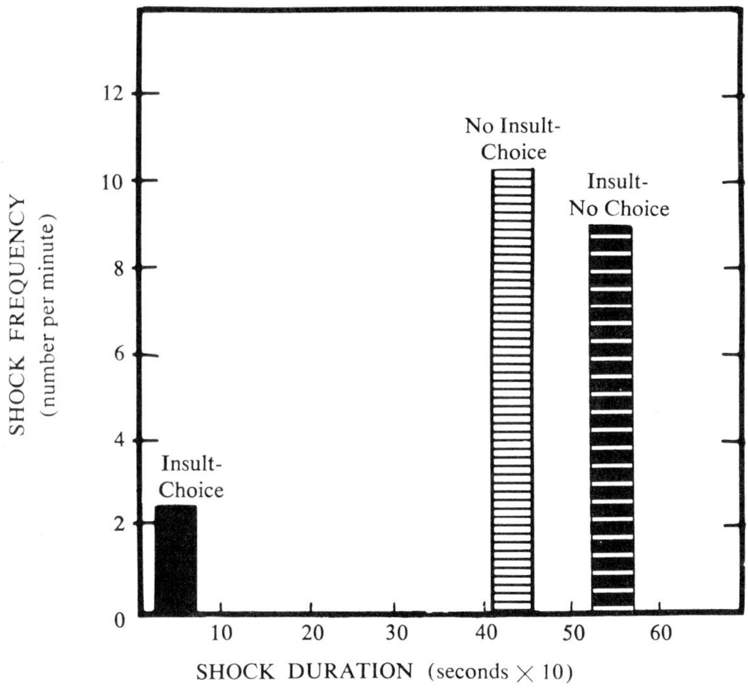

FIGURE 3

Differential effects of provocation on aggression toward partner. The location and height of each bar represent for that group the mean *difference* between the duration and frequency (respectively) of shocks delivered under High and Low Provocation.

In response to Low Provocation, those who were insulted shocked their partners more than did those who were not insulted ($p < 0.025$); they also maintained the shock duration slightly longer ($p < 0.15$). There were no differences in response to Low Provocation between the two Insult groups, Choice and No Choice.

Those under High Provocation in the No Insult-Choice group almost doubled the level of aggression employed by those under Low Provocation. A similar increased aggression was noted for the Insult-No Choice group under High Provocation. Figure 3 presents a graph of this data, showing the difference between aggression under High and Low Provocation for those groups and the Insult-Choice (High Dissonance) group. The effect is quite clear: High Dissonance subjects under High Provocation responded with significantly less aggression than the Insult-Choice subjects and with even less aggression than the No Insult subjects. In fact, these High Dissonance subjects responded to the High Provocation as if it were minimal: the frequency and duration of shocks they gave their partners in response to intense provocation were no greater than when provocation was low.

These data are consistent with the hypothesis that the High Provocation treatment following dissonant choice arouses further dissonance, which acts to inhibit the intensity of aggressive responses. The presence of a provocation effect in both the Insult-No Choice and the No Insult-Choice groups, contrasted with the absence of such an effect in the Insult-Choice groups, suggests that greater tolerance for High Provocation was conferred only by the dissonant choice.

Postaggression Liking for Partner. The final measures of the desire to work with the partner again in a future study and of the willingness to admit him into one's circle of friends reflect evaluation of the partner after he insulted and provoked the subject and was shocked in return. Subjects who were not insulted were most willing to work with their partners and admit him to a circle of friends. Among the insulted subjects, the effects of choice and provocation were predictable from our dissonance model. Insult-No Choice subjects were more negative toward their partners on both measures under High than under Low Provocation. The Insult-No Choice (High Dissonance) group desired to work with the partner *more* and were *more* willing to admit him into a circle of friends under High than under Low Provocation! Under High Provocation, the difference between the two insulted groups (Choice and No Choice) on the future-interaction measure was statistically significant, ($p < 0.05$), while the difference between them on the sociometric friendship measure approached significance ($t = 2.03$; $p < 0.10$). Of major theoretical and practical consequence is the finding that on the measure of *change* in desire to work with the partner (from after Part 1 to after the end of Part 2), the only group that showed an *increase* in willingness to re-enter the interaction was the Insult-Choice group given High Provocation. Their increase in desire to maintain contact with the antagonistic partner is significantly greater ($p < 0.05$) than the decrease shown by the other two groups.

DISCUSSION

The present experiment provides strong evidence for the importance of choice and commitment in interpersonal relations. As predicted, subjects who made a dissonant choice to continue interaction with the disliked partner showed a greater improvement in their evaluation of the partner's personality than did subjects in all other groups. In addition, the findings regarding aggressive behavior revealed that the High Provocation treatment elicited considerably fewer aggressive responses from the Insult-Choice subjects than it did from the Insult-No Choice Controls. Finally, among the Insult subjects, those making the dissonant choice concerning the offensive partner and subsequently receiving the strongest additional provocation for aggression were the ones who emerged liking this partner the most. These effects—increased liking and less aggression—are contrary to expectations derived from frustration-aggression theory. They also provide an exception to Berkowitz' (1964) "cue-value" theory of aggression. The predictions from this theory are that intensity of aggression is positively correlated, other things being equal, with both the magnitude of provocation and the strength of the hostile attitude evoked by the antagonist.

The data from our study on frequency and duration of shock under varied levels of initial insult (and thus of hostile attitude) and provocation support this position for both the No Insult-Choice group and the Insult-No Choice group. However, the Insult-Choice (High Dissonance) group provides an exception to Berkowitz' theory—an exception that can be understood by an analysis of dissonant choice as a dynamic motivational process.

The findings regarding response to provocation were consistent with our initial speculation that dissonance arousal and reduction was an *ongoing process*. It will be recalled that this analysis was proposed to test whether the consequences of choosing, and therefore the amount of postdecisional dissonance aroused, are matters simply of the act of choice per se or whether they depend also on subsequent events (cf. Rosenau, 1964). To maintain a reduced level of dissonance, subjects are motivated to secure outcomes in the interaction that are consistent with having chosen to enter it (e.g., minimizing its unpleasantness). The behavior of the partner in the High Provocation condition is inconsistent with the choice to continue and thus presumably arouses further dissonance. Strong aggressive responses to this provocation are incompatible with this dissonance motivation, since such responses would be likely to intensify the conflict between the subject and his partner. As predicted, then, the subjects in the Insult-Choice condition were less aggressive to the highly provocative partner than were the subjects in the Insult-No Choice group.

Sources of Bias

The inclusion in the research design of the No Insult-Choice subjects helps exclude the possibility of any simple error effect due to the presence of biasing demand characteristics; these subjects, given the same choice condition as the High Dissonance group, failed to show any systematic change in attitudes toward their partners.

It is more difficult, however, within the limits of the present research design, to rule out the influence of experimenter bias. Both experimenters were aware of the treatment assignment of each subject and of the experimental hypotheses, so that it is conceivable that they could have communicated some information about these hypotheses during the critical choice interview. To minimize the possibility of such influence, great care was taken to eliminate evaluative references to the partner during the choice period. Intensive interviews with the subjects at the end of the experiment failed to elicit any awareness of the relation between choice and attitude change. Indeed, many of the subjects were quite skeptical about this hypothesis when it was explained to them. Thus, while the possibility of an experimenter-bias effect accounting for the observed changes in evaluation cannot be dismissed completely, it seems unlikely that this bias was operative to any great extent in the present experiment.

All conclusions regarding the effects of choice must be restricted to those subjects who accepted this induction, since one third of the subjects in the Insult-Choice group refused to re-enter interaction with the partner and had to be dropped from Part 2 of the experiment.

The existence of such a substantial refusal rate provides valuable behavioral confirmation of the assumed unwillingness to continue interaction with the offensive coworker.[4] The absence of refusals among the No Insult-Choice subjects indicates that liking is an important determinant of interpersonal choice. On the other hand, the high proportion of Refusal subjects within the Insult-Choice group introduces the factor of self-selection in participation in Part 2 of the experiment, which may limit the generality of our findings. What is the nature of this sampling bias? Comparison of the reactions of subjects in the Insult-Refusal and Insult-Choice groups reveals few statistically reliable differences.

The initial evaluation of the partner by subjects in the Refusal group tended to be slightly more positive than that of subjects in other groups (see Table 2). Their reaction to the Insult treatment is quite comparable to that of the Insult-Choice group on two of the three attitude measures. The Refusal subjects did show significantly greater increases in the attribution of negative speech characteristics (see Table 2), but even this difference was largely eliminated when an analysis covarying pre-insult differences in attitude was performed. The most striking difference between the accepting and refusing Insult subjects is associated with the effects of this decision on their attitude toward the partners. Insult-Choice subjects showed significant (relative to zero) positive change in their evaluation of the partner ($p < 0.001$), while the Refusal subjects showed a "boomerang" effect, changing their evaluation of the partner's personality in a negative direction ($t = 1.97$; $p < 0.10$).[5]

It would appear, then, that except for the effects of the choice itself, the reactions of the Refusal group were fairly similar to those of the Insult-Choice group. Still, there may be important, but unmeasured, differences between these two groups (e.g., self-esteem, social desirability) that restrict the scope of our findings. Therefore, within the limits of the present research, our generalizations are clearly confined to subjects who chose. Comparison of Insult-Choice with Insult-No Choice subjects are biased to the extent that there exist, in the latter group, individuals who would have chosen not to continue had they been offered the option to do so. The influence of this self-selection factor as a bias on the aggression data is probably small. The most obvious hypothesis, that only relatively more compliant individuals would choose to continue work with the insulting partner, leads to the prediction of less intense aggression among these subjects than among those in the Insult-No Choice group, which lack this self-selection. The data of Table 3 help to rule out this alternative explanation. We saw that there were no differences between Insult-Choice and Insult-No Choice subjects in the frequency or duration of shocks meted out to the partner in the Low Provocation conditions. It was only at the higher level of provocation

4. It is interesting to note at this point that only one of the Refusal subjects indicated dislike of the partner or gave his bizarre, insulting evaluation as the reason for not continuing with the "second" experiment. The other 11 subjects excused themselves because of "other appointments," examinations, and the like.

5. This divergence in the evaluation of the partner between Insult-Choice and Refusal groups is quite consistent with the effects of choice on the attractiveness of chosen and rejected alternatives demonstrated by studies using within-subjects designs (Brehm & Cohen, 1962; Festinger, 1964).

that the predicted diminution of aggression among choosing subjects was observed.

CONCLUSIONS

The work of Thibaut and Kelley (1959) and Homans (1961) has indicated that interpersonal attraction may profitably be viewed in terms of a social-exchange process. Clearly, the rewards gained and the costs incurred during the interaction are important considerations in predicting the future of any interpersonal relation. The contribution of dissonance theory here lies in its emphasis on the role played by choice and personal commitment in motivational change. Such change may result not only in the immediate modification in one's evaluation of another person but also in long-lasting change in tolerance of frustration and inhibition of physical aggression.

Editor's Comments

In this study, not only did the conditions under which dissonance was reduced result in lessened feelings of hostility toward an insulting person and limit aggression toward him when he was provoking it, but in the end, it even produced a conciliatory attitude that would allow further social contact and communication and perhaps even the development of the kind of interpersonal bond that Lorenz describes as essential for the long-term control of aggression. These results, when contrasted with those detailed by Brock and Pallak (Article 13) and supplemented by Glass and Wood (Article 14), highlight the diverse behavioral reactions that can be understood and predicted knowing the cognitive conditions associated with an individual's commitment to a given behavior. While the previous work on aggression revealed consequences of dissonant choices that were reminiscent of the reactions of the Nazi captors to their concentration-camp victims—such as devaluing the victim, minimizing his pain, and feeling more obligated to act aggressively—the present research points to a different ethic, a tolerant turning of the other cheek.

How long would the dissonant individual continue to take insults, endure frustration, and experience provocation without striking back? Real-life analogues direct our attention to the obvious fact that the immediacy and directness of such reactions vary across a broad continuum: some people retaliate as soon as they have the opportunity, others forebear until restraint can no longer be reasonably exercised, while still others appear to have limitless acceptance and tolerance of frustration and provocation.

The interesting question is not how much any given individual can put up with before he "explodes," but rather what are some of the causes and consequences of this nonretaliatory behavior. There is, for example, the person whose restraint is reinforced by social approval and who comes to value the approbation of being cool, calm, and composed when others would be provoked into action. A different process characterizes the "chronically overcontrolled type," who has learned to control *all* signs of outward hostility. "His inhibitions against the expression of aggression are extremely rigid, so he rarely, if ever, responds with aggression no matter how great the provocation" (Megargee, 1966, p. 2).

The pattern that distinguishes the potentially assaultive overcontrolled person is outward conformity coupled with inner alienation. This pattern may arise from a socialization process that exaggerates conformity to the rules of the social system: to gain affection from their parents, such individuals have to deny or repress all hostility, however slight. This interpretation comes from a study of people who committed a homicide without any prior record of anti-social behavior (Weiss, Lamberti, & Blackman, 1960). Of special relevance to Firestone's research is the evidence that such persons are *generally* unresponsive even to extreme provocation; but when they do finally aggress (clearly a necessary criterion to define them post hoc as overcontrolled), their actions tend to be extremely assaultive and in response to some minor provocation that just happened to be the last straw.

What about the person who seems to be continually frustrated and disappointed in all areas of his life and who is blocked in attaining many of his goals? Such a person may become a fatalist who believes that bad luck follows him; in Yiddish (which has a vocabulary that finely differentiates among a variety of similar types), he is a *shlemazel*. He becomes vested with the attribute of somehow calling forth frustration upon his own head by his very existence, as if it is attracted by an invisible lightning rod. One possible consequence of adopting this view is that by defining oneself as someone who always gets "dumped" on, the person begins to act so as to increase the likelihood that he will elicit aggression and provocation from others. What develops, then, is the destructive, self-fulfilling prophecy characteristic of this "*shlemazel-shlemiel* syndrome."

Then there is the Caspar Milquetoast, who, in his resignation to his wife's constant abuse and in his abject meekness, provokes her to even greater excesses while he passively waits to receive his promised inheritance. One final type to mention in passing is The Mother, who takes out on her family all her frustrations, her lifelong burdens, her lack of recognition and endless privations without ever a sign of direct aggression. Nevertheless, she destroys her children through ingeniously subtle techniques of overprotectiveness fortified by small doses of guilt, which may be delayed in onset but continue to be active for a long time (cf. Roth, 1968). The reader is invited to fill in other nonaggressive types, an area of systematic investigation largely ignored by psychologists.

Another question raised by Firestone's study is whether people try to make the best of a bad situation even if they did not choose it. The following design of a study by Grebstein (1967) yielded experimental evidence of the answer to that question. First, each subject was told that in the second part of the experiment he would have to work with one partner, but first he would have to get to know him along with a second person (with whom he would have no future interaction). The subjects in one condition were assigned Partner A and in another, Partner B;

in a third condition, they were assigned neither but were told they could choose their partner after a series of information-exchange rounds (like those used by Firestone). From the outset, A was an extremely threatening person (arrogant, condescending, egotistical, and progressively more obnoxious and hostile throughout the rounds), while B was a nonthreatening person (placid and easy-going, who maintained a good-natured disposition throughout the five rounds). The subjects in each of the three conditions frequently evaluated (over 30 times) each of these target persons on a series of simple good-bad personality traits throughout the information exchanges.

Did those assigned the threatening partner try to salvage a bad situation by minimizing the differences between him and the nice guy, either by perceiving their partner as less bad or the other as less good? The data, presented in Figure 4, show that the threatening person (A) was rated more negatively than person B by all subjects from the first round, and he was seen as increasingly more unattractive as the rounds progressed. It is clear, however, that when subjects know they are required to interact with the threatening person, they do not distort their evaluation of him relative to the nonthreatening person; rather they emphasize the differences between the two, especially on the early rounds.

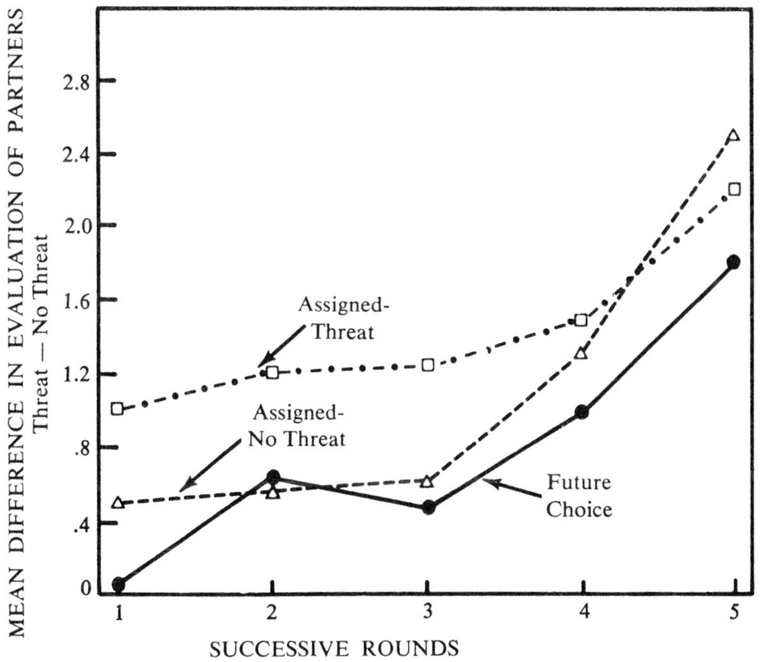

FIGURE 4

The mean differences in subjects' evaluation of the personality of threatening and nonthreatening partners after each of five rounds of information exchange under conditions where the partner had previously been assigned or where the subject expected to choose his partner after the fifth round. (Adapted from Grebstein, 1967.)

According to Grebstein, denial of the negative aspects of person A was made difficult because the information about him was so extreme.

However, consider the ratings of the subjects who listened to A and B knowing that they would be free to choose either and had no constraints placed upon them. Apparently, the operation of choice resulted in their being less evaluative than in either of the other conditions and enabled them to minimize the personality differences between the prospective partners (over all trials and especially on Trial 1). It is as if prior to the actual commitment to one of the two target persons, subjects in the Choice condition kept themselves receptive to new information and, by not exaggerating the differences between A and B, maintained a greater flexibility in their responsiveness to them than subjects already assigned a partner.

On the basis of dissonance theory and the extensive research on re-evaluation of alternatives following a decision, we would expect that this "open channel" information processing would become distorted by the act of decision making, resulting in a spreading apart of the alternatives such that the chosen person would be seen as more attractive and the rejected one less attractive (cf. Brehm & Cohen, 1962; Cohn, 1964; Festinger, 1964). Grebstein's data suggest that prior to commitment to a specific course of action there is not a biased scanning of the alternatives, rather the opposite, a surprisingly unbiased, limited evaluative orientation. It is only the need to justify the decision that introduces the noise into the system that comes out as music the subject wants to hear.

What is needed at this point in our era of an already distorted world perspective based on dissonance commitments is more research directed toward formulating the situational and personal factors that allow a person either to refuse such commitments or, once having undertaken them, to be able to say, "Enough. I was wrong. I made a mistake, but I don't have to change the world to make it follow from my irrational action." The final study in this volume represents an exploratory attempt in that general direction by investigating one type of person for whom dissonance processes do not appear to work as they do for others—the Machiavellian.

16. NO DISSONANCE FOR MACHIAVELLIANS?

Karen Bogart, Florence Geis, Marguerite Levy, and Philip G. Zimbardo

Are there people who do not experience dissonance in the kinds of situations described in this monograph? The dissonance paradigm of forced public compliance employed in the previous studies in this series is basically one of irrationality. An individual finds himself doing something he normally would not want to do and doing it for insufficient justification. In fact, most of these subjects make a commitment to behave publicly in a manner that is not predictable from prior knowledge of their relevant beliefs, attitudes, values, or even drive level. Moreover, under the the appropriate dissonance-arousing conditions (of choice and insufficient justification), these subjects typically resolve the problem by a further process involving the cognitive and perceptual modification of reality.

However, in each study there is a persistent minority whose behavior does not "fit" the theoretical expectations. Some subjects refuse to comply with a request to engage in irrational behavior, while others who do comply publicly do not modify their subjective state to make it agree with their behavior. Admittedly, these individuals comprise only a small part of the population studied; but can their behavior be understood in terms of systematic individual differences, or is it simply attributable to the effects of random influences? If the former, then we may be able to refine the theory of cognitive dissonance by specifying more precisely its conditions of applicability and, at the same time, increase our understanding of the operation of the relevant personality variables.

In studies on social motives and interpersonal behavior, it seems that the arousal of dissonance following a discrepant choice should, in part, depend upon the subject's orientation toward other people. Dissonance in these situations should be greatest for those persons who become personally involved with the relevant others (the experimenter, the source of social deprivation or reinforcement, the victim, the provocateur, etc.); dissonance should be least for those who cannot get involved with other individuals, because of an asocial, instrumental orientation in which people are objects to be exploited or manipulated. Such persons focus entirely upon the task activity and its goal, and other people in the situation assume meaning only in relation to that goal. Furthermore, it ought to be the case that dissonance arousal is more probable among those people whose cognitions are shaped by their behavior than among those who might be differentiated as having their behavior shaped (guided) by their cognitions.

Consequently, it seemed to us that these differences in orientation, evaluation, and strategy are manifest among persons who differ in Machiavellian attitudes. If so, it should follow that people with high Machiavellian attitude scores should be more successful at avoiding dissonant situations than persons

Source: Bogart, Karen, Florence Geis, Marguerite Levy, and Philip G. Zimbardo, "No Dissonance for Machiavellians?" Unpublished selection written for this volume.

who do not have this attitude pattern. Moreover, once engaged in dissonant behavior, Machiavellian individuals should be better able to tolerate it or restore consonance in ways different from those employed by individuals without Machiavellian attitudes.

WHAT IS MACHIAVELLIANISM AND HOW IS IT RELATED TO DISSONANCE?

Machiavellianism is a personality variable operationally defined by scores on the Mach Scales (see Christie & Geis, 1968). The Mach Scales are attitude scales consisting of a series of statements in Likert (Mach IV) and Forced-Choice (Mach V) format which expound a Machiavellian philosophy. These statements are drawn from Machiavelli's *The Prince* and *The Discourses*. The Mach Scales[1] differentiate between High and Low Machiavellians on the basis of the extent to which they endorse Machiavelli's rules of conduct in human relations. In effect, the Scales distinguish between persons with relative standards of behavior (e.g., "Never tell anyone the real reason you did something unless it is useful to do so") at one end of the continuum and persons with absolute standards (e.g., "Honesty is the best policy in all cases") at the other.

The Machiavellian philosophy is a philosophy of pragmatism. It advocates behavior inconsistent with private belief (e.g., telling people what they want to hear) when that behavior works. Thus, it might be expected that high scorers on the Mach Scales (hereafter, *High Machs*) may in general be better able to tolerate cognitive inconsistency or dissonance produced by a discrepancy between behavior and attitudes than Low Mach scorers are.

It has been hypothesized (Geis, 1968) that the behavior of High Machs is influenced by what they know (cognition) and that of Low Machs, by how they feel (emotion). Thus, High Machs have been characterized as being extremely rational, and as such they may be more successful than Low Machs in avoiding dissonance situations, which are essentially irrational. The most salient behavioral difference between High and Low Mach individuals is that High Machs are manipulative. They willingly and successfully manipulate other subjects (especially Low Machs) in experimental situations, and they've often been suspected of trying to manipulate the experimenter as well. As might be expected, they resist attempts to be manipulated—either by fellow subjects or an experimenter. On the other hand, if one does succeed in deceiving them—for example, when they are subjects in an experiment—they respond not with anger or embarrassment but with enthusiasm, redoubled interest, curiosity, and appreciation. A characteristic that seems to underlie all these behaviors is the maintenance of emotional distance. High Machs do not get emotionally involved in others' behavior, or even in their own behavior. This emotional detachment or coolness

1. The Mach Scales are as reliable as other personality tests in which items are balanced for direction of wording to eliminate agree-disagree response sets. Split-half reliability coefficients for the Mach IV, in Likert format, range from 0.70 to 0.90. For the Mach V, in Forced-Choice format, they range from 0.60 to 0.80. Mach Scale score has been demonstrated to relate to congruent differences in behavior in a variety of experimental situations (Christie & Geis, 1968).

leaves them free to concentrate on the cognitive, rational implications of the situation. It should be noted, however, that High Machs are *not* more intelligent than Lows by standard intelligence tests.

In dissonance experiments like those reported earlier although the subject is ostensibly given a choice not to eat grasshoppers or endure any more painful electric shocks or to go without water for twenty-four hours, subtle but strong pressures are usually successful in getting the individual to choose to do so without his becoming aware that he is being manipulated. The data for some subjects must be discarded in any dissonance experiment, however, either because those individuals do become suspicious or because without becoming suspicious they nevertheless refuse to make the choice that is subtly demanded. The possibility exists that those subjects who resist dissonance manipulations, and as a result are lost from the dissonance analysis, are, in fact, High Machs who will not allow themselves to be pressured into irrational behavior. But even High Machs who do commit themselves may not experience cognitive inconsistency in the same way as Low Machs under identical circumstances. Perhaps consistency has value for such subjects only to the extent that it has implications for manipulation (exploitation of others) and not for any intrinsic homeostatic function it may normally serve for other people. Thus it may be that inconsistency is not a *generalized* source of pressure that motivates change but that it has implications for behavior modification only when it is relevant to the prevailing cognitive orientation—in this case, of exploiting others.

Another way of looking at dissonance in High Machs is to consider the possibility that they do not experience dissonance because of the dominant tactic in Machiavellian strategy that involves "conning" and deceiving others (when straight power plays are not appropriate). Such an approach involves the controlled use of discrepancy and inconsistency in the service of their own gratification. Their behavior is guided and controlled by such cognitive strategies. Unlike other people, their *cognitions* are not readily changed by feedback received from their *behavior*, but their behavior is modified by their cognitions.

COHESIVENESS, DISSONANCE, AND ATTITUDE CHANGE

Given these theoretical considerations about the relationship between individual differences in Machiavellianism and dissonance, the implications for testing are obvious: Put High and Low Machs in a situation where there is inconsistency between behavior and values or attitudes and look for differential patterns of response in the two groups. However, we may increase the yield from our research by exploring this relationship between dissonance and Machiavellianism in the context of a study on group cohesiveness.

Cohesiveness is one of the truly "social" concepts in social psychology and was central in the early research of the Group Dynamics School (see Cartwright & Zander, 1960). Group cohesiveness is the answer to the question, "What is it about some functioning groups that causes members to make more sacrifices for the group, to work harder, to extol its virtues, to feel happier in its presence, to interact with other members more, and to agree more readily with the ideas of, and accept the behavior of, one another?" Lewin, Lippitt, and White (1939), for example, showed that in groups with a democratic atmosphere and leader there were more "we" than "I" remarks as contrasted with autocratic groups. Kurt Back (1951) experimentally manipulated three aspects of cohesiveness (prestige of the group, group mediation of individual goals, and attraction to the other members) and demonstrated that regardless of the basis for cohesiveness, there were more influence attempts and more acceptance of influence in highly cohesive than in noncohesive groups.

If cohesiveness is a product of interpersonal attraction between interacting individuals, then the derivation and results of the grasshopper experiments (Zimbardo, Weisenberg, Firestone, & Levy, 1965 [Article 3]; also Smith, 1961) call into question the generalization that attitude change is positively related to feelings of cohesiveness. In those studies, dissonant compliance to the request from a positive source produced greater liking of the source but little real change in attitude toward the object of the compliance (i.e., grasshopper). In contrast, the same behavior elicited by a negative source produced marked changes in subjects' attitude toward liking the previously disliked food but no changes in their dislike for the source.

If an individual publicly behaves contrary to his attitudes or values, not in response to authority, but in response to pressure brought to bear by various of his peers, then we are in a position to assess the effects upon attitude change of complying with pressures from groups varying in cohesiveness. An individual's compliance with a request from peers who are personally liked, have prestige, help mediate the individual's goals—in short, peers to whom he is attracted—should produce little dissonance because invoking such attributes of the "agent" of coercion should provide adequate justification for the discrepant act. Obviously this is not true if the peers are not well liked, have low prestige, etc. Under these conditions, discrepant behavioral compliance should arouse dissonance which will be reduced by modifying the relevant private attitudes to make them fit the public behavior.

DISSONANCE PREDICTIONS

Attitude change following public compliance in performing a discrepant act should be *less* for individuals responding to pressure from attractive peer-group members (highly cohesive groups) than from unattractive ones (low-cohesive groups). This dissonance-produced change in attitude will occur for those low in Machiavellianism but not for High Machs. Thus, we are predicting an interaction effect of the Mach predispositional variable and the manipulated cohesiveness variable.

OVERVIEW OF EXPERIMENTAL DESIGN

Adequate test of this prediction and the interaction of Machiavellianism and dissonance required an experiment with the following features:

1. Initial determination of a private attitude
2. Preselection of High and Low Mach subjects
3. Manipulation of cohesiveness on a dimension irrelevant (orthogonal) to the attitude in question or to Machiavellianism
4. Assessment of the success of this manipulation
5. An experimental task on which two subjects can work simultaneously
6. A request by the peer-group member to the subject to engage in the attitude-discrepant behavior
7. A behavioral measure of compliance with this influence attempt
8. A final measure of change in the relevant private attitude
9. A measure of any subsequent change in attraction toward the peer-group member

The basic design was therefore quite simple. High and Low Mach subjects were put into a dissonant situation by having their partners pressure them to cheat on a test. It was assumed that for most subjects cheating would be a value-discrepant act, especially where it had relatively little utility, e.g., cheating in an experiment compared to cheating on an important final examination. For half of each of these Mach groups the partner was a high-prestige, attractive partner, while for the others he was a low-prestige, unattractive partner. Thus, Low Dissonance was a function of adequate justification for cheating, operationalized as influence from an attractive partner, while High Dissonance required the low justification attributable to influence from an unattractive partner.

PROCEDURE

At the beginning of the semester, 74 male undergraduates, recruited from the subject pool of the introductory psychology course at Washington Square College of New York University, were pretested on the Mach Scale, which was described to them as a "personality test." It was preceded by four genuine, original ink-blots to interpret, to convince even the skeptics that it *was* a personality test. Subsequently, 61 subjects—33 High Machs and 28 Lows (above and below the common median)—participated in the experiment. Each session was conducted by a female experimenter, with a naïve subject and a pretrained confederate playing the role of the partner. Subjects were told that the purpose of the experiment was to determine whether teams of people who were similar to each other in personality were more or less efficient on a group task than teams of people who were quite unlike each other in personality. Accordingly, they were told, some of the teams in the experiment were selected so that the two members were very much alike and others had two members very different from each other.

The subject was then privately given the alleged results of his own personality test. This consisted of a mimeographed page, entitled "Individual Diagnostic Evaluation," that showed scales labelled "Creativity," "Self-actualization," "Neurotic tendencies," "Intelligence estimate," etc. The subject's name was on the sheet, and the scales were all hand-marked to show a highly desirable personality pattern. This was to prevent the subjects from identifying or sympathizing later with Low Prestige partners.

Prestige and Attraction of Partner

Each subject was given a form that contained his own (factual) and his partner's (fictional) name, school, major, interests, hobbies, organizational memberships, prizes, and honors. The High Prestige partner was described as a graduate law student of diversified interests and high academic achievement. In addition, since pretesting had shown that New York University students were more attracted to partners who were "different" from themselves, the experimental subjects in this condition were told that their partner was "pretty much different from you in personality."

The Low Prestige partner was described as an industrial arts major in the school of education, undistinguished by any interests or academic honors. In addition, he was said to be "pretty much similar" to the subject according to the previously administered personality test.

Naturally, the confederate partner never knew which of the descriptions had been used, and he was totally unaware of the Machiavellianism variable. Immediately after the prestige manipulation, an evaluation of its effectiveness was obtained on the pretext that we needed to know the subject's attitudes and feelings toward his partner to understand the results of the study.

A Chance to Cheat

After a pretended duplication of this procedure with the partner, the experimenter brought the two together for their team task; they were each to respond to questions on a specially constructed, multiple-choice, human relations problems test. In the first group of questions, the answers were obvious and reasonable; the second group of questions was more difficult; in the last third of the test, the problems had no solutions.

As the two subjects finished the first set of questions, the experimenter received an apparently unexpected telephone call, obviously demanding her presence elsewhere at once. After first protesting that she was in the middle of a testing session, she asked the subject and partner to continue the test without her, explained that she might be gone for some time, and finally asked the subject to bring both test papers to her on another floor in the building when they had finished.

She left, with footsteps echoing down the stairway, and the two subjects worked in silence on the second set of questions. Shortly after beginning the impossible problems in the third set, the partner sighed, groaned, wriggled in his seat, and looked generally distressed. Breaking his pencil, he went to get another from the experimenter's desk, and discovered there the answer key to the test. He announced his find, hesitated, finally decided out loud to use it, and offered it casually to the subject. If the subject refused, the partner used it alone but later urged the subject to use it on the next problem. If the subject still refused, the partner continued cheating alone. At the final opportunity for the subject to cheat, the partner said, "You'll *never* get this one; you've *gotta* look." At no time did the partner announce answers out loud or otherwise force or trick the subject into cheating. His pressure to cheat consisted of advising, urging, and setting the example, but the subject was really free to comply or not. Since we were interested in individual differences in compliance, the pressure situation was designed so that about half the subjects, overall, would comply.

Final Assessment of Attitude Change

When the subject appeared at the experimenter's office with the completed test papers, he was given a second administration of the Mach Scale. Since scores on the Mach Scale represent a continuum of attitudes toward conventional morality from endorsement to rejection, the difference between the subject's Mach score just after the cheating session and his score at the beginning of the semester provided the measure of change in attitude toward conventional morality. After the Mach Scale came a second check on the prestige manipulation, then an open-ended opportunity to express suspicion or to confess to cheating. Finally, all the experimental procedures were fully explained.

RESULTS

Attraction to Team Partner

The prestige manipulation was successful, as is shown in Table 1. Subjects given the High Prestige description were significantly more attracted to their partner, both before and after the cheating session, than subjects given the Low Prestige

TABLE 1

CHECK ON THE PRESTIGE MANIPULATION*

Rating	High Prestige Condition		Low Prestige Condition		t	p
	n	Mean Score	n	Mean Score		
Presession	28	6.42	32	4.77	8.92	<0.01
Postsession†	18	6.29	11	4.81	3.93	<0.01
Difference‡		0.11 (t = 0.53; n.s.)		−0.04 (t = −0.12; n.s.)		

* The data presented here represent responses to only one of three measures used: "How well do you [did you] like your partner, personally?" The answers, on a 10-point scale, ranged from 1 = "Not at all" to 10 = "Very much." The results on the other two measures were in accord with the data displayed here.

† Based only on those subjects who complied (i.e., cheated).

‡ A positive value indicates a decrease in liking for the partner from the pre- to postsession rating; a negative value indicates an increase.

description (on three different measures, only one of which is presented here). Most important, subjects given the Low Prestige treatment did not like their partner any more after the cheating session than they had before it. Thus, subjects who complied did not reduce dissonance by perceiving their partner as more attractive. With this avenue of dissonance reduction not utilized, the predicted effects of the independent variables on attitude change can be assessed more clearly.

Among the subjects who *refused* to comply, however, there was a consistent significant lowering of attraction toward, interest in, and personal liking for the partner. Moreover, this "rejection" of the partner was significantly greater for the High Prestige partner! Thus, it appears that one means of reducing the dissonance produced by deciding not to accept the influence of a High Prestige partner is to perceive him as not worthy. In fact, noncompliers in the High Cohesive condition liked their partner even less than did subjects in the Low Cohesive condition who complied, although prior to the influence attempt they liked him significantly more.

Public Compliance

First let's look at the results in terms of cheating and refusing to cheat in this situation. In spite of the difference between High and Low Machs in reported initial attitudes toward morality, the High Machs did not cheat more than the Lows; about half of each group complied and cheated. Of the 33 High Machs 16 cheated and 16 refused. One became suspicious of the bogus telephone call, ending the session before the cheating induction (his data were deleted from the analyses). Of the 28 Low Machs, 13 cheated and 15 refused.

Selective Cheating

Although the total frequency of cheating was the same for both Mach groups, High and Low Machs distributed their cheating and refusals between the High and Low Dissonance conditions quite differently, as is shown in Table 2. Low Machs cheated, as urged, about half the time, regardless of the dissonance condition. High Machs, on the other hand, discriminated between the two conditions. First, it proved almost impossible to pressure them into the dissonant cheating behavior in the High Dissonance condition (where they had Low Prestige partners and little justification for compliance). Less than a third of the High Machs cheated in this condition (5 out of 18), while more than three fourths of them cheated under the Low Dissonance condition (11 out of 14).

This finding makes sense in terms of the personality characteristics of High Machs described earlier. Allowing oneself to be manipulated into dissonant behavior with low justification is irrational by definition, and cheating in response to the partner's pressure involves allowing oneself to be manipulated. The special talent of the High Machs is manipulating others and resisting attempts by others to manipulate them. One way they do this is by remaining cool, de-

TABLE 2

NUMBER OF SUBJECTS WHO COMPLIED (CHEATED) AND REFUSED TO COMPLY, BY MACH AND DISSONANCE CONDITION

	High Machs		Low Machs	
	Cheated	Refused to Cheat	Cheated	Refused to Cheat
High Dissonance (Low Justification)	5	13	6	8
Low Dissonance (High Justification)	11	3	7	7
	16	16	13	15
	$\chi^2 = 6.22, p < 0.02$		$\chi^2 < 1.00$, n.s.	

tached, and emotionally uninvolved. They act on the basis of rational strategies, not impulses or feelings. Obviously, one rational way to avoid dissonant behavior is to refuse to engage in it.

In fact, those (5) subjects in the High Mach group who cheated when there was little justification (High Dissonance treatment) were *less* Machiavellian (on initial Mach scores) than those (11) who refused to comply ($p < 0.05$). Moreover, when there was adequate justification for cheating (Low Dissonance treatment), those (11) High Machs who complied were initially *more* Machiavellian than those (3) who did not ($p < 0.10$). For the Low Machs, there was no relationship between compliance and initial Mach scores.

Change in Private Attitudes After Cheating

Having publicly complied to the pressure exerted by one's partner to cheat, the dominant dissonance-reducing mechanism expected would be to change one's private attitudes to make them consistent with being a cheater. A consonant outcome could be produced by perceiving oneself as less moral, even though such a change in self-attitudes should conflict with one's self-esteem.

The data presented in Figure 1 offer confirmation of this dissonance prediction. Low Mach subjects who complied with the request to cheat under High Dissonance conditions (i.e., low justification due to a low-prestige, unattractive partner) subsequently *lowered* their endorsement of conventional morality. Those who cheated under Low Dissonance conditions (i.e., high justification due to a high-prestige, attractive partner) did just the opposite and raised their endorsement. Even with a small cell size, the difference between these two divergent patterns of response is significantly greater than the 0.01 level of probability. In addition, both of these changes are significantly different from zero ($p < 0.05$). Thus, the Low Machs who complied clearly behaved in accordance with expectations based upon a dissonance formulation.

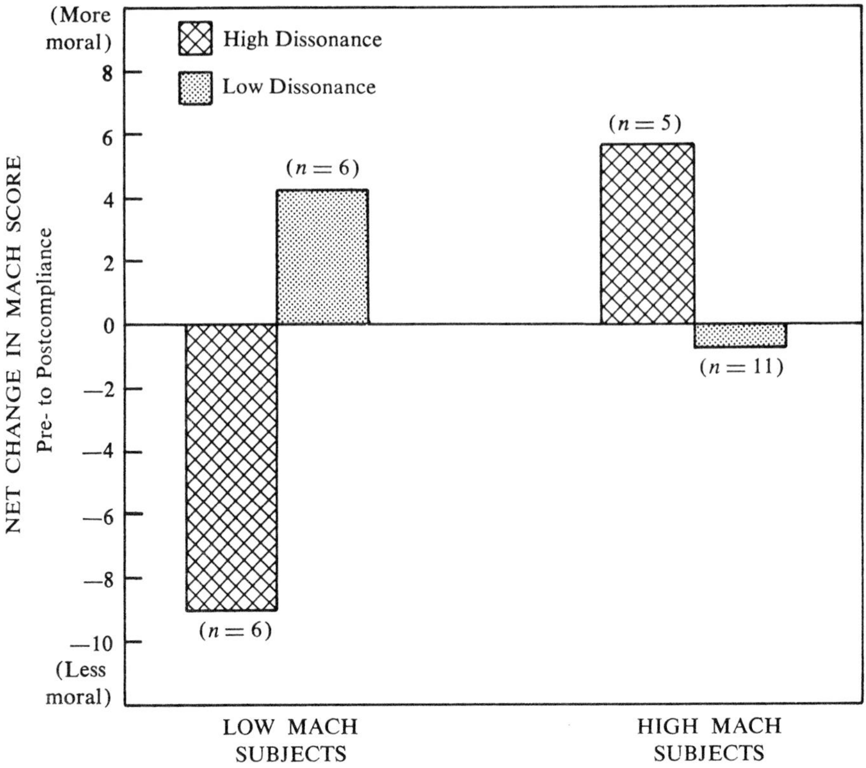

High vs. Low Dissonance:
For Low Mach subjects: $t = 4.35$, $p < .01$
For High Mach subjects: $t = 2.10$, $p < .10$

High vs. Low Mach subjects:
In the High Dissonance condition: $t = 4.05$, $p < .01$
In the Low Dissonance condition: $t = 1.95$, $p < .10$

FIGURE 1

Net change in attitude toward conventional morality after compliance (cheating), as measured by mean change in Mach Scale score.

What about the High Machs? They responded to the dissonance conditions in exactly the opposite way from the Low Machs. For the High Machs, compliance under High Dissonance conditions resulted in *greater* endorsement of conventional moral precepts, while under Low Dissonance there was no group change in attitudes ($p < 0.10$). Thus, neither the main effect of Machiavellianism nor the level of dissonance is significant, but the interaction between them is significant in precisely the manner predicted.

It should also be mentioned that those refusing to comply with the request to cheat not only derogated their partner (especially in the High Prestige condition) but also *increased* their endorsement of conventional morality (although not statistically significant).

DISCUSSION

It appears, then, that individuals who have adopted an interpersonal response style of manipulating others and resisting attempts by others to manipulate them avoid dissonant behavior by refusing to be "conned" into it. They act according to rational, pragmatic considerations and are not distracted by emotional involvements. In this study, their cheating or refusing to cheat was not based upon moral considerations but rather upon social conditions that provided appropriate justification. The High Machs ignored or were not sensitive to the additional cues provided by the physical presence of the partner. Their behavior was guided by the deceptive labels (cognitive cues) explicitly provided by the experimenter. When they did behave irrationally, they did not try to achieve the homeostasis posited by dissonance theory. In fact, just the opposite was true. They changed their attitudes to make them even more inconsistent with their behavior, becoming more moral after having cheated with insufficient justification. This raises a provocative issue of the possible utility of "dissonance therapy" for changing High Machs into Lows (i.e., as indicated by more moral Scale scores).

The Low Mach individuals evidently cheated or refused partly on the basis of moral principles and partly because of personal feelings for their partner that developed in the face-to-face situation—regardless of the verbal label and printed "demographic" information provided by the experimenter. Once having behaved in a way that should have aroused dissonance, they did reduce the cognitive inconsistency in the way predicted by dissonance theory: they changed their attitudes to define themselves as less moral.

Since High Machs more often refuse to comply under High Dissonance conditions and become more suspicious about experimental deceptions, it is likely that relatively more High than Low Mach subjects are likely to be lost or selectively excluded in forced public compliance dissonance experiments. Thus, it is possible that it is the overrepresented Low Machs who have provided much of the empirical data supporting dissonance predictions.

Awareness of this possible source of "bias" may help to increase the precision of the predictions made by dissonance theory as well as to suggest new areas or loci of dissonance research—for example, the study of cognitive-consistency reinforcement histories of individuals in subcultures characterized as being Machiavellian.

Editor's Comments

The results of this study indicate that High Machiavellians respond to dissonance situations differently from Low Machs and that it is only this latter group that behaves according to predictions derived from dissonance theory. However, we are still in the dark as to what is the crucial point in the dissonance sequence at which these groups diverge. Is it in the precommitment information processing, orientation, and evaluation stage? Or is it in the initial experience of confronting the dissonant cognitions, in the development of a tolerance for maintaining dissonance, or in more subtle and complex behavioral consequences of dissonance reduction than were measured in this research? Future research relying upon increased sophistication in technique and research design must address itself to uncovering the psychological process by which gross stimulus variables interact with subject dispositional variables to produce behavior change. Social psychologists will have to direct more attention to basic intra-individual processes if they are truly to understand human behavior as a function of social stimulus variables.

But is there enough evidence to suggest that it is worth-while to invest further energy and intellect in this way with regard to the variable of Machiavellianism? After all, this study is really little more than a pilot experiment with a small number of subjects, a theoretically "unpure" manipulation of dissonance, and an unusual measure of attitude change. However, the results of two recent doctoral dissertations offer an affirmative "go ahead."

Gilda Epstein (1966) varied Machiavellian level, dissonant activity, and type of sponsorship of a communication in a $2 \times 2 \times 2$ factorial design with 80 males from Columbia College. High and Low Machs either silently read speeches (Low Dissonance activity) or actively role played and improvised speeches (High Dissonance activity) arguing against their own initial attitudes toward fluoridation. The arguments used in the speeches were attributed to either a positive sponsor (scientific organization) or a negative one (layman). The results are clear, and they confirm the general finding of our cheating study. There was a significant interaction ($p < 0.025$) between Mach level and dissonance level: High Machs changed their attitudes slightly more under Low than High Dissonance, while Low Machs changed much more under High Dissonance. While there was no main effect of sponsor, there was greater attitude change produced by the negative sponsor than the positive sponsor under High Dissonance conditions. Moreover, most attitude change was found in the cell where dissonance effects should have been maximal—with Low Machs in a role-playing, effortful activity with a negative sponsor (weak justification). These findings not only increase our confidence in the relevance of Machiavellianism for our dissonance formulation, but they provide further support for the assumptions underlying the use of negative communicators in the grasshopper study and low cohesiveness in the present study. However, they do stand in opposition to the research of Janis and Gilmore (1965), which reports more opinion change for favorable sponsors under role-playing conditions.

Karen Bogart has clarified the questionable issues arising out of the present study in a carefully designed and rigorously executed experiment (1967). First, she provides a Control group of subjects who were not urged to cheat but who were treated identically and whose attitudes were measured at the same time as the experimental subjects. Then, because the prestige manipulation in our pilot study might have carried the implication that the partner was also more successful in carrying out the prohibited behavior, she separated the perceived prestige from the Machiavellianism of the *partner* by describing a High and Low Mach partner within each of the two prestige levels—e.g., a law student as High

Prestige, High Mach; a graduate physics major as High Prestige, Low Mach; a business administration student as Low Prestige, High Mach; and an industrial arts major as Low Prestige, Low Mach. In addition, she used a task where the partners had to cooperate closely in planning a speech (which makes a cohesiveness interpretation more relevant). The dissonance dilemma used was one in which subjects had to comply either with the rules of the experiment to argue a given position or with their partner's pressure to violate these rules by arguing a different position—one likely to produce a better evaluation for the team.

Her results (with a sample of 105 New York University undergraduate males, of whom 46 cheated, 41 did not, and 18 served as Controls) indicate that: (1) High Machs cheated more than Low Machs overall ($p < 0.05$); (2) High Machs were discriminating in their cheating while Lows were not; the Highs cheated significantly more frequently in response to pressure from High than from Low Prestige partners ($p < 0.025$); (3) once having engaged in the dissonant behavior, Low Machs under High Dissonance (Low Prestige) changed their attitudes significantly ($p < 0.05$) to make them consistent with their "immoral" behavior; (4) complying High Machs showed the opposite effect, becoming more moral under High Dissonance conditions and less under Low Dissonance (though not significantly); (5) the prestige effect was not influenced by differences in partner's manipulated Machiavellianism; and (6) in the Control group, there was no attitude-change difference between High and Low Machs, and the only group that differed significantly from these Controls was the Low Machs who cheated under High Dissonance conditions ($p < 0.05$).

Thus, the interaction of this type of individual-difference variable with dissonance conditions is not limited to a specific situation of dissonance arousal, type of compliant act, or unique response. Understanding of this relationship permits prediction of social behavior (selective cheating guided by perceived sources of justification) as well as of attitude change on important self-attitudes (morality) and opinion issues.

Brehm and Cohen (1962) cogently point up the manifold problems facing any attempt to interrelate personality characteristics and issues of dissonance arousal and reduction. However, such attempts might justify the risks involved since "it should be clear that there are advantages to be gained by both personality theory and dissonance theory if such coordination is made" (Brehm & Cohen, 1962, p. 177).

CONCLUSION

The reader, who is now cast in the role of juror to evaluate the validity of the claims we have made about psychological reality, is aware of the basic problem facing the defense in this concluding chapter of our testimony. It might seem that the extensive variety of evidence already advanced would dictate a strategy of resting the case with little more than a factual summation and a plea for a verdict of "proven." However, in the process of gathering, presenting, and evaluating the evidence, the scope of our inquiry has gradually widened, generating implications that extend far beyond our original focus. In fact, it is now difficult to think of expert testimony in almost any area of psychology, as well as some in related disciplines, that would not have some bearing upon this case.

Let us first review what we can conclude at a purely empirical level; that is, let us examine the phenomena that have been reliably demonstrated in this series of experiments. Then, given this data base, we may examine the theoretical conclusions that seem justified and, finally, reconsider the broader conceptual issues raised in the Introduction to this volume. Although we will present some additional evidence, observations, and speculations here to extend the sphere of application of our conclusions, we will not be able to explore in this text all of the available data and implications that may be relevant to an understanding of the cognitive control of motivation.

EMPIRICAL PHENOMENA

In cataloguing the relationships obtained experimentally between our independent variables and dependent measures, our primary attention will be centered upon those subjects who voluntarily committed themselves to a further state of deprivation or to more aversive stimulation or who agreed to engage in behavior that was discrepant with their attitudes or values—and did so for minimal incentives (namely little or no monetary reward or relatively few explicitly presented reasons supporting this commitment). Their behavior will be compared to groups of subjects randomly drawn from the same population who differ only either in being given no explicit choice in making the commitment or in being given choice but provided with more substantial incentives for the commitment (i.e., larger monetary rewards or more compelling reasons consistent with the commitment).

Articles 1 *and* 2. Subjects who had already missed two meals and who reported feeling hungry at the time they voluntarily committed themselves to forego another meal (for no money and few explicit reasons) subsequently reported themselves to be less hungry, ordered fewer items of food (for an anticipated free meal following deprivation), and exhibited less of a release of free fatty acids (FFA) into the blood than did the comparison groups (choice and \$5.00 incentive, no choice Controls, or choice and high rational justification).

Article 3. Subjects whose initial attitude toward eating Japanese grasshoppers was one of strong dislike reported liking them more and approved of more strongly worded personal endorsements for them after having eaten some at the request of a disliked, negatively evaluated communicator, as compared to the attitude change of Eaters responding to the inducement of a positive communicator and of Controls not given the experimental treatment. There was a trend for this result to be strongest with no monetary incentive for eating the grasshoppers and weakest when a 50-cent incentive was added.

Article 4. Thirst ratings were lower and water consumption less when subjects who had not drunk any liquids from bedtime to the afternoon of the next day voluntarily agreed to an additional 24-hour period of liquid deprivation for $1.00 (compared to those in a $5.00 condition). The effects (only a trend for water consumption) were greater when the presence of water was made salient during the commitment phase of the experiment.

Article 6. Similar, though more conclusive, results were found when subjects whose mouths were experimentally made to feel hot and dry voluntarily agreed to a 24-hour (versus a 4-hour) period of further deprivation with minimal rational justification (versus more extensive supporting reasons). Not only was their perceived thirst less and their water consumption reduced, but these subjects revealed the following behaviors that were more characteristic of No Thirst Controls than of Thirst Controls (no choice or future deprivation manipulation): slower learning on a paired-associate task involving liquid-related stimuli; perception of fewer liquid-related words than neutral ones on a perceptual task; fewer reports of themas expressing a need for water in response to a TAT-like projective stimulus with salient water-related cues; and more themas reflecting a generally troubled feeling.

Article 5. When the same experimental induction of thirst via a hot, dry mouth was coupled with the (hypnotically induced) inconsistent cognition of feeling one's stomach bloated with water, subjects rated their thirst lower and drank less (actually almost not at all) than comparable Hypnotic subjects given a thirst-irrelevant suggestion or than nonhypnotized Controls who role-played the bloated-stomach condition.

Articles 7 *and* 9. In a situation in which perceived pain, serial-anticipation learning, and GSR were related to the intensity of unavoidable electric shocks administered to the fingers of subjects, all three response measures were modified when individuals agreed to endure a second series of shocks after being explicitly given the option of refusing and few reasons for continuing. These subjects perceived an invariant level of painful shock to be somewhat less painful, their learning improved significantly, and their GSR to shock decreased significantly. Their pattern of response was more comparable to that of Control subjects for whom the shock intensity had been lowered by over 20 volts than it was to that of subjects given the same level of shock but no choice in continuing, or that of subjects given the same shock level, choice, and many reasons for continuing. In fact, their pattern of less perceived pain, smaller GSR, and improved learning was reproduced in a group of subjects given an hypnotic analgesia induction but was not replicated in role-playing analgesia subjects or in an achievement-oriented hypnotic group.

Articles 8 *and* 2. Following an acquisition period in an eyelid-conditioning task, subjects who were led to anticipate that the intensity of the UCS (air puff) would be increased showed a significant increment in percentage of conditioned eye-blink responses on the next ten trials. This effect was limited to those given no choice in whether to be exposed to the more noxious UCS and those given a choice to refuse but supplied with a series of rational arguments for continuing. This increase in conditioning was suppressed, however, in the group of subjects who voluntarily committed themselves to the increased UCS with only minimal supportive arguments provided by the experimenter.

This control of emotional arousal was also shown in an earlier study on stress. Subjects who showed most stress reaction (greatest release of free fatty acids, or FFA) to an initial needle puncture of an indwelling needle subsequently showed significantly less physiological arousal (as measured by FFA release) after they had voluntarily agreed to further needle puncture (in the course of a fasting experiment) for no monetary and only minimal rational incentives, relative to the comparison groups.

Article 10. Subjects desiring to perform well first experienced the difficult and unpleasant task of trying to recite and explicate a poem under conditions of delayed auditory feedback (DAF), then were asked to commit themselves to a second longer session in which they could expect to perform either about average or very poorly. Those who agreed to the task anticipating only moderate success, set a dial on the DAF apparatus at a level that would increase their chances of performing well, while those who made a discrepant commitment expecting failure set the dial at a level that they knew would increase both the difficulty of the task and their probability of failure.

Article 11. Greater recall of and shorter reaction times to failure-related than to nonfailure-related stimuli (in an incidental learning paradigm) were shown by subjects whose task achievement had been emphasized but who had voluntarily committed themselves, for a small monetary incentive of $1.00, to a task promising a high probability of failure. In addition, these subjects reported themselves as being less uncomfortable during the failure task and they had the poorest scores on a test measuring general level of task-persistent motivation (compared to No Choice Controls and those given either a low-probability-of-failure induction or a larger incentive of $5.00 for commitment).

Article 12. The effectiveness of verbal reinforcers for increasing the emission rate of reinforcement-contingent pronouns was shown to be enhanced by a prior operation of abrupt deprivation of social approval. However, subjects given this initial social-deprivation treatment who then voluntarily committed themselves to a second period of anticipated social disapproval for a small monetary incentive failed to show the conditioning effect. They behaved like a group of subjects who had not experienced any prior social deprivation and were significantly different from the comparison groups that did demonstrate a reliable acquisition curve (i.e., subjects given only the initial deprivation treatment and subjects given, in addition, a $5.00 rather than a $1.00 incentive for voluntary commitment to the interview with a disapproving interviewer).

Articles 13 *and* 14. Under certain specifiable conditions, the administration of a series of presumably intense shocks to, or the verbal derogation of, a helpless nonprovocative victim resulted in marked attitudinal, perceptual, and behavioral effects. The victim was evaluated more negatively and his pain was minimized, while the subject evaluated himself more negatively, felt more obligated to behave as he did, and recalled fewer negative consequences of using electric shock as functions of the following manipulated variables: high choice to aggress, high level of aggression, minimal external reasons given to support the aggression, and no anticipated future interaction with the victim. When the victim could not readily be devalued because the aggressor was initially attracted to him, then, instead, attitudes toward the use of shock in human research became more favorable. The individual-difference variable of self-esteem was related to the victim derogation noted above, with those having higher levels of self-esteem derogating the victim more.

Article 15. When subjects attempting to create a favorable public impression were frustrated by being insulted by a stranger, they developed a dislike for that stranger. However, when these subjects were given the opportunity to interact closely with that person on a second task, their attitudes toward him became more favorable when they could explicitly choose whether or not to do so. Moreover, this attitude change was carried over into behavioral responses to this person. Retaliatory aggression (frequency and duration of shocks given to the partner) did not increase as the agent of frustration increased his provocation of these subjects (i.e., delivered many rather than few blasts of white noise to the subject during a problem-solving task). In contrast, those not insulted but given the choice to interact with the partner and those not given a choice to work with the insulting partner delivered more shocks as provocation increased.

Article 16. When subjects were induced by their partners to engage in the value-discrepant behavior of cheating on an experimental task, they changed their degree of endorsement of conventional morality as a function of the attractiveness of the partner and their own initial level of Machiavellianism. Those subjects who were low on a Mach Scale found cheating more acceptable if they had voluntarily agreed to cheat at the request of a low-prestige, unattractive partner (compared to a high-prestige, attractive one). On the other hand, High Mach subjects who cheated under these conditions came to espouse a more moral position.

From these findings we may conclude that under the experimental conditions described, the following spectrum of behavior can be effectively modified by the manipulation of the variables of choice, incentive for commitment, pre-commitment level of motivation, anticipated severity of future deprivation or of the expected aversive-stimulus situation, and the attributes of the agent of influence:

1. *Subjective:* attitudes toward self, others, specific foods, cheating, and administering shock; perception of feelings of hunger, thirst, pain, obligation, self-comfort; perception of thirst-related stimuli and projected themas.

2. *Behavioral:* amount of food requested and water consumed; reaction time; task persistence; setting a task level of difficulty; recall of negative attrib-

utes; recall in incidental learning; speed of paired-associate and serial-anticipation learning; amount of verbal and eyelid conditioning; frequency and duration of shocks given to another person.

3. *Physiological:* release of free fatty acids in response to hunger and stress, galvanic skin response to electric shock, and basal skin resistance to situational demands.

Lack of Research on Sexual Deprivation

In any program of research, such as this one, that purports to say something about the extent to which the phenomena just described can be generalized to all motivational states, research on commitment to sexual deprivation is conspicuously absent. However, our failure (and that of our colleagues) to engage in controlled laboratory research on human sexual motivation is the result of a number of practical considerations and a few ethical ones rather than a lack of significant theoretical problems. Therefore, at present, we must rely upon the less than adequate evidence gathered in field studies, which is usually incidental to the major purpose of the study. The following remarks, then, should be taken as only tentative clues to the relevance of our general paradigm for an understanding of the control of sexual motivation. The reader can perhaps supplement them with his own uncontrolled observations.

In the Antarctic, there are research and military stations that are totally isolated from the outside world for eight to ten months a year, where temperatures drop as low as −104°F. and winds go up to 130 knots per hour. One recent psychiatric evaluation of the reactions of 163 men who had volunteered for Operation Deep Freeze concluded:

> Acceptance by an individual of commitment to isolation, with the knowledge that there is no escape, results in concern with a different class of adjustment problems than those problems experienced by people in isolation who are not so committed (Rohrer, 1960, p. 23).

One of the adjustment problems alluded to was a rather dramatic change in sexual attitudes and behavior, as revealed in these statements by the men themselves:

> "You put women out of your mind."
>
> "Down here you handle sex by trying to keep it off your mind. It isn't here, so you might as well forget about it and that's what I did."
>
> "I came down here to prove something to myself and I failed. I'm just no good as a man, I guess."
>
> "The day I jumped off the boat and landed here, my virility jumped up four times as strong. I'll be honest, sometimes I was masturbating four or five times a day at first, and did it daily, sometimes twice daily, until August, and then the need for it completely disappeared."
>
> (Rohrer, 1960, p. 13)

A similar set of incidental observations was made on the conscientious objectors who volunteered for the Minnesota semistarvation studies during World War II (cf. Keys, Brozek, Henschel, Mickelson, & Taylor, 1950). Sexual urges decreased markedly during their period of confinement and then were slow to return during the rehabilitation period. Subjects reportedly "cooled noticeably" toward their girl friends, and their courtships collapsed.

Could we demonstrate that voluntary commitment for minimal incentives to a prolonged period of heterosexual deprivation among normally arousable subjects would result in reduced sexual drive? Would sexual stimuli become less effective as reinforcers? Would the incidence of sexual dreams and sexual arousal during sleep decrease? Would there be underestimations in judgments of the erotic zones of the body of opposite-sex members? Our theoretical model would probably predict affirmative answers to these and related queries. The systematic study of sexual motivation might enable the investigator to address himself more clearly than we have been able to in our research to the problem of distinguishing between true reduction of motivation and suppression or denial of it, which might be revealed in a variety of displaced, indirect indicators of sexual arousal.

THEORETICAL ANALYSIS

Recently at the University of Canterbury, New Zealand, a simple experiment was conducted to determine whether psychophysical judgments could be influenced by the disproportionality of reward to the effort involved in making the judgments (Wilson & Russell, 1966). Subjects had to estimate the vertical height to which they lifted a light and a heavy weight (the actual lifted height, specified by the experimenter, was held constant). Some subjects performed the task without remuneration; for some, a larger reward (a shilling) was paired with the heavier weight and a smaller reward (a penny) with the lighter; the members of a third group received only a penny for lifting the heavy weight and a shilling for lifting the light one. This last, disproportionate reward-to-effort group overestimated (to five times the actual amount) the height to which they lifted the light weight (high reward) while underestimating that of the heavy weight (low reward) and they did so significantly more ($p < 0.025$) than the other groups. Although Wilson and Russell were not working from a dissonance theory orientation, they interpreted their findings in terms of a dissonance model, according to which the cognitive dissonance created by working hard for small rewards and receiving relatively large rewards for easy work is reduced by a "perceptual and/or judgmental distortion effect."

Investigator Wilson provides (in a personal communication to this author) what may be considered the keynote statement for introducing the appropriateness of a dissonance theory analysis for both his and our empirical findings:

> As one whose interests and activities are predominately psychophysical and sensory, it was somewhat disturbing to find that

> dissonance reduction, or the phenomenon we demonstrated and never mind what it is called, could alter a set of judgments in a way which is not currently recognized by experimental psychologists. I should undertake the exercise of examining a large body of experimental literature for the sole purpose of unearthing incidents where responses and consequently the results could in part at least be a manifestation of dissonance reduction. For most subjects there is a lot to be lost and gained personally in the few minutes they act as guinea pigs and when something personal is at stake we can expect mechanisms such as dissonance to operate.

Unless there is some unknown error structure (cf. Kruskal, 1967) common to all studies we have examined, we have demonstrated a real phenomenon in which a diverse set of responses is functionally related to a variety of antecedent variables. To maintain the conservative focus of the empiricist and thereby avoid the risks involved in drawing theoretical inferences would be to ignore the heuristic power of Festinger's theory of cognitive dissonance, which generated this entire body of results, as well as its integrative facility in meaningfully relating the cognitive input variables to the behavioral consequences via the constructs of dissonance arousal and reduction.[1] To be sure, not all of the hypotheses tested in these studies were rigorously derived from the explicitly formulated statement of dissonance theory (Festinger, 1957); but they were directly suggested by, or the research was clearly stimulated by, the theory and its subsequent reformulations (notably Brehm & Cohen, 1962). Especially at the stage of translating the abstract propositions of the theory into specific, experimental operations, many extratheoretical assumptions were required. However, while it is possible to erect an alternative theoretical explanation to account for the results of any one experiment or subset of them, only dissonance theory can satisfactorily and parsimoniously account for all of them. Moreover, it can be shown that the predictive precision of the theory is further improved by taking into account theoretically relevant individual-difference variables.

The Dissonance Explanation: A Modified Version

Although Emerson claimed that "consistency is the hobgoblin of little minds," the basic assumption of dissonance theory, which is underscored by our research, is that people do in fact strive for consistency. Thus, whenever one has made a decision, it becomes important that it appear to oneself and to others that the decision is consistent with the information available and that its consequences are consistent with the premises on which it was based. Dissonance can be viewed as a probability function of the likelihood of a particular decision given only the individual's cognitions of his internal state and of the external stimulus

1. A recent, thorough, but not exhaustive, search of the published American literature reveals about three hundred items pertaining to the theory of cognitive dissonance; a bibliography is in preparation by S. Margulis and Francis Cathcart, University of Florida.

conditions relevant to that decision. If dissonance is so viewed, then the magnitude of dissonance created by the decision to engage in the motive- and attitude-discrepant behaviors we have investigated here becomes a function of the combined magnitude of those variables that could be used as evidence supporting the *contrary* decision, or lowering the probability of the chosen action. If a man is hungry and food is available, it is highly likely that he will eat; therefore, the probability that he will refuse the food and agree to fast for an extended period of time is low. Obviously, however, there can be extenuating circumstances that increase the probability of this occurrence—such as the constraints provided by threats or by promises of large rewards, the existence of some unusual state of mind in which "reason is suspended" (insanity, intoxication, etc.), or the operation of religious, political, dietary, or cosmetic reasons to support voluntary fasting. On the other hand, the fasting of this hungry person is more inconsistent with a rational model of behavior predictability the greater his initial drive level, the more severe his anticipated deprivation, the greater his freedom of choice, and the fewer the number of supporting justifications.

Within the drive-reduction process postulated by Festinger's theory, incongruity then becomes a proximal stimulus for the instigation of operations and behaviors directed toward its own removal (cf. Levy, 1963). The intensity of attempts at dissonance reduction are reflections of the inferred magnitude of dissonance aroused. In our research we have both assumed and arranged experimental conditions such that a dominant dissonance-reducing reaction would be to alter one's motivational state to make it consistent with the discrepant behavioral commitment. It is this presumed basic change in motivation that accounts for (is reflected in) the host of phenotypically dissimilar behaviors observed. Thus, at a theoretical level, this research purports to demonstrate that in the process of dissonance reduction, biologically-based drive states and socially-learned motives may be altered and brought under the control of those cognitive variables that influence dissonance arousal.

The Dissonance-Reduction Phenomenon

The basic behavioral process we have been studying can be thought of as a "response effect" and is nicely illustrated in the following excerpt:

> . . . and whistle a happy tune, so no one will suspect I'm afraid. The result of this deception is very strange to tell, for when I fool the people I fear, I fool myself as well (Oscar Hammerstein, "The King and I").

and in J. M. Barrie's sweet lemon philosphy of life which consists "not in doing what you like, but in liking what you do."

A more precise statement about how responses may feed back to modify the stimulus conditions that initiated them—the most fascinating process in the forced-compliance situations reported in this volume—comes from the systematic research of Block and Reiser (1962) and Reiser and Block (1965) on discrimination and recognition of weak stimuli. When visual stimuli are too weak to elicit correct verbal identification because they are presented below visual threshold, autonomic (GSR) responses may still reflect both the nature of the stimuli and/or the nature of the mistaken identifications. Block and Reiser have repeatedly found that when a subject makes an immediate commitment to a given identification, autonomic mobilization is in accord with the mistaken identification rather than with the nature of the stimulus; *the effect of the response overrides the effect of the true stimulus!* When an immediate commitment is not required, then subliminal information regarding the true nature of the stimulus is made full use of and gains exclusive access to autonomic centers.

This physiological response to one's own decision enables the person to create a new level of reality that may in turn be used to provide a firmer basis for validating both the wisdom and internal consistency of the decision. We have carried this argument further by assuming that in the process of denying the "objective" impact of drive stimuli upon himself, the dissonant individual functionally lowers the drive itself.

Drive Reduction versus Drive Suppression. The question of whether dissonance reduction actually weakens a drive or merely temporarily suppresses its manifestation was made salient by Mansson's data, which showed that thirsty High Dissonance subjects overreacted in denying their thirst. On a number of measures they appeared to be even less thirsty than Control subjects known not to be thirsty. However, on a projective measure in which they gave few need-for-water responses to an obviously water-related picture, they gave more such responses to a picture without water cues and they revealed themselves to be more generally troubled or upset. This finding is reminiscent of those reported in two earlier studies on anxiety. Zimbardo, Barnard, and Berkowitz (1963) found that highly defensive, test-anxious children were better able to control their verbal behavior (that is, appear not anxious) under normally anxiety-provoking evaluative-interview conditions than under permissive conditions where the lack of structure eliminated discriminative cues used in defending against (suppressing) anxiety. Fenz (1964) showed that in TAT stories constructed on the day of their jump, novice parachutists denied any fear of jumping. This effect was limited, however, to a highly relevant stimulus picture of a man about to parachute, and they did express considerable fear in reacting to a picture unrelated to parachuting. That they were in fact made anxious by the impending jump was evidenced by their increasingly steep GSR gradients produced only to parachute-relevant words with increasing proximity to jump time.

This general question of weakened drive versus suppressed drive manifestation is difficult to answer, then, as long as reactive measures with high face validity are used to assess dissonance. However, we have been able to show dissonance-reduction effects on GSR measures to pain, on free-fatty-acid release to hunger and stress, and on eyelid conditioning, as well as on other measures involving minimal self-descriptive aspects. In addition, two recent dissertations have replicated our GSR finding. Lewin (1965) found a highly significant ($p < 0.001$) linear trend of pain tolerance to electric shocks increasing as monetary incentives associated with the shocks decreased (over five levels). Penner (1966) in a supplementary finding to his excellent study (demonstrating the superiority of dissonance to counterconditioning theory in predicting resistance to extinction effects) also shows that the less one is rewarded for pain, the less it hurts. The dissonance aroused by working for a low reward under high shock was reduced in part by minimizing the pain: GSR decreased from the first to the last of 21 shocks in 62 per cent of the Low Reward group, 50 per cent of the Moderate Reward group, and only 30 per cent of the High Reward group ($p < 0.02$). Also relevant is Gerard's (1967) finding of greater constriction in pulse amplitude immediately after (but not before) a decision involving similar (high dissonance) alternatives than after such a decision between dissimilar ones.

Finally, the complexity of thinking in terms of "real" drive reduction (raised initially when we considered whether Aesop's "sour grapes" fox was really not hungry when he said he wasn't) can be seen from the research on obesity by Stunkard (1959). He reports that obese women don't report hunger contractions when they occur because they experience intense social pressure about eating and are in a conflict about eating. Their "denial of hunger extended to denial of sensations of epigastric emptiness and of desire to eat—fundamental characteristics of the hunger experience among nonobese women" (Stunkard, 1959, p. 288). But in order for these women to remain obese, they must eat more than nonobese women. Should we conclude that they are suppressing the hunger or are less hungry? Or is it more valuable to recast the formulation as Schachter (1967) has done and view their denial of hunger as shifting the locus of control of eating behavior from the internal cues related to the physiology of the hunger experience to external stimulus cues related to characteristics of the food and conditions associated with eating? In choosing the latter explanation, we might say then not that dissonance changes drive states but rather that it weakens the control of stimuli that normally direct behavior in favor of others that reflect more central, cognitive control.

Some Experimental Exceptions: Factors Involved

In our validation of dissonance theory, we have employed a method of experimental proof based upon demonstration of statistically significant differences among group averages—an approach that has ignored the persistent minority of individual cases that do not fit the dissonance prediction.[2] The apparent challenge these exceptions pose to the adequacy of the theory can be turned to an advantage if this "unexplained" variance can be accounted for by theoretically relevant principles. Although we have not as yet made a systematic study of deviant cases, a number of recent investigations have sought to explain individual differences in the perception and interpretation of dissonance-related stimulus conditions and in mode of response to dissonance.

Personality Type. Evidence of the occurrence of "choiceless" dissonance

2. Obviously individual exceptions to the principal results of any of the experiments presented in this text are to be expected because the research strategy was not tailored to individual differences in background, responsiveness, or any other variables that might affect reactions on the dependent measures. Instead, we used uniform presentation and manipulation of the stimulus and the experimental treatments across all subjects within each group.

was uncovered as an incidental finding in Neulinger's dissertation research (1965). He was able to track down and identify a subgroup of subjects whose atypical (though uniform) reaction to engaging in discrepant behavior under No-Choice conditions initially resulted in an apparent disconfirmation of the dissonance prediction. The hypothesis under investigation was that individuals would react with less negative effect to the unpleasant aspects of a given situation (*Press*) which is more incongruent than congruent with their dominant personality typology (*Type*) if they enter the Press under High Choice (dissonance-creating) conditions. Under the guise of a study on the effects of fatigue on aesthetic judgments (the "too long at the museum" effect), subjects of each of two personality types responded to a series of slides under Congruent and Incongruent conditions while standing on one leg at a time (for a total of 40 minutes). The dependent measure was the perceived difficulty of standing on one leg. The personality types (determined by Stein's, 1963a, need typology) were: "*Socially Oriented Type* (IBR)—characterized by a need to please others, apprehension at being critical, fear of being criticized, preference of a structured, familiar environment requiring little initiative"; and "*Intellectually Oriented Type* (IIEQ)—concerned with achievement, independence, novelty, and little concern about being critical." Therefore, in order to introduce the incongruity between Type and Press, a task requiring extensive criticism or praise was chosen.

As predicted, incongruity resulted in less perceived difficulty (of standing on one leg) for both types (taken together) under High Choice conditions than did Type-Press congruity. However, the same result occurred under Low Choice conditions. Neulinger then showed that the Socially Oriented Type behaved as theoretically expected, responding to the two choice situations differently, but the Intellectually Oriented Type did not. When this group, which generally is characterized by their need for autonomy, was dichotomized into those high and low in this need, a clear pattern emerged. The data for those low in need for autonomy was in line with the data for the other groups and followed the prediction of differential reaction to incongruity depending upon differences in choice. In contrast, those with high need for autonomy showed even greater dissonance effects under Low Choice than under High! For them, the freedom to satisfy one's need for autonomy is always the critical dimension of response in any interaction. Therefore, being induced to function in a situation where they perceive they have little or no choice is maximally discrepant with their self-image. Such subjects, then, react to dissonance under High Choice as do other subjects, but they react to a limitation of their autonomy differently from the way others do.

Awareness of the relationship between dominant personality styles and situational characteristics is also important for locating systematic sources of bias in sampling. For example, Neulinger's study revealed that the Socially Oriented Type is significantly less likely to volunteer for an experiment than is the Intellectually Oriented Type (47 per cent versus 13 per cent, $p < 0.01$), probably because of the former's apprehension of self-exposure and novelty contrasted with the latter's intellectual curiosity. Thus, in research using volunteer populations, the former type will be underrepresented; however, once in the experimental situation, this Socially Oriented Type should be less likely to refuse to engage in dissonant behavior than the more autonomous Intellectually Oriented Type. Moreover, we might infer that when subjects (from the traditional introductory psychology pool) are allowed to select the experiments in which they will serve, the more curious Intellectually Oriented Type will be overrepresented in research done early in the school term, while research performed closer to the deadline for fulfilling the subject requirement will be biased with relatively more of the Socially Oriented Type.

Cognitive Style. The results of a study by Harvey and Ware (1967) suggest that "concreteness of conceptual functioning disposes toward a low tolerance of dissonance and toward resolving cognitive inconsistency in ways different from the modes of resolution that result from abstract functioning" (pp. 229–230). "Concrete" and "abstract" subjects (characterized by a test of how they differentiated and organized concepts of relevant aspects of their world) evaluated an object person on the basis of two inconsistent sets of information: the first showed the person to have been bad in the past, while the second revealed him to be good now (and vice versa for half the subjects). The greater need for cognitive consistency and lowered tolerance for dissonance among the Concrete subjects (compared to the Abstract subjects) was illustrated in a series of self-report measures, where they were more aware of and disturbed by the inconsistency, couldn't integrate it, gave fewer explanations for it, used stereotypic labels in their explanations, and reacted differently on still other dimensions.

Wollitsky (1967) formulated a similar continuum to characterize his subjects according to cognitive style. After he failed to find the expected greater denial of the cigarette-smoking–cancer link among smokers than nonsmokers, Wollitsky showed that this dissonance-reducing reaction did occur in subjects whose cognitive style could be characterized as "flexible" but not in subjects who were cognitively "constricted." Subjects were identified along a constricted-flexible dimension on the basis of their susceptibility to the interference of compelling, irrelevant stimuli on a color-word task (i.e., they had to read the verbal labels of color names written in different colors; see Stroop, 1935). Constricted subjects, who are interference prone, were more likely to believe in smoking as a cause of cancer and to have tried to reduce their cigarette consumption. On the other hand, flexible subjects, who avoided or denied instrusions on the predictor task (thus reacting adaptively), also tended to deny the causal link between smoking and cancer (thus acting maladaptively) and to carry this belief denial into behavior, maintaining their smoking habit.

In the studies reported in this volume by Cohen and Zimbardo (Article 10) and by Schlachet (Article 11), not all subjects who committed themselves to an anticipated failure experience reacted in a way that could be interpreted as lowering their achievement motivation. Subsequent research has shown that perhaps these subjects were members of a subset of individuals who use the sensitizing defenses of intellectualization and projection when faced with threatening stimuli. Glass, Canavan, and Schiavo (1968), using female subjects, replicated the basic finding of the two earlier studies, using even more direct measures of achievement motivation, but they did not find any dissonance effect for "sensitizers." It was only among subjects characterized as "repressors" (by a prior self-report test) that commitment to failure for minimal incentives resulted in a "reduction in cognized intensity of motivation to succeed," as well as a devaluation of the task and test situation.

Threat of Being Wrong. The mode of dissonance reduction employed is not only a function of learned response preferences or cognitive styles but also depends upon certain stimulus properties and expectations. Individuals tend to choose the mode of dissonance reduction that has the most perceived stability—the one that is not challenged by presently available information nor likely to come under reality attack in the future. Walster, Berscheid, and Barclay (1967) support this proposition with the finding of a significant triple-order interaction in the way nursery-school children changed their ratings of each of two toys after choosing one and rejecting the other on the basis of their expectation of receiving objective information about one of them. The children increased their liking of the toy that couldn't be devalued by future information, and the often-found dissonance effect—the spreading apart in attractiveness of the chosen and rejected alternatives—was considerably weakened when they expected information that *might* prove they made the wrong decision.

Socio-Economic Class. The response to dissonance may also vary as a function of the subjects' socio-economic class. Ostfeld and Katz (1967) offer evidence that in the situation they studied, lower-class children do not experience or respond to dissonance in the same way as middle-class children. In their study, nursery-school children were forbidden to play with a favorite toy under conditions of mild threat (Low Justification) or severe threat (High Justification). According to dissonance theory (cf. Aronson & Carlsmith, 1963), the behavior of not playing with a valued toy is more dissonant the weaker the threats used to enforce this commitment. The dissonance-reducing response was shown by all the middle-class children, who devalued their toys under mild threat but not under severe; the lower-class children, however, found their toys equally less attractive following both threats. In an ingenious use of an unobtrusive response measure, the authors also had the children color pictures of toys with crayons whose colors were also ranked. All the children colored their favorite toys with their favorite crayon colors before the dissonance manipulation; however, after it, middle-class children used a less-favored crayon for the picture of the taboo toy more after mild than after severe threat. A significant triple-order interaction also occurred in this study when for lower-class children this nonverbal measure was found to be unrelated to severity of threat or to changes in verbal statements about the attractiveness of the toys.

The studies cited above and those presented earlier relating self-esteem and also Machiavellianism to dissonance processes represent only part of the growing body of experimentation on the complexities underlying the superficial simplicity of the dissonance theory formulation (see especially Bishop's 1967 analysis of the special meaning of monetary incentives to "anal" subjects). Although it is clear that some behavior can be predicted knowing only the nature of the significant prevailing social-stimulus conditions, a better understanding and more refined and complex predictions result from studying the interaction of current social stimuli with relevant individual-difference variables reflecting prior response histories, perceptual orientations, skills, and capabilities. Obviously, what is needed is a theoretical formulation of these processes rather than more of the piecemeal approach arbitrarily yoking together "personal" and social variables.

The Nature of Decision Making

There is much critical contention over the importance of the act of deciding in generating the changes in perception, judgment, behavior, and motivation that we have seen in our research. Although the research of Festinger (1964) and his students has rather effectively differentiated the conflict occurring prior to the decision from the dissonance that follows it, nevertheless one reviewer of these studies concludes that the predecision process may be thought to be continuous with the postdecision process unless it can be demonstrated that attention to and evaluation of the alternatives is different in these two temporarily distinct stages (Rosenberg, 1966a). Similarly, Deutsch and Krauss (1965) maintain that the arousal of dissonance can occur with or without there having been a decision made and that dissonance thus is not an inevitable consequence of decisions.

By continuously monitoring the momentary changes in attention toward each of the alternatives involved in a decision, Gerard (1967) suggests one methodological approach to this theoretical question. He shows that decision making is a discontinuous process in which behavior following an overt decision is qualitatively different from that preceding it. Prior to decision, Gerard's subjects focused on the alternative that they eventually *rejected* more than the one they accepted, but the act of deciding shifted their focus to the chosen alternative. Thus, the process of accumulating evidence and establishing a preference, which enables one to make a decision, becomes extremely biased following the decision, presumably to justify it.

Not only do pre and postdecision processes differ qualitatively, but the act of decision making itself is different from the act of establishing a preference. Preferences are necessary to locate a suitable construction site, but decisions become the blueprints which determine the very shape of the construction. Attention to alternatives should be equally divided and information seeking should be open and objective when evaluation has no consequences other than the establishment of a personal preference. The demand imposed by having to make a decision to reject one alternative while accepting the other biases the information processing. Gerard's data suggest that the initial concern of the subject is with what he has to lose in the potentially rejected alternative but that the decision then reverses the orientation toward what has been gained with the chosen alternative. It might be interesting to study this process and the dissonance consequences while varying the anticipated time available prior to overt decision making and then forcing a "premature" decision.

We assume, then, that decisions do not create dissonance when they are, in effect, no different from preferences—that is, when they do not have meaningful consequences for the individual. Moreover, since we acknowledge individual variations in preferences (as "taste"), they do not have to be defended or justified as do decisions.[3] Dissonance processes can be definitely assumed to operate only when decisions become commitments.

The Importance of Choice and Commitment

In our introductory remarks, we pointed to the vital role of choice in influencing the direction of human behavior. Brehm and Cohen have said that "it may be that volition is implicit in any situation of unequivocal dissonance arousal" (1962, p. 302). This is true because, as in criminal proceedings, it is necessary to determine volition in the decision in order to assign responsibility for its consequences. When a decision has (potentially) negative consequences, then the exercise of one's volition in that decision—even if there is only an "illusion of choice" (as Kelley, 1968, describes the situation we have used)—makes salient one's initiative and involves one in all of the consequences, even those unanticipated. Similarly, in legal proceedings, the lack of anticipation of negative consequences does not preclude the assignment of direct responsibility: as long as past volition *could have* prevented the consequences, the person is guilty of criminal negligence (an interesting area for psychological investigation).

Freedman's (1963) view that dissonance may be aroused even when choice is negligible is supported in a recent study by Brock (1968). However, Brock's experimental design also enabled him to demonstrate that "volition may be a more powerful determinant of dissonance than any others studied thus far" (p. 60). His data show that dissonance reduction at each of three levels of justification (with eight, three, or no reasons to engage in a boring task) increases with increases in volition.

Although volition in decision making is an important determinant of dissonance, it is not a necessary condition, because dissonance (like relatives) can be inherited. Responsibility for *maintaining*, rather than initiating, a given decision can be inherent in a given role and can create dissonance to the degree that the individual takes his self-definition from his role behavior and a vital part of that role involves keeping commitments. The obvious applicability of this principle to political and international commitments requires no further comment for the reader aware of the potential force behind these dissonance-laden, inherited commitments.

Before considering *why* individuals strive toward consistency, let us mention in passing several characteristics of commitment that make it indispensable in the generation of dissonance. Commitment to a given alternative or course of

3. In passing, it should be observed that even preferences and value judgments may have consequences when they are communicated by people in the public eye and others act upon them. Thus, those in "positions of responsibility" are held responsible for the public effects of their private behavior because their preferences may have the status of decisions for others. Looked at differently, the extent to which an individual's preferences or decisions have consequences for others is one measure of social power and influence.

action involves the risk of being wrong, of self-exposure, of potential loss. Commitment, then, always involves one action at the expense of others, with the knowledge that the rejected alternative has positive features that others may find more acceptable or that it has nonobvious aspects that may be discovered and preferred by others. This is why there can be no such process as an approach-approach conflict (except in the most trivial sense). The act of deciding always incurs some loss. Commitment also involves setting oneself in opposition to real or imagined others. The very act of making a commitment for which one assumes responsibility *individuates* the decision maker and sets him apart from the tribe.[4] The committed man must be prepared to become the enemy of the people in order to defend his commitment. Commitment invariably leads to dissonance when it becomes inextricably linked with one's self-definition. When one perceives that his choice places him on the same evaluative continuum as the object of his choice, then he becomes involved with the instrumental function of his response in defining his personal worth, intelligence, sensitivity, etc. (cf. Zimbardo, 1960). Commitment forces one to articulate his position, thereby increasing the chance of a definitive test of its validity and of being proven wrong.

Finally, commitment is essentially an investment of energy to cope with the perceived demands of the environment, in an attempt to control that environment. If the expectations that fostered the commitment are in danger of being disconfirmed, the individual's feeling of control is diminished. Dissonance then operates by providing an appropriate set of preprogrammed efferent instructions ready for immediate use (cf. Festinger, Ono, Burnham, & Bamber, 1967) which enable the individual to defend his commitment and maintain, at least temporarily, some feeling of control and autonomy.

The Value of Consistency: Social and Personal

What are the issues confronting the subject in any one of these experiments at the moment when he makes the commitment to engage in the motive-discrepant behavior with minimal justification? Most obvious, but not necessarily most potent, is his concern about the direct implications for his well-being and functioning of the deprivation state or aversive stimulus. However, there are two other general areas of concern: the social-psychological implications of making commitments in the face of inconsistency and the personal implications of behaving irrationally.

Inconsistency motivates behavior not because of some innately determined perception of structural inconsistency between cognitive elements but because

4. Special conditions of time distortion and anonymity enable the individual to eschew responsibility, result in suspension of concern over negative evaluation by others (shame) and by one's self (guilt), and create a state of *de-individuation* (cf. Festinger, Pepitone, & Newcomb, 1952). Thus, perceived loss of personal identity or excessive stimulus arousal may temporarily overwhelm the cognitive controls that normally individuate people, restrain antisocial behavior, and limit self-gratification (as in Mardi Gras, primitive rituals, orgies, mob hysteria, or the aggressive behavior of deindividuated subjects described by Zimbardo, Abric, Lange, Rijsman, Bokorova, Potocka-Hoser, and Honai, 1967).

of the learned value and significance of consistency. In most cultures, consistency, if it is not prized in and for itself, is certainly reinforced as a general behavior underlying a multitude of specific responses. In our society, the "golden rule" stresses interpersonal consistency, the hypocrite is derided because his actions are inconsistent with his words, our child-rearing practices build consistency into almost every aspect of human functioning, and our educational systems emphasize logical consistency and historical continuity. The imposition of the human concept of time on the flow of events makes causal consistency a reality and traps present behavior between past commitments and future obligations and expectations. Consistency is nurtured not only directly by being reinforced but also indirectly by being observed as a pattern in which reinforcements are related to responses. The importance of this "learning" of consistency will become blatantly obvious if, as it now appears, one of the determinants of childhood schizophrenia is proven to be parental inconsistency in reinforcing the child's behavior.

Therefore, when a person makes a decision that has a low probability of occurrence given the available information, he should feel *atypical.* Without knowledge of the decisions of others (a variable that ought to be manipulated in future research), his discrepant commitment should result in his feeling noncomparable with those to whom he usually refers his behavior. The individual wants to be perceived as "normal" (in a statistical sense), to be similar to other members of his reference group—not to be a deviant. In the absence of social-comparison information to establish the normality of his act, he must establish its rationality. He reasons that others would have behaved as he did if they saw the situation as he does and that although his behavior may at first glance seem unusual, it actually follows rationally from the stimulus conditions (as he has reinterpreted them). A systematic integration of social-comparison theory (Festinger, 1954), Bem's (1967) provocative self-perception model, and dissonance theory is needed to develop the social implications of this aspect of dissonance generated by inconsistency between a discrepant commitment and concern for evaluation of the self by others.

Consistency is also valued because of its role in social control and for what it implies about personal control. By increasing the predictability of behavior (on an actuarial basis), consistency oils the machinery of social interaction and facilitates the management of behavior. Moreover, behavior that is not under the spurious control of interpersonal predictability appears as a danger to others, and they will take steps either to increase its predictability (i.e., make it consistent with rationally perceived causes, with past behavior, or with their own behavior), or to reject or even isolate the inconsistent offender from the society.

On a more primitive, personal level, consistency is a safeguard against chaos, it is the ordering aspect of rationality that is in constant struggle with the irrational forces within and outside the individual. Thus, consistency becomes a self-imposed principle in order for the individual to maintain a conception of himself as a normal member of society, who in behaving as others expect him to gains their social recognition (the most potent of all reinforcers) as a rational decision maker, whose decisions help him to control his environment.

GENERAL CONCEPTUAL CONCLUSIONS

The broader implications of the research and views we have presented are probably best reflected in an early statement by Carl Rogers on how the social sciences should regard the object of their inquiry:

> [The] ability of the person to discover new meaning in the forces which impinge upon him and in the past experiences which have been controlling him, and the ability to alter consciously his behavior in the light of this new meaning, has a profound significance for our thinking which has not been fully realized. We need to revise the philosophical basis of our work to a point where it can admit that forces exist within the individual which can exercise a spontaneous and significant influence upon behavior which is not predictable through knowledge of prior influences and conditioning (1946, p.422).

The cognitive approach developed in the introduction to this volume must be restated at this point. Our dissatisfaction with behaviorism and traditional experimental psychology can be attributed to their attempt to formalize a system of behavior in which the structure of processes was primary, while relevant content and important cognitive variables were neglected. Thus, we would argue that this limited focus be expanded by integrating the cognitively oriented view of behavior into the presuppositions and postulates of a new set of principles of behavior.

Pribram (1967) has cogently demonstrated such a possibility by building a model of a new neurology in which cognitive variables play a crucial function. He shows that "until recently a cognitive term such as 'expectancy' had little to support it in the way of hard fact" but that now it, along with the neurology of novelty and the basis of "interest," has been demonstrated electroneurally and psychophysiologically as well as behaviorally.

The central issue emerging from our work goes beyond the humanism initially espoused. It is not whether man differs from lower animals that is most important; rather, the main concern of all psychologists should be the ways in which all living organisms attempt to cope with and control their environment. Man's striving for this kind of environmental control is dramatically brought home by Cannon's (1942) study of voodoo death. Cannon's thorough analysis of reports of sudden, psychogenic death among physically healthy, primitive people who have been tabooed not only convinced him of the validity of the phenomenon of voodoo death, but it enabled him to infer that the mediating agent was overactivity of the parasympathetic nervous system. Richter (1957) substantiated this suggestion in controlled research with wild rats placed in threatening situations with no chance of escape. He concluded that in human beings as well as in rats, sudden death may occur when the victim resigns himself to a situation that seems hopeless rather than attempting to fight against it or flee from it. "Hopelessness is postulated as the psychological condition which then induces the parasympathetic death observed in rats, and assumed in man. Apparently, belief in the inevitability of one's doom also results in a number of individuals dying each year from minor wounds or small, sublethal doses of poison" (according to Dr. R. S. Fisher, Coroner of Baltimore, reported by Richter, 1957, p. 197).

Recent medical studies have indicated that there is a vital contribution to our understanding of behavior yet to be made from the systematic investigation of the social, behavioral, and physiological correlates of hopelessness and resignation (the antithesis of control), even in their less dramatic occurrences among civilized, modern men. Medical investigators have begun to accumulate evidence suggesting that when a person responds to events in his life with helplessness or hoplessness he initiates a complex series of biological changes that fosters the development of *any* disease potential which is present—even diabetes, heart disease, and cancer. Dr. Schmale (University of Rochester Medical Center) explains these findings with concepts similar to those we have used to understand the basic dynamics of cognitive control:

> Man is constantly interacting within his many environments, and at many levels of organization—from the subcellular and biochemical to the most external or peripheral, that of family, work and now even his universe. We postulate that when a person gives up psychologically, he is disrupting the continuity of his relatedness to himself and his many environments or levels of organization.
>
> In making such a break, or with this loss of continuity, he may become more vulnerable to the pathogenic influences in his external environments and/or he may become more cut off from his external environments and more predisposed to internal derangements. Thus, disease is more apt to appear at such time of disruptions and increased vulnerability. (Cited by Brody, 1968, p. E. 11; see also Engel, 1968.)

The significant motivation for behavior, then, comes not from appetite or aversion but from the tensions felt by all organisms who strive for autonomy and control, who search for ways to free themselves from dependence upon their environment. This is one way of interpreting Zimbardo and Montgomery's (1957) finding that even very hungry and thirsty rats will explore a novel environment for a relatively long period of time rather than stop to eat or drink. Such tensions, however, are not to be thought of in the simplistic homeostatic terms of our classical drive-reduction theories (which have been proven inadequate to explain even simple hunger-eating relationships; see Jacobs & Sharma, 1968). These tensions vary in intensity as a function of one's actual or perceived degree of control over the environment, a dynamic process and not one in which the organism seeks a state of quiescent equilibrium. We have suggested some of the reasons why inconsistency motivates behavior, but striving toward consistency does not necessarily imply seeking a static paradise in which balanced cognitions languish in blissful harmony.[5] Cognitive dissonance has recently been shown to possess the energizing properties of a general drive (by modifying perform-

5. Levy (1963) beautifully outlines a model of therapeutic interpretation in which the key element for successful behavior change involves a planned progressive *increase* in dissonance.

ance on tasks that are contiguous but unrelated to the presumed dissonance-arousing task; cf. Waterman & Katkin, 1967, as well as Cottrell & Wack, 1967); however, the drive-reduction assumptions of the theory only serve to mask its vast heuristic power. The state of psychological equilibrium implicit in striving for consistency is not an end but a means toward minimizing dependency on the environment and maximizing control over it by means of reliance upon internal rather than external controls.

We have also posited that in exercising his capacity to choose, man transforms himself by rejecting reality as a given and creating instead a new social and physical reality. In doing so, man may not only come to recognize his true potential to make innovations that advance society and even fulfill his desire to transcend himself, but he may reveal his darker side as well—his survival needs, his desire for self-gratification at any cost, and his maladaptive coping with environmental realities. These are the alternatives posed for man and society by the existence of freedom.

It is interesting to note that we have arrived at the same premise that is basic to Brehm's (1966) recent research on "reactance." The hypothetical problem Brehm initially posed to illustrate the relevance of dissonance theory for an understanding of motivation—namely, how a hungry professor might respond to the choice of finishing a paper or stopping for lunch—must now be seen in the larger perspective of the attempt by the individual to be free to make up his own mind, to decide for himself. Whenever individual freedom to choose is threatened or eliminated, reactance processes are aroused and behaviors are initiated that function to increase feelings of mastery over one's fate. The prime importance of such freedom is captured in Merryman's analysis of the dangers of censorship laws: "In a free society a citizen has the power to choose, and bears responsibility for the choices he makes—censorship laws deprive us of choice and responsibility. They diminish us and they diminish our society" (1966, p. 17).

We have not yet come to appreciate the degree of cognitive control man possesses over both external stimuli and his internal environment (cf. Melzack's 1961 analysis of pain control, as well as *Life Magazine*'s 1953 report on painless dentistry, yoga style; Schachter's analysis of emotion, 1964, and Ross, Rodin, & Zimbardo's 1968 study of fear reduction through cognitive manipulation of its symptoms). It is hoped that the present body of research will be a step in the direction envisioned centuries ago by the Roman poet, Marcus Manilius:

> No barriers, no masses of matter however enormous, can withstand the powers of the mind; the remotest corners yield to them; all things succumb; the very Heaven itself is laid open (*Astronomica* I, c. 40 B.C.).

REFERENCES

Abelson, R. P., Aronson, E., McGuire, W. J., Newcomb, T. M., Rosenberg, M. J., & Tannenbaum, P. H. (Eds.) *Theories of cognitive consistency: A sourcebook.* Chicago: Rand McNally, 1968.

Archer, E. J. Re-evaluation of the meaningfulness of all possible CVC trigrams. *Psychol. Monogr.*, 1960, *74*, No. 497.

Aronson, E. The psychology of insufficient justification: An analysis of some conflicting data. In S. Feldman (Ed.), *Cognitive consistency.* New York: Academic Press, 1966, pp. 109–133.

Aronson, E., & Carlsmith, J. M. Effect of the severity of threat on the devaluation of forbidden behavior. *J. abnorm. soc. Psychol.*, 1963, *66*, 584–588.

Aronson, E., & Golden, B. W. The effect of relevant and irrelevant aspects of communicator credibility on opinion change. *J. Pers.*, 1962, *30*, 135–146.

Aronson, E., Turner, J., & Carlsmith, J. M. Communicator credibility and communication discrepancy as determinants of opinion change. *J. abnorm. soc. Psychol.*, 1963, *67*, 31–36.

Atkinson, J. W. Motivational determinants of risk-taking behavior. *Psychol. Rev.*, 1957, *64*, 359–372.

Atkinson, J. W., & Litwin, G. H. Achievement motive and test anxiety conceived as motive to approach success and motive to avoid failure. *J. abnorm. soc. Psychol.*, 1960, *60*, 52–63.

Atkinson, J. W., & McClelland, D. C. The projective expression of needs: II. The effect of different intensities of the hunger drive on thematic apperception. *J. exp. Psychol.*, 1948, *38*, 643–658.

Back, K. W. Influence through social communication. *J. abnorm. soc. Psychol.*, 1951, *46*, 9–23.

Back, K. W., Bogdonoff, M. D., Shaw, D. M., & Klein, R. F. An interpretation of experimental conformity through physiological measures. *Behavioral Science*, 1963, *8*, 34–40.

Baer, D. J. Smoking attitude, behavior, and beliefs of college males. *J. soc. Psychol.*, 1966, *68*, 65–78.

Barber, T. X. Hypnosis as perceptual-cognitive restructuring: IV. "Negative hallucinations." *J. Psychol.*, 1958, *46*, 187–201.

Barber, T. X. Physiological effects of "hypnotic suggestions": A critical review of recent research (1960–1964). *Psychol. Bull.*, 1965, *63*, 201–222. (a)

Barber, T. X. The effects of "hypnosis" on learning and recall: A methodological critique. *J. clin. Psychol.*, 1965, *1*, 19–25. (b)

Barber, T. X. Toward a theory of pain. *Psychol. Bull.*, 1959, *56*, 430–460.

Barber, T. X., & Calverley, D. S. Experimental studies in hypnotic behavior: Suggested deafness evaluated by delayed auditory feedback. *Brit. J. Psychol.*, 1964, *55*, 439–446.

Barber, T. X., & Calverley, D. S. The relative effectiveness of task-motivating instructions and trance induction procedure in the production of "hypnotic-like" behaviors. *J. nerv. men. Dis.*, 1963, *137*, 107–116.

Barber, T. X., & Hahn, K. W., Jr. Physiological and subjective responses to pain-producing stimulation under hypnotically suggested and waking-imagined "analgesia." *J. abnorm. soc. Psychol.*, 1962, *65*, 411–418.

Baron, R. M. Social reinforcement effects as a function of social reinforcement history. *Psychol. Rev.*, 1966, *73*, 527–539.

Barry, H., Jr., Mackinnon, D. W., & Murray, H. A., Jr. Studies in personality: A. Hypnotizability as a personality trait and its typological relations. *Human Biology*, 1931, *3*, 1–16.

Beach, F. A. The descent of instinct. *Psychol. Rev.*, 1955, *62*, 401–410.

Beecher, H. K. *Measurement of subjective responses.* New York: Oxford University Press, 1959.

Bell, C. R. Personality characteristics of volunteers for psychological studies. *Brit. J. soc. clin. Psychol.* 1962, *1*, 81–95.

Bem, D. Self-perception: An alternative interpretation of cognitive dissonance phenomena. *Psychol. Rev.*, 1967, *74*, 183–200.

Bergin, A. E. The effect of dissonant persuasive communications upon changes in self-referring attitudes. *J. Pers.*, 1962, *30*, 423–438.

Berkowitz, L. *Aggression: A social psychological analysis.* New York: McGraw-Hill, 1962.

Berkowitz, L. Aggressive cues in aggressive behavior and hostility catharsis. *Psychol. Rev.*, 1964, *71*, 104–122.

Berkowitz, L. Repeated frustrations and expectations in hostility arousal. *J. abnorm. soc. Psychol.*, 1960, *60*, 422–429.

Berkowitz, L., & Holmes, D. S. A further investigation of hostility generalization to disliked objects. *J. Pers.*, 1960, *28*, 427–442.

Binder, A., McConnell, D., & Sjoholm, N. A. Verbal conditions as a function of experimenter characteristics. *J. abnorm. soc. Psychol.*, 1957, *55*, 309–314.

Bishop, F. V. The anal character: A rebel in the dissonance family. *J. Pers. Soc. Psychol.*, 1967, *6*, 23–36.

Blackman, R. B., & Tukey, J. W. *The measurement of power spectra.* New York: Dover, 1959.

Block, J. D., & Bridger, W. H. The law of initial value in psycho-physiology: A reformulation in terms of experimental and theoretical considerations. *Ann., N.Y. Acad. Sci.*, 1962, *98*, 1229–1241.

Block, J. D., & Reiser, M. F. Discrimination and recognition of weak stimuli. *Arch. Gen. Psychiat.*, 1962, *6*, 25–36.

Blum, G. S. *A model of the mind.* New York: Wiley, 1961.

Bogart, Karen. Machiavellianism and individual differences in response to cognitive dissonance. Unpublished doctoral dissertation, New York University, 1967.

Bogdonoff, M. D., Estes, E. H., Jr., & Trout, D. L. Acute effect of psychologic stimuli upon plasma non-esterified fatty acid levels. *Proc. Soc. exp. Biol. Med.*, 1959, *100*, 503–504.

Brady, J. V. Emotion and the sensitivity of psychoendocrine systems. In D. G. Glass (Ed.), *Neurophysiology and emotion.* New York: Rockefeller University Press and Russell Sage Foundation, 1967.

Brady, J. V. Psycho-physiology of emotional behavior. In A. Bachrach (Ed.), *Experimental foundations of clinical psychology.* New York: Basic Books, 1962.

Bramel, D. A dissonance theory approach to defensive projection. *J. abnorm. soc. Psychol.*, 1962, *64*, 121–129.

Bramel, D. Selection of a target for defensive projection. *J. abnorm. soc. Psychol.*, 1963, *66*, 318–324.

Brehm, J .W. A dissonance analysis of attitude-discrepant behavior. In M. J. Rosenberg & C. I. Hovland (Eds.), *Attitude organization and change.* New Haven: Yale University Press, 1960, pp. 164–197.

Brehm, J. W. Motivational effects of cognitive dissonance. In M. Jones (Ed.), *Nebraska Symposium on Motivation.* Lincoln, Nebraska: University of Nebraska Press, 1962, pp. 51–77.

Brehm, J. W. *A theory of psychological reactance.* New York: Academic Press, 1966.

Brehm, J. W., & Cohen, A. R. Choice and chance relative deprivation as determinants of cognitive dissonance. *J. abnorm. soc. Psychol.*, 1959, *58*, 383–387.

Brehm, J. W., & Cohen, A. R. *Explorations in cognitive dissonance.* New York: Wiley, 1962.

Brock, T. C. Relative efficacy of volition and justification in arousing dissonance. *J. Pers.*, 1968, *36*, 49–66.

Brock, T. C., & Buss, A. H. Dissonance, aggression and evaluation of pain. *J. abnorm. soc. Psychol.*, 1962, *65*, 197–202.

Brock, T. C., & Buss, A. H. Effects of justification for aggression and communication with the victim on post-aggression dissonance. *J. abnorm. soc. Psychol.*, 1964, *68*, 403–412.

Brody, J. E. When illness follows a "giving up." *The New York Times*, April 7, 1968, Sec. E, p. 11.

Brown, R. Models of attitude change. In R. Brown, E. Galanter, E. H. Hess, & G. Mandler, *New directions in psychology.* New York: Holt, Rinehart & Winston, 1962, pp. 3–85.

Brown, R. *Social psychology.* New York: Free Press, 1965.

Brozek, J., Guetzkow, H., & Baldwin, M. V. A quantitative study of perception and association in experimental semi-starvation. *J. Pers.*, 1951, *19*, 245–264.

Bush, I. E. Chemical and biological factors in the activity of adrenocortical steroids. *Pharmacol. Revs.*, 1962, *14*, 317.

Buss, A. H. *The psychology of aggression.* New York: Wiley, 1961.

Buss, A. H., & Brock, T. C. Repression and guilt in relation to aggression. *J. abnorm. soc. Psychol.*, 1963, *66*, 345–350.

Cannon, W. B. "Voodoo" death. *Psychosomatic Medicine*, 1957, *XIX*, 182–190.

Cardon, P. V. L., & Gordon, D. S. J. Rapid increase of plasma nonesterified fatty acids in man during fear. *J. psychosom. Res.*, 1959, *4*, 5–10.

Carson, R. C. Intralist similarity and verbal rote learning performance of schizophrenic and cortically damaged patients. *J. abnorm. soc. Psychol.*, 1958, *57*, 99–106.

Cartwright, D., & Zander, A. *Group dynamics*. New York: Harper & Row, 1960.

Chapanis, Natalia, & Chapanis, A. Cognitive dissonance: Five years later. *Psychol. Bull.*, 1964, *61*, 1–22.

Christie, R., & Geis, F. (Eds.) *Studies in Machiavellianism*. New York: Academic Press, 1968.

Church, R. Effects of competition on reaction time and skin conductance. *J. abnorm. soc. Psychol.*, 1962, *65*, 32–40.

Cobb, L. A., Ripley, H. S., & Jones, J. W. Role of the nervous system in free fatty acid mobilization as demonstrated by hypnosis. In M. J. Karvonen and A. J. Barry (Eds.), *Physical activity and the heart*. Springfield, Ill.: Thomas, 1967, pp. 192–199.

Cofer, C. N., & Appley, M. H. *Motivation: Theory and research*. New York: Wiley, 1964.

Cohen, A. R. Attitudinal consequences of induced discrepancies between cognitions and behavior. *Publ. Opin. Quart.*, 1960, *24*, 297–328.

Cohen, A. R. Some implications of self-esteem for social influence. In C. I. Hovland & I. L. Janis (Eds.), *Personality and persuasibility*. New Haven: Yale University Press, 1959, pp. 102–120.

Cohen, J. Multiple regression as a general data-analytic system. Unpublished paper, New York University, March 1967.

Cohn, A. Behavior with and attractiveness of a partner as functions of choice and negative information. Unpublished doctoral dissertation, New York University, 1964.

Conn, L. K., & Crowne, D. P. Instigation to aggression, emotional arousal, and defensive emulation. *J. Pers.*, 1964, *32*, 163–179.

Cottrell, N. B., & Wack, D. L. Energizing effects of cognitive dissonance. *J. pers. soc. Psychol.*, 1967, *6*, 132–138.

Crowne, D. P., & Marlowe, D. A new scale of social desirability independent of psychopathology. *J. consult. Psychol.*, 1960, *24*, 349–354.

Davis, K. E., & Jones, E. E. Changes in interpersonal perception as a means of reducing cognitive dissonance. *J. abnorm. soc. Psychol.*, 1960, *61*, 402–410.

Davis, L. W., & Husband, R. W. A study of hypnotic susceptibility in relation to personality traits. *J. abnorm. soc. Psychol.*, 1931, *26*, 175–182.

DeCharms, R., & Wilkins, E. J. Some effects of verbal expression of hostility. *J. abnorm. soc. Psychol.*, 1963, *66*, 463–470.

Deutsch, M., & Krauss, R. M. *Theories in social psychology*. New York: Basic Books, 1965.

Deutsch, M., Krauss, R. M., & Rosenau, N. Dissonance or defensiveness? *J. Pers.*, 1962, *30*, 16–28.

Diven, K. Certain determinants in the conditioning of anxiety reactions. *J. Psychol.*, 1937, *3*, 291–308.

Dole, V. P. A relation between non-esterified fatty acids in plasma and the metabolism of glucose. *J. clin. Invest.*, 1956, *35*, 150–152.

Dollard, J., Miller, N. E., Doob, L. W., Mowrer, O. H., & Sears, R. R. *Frustration and aggression.* New Haven: Yale University Press, 1939.

Dulany, D. E., Jr. Hypotheses and habits in verbal operant conditioning. *J. abnorm. soc. Psychol.*, 1961, *63*, 251–263.

Edwards, A. L. *Experimental design in psychological research.* New York: Holt, Rinehart & Winston, 1960.

Edwards, A. L. *Manual for the Edwards Personal Preference Schedule* (Rev. ed.). New York: Psychological Corporation, 1957.

Engel, B. T. Stimulus-response and individual-response specificity. *Arch. gen. Psychiat.*, 1960, *2*, 305–313.

Engel, G. L. A life setting conducive to illness: The giving up-given up complex. *Ann. Intern. Med.*, 1968, in press.

Epstein, G. F. Machiavellianism, dissonance and the devil's advocate. Unpublished doctoral dissertation, Columbia University, 1966.

Epstein, R. The effects of commitment to social isolation on children's imitative behavior. *J. of pers. soc. Psychol.*, 1968, *9*, in press.

Epstein, S., & Lewitt, H. Influence of hunger on the learning and recall of food selected words. *J. abnorm. soc. Psychol.*, 1962, *64*, 130–135.

Eriksen, C. W. (Ed.) Behavior and awareness: A symposium of research and interpretation. *J. Pers.*, 1962, *30*, 1–158.

Exline, R. V., Thibaut, J., Brannon, Carole, & Gumpert, P. Visual interaction in relation to Machiavellianism and an unethical act. In R. Christie & F. Geis (Eds.), *Studies in Machiavellianism.* New York: Academic Press, 1968.

Farber, I. E. The things people say to themselves. *Amer. Psychologist*, 1963, *18*, 185–197.

Fenz, W. D. Conflict and stress as related to physiological activation and sensory, perceptual, and cognitive functioning. *Psychol. Monogr.*, 1964, *78*, Whole No. 585.

Feshbach, S. Aggression, accident, anger and hostility. *Contemp. Psychol.* 1962, *7*, 268–269.

Feshbach, S. The catharsis hypothesis and some consequences of interaction with aggressive and neutral play objects. *J. Pers.*, 1956, *24*, 449–462.

Festinger, L. *A theory of cognitive dissonance.* Stanford: Stanford University Press, 1957.

Festinger, L. A theory of social comparison processes. *Human Relations*, 1954, *7*, 117–140.

Festinger, L. *Conflict, decision and dissonance.* Stanford: Stanford University Press, 1964.

Festinger, L. Informal social communication. *Psychol. Rev.*, 1950, *57*, 271–282.

Festinger, L., Ono, H., Burnham, C. A., & Bamber, D. Efference and the conscious experience of perception. *J. exp. Psychol. Monogr.*, 1967, *74*, Whole No. 637.

Festinger, L., Pepitone, A., & Newcomb, T. Some consequences of deindividuation in a group. *J. abnorm. soc. Psychol.*, 1952, *47*, 382–389.

Fishbein, H. D. Studies in efficiency: Muscle-action patterns in reaction time as related to inhibition of eyelid conditioning. *J. Pers. soc. Psychol.*, 1965, *2*, 180–187.

Freedman, J. L. Attitudinal effects of inadequate justification. *J. Pers.*, 1963, *31*, 371–385.

Friedlander, J. W., & Sarbin, R. T. The depth of hypnosis. *J. abnorm. soc. Psychol.*, 1938, *33*, 281–294.

Friedman, S. B., Ader, R., & Glasgow, L. A. Effects of psychological stress in adult mice inoculated with coxackie B viruses. *Psychosom. Med.*, 1965, *27*, 361–368.

Friedman, S. B., & Glasgow, L. A. Psychologic factors and resistance to infectious disease. *Pediatric Clinics of North America*, 1966, *13*, 315–335.

Gardner, R. W., Holzman, P. S., Klein, G. S., Linton, Harriet B., & Spence, D. P. Cognitive control: A study of individual consistencies in cognitive behavior. *Psychol. Issues*, *1*, (4). New York: International Universities Press, 1959.

Geis, F. The con game. In R. Christie & F. Geis (Eds.), *Studies in Machiavellianism.* New York: Academic Press, 1968.

Gelfand, D. M. The influence of self-esteem on rate of verbal conditioning and social matching behavior. *J. abnorm. soc. Psychol.*, 1962, *65*, 259–264.

Gelfand, S. The relationship of experimental pain tolerance to pain threshold. *Canad. J. Psychol.*, 1964, *18*, 36–42.

Gerard, H. B. Choice difficulty, dissonance and the decision sequence. *J. Pers.*, 1967, *35*, 91–108.

Gewirtz, J. Deprivation and satiation as setting conditions determining the reinforcing efficacy of non-appetitive (social) stimuli. *Minn. Sympos. on Child Psychol.* Minneapolis: University of Minnesota Press, 1967, *1*, in press.

Gewirtz, J. L., & Baer, D. M. Deprivation and satiation of social reinforcers as drive conditions. *J. abnorm. soc. Psychol.*, 1958, *57*, 165–172.

Gibbon, J. Discriminated punishment: Avoidable and unavoidable shock. *J. exp. anal. Behav.*, 1967, *10*, 451–460.

Gibson, E. J. A systematic application of the concepts of generalization and differentiation to verbal learning. *Psychol. Rev.*, 1940, *47*, 196–229.

Glass, D. C. Changes in liking as a means of reducing cognitive discrepancies between self-esteem and aggression. *J. Pers.*, 1964, *32*, 531–549.

Glass, D. C. Theories of consistency and the study of personality. In E. F. Borgatta & W. W. Lambert (Eds.), *Handbook of personality theory and research.* Chicago: Rand McNally, 1965.

Glass, D. C., Canavan, Donnah, Schiavo, S. Achievement motivation, dissonance and defensiveness. *J. Pers.*, 1968, in press.

Glass, L. B., & Barber, T. X. A note on hypnotic behavior, the definition of the situation and the placebo effect. *J. nerv. ment. Disorders*, 1961, *132*, 539–541.

Goffman, E. *The presentation of self in everyday life*. Garden City, New York: Doubleday, 1959.

Gormezano, I. Classical conditioning. In J. B. Sidowski (Ed.), *Experimental methods and instrumentation in psychology*. New York: McGraw-Hill, 1966, pp. 383–420.

Grebstein, L. D. Defensive behavior in an interpersonal situation: A functional approach. *J. consult Psychol.*, 1967, *31*, 529–534.

Green, D. R. Volunteering and the recall of interrupted tasks. *J. abnorm. soc. Psychol.*, 1963, *66*, 397–401.

Grinker, J. The control of classical conditioning by cognitive manipulation. Unpublished doctoral dissertation, New York University, 1967.

Haas, H., Fink, H., & Hartfelder, G. "Das placebo-problem" which appears in Fortschritte der Arzneimittelforchung, 1959, *1*, 279–454. Verlag, Basel, Switzerland. A translation of selected parts appeared in the *Psychopharmacology Service Center Bulletin*, 1963, *8*, 1–65.

Halliday, A. M., & Mingay, R. Retroactive raising of a sensory threshold by a contralateral stimulus. *Quart. J. exp. Psychol.*, 1961, *13*, 1–11.

Hardy, J. D., Wolff, H. G., & Goodell, H. *Pain sensations and reactions*. Baltimore: Williams & Wilkins, 1952.

Harlow, H. F., Harlow, M. K., & Meyer, D. R. Learning motivated by a manipulation drive. *J. exp. Psychol.*, 1950, *40*, 228–234.

Harvey, O. J., & Ware, R. Personality differences in dissonance resolution. *J. pers. soc. Psychol.*, 1967, *7*, 227–230.

Heider, F. *The psychology of interpersonal relations*. New York: Wiley, 1958.

Hershkowitz, A. Naturalistic observations on chronically hospitalized patients. *J. nerv. ment. Disorders*, 1962, *135*, 258–264.

Hilgard, E. R. Hypnosis. *Annu. Rev. Psychol.* Stanford: Stanford University Press, 1956, pp. 157–180.

Hill, K. T., & Stevensen, H. W. The effectiveness of social reinforcement following social and sensory deprivation. *J. abnorm. soc. Psychol.*, 1964, *68*, 579–584.

Hinkle, L. E., Jr., & Plummer, N. Life stress and industrial absenteeism. *Industr. Med. Surgery*, 1952, *21*, 363–375.

Hokanson, J. E. The effects of frustration and anxiety on overt aggression. *J. abnorm. soc. Psychol.*, 1961, *62*, 346–351.

Holt, R. R Cognitive controls and primary processes. *J. Psychol. Res.*, 1960, *4*, 1–8.

Homans, G. C. *Social behavior: Its elementary forms*. New York: Harcourt, Brace, 1961.

Horn, D. Behavioral aspects of cigarette smoking. *J. Chronic Diseases*, 1963, *16*, 383–395.

Hovland, C. I., Janis, I. L., & Kelley, H. H. *Communication and persuasion.* New Haven: Yale University Press, 1953.

Hovland, C. I., Lumsdaine, A. A., & Sheffield, F. D. *Experiments on mass communication.* Princeton: Princeton University Press, 1949.

Hovland, C. I., & Weiss, W. The influence of source credibility on communication effectiveness. *Publ. Opin. Quart.*, 1951, *15*, 635–650.

Hull, C. L. *Hypnosis and suggestibility—an experimental approach.* New York: Appleton-Century, 1933.

Ikemi, Y., & Nakagawa, S. A psychosomatic study of contagious dermatitis. *Kyushu J. Med. Sci.* 1962, *13*, 335–350.

Ito, M. The relation between success-failure and completed-incompleted tasks. *Japanese J. of Psychol.*, 1957, *27*, 259–269.

Jacobs, H. J., & Sharma, K. N. Taste versus calories: Sensory and metabolic signals in the control of food intake. *Ann., N.Y. Acad. Sciences*, 1968, in press.

Janis, I. L. *Psychological stress.* New York: Wiley, 1958.

Janis, I. L., & Fields, P. B. Sex differences and personality factors related to persuasibility. In C. I. Hovland & I. L. Janis (Eds.), *Personality and persuasibility.* New Haven: Yale University Press, 1959, pp. 55–68, 300–301.

Janis, I. L., & Gilmore, J. The influence of incentive conditions on the success of role playing in modifying attitudes. *J. Pers. soc. Psychol.*, 1965, *1*, 17–27.

Jones, E. E. *Ingratiation.* New York: Appleton-Century-Crofts, 1964.

Jordan, N. The mythology of the non-obvious: Autism or fact? *Contemporary Psychol.*, 1964, *9*, 140–142.

Kanfer, F. H., & Karas, S. C. Prior experimenter-subject interaction and verbal conditioning. *Psychological Reports*, 1959, *5*, 345–353.

Katz, D. The functional approach to the study of attitudes. *Publ. Opin. Quart.*, 1960, *24*, 163–200.

Kelley, H. H. Attribution theory in social psychology. Paper prepared for the Nebraska Symposium on Motivation, 1967.

Kelman, H. C., & Hovland, C. I. "Reinstatement" of the communicator in delayed measurement of opinion change. *J. abnorm. soc. Psychol.*, 1953, *48*, 327–335.

Keys, A. B., Brozek, J., Henschel, A., Mickelson, O., & Taylor, H. L. *The biology of human starvation.* Minneapolis: University of Minnesota Press, 1950.

Kimble, G. A. Attitudinal factors in eyelid conditioning. Presidential address, Division 3, Amer. Psychol. Ass., 1964. In G. A. Kimble (Ed.), *Foundations of conditioning and learning.* New York: Appleton-Century-Crofts, 1967.

Kimmel, H. D. Instrumental inhibitory factors in classical conditioning. In W. F. Prokasy (Ed.), *Classical conditioning: A symposium.* New York: Appleton-Century-Crofts, 1965, pp. 148–171.

King, J. H. Brief account of the sufferings of a detachment of United States Cavalry, from deprivation of water, during a period of eighty-six hours, while scouting on the "Llano Estacado" or "Staked Plains," Texas. *Am. J. Med. Sci.*, 1878, *75*, 404–408. Cited in Wolf, 1958, pp. 375–380.

Kipnis, D. A noncognitive correlate of performance. *J. Appl. Psychol.*, 1962, *46*, 76–80.

Klein, G. S. Need and regulation. In M. R. Jones (Ed.), *Nebraska Symposium on Motivation.* Lincoln, Nebraska: University of Nebraska Press, 1954.

Klein, G. S., Schlesinger, H. J., & Meister, D. E. The effect of personal values on perception: An experimental critique. *Psychol. Rev.*, 1951, *58*, 96–112.

Klein, R. F., Bogdonoff, M. D., Estes, E. H., Jr., & Shaw, D. M. Analysis of the factors affecting the resting FFA level in normal man. *Circulation*, 1960, *22*, 772.

Kline, M. V. (Ed.) *Clinical correlations of experimental hypnosis.* Springfield, Ill.: Thomas, 1963.

Klinger, B. I. The effects of peer model responsiveness and length of induction procedure in hypnotic responsiveness. Paper presented at the meeting of the Eastern Psychol. Ass., April 1968.

Kowalowski, A. Studien zur Psychologie des Pessimismus. *Grenzfragen des Nerven und Seelenlebens*, 1904, *4*, 100–122.

Kruglov, L. P., & Davidson, H. H. The willingness to be interviewed: A selective factor in sampling. *J. soc. Psychol.*, 1953, *38*, 39–47.

Kruskal, W. Statistics, Moliére, and Adams. *Amer. Scientist*, 1967, *55*, 416–428.

Lacey, J. I., & Lacey, B. C. Verification and extension of the principle of autonomic response stereotypes. *Amer. J. Psychol.*, 1958, *71*, 50–73.

Lambert, W. E., Libman, E., & Posner, E. G. The effect of increased salience of a membership group on pain tolerance. *J. Pers.*, 1960, *38*, 350–357.

Lawrence, D., & Festinger, L. *Deterrents and reinforcement.* Stanford: Stanford University Press, 1962.

Lazarsfeld, P. F., Berelson, B., & Gaudet, H. *The people's choice.* New York: Columbia University Press, 1944.

Levine, R., Chein, I., & Murphy, G. The relation of the intensity of need to the amount of perceptual distortion. *J. Psychol.*, 1942, *13*, 283–293.

Levy, L. H. *Psychological interpretation.* New York: Holt, Rinehart & Winston, 1963.

Lewin, I. The effect of reward on the experience of pain. Unpublished doctoral dissertation, Wayne State University, 1965.

Lewin, K., Dembo, Tamara, Festinger, L., & Sears, Pauline, Level of aspiration. In J. McV. Hunt (Ed.), *Personality and the behavior disorders.* New York: Ronald, 1944.

Lewin, K., Lippitt, R., & White, R. K. Patterns of aggressive behavior in experimentally created social climates. *J. soc. Psychol.*, 1939, *10*, 271–299.

Livingston, W. K. What is pain? *Scientific Amer.*, 1953, *188*, No. 3, 59–66.

Loomis, H., & Moskowitz, S. Cognitive style and stimulus ambiguity. *J. Pers.*, 1958, *26*, 349–364.

Lorenz, K. *On aggression.* New York: Harcourt, Brace & World, 1966.

McClelland, D. *The achieving society.* New York: Free Press, 1967.

McClelland, D., Atkinson, J. W., Clark, R. A., & Lowell, E. L. *The achievement motive.* New York: Appleton-Century, 1953.

McCoy, N., & Zigler, E. Social reinforcer effectiveness as a function of the relationship between child and adult. *J. Pers. soc. Psychol.*, 1965, *1*, 604–612.

McGranahan, D. A critical and experimental study of repression. *J. abnorm. soc. Psychol.*, 1940, *35*, 212–225.

McGuire, W. J. Personality and susceptibility to social influence. In E. F. Borgatta & W. W. Lambert (Eds.), *Handbook of personality theory and research.* Chicago: Rand McNally, 1967.

McKinney, F. Studies in the retention of interrupted learning activities. *J. of Comp. Psychol.*, 1935, *19*, 265–296.

Mahran, A. Individual differences in delayed and reduced auditory feedback. Unpublished doctoral dissertation, New York University, 1966.

Mandler, G. Comments on uncertainty. Paper presented at Russell Sage Conference on Neurophysiology and Emotion, December 1965.

Mandler, G. The conditions for emotional behavior. In D. C. Glass (Ed.), *Neurophysiology and emotion.* New York: Rockefeller University Press, 1967, pp. 96–102.

Mansson, H. H., & Greenbaum, C. W. A possible situational determinant of the relationship between need for approval and verbal conditioning. *Amer. Psychologist*, 1963, *18*, 395 (Abstract).

Mason, J. W., & Brady, J. V. The sensitivity of psychoendocrine systems to social and physical environment. In P. H. Leiderman & D. Shapiro (Eds.), *Psychobiological approaches to social behavior*. Stanford: Stanford University Press, 1964, pp. 4–23.

Megargee, E. I. Undercontrolled and overcontrolled personality types in extreme anti-social aggression. *Psychol. Monogr.*, 1966, *80*, No. 3.

Melzack, R. The perception of pain. *Scientific Amer.* 1961, *204*, (2), 41–49.

Melzack, R., & Wall, D. D. Pain mechanisms: A new theory. *Science*, 1965, *150*, 971–979.

Merrill, R. M. The effect of pre-experimental and experimental anxiety on recall efficiency. *J. exp. Psychol.*, 1954, *48*, 167–172.

Merryman, J. H. The fear of books. *Stanford Today.* Stanford Univ. Alumni Magazine, Autumn, 1966, pp. 14–17.

Meyer, R. J., & Haggerty, R. J. Streptococcal infections in families: Factors altering individual susceptibility. *Pediatrics*, 1962, *29*, 539.

Milgram, S. Behavioral study of obedience. *J. abnorm. soc. Psychol.*, 1963, *67*, 371–378.

Miller, J. The effect of facilitory and inhibitory attitudes on eyelid conditioning. *Psychol. Bull.*, 1939, *36*, 577–578.

Miller, N. E. Experiments on motivation. *Science*, 1957, *126*, 1271–1278.

Miller, N. E. Liberalization of basic S-R concepts: Extensions to conflict behavior, motivation and social learning. In S. Koch (Ed.), *Psychology: A study of a science.* V *2*. New York: McGraw-Hill, 1959, pp. 196–292.

Moore, J. W., & Gormezano, I. Yoked comparisons of instrumental and classical eyelid conditioning. *J. exp. Psychol.*, 1961, *62*, 552–559.

Mosteller, F., & Bush, R. R. Selected quantitative techniques. In G. Lindzey (Ed.), *Handbook of social psychology.* V*1*. *Theory and method*. Cambridge, Mass.: Addison-Wesley, 1954, pp. 289–334.

Moyer, K. E., & Lindley, R. H. Supplementary report: Effects of instructions on fixation and recovery of a conditioned avoidance response. *J. exp. Psychol.*, 1962, *64*, 95–96.

Murray, H. A., et al. *Explorations in personality*. New York: Science Editions, 1962 (copyright 1938).

Neulinger, J. Person types, environment types and resultant forces. Unpublished doctoral dissertation, New York University, 1965.

Newcomb, T. *The acquaintance process*. New York: Holt, Rinehart & Winston, 1961.

Newman, M. Personality differences between volunteers and nonvolunteers for psychological investigations: Self-actualization of volunteers and nonvolunteers for researches in personality and perception. *Dissertation Abstracts*, 1957, *17*, 684.

Norris, E. B., & Grant, D. A. Eyelid conditioning as affected by induced inhibitory set and counter reinforcement. *Amer. J. Psychol.*, 1948, *61*, 37–49.

O'Connell, D. N., & Tursky, B. Silver-silver chloride sponge electrodes for skin potential recording. *Amer. J. Psychol.*, 1960, *73*, 302–304.

Orne, M. T. On the social psychology of the psychological experiment: With particular reference to demand characteristics and their implications. *Amer. Psychol.*, 1962, *17*, 776–785.

Orne, M. The nature of hypnosis: Artifact and essence. *J. abnorm. soc. Psychol.*, 1959, *58*, 277–299.

Ostfeld, Barbara, & Katz, Phyllis A. The effect of threat severity in children of varying socio-economic levels. Paper presented Soc. Res. Child Develop. Assoc., 1967.

Pallak, M. S. The effect of aggression on interpersonal attractiveness. Paper presented at meeting of Eastern Psychol. Assoc., New York, April 1966.

Patker, P. D. An experimental investigation of the relative effects of direct and hypnotic suggestions for improved performance in learning tasks varied in complexity. Unpublished doctoral dissertation, Boston University, 1963.

Parker, P. D., & Barber, T. X. Hypnosis, task-motivating instructions, and learning performance. *J. abnorm. soc. Psychol.*, 1964, *69*, 499–504.

Passey, G. E. The influence of intensity of unconditioned stimulus upon acquisition of a conditioned response. *J. exp. Psychol.*, 1948, *38*, 420–428.

Pavlov, I. P. *Conditioned reflexes*. Oxford: Milford, 1927.

Peak, H. Attitude and motivation. In M. Jones (Ed.), *Nebraska Symposium on Motivation*. Lincoln, Nebraska: University of Nebraska Press, 1955, *3*, 149–188.

Penner, D. D. Cognitive dissonance or counterconditioning: An experimental test of two predictors of resistance to extinction. Unpublished doctoral dissertation, Purdue University, 1966.

Perry, W. R. Post-aggression cognitive dissonance, victim response style, and hostility-guilt. Unpublished doctoral dissertation, Ohio State University, 1965.

Pervin, L. A., & Yatko, R. J. Cigarette smoking and alternative methods of reducing dissonance. *J. of pers. soc. Psychol.*, 1965, *2*, 30–36.

Peryman, D. R., Polemis, Bernice W., Kamen, J. W., Eindhoven, J., & Pilgrim, F. J. *Food preferences of men in the U.S. Armed Forces*. Publication of the Quartermaster Food and Container Institute for the Armed Forces, Chicago, 1960.

Posner, E. G. Some psycho-social determinants of pain tolerance. Paper presented at the XVI International Congress of Psychology, Washington, D.C., 1963.

Prentice, W. C. H. Some cognitive aspects of motivation. *Amer. Psychologist*, 1961, *16*, 503–511.

Pribram, K. H. The new neurology and the biology of emotion. *Amer. Psychologist*, 1967, *22*, 830–838.

Prokasy, W. F. Classical eyelid conditioning: Experimenter operations, task demands, and response shaping. In W. F. Prokasy (Ed.), *Classical conditioning: A symposium*. New York: Appleton-Century-Crofts, 1965, pp. 208–225.

Rapaport, D. *Emotions and memory* (2nd ed.). New York: Science Editions, 1961.

Reik, T. *The compulsion to confess*. New York: Grove Press, 1961.

Reiser, M. F., & Block, J. D. Discrimination and recognition of weak stimuli, III. *Psychosomatic Med.*, 1965, *27*, 274–285.

Richter, C. P. On the phenomenon of sudden death in animals and man. *Psychosomatic Med.*, 1957, *19*, 191–198.

Rogers, C. R. Significant aspects of client-centered therapy. *Amer. Psychol.*, 1946, *1*, 415–422.

Rohrer, J. H. Human adjustment to Antarctic isolation. Mimeo report for the Group Psychol. Branch Office of Naval Research, September 1960.

Rosen, E. Differences between volunteers and nonvolunteers for psychological studies. *J. of appl. Psychol.*, 1951, *35*, 185–193.

Rosen, S. Post-decision affinity for incompatible information. *J. abnorm. soc. Psychol.*, 1961, *63*, 188–190.

Rosenau, Norah. Decisional importance, dissonance and information. Unpublished doctoral dissertation, New York University, 1964.

Rosenbaum, M. E., & DeCharms, R. Direct and vicarious reduction of hostility. *J. abnorm. soc. Psychol.*, 1960, *60*, 105–111.

Rosenberg, M. Deciding about dissonance. *Contemp. Psychol.*, 1966, *11*, 4–7. (a)

Rosenberg, M. J. Some limits of dissonance: Toward a differentiated view of counter-attitudinal performance. In S. Feldman (Ed.), *Cognitive consistency.* New York: Academic Press, 1966, pp. 135–170. (b)

Rosenberg, M. J., & Hovland, C. I. (Eds.), *Attitude organization and change.* New Haven: Yale University Press, 1960.

Rosenberg, M. J. When dissonance fails: On eliminating evaluation apprehension from attitude measurement. *J. pers. soc. Psychol.*, 1965, *1*, 28–43.

Rosenthal, R. The effects of the experimenter on the result of psychological research. In B. A. Maher (Ed.), *Progress in experimental personality research.* New York: Academic Press, 1964.

Rosenzweig, S. An experimental study of "repression" with special reference to need-persistive and ego-defensive reactions to frustration. *J. exp. Psychol.*, 1943, *32*, 64–75.

Ross, L., Rodin, J., & Zimbardo, P. G. Fear reduction through symptom misattribution. Unpublished mimeographed report, Columbia University Social Psychol. Dept., 1968.

Roth, P. Civilization and its discontents. In *New American Review.* New York: New American Library, 1968, pp. 7–81.

Safford, R. R., & Rockwell, J. H. Performance decrement in twenty-four hour driving. Unpublished manuscript, Systems Research Group, Ohio State University, 1966.

Saltz, G., & Epstein, S. Thematic hostility and guilt responses as related to self-reported hostility, guilt, and conflict. *J. abnorm. soc. Psychol.*, 1963, *67*, 469–479.

Salzinger, K. Experimental manipulation of verbal behavior: A review. *J. gen. Psychol.*, 1959, *61*, 65–94.

Sanford, R. N. The effect of abstinence from food upon imaginal processes. *J. Psychol.*, 1936, *2*, 129–136.

Sarnoff, I. *Society with tears.* New York: Citadel, 1966.

Sarnoff, I. *Personality dynamics and development.* New York: Wiley, 1962.

Sarnoff, I., & Zimbardo, P. G. Anxiety, fear and social affiliation. *J. abnorm. soc. Psychol.*, 1961, *62*, 356–363.

Sartre, Jean-Paul. *Existentialism and human emotions.* New York: Philosophical Library, 1957.

Schachter, S. Cognitive effects of obesity on bodily functioning: studies of obesity and eating. In D. C. Glass (Ed.), *Neurophysiology and emotion.* New York: Rockefeller University Press and Russell Sage Foundation, 1967.

Schachter, S. The interaction of cognitive and physiological determinants of emotional states. In P. H. Leiderman and D. Shapiro (Eds.), *Psychobiological approaches to social behavior.* Stanford: Stanford University Press, 1964.

Schachter, S. *The psychology of affiliation.* Stanford: Stanford University Press, 1959.

Scheerer, M. Cognitive theory. In G. Lindzey (Ed.), *Handbook of social psychology.* Cambridge, Mass.: Addison-Wesley, 1954.

Scheffé, H. *The analysis of variance.* New York: Wiley, 1959.

Schnore, M. M. Individual patterns of physiological activity as a function of task differences and degree of arousal. *J. exp. Psychol.*, 1959, *58*, 117–127.

Scotch, N. A. Sociocultural factors in the epidemiology of Zulu hypertension. *Amer. J. of Publ. Health*, 1963, *53*, 1205–1213.

Shor, R. E. Physiological effects of painful stimulation during hypnotic analgesia under conditions designed to minimize anxiety. *International J. of Clinical and Experimental Hypnosis*, 1962, *10*, 183–202.

Sidman, M., & Boren, J. J. The relative aversiveness of warning signal and shock in an avoidance situation. *J. abnorm. soc. Psychol.*, 1957, *55*, 339–344.

Sidman, M., Mason, J. W., Brady, J. V., & Thach, J. S., Jr. Quantitative relations between avoidance behavior and pituitary-cortical activity in rhesus monkeys. *J. of the Experimental Analysis of Behavior*, 1962, *5*, 353–362.

Silverman, L. H., & Silverman, D. K. A clinical-experimental approach to the study of subliminal stimulation: The effects of a drive-related stimulus upon Rorschach responses. *J. abnorm. soc. Psychol.*, 1964, *69*, 158–172.

Simon, H. A. Motivational and emotional controls of cognition. *Psychol. Rev.*, 1967, *74*, 29–39.

Simon, H. A., & Newell, A. Information processing in computer and man. *Amer. Scientist*, 1964, *52*, 281–300.

Sinclair, D. C. Cutaneous sensation and the doctrine of specific energy. *Brain*, 1955, *78*, 584–614.

Skinner, B. F. *Verbal behavior.* New York: Appleton-Century-Crofts, 1957.

Smith, E. E. The power of dissonance techniques to change attitudes. *Publ. Opin. Quart.*, 1961, *25*, 626–639.

Smith, K. V. *Delayed sensory feedback and behavior.* Philadelphia: Saunders, 1962.

Spence, D. P. The multiple effects of subliminal stimuli. *J. Pers.*, 1961, *29*, 40–43.

Spence, D. P., & Ehrenberg, B. Effects of oral deprivation on responses to subliminal and supraliminal verbal food stimuli. *J. abnorm. soc. Psychol.*, 1964, *69*, 10–18.

Spence, K. W. Anxiety (drive) level and performance in eyelid conditioning. *Psychol. Bull.*, 1964, *61*, 129–139.

Spence, K. W. A theory of emotionally based drive and its relation to performance in simple learning situations. *Amer. Psychologist*, 1958, *13*, 131–141. (a)

Spence, K. W. Behavior theory and selective learning. In M. R. Jones (Ed.), *Nebraska Symposium on Motivation, 1958*. Lincoln, Nebraska: University of Nebraska Press, 1958, pp. 73–107. (b)

Spence, K. W. Cognitive and drive factors in the extinction of the conditioned eyeblink in human subjects. *Psychol. Rev.*, 1966, *73*, 445–458. (a)

Spence, K. W. Cognitive factors in the extinction of the conditioned eyelid response in humans. *Science*, 1963, *140*, 1224–1225.

Spence, K. W. Extinction of the human eyelid CR as a function of presence or absence of the UCS during extinction. *J. exp. Psychol.*, 1966, *71*, 642–648. (b)

Spence, K. W. Learning and performance in eyelid conditioning as a function of intensity of the UCS. *J. exp. Psychol.*, 1953, *45*, 57–63.

Spence, K. W., & Goldstein, H. Eyelid conditioning performance as a function of emotion-producing instructions. *J. exp. Psychol.*, 1961, *62*, 291–294.

Spence, K. W., Homzie, M. J., & Rutledge, E. F. Extinction of the human eyelid CR as a function of the discriminability of change from acquisition to extinction. *J. exp. Psychol.*, 1964, *67*, 545–552.

Spence, K. W., & Platt, J. R. UCS intensity and performance in eyelid conditioning. *Psychol. Bull.*, 1966, *65*, 1–10.

Spence, K. W., & Ross, L. E. A methodological study of the form and latency of eyelid responses in conditioning. *J. exp. Psychol.*, 1959, *58*, 376–381.

Spielberger, C. D. The role of awareness in verbal conditioning. In C. W. Eriksen (Ed.), *Behavior and awareness*. Durham, N. C.: Duke University Press, 1962, pp. 73–101.

Stamler, R. Acculturation and Negro blue-collar workers. In A. R. Shostak & W. Gomberg (Eds.), *The blue collar world*. New York: Prentice-Hall, 1964.

Stein, M. Explorations in typology. In R. W. White (Ed.), *The study of lives*. New York: Atherton Press, 1963. (a)

Stein, M. Final technical report. Washington, D. C.: Peace Corps, 1963. (b)

Sternback, R. A., & Tursky, B. Ethnic differences among housewives in psychophysical and skin potential responses to electric shock. *Psychophysiology*, 1965, *1*, 241–246.

Stevensen, H. W., & Odom, R. D. The effectiveness of social reinforcement following two conditions of social deprivation. *J. abnorm. soc. Psychol.*, 1962, *65*, 429–431.

Stroop, J. R. "Studies in interference in serial verbal reaction." *J. exp. Psychol.*, 1935, *18*, 643–661.

Stunkard, A. Obesity and the denial of hunger. *Psychom. Med.*, 1959, 281–289.

Sutcliffe, J. P. "Credulous" and "skeptical" views of hypnotic phenomena: Experiments in esthesia, hallucination, and delusion. *J. abnorm. soc. Psychol.*, 1961, *62*, 189–200.

Sweet, W. H. Pain. In John Field (Ed.), *Handbook of physiology*. Washington, D. C.: American Physiological Society, 1959, *1*, Chap. 26, pp. 459–506.

Taffel, C. Anxiety and the conditioning of verbal behavior. *J. abnorm. soc. Psychol.*, 1955, *51*, 496–501.

Thibaut, J. W., & Kelley, H. H. *The social psychology of groups*. New York: Wiley, 1959.

Trout, D. L., Estes, E. H., Jr., & Friedberg, S. J. Titration of free fatty acids of plasma: A study of current methods and a new modification. *J. of Lipid Research*, 1960, *1*, 199–202.

Truax, C. B. The repression response to implied failure as a function of the hysteria-psychasthenia index. *J. abnorm. soc. Psychol.*, 1957, *55*, 188–193.

Underwood, B. J. *Experimental psychology.* New York: Appleton-Century, 1949.

Van Pelt, S. J. Hypnotism and its importance in medicine. *Brit. J. Med. Hypnotism*, 1949, *1*, 19–34.

Verplanck, W. S. A glossary of some terms used in the objective science of behavior. *Psychol. Rev. Suppl.*, 1957, *64*, 1–42.

Vinacke, E. W. The complexities of thinking. *Psychol. Bull.*, 1962, *59*, 450–457.

Wallach, H. Some considerations concerning the relation between perception and cognition. *J. Pers.*, 1949, *18*, 6–12.

Walster, E. The temporal sequence of post-decision processes. In L. Festinger, *Conflict, decision, and dissonance.* Stanford: Stanford University Press, 1964, pp. 112–128.

Walster, E., Berscheid, E., & Barclay, A. M. A determinant of preference among modes of dissonance reduction. *J. pers. soc. Psychol.*, 1967, *7*, 211–216.

Walters, R. H., & Karal, P. Social deprivation and verbal behavior. *J. Pers.*, 1960, *28*, 89–107.

Waterman, C. K., & Katkin, E. S. Energizing (dynamo-genic) effect of cognitive dissonance on task performance. *J. pers. soc. Psychol.*, 1967, *6*, 126–131.

Weiss, J. W. A., Lamberti, J. W., & Blackman, N. The sudden murderer. *Arch. Gen. Psychiat.*, 1960, *2*, 669–678.

Weitzenhoffer, A. M. *Hypnotism: An objective study in suggestibility.* New York: Wiley, 1953.

Weitzenhoffer, A. M., & Hilgard, E. R. *Standard hypnotic susceptibility scale.* Palo Alto, Calif.: Consulting Psychologists Press, 1959.

White, Elna H. Autonomic responsivity as a function of level of subject involvement. *Behav. Sci.*, 1965, *10*, 39–50.

Wilson, P. R., & Russell, P. N. Modification of psychophysical judgments as a method of reducing dissonance. *J. pers. soc. Psychol.*, 1966, *3*, 710–712.

Winer, B. J. Statistical principles in experimental design. New York: McGraw-Hill, 1962.

Wispé, L. G. Physiological need, verbal frequency, and word association. *J. abnorm. soc. Psychol.*, 1954, *49*, 229–234.

Wolf, A. V. *Thirst: Physiology of the urge to drink and problems of water lack.* Springfield, Ill.: Thomas, 1958.

Wolff, B. B., & Jarvik, M. E. Variations in cutaneous and deep somatic pain sensitivity. *Canad. J. Psychol.*, 1963, *17*, 37–44.

Wolff, B. B., Krasnegor, N. A., & Farr, Roberta S. Effect of suggestion upon experimental pain response parameters. *Perceptual and Motor Skills*, 1965, *21*, 675–683.

Wolff, C. T., Hofer, M. A., & Mason, J. W. Relationship between psychological defenses and mean urinary 17-OH-CS excretion rates: II. Method and theoretical considerations. *Psychosom. Med.*, 1964, *26*, 592–609.

Wolff, H. G., & Goodell, H. The relation of attitude and suggestion to the perception of and reaction to pain. *Research Publication of the Assoc. of Nervous and Mental Disorders*, 1943, *23*, 434–448.

Wollitzky, D. Cognitive control and cognitive dissonance. *J. pers. soc. Psychol.*, 1967, *5*, 486–490.

Woodworth, R. S., & Schlosberg, H. *Experimental psychology*. New York: Holt, 1954.

Worchel, P. Anxiety and repression. *J. abnorm. soc. Psychol.*, 1955, *50*, 201–205.

Yates, A. Delayed auditory feedback. *Psychol. Bull.*, 1963, *60*, 213–231.

Zajonc, R. B. Cognitive structure and cognitive tuning. Unpublished doctoral dissertation, University of Michigan, 1955.

Zajonc, R. B. Cognitive theories of social behavior. In G. Lindzey & E. Aronson (Eds.), *Handbook of social psychology*. Cambridge, Mass.: Addison-Wesley, 1967.

Zborowski, M. Cultural components in responses to pain. *J. soc. Issues*, 1952, *8*, 16–30.

Zeigarnik, Bluma. Über das behalten von erledigter und unerledigter Handlungen. *Psychol. Forsch.*, 1927, *9*, 1–85. In K. Lewin (Ed.), *A dynamic theory of personality*. New York: McGraw-Hill, 1935.

Zeller, A. F. An experimental analogue of repression: II. The effect of individual failure and success on memory measured by relearning. *J. exp. Psychol.*, 1950, *40*, 411–422.

Zeller, A. F. An experimental analogue of repression: III. The effect of induced failure and success on memory measured by recall. *J. exp. Psychol.*, 1951, *42*, 32–38.

Zimbardo, P. G. The effects of effort and improvisation on self-persuasion produced by role-playing. *J. exp. soc. Psychol.*, 1965, *1*, 103–120.

Zimbardo, P. G. Involvement and communication discrepancy as determinants of opinion conformity. *J. abnorm. soc. Psychol.*, 1960, *60*, 86–94.

Zimbardo, P. G., Abric, J. C., Lange, F., Rijsman, J., Bokorova, V., Potocka-Hoser, A., & Honai, R. The aggressive consequences of loss of personal identity. Mimeo technical report, European Research Training Seminar in Experimental Social Psychology, 1967.

Zimbardo, P. G., Barnard, J. W., & Berkowitz, L. The role of anxiety and defensiveness in children's verbal behavior. *J. Pers.*, 1963, *31*, 79–96.

Zimbardo, P. G., Dworkin, L., Ebbesen, E., & Fraser, S. C. Objective measurement of attitudes and subjective states. Unpublished paper presented to Eastern Psychol. Ass., 1966.

Zimbardo, P. G., & Formica, R. Emotional comparison and self-esteem as determinants of affiliation. *J. Pers.*, 1963, *31*, 141–162.

Zimbardo, P. G., & Montgomery, K. D. The relative strengths of consummatory responses in hunger, thirst and exploratory drive. *J. comp. physiol. Psychol.*, 1957, *50*, 504–508.

1 2 3 4 5 6 7 8 9 10 11 12 13 14 15 16 17 18 19 20 21 22 23 24 25 SH 75 74 73 72 71 70 69